PIMLICO

822

UNDER TWO DICTATORS

Margarete Buber-Neumann was born in 1901 in
Potsdam, Germany. She married Rafael Buber – the
son of Martin Buber – and had two daughters with
him. After their divorce, she joined the Communist
Party, married Heinz Neumann and was sent to a
Soviet labour camp and, later, to Ravensbrück. After
the war, she was invited to Sweden for recuperation
where she took an office job and wrote, in the
evenings, *Als Gefangene bei Stalin und Hitler* (*Under
Two Dictators*). In 1949 and 1950 she was a key witness
in the Krawtschenko and Rousset trials in Paris,
disproving the Communist denial of the existence of
the Gulag. She spent the rest of her life in Frankfurt,
writing and lecturing widely. The author of eight
books, she died in Frankfurt in November 1989.

Nikolaus Wachsmann is Reader in modern European
history at Birkbeck (University of London), where
he is directing a major research project on the Nazi
camps. He has written widely on terror and repression in the Third Reich. His book *Hitler's Prisons*
won the Royal Historical Society Gladstone Prize
and was jointly awarded the Longman-History Today
Book of the Year Award.

D1354988

UNDER TWO DICTATORS

Prisoner of Stalin and Hitler

———

MARGARETE BUBER-NEUMANN

Translated by
EDWARD FITZGERALD

With an introduction by
NIKOLAUS WACHSMANN

PIMLICO

Published by Pimlico 2009

2 4 6 8 10 9 7 5 3 1

Copyright © The Literary Estate of Margarete Buber-Neumann 2008
Translation copyright © Edward Fitzgerald 1949
Introduction copyright © Nikolaus Wachsmann 2008
Part III and Part IV copyright © Judith Buber Agassi 2008

First published in Great Britain by Victor Gollancz Ltd in 1949

Revised Pimlico edition published in 2008

Pimlico
Random House, 20 Vauxhall Bridge Road,
London SW1V 2SA

www.rbooks.co.uk

Addresses for companies within The Random House Group Limited can be found at:
www.randomhouse.co.uk/offices.htm

The Random House Group Limited Reg. No. 954009

A CIP catalogue record for this book
is available from the British Library

ISBN 9781845951030

The Random House Group Limited supports The Forest Stewardship
Council (FSC), the leading international forest certification organisation. All our titles that are
printed on Greenpeace approved FSC certified paper carry the FSC logo. Our paper procurement
policy can be found at www.rbooks.co.uk/environment

Typeset in Galliard by Palimpsest Book Production Limited,
Grangemouth, Stirlingshire

Printed and bound in Great Britain by
Clays Ltd, St Ives plc

CONTENTS

INTRODUCTION

In the summer of 1947, Margarete Buber-Neumann spent several sun-drenched weeks on a remote Norwegian island, south of Oslo. She was living in a friend's holiday home, with majestic fjord views. But the background to this idyllic picture was stained with tragedy. Just two years earlier, Buber-Neumann had still been a prisoner in the SS camp in Ravensbrück. And this had not been her first experience of life and deaths in camps. She had already endured the Gulag, making her one of the few prisoners to survive both Nazi and Soviet camps.

During her stay on the island in 1947, Margarete Buber-Neumann was forcing herself to think about the camps. She was working hard on a memoir about her imprisonment in Nazi Germany and the Soviet Union between 1938 and 1945 – seven long years, she wrote, which added up to a whole life. The idea for such a book, she later recalled, had first emerged when she was a prisoner in Ravensbrück, during a conversation with another inmate and close friend, the Czech journalist Milena Jesenska, who later died in the camp. Soon after the end of the Second World War, Buber-Neumann started to put some of her experiences on paper, but it was only in 1947 that her book took shape. In early August 1947, when she returned from her writer's retreat to Stockholm – where she had moved in the previous year, hoping to start a new life – Buber-Neumann had already completed some 250 pages of a rough draft. Over the following months she poured all her energy into 'the horrific task of completing the manuscript', as she wrote at the time. The book was published in 1948 in

Swedish translation and later that year in German, under the matter-of-fact title *Prisoner of Stalin and Hitler*.[1]

The book opens dramatically with the arrest of Buber-Neumann's husband Heinz in Moscow in 1937, soon followed by her own detention. But her political life had begun almost two decades earlier, during one of the most tumultuous periods of German history. In autumn 1918, when she was just seventeen years old, Germany was turned upside down. Exhausted from the unprecedented bloodshed and destruction of the First World War, the German Empire finally sued for peace – unwittingly sparking a revolution, spearheaded by soldiers and workers demanding an immediate armistice. The mass protests quickly gained irresistible momentum and toppled the Emperor. Almost overnight, Germany had become a Republic. But the speed of the transition was deceptive. It did not end the political upheaval. On the contrary: over the next fifteen years the young democracy was repeatedly pushed to the brink of civil war. Forced to sign the hated Treaty of Versailles and facing an increasingly desperate economic crisis, the Republic haemorrhaged popular support from early on – to the delight of the radical parties on right and left, who placed the blame for the national crisis on the fragile shoulders of the democratic government, all the while peddling simple and drastic solutions for Germany's malaise.

Living in this highly charged atmosphere, it was hard to ignore politics – nowhere more so than in Berlin, the German capital. Grete Thüring (as she was then called) had grown up in nearby Potsdam, with its sumptuous residence of the Prussian royalty, and moved to Berlin shortly after the revolution, leaving behind the old world, embodied by her father, with his devotion to all things Prussian. In Berlin, she witnessed the violent birth of the new state. The city was in turmoil, shaken by strikes, demonstrations, uprisings and assassinations. Soon, she too became an actor in Germany's political drama. Turning away from her bourgeois upbringing – her father was manager of a local brewery – she slowly

---

[1] For the quote, see Buber-Neumann to Helmuth Faust, 20 November 1947, in Nachlass Margarete Buber-Neumann, Deutsche Nationalbibliothek, Deutsches Exilarchiv 1933–1945, Frankfurt am Main. See also ibid., Babette Gross to Buber-Neumann, 16 November 1946; Buber-Neumann to Helmuth Faust, 11 July 1947, 31 July 1947, 3 August 1947, 9 September 1947; Margarete Buber-Neumann, *'Freiheit, du bist wieder mein . . .' Die Kraft zu überleben* (Munich, 1978), pp. 185–6, 202–10; Buber-Neumann to her daughter Judith, 7 February 1946, reprinted in Margrid Bircken, Elke Liebs (eds), *Von Potsdam nach Moskau und Zurück* (Schkeuditz, 2002), p. 221. For all bibliographical details on Buber-Neumann's work, see ibid., pp. 231–2. I want to thank Judith Buber-Agassi, Jürgen Zarusky and Christian Goeschel for their comments on different aspects of this introduction.

drifted towards the German Communist Party (KPD), joining its youth movement in spring 1921. Many years later she recalled that what had attracted her was not Marxist theory, of which she was ignorant, but its emotional appeal: the promise that a revolution would bring heaven on earth, putting an end to poverty, exploitation and injustice. Marching in her first demonstration in 1921, among a sea of red flags, she was swept along by the fanaticism of the masses, with their chants and hymns celebrating the ardently anticipated victory of the working class and mourning its fallen martyrs.

But she was not yet consumed by politics. She trained as a nursery-school teacher and soon started a family of her own, giving birth to two daughters with her husband Rafael Buber, son of the Jewish religious philosopher Martin Buber. It was only after the failure of her short marriage that she threw herself completely into politics (in 1928 after a bitter court battle, she also lost custody of her children, who later emigrated to Palestine with her parents-in-law). By the late 1920s, she had dedicated herself full-time to Communism. She was employed in the Berlin headquarters of the KPD, in the office of a paper of the Communist International (Comintern). In her spare time she devoted herself to local agitation for the KPD, having joined the party in 1926. She was now a true believer with an unshakeable faith in the Soviet Union, which she saw as the 'model for a better world, come true'. Her social life, too, revolved around the Party. Her sister, for example, was a committed activist and lived with Willi Münzenberg, the maverick Communist publisher and propagandist.[2] Given her commitment to the cause, it was not surprising that Margarete Buber met the love of her life inside the movement. For German Communists like her, the private was very much political.

Heinz Neumann was a political celebrity, the shooting star of the German Communists. He was young, clever and charismatic, and his reputation as a man of ideas and action – he was known as a sharp theoretician and writer, and as a fiery orator and agitator – won him friends (and enemies) across the movement, from rank-and-file activists in Germany all the way to Stalin, whom he first met in 1922, during his maiden trip to the USSR. Neumann had pledged his life to Communism from an early age. Born in 1902 into a middle-class family in Berlin, his rise in the Communist

---

[2] Quote in Margarete Buber-Neumann, *Von Potsdam nach Moskau – Stationen eines Irrweges* (Frankfurt am Main, 1985), p. 213. See also ibid., pp. 7–147. For details on her political life in the 1920s, see her curriculum vitae (dated 22 September 1936), which has been reprinted in Reinhard Müller, 'Linie und Häresie', in *Exil. Forschung, Erkenntnisse, Ergebnisse* 11 (1991), pp. 46–69, here pp. 67–9.

movement was meteoric. He joined the KPD as a teenager in 1920, when it was still a small, fledgling party, becoming a full-time functionary in 1922. In the mid 1920s he represented the KPD in Moscow, on the executive committee of the Comintern. It was as a Comintern agent that he participated in the disastrous Canton revolt in December 1927, which was brutally put down, claiming the lives of several thousand Chinese Communists. But this did not derail Neumann's career. In 1928 the ambitious young man was ordered back to Germany, where he became one of the KPD leaders. Still in his twenties, he held several key positions and edited the incendiary Communist daily newspaper *Red Flag*, which called for a violent battle against both the rising Nazi movement and the Republic. He seemed destined for a stellar career as a professional revolutionary, at a time when his party attracted more votes than ever, as the German Republic slumped to yet another catastrophic crisis in the early 1930s.[3]

Meeting Heinz Neumann in 1929 was a turning point in Margarete Buber's life. They quickly fell in love and within weeks had become inseparable (though their marriage was never officially registered). From now on their fates were intertwined and when Neumann's world collapsed – forcing him into exile, isolation and poverty – so did hers. The fall of Heinz Neumann was no less spectacular than his rise. The KPD always provided fertile ground for political intrigues and, in spring 1932, it was Neumann who became a casualty of the constant infighting, losing a struggle with his main rival, party chief Ernst Thälmann. Stripped of his powers and back in the Soviet Union, he had to watch from afar as the German Republic started to collapse completely – eventually destroyed in early 1933 by the Nazi movement and its nationalist allies, not by the Communist revolution, as Neumann and his comrades had always confidently predicted. Even worse, it was Neumann who was later blamed internally: although the KPD leadership had been in broad agreement about tactics, party bosses looked for a scapegoat for their collective failures and Neumann, recently sacked, made a convenient target. He was duly accused of having led the party astray by 'deviating' from the fictitious 'correct' line. But back in summer 1932 Neumann was not yet a total outcast. He was still hoping for redemption and repeatedly met with Stalin, holidaying on the Black Sea coast. Effectively 'on probation', Neumann was then sent to Spain as a Comintern agent.

---

[3] Hermann Weber, 'Heinz Neumann', in Wolfgang Benz, Hermann Graml (eds), *Biographisches Lexikon zur Weimarer Republik* (Munich, 1988), pp. 237–8; Margarete Buber-Neumann, *Kriegsschauplätze der Weltrevolution* (Frankfurt am Main, 1973), pp. 104–21; Buber-Neumann, *Potsdam*, pp. 149–65; Eve Rosenhaft, *Beating the Fascists? The German Communists and Political Violence 1929–1933* (Cambridge, 1983), esp. pp. 60–87.

But during 1933 he fell foul of the Communist ideological watchdogs again. Ordered to stay out of German politics, he had not been able to stop himself from writing to an old party friend. This cost him dearly: he was accused of wanting to split the KPD and was ritually denounced by his former comrades. The German party executive described him as a 'troublemaker' who had to be eliminated, while Georgi Dimitrov – soon to head the Comintern – attacked him as 'a political degenerate'. Completely humiliated, Heinz Neumann was ordered to Switzerland, arriving in Zurich in late 1933. During her husband's fall from grace Margarete Buber-Neumann was with him, moving from one European city to another – Berlin, Moscow, Madrid, Paris – often living like a fugitive, with a false passport, and putting her life on the line for the Communist cause. Settling illegally in neutral Switzerland, the couple found no peace either. Cut off from the Communist movement, Neumann was restless, a political junkie suffering withdrawal symptoms: without the party, he explained to his wife, his life was simply not worth living. Matters soon got even worse. In December 1934 he was arrested by the Swiss police. Margarete Buber-Neumann herself only just managed to escape over the French border. Eventually, Moscow came to the rescue – or so it seemed – and intervened with the Swiss authorities, offering to take in Heinz Neumann. He was released from prison and expelled to France, where he was reunited with his wife. Together, they boarded a Soviet freighter in Le Havre, taking them to the Soviet Union and towards an uncertain future.[4]

The couple arrived in Moscow in early summer 1935, moving to the Hotel Lux, the Comintern guesthouse for senior Communists from around the world. They knew the place well, having stayed there several times before. This time, though, the atmosphere was different: fear haunted the corridors, just as it did Soviet society at large. Witch-hunts among party members were already under way and state terror intensified after the first show trial in summer 1936, which ended with the first execution of former members of the Party Central Committee. Heinz Neumann and his wife were all too familiar with the ruthless methods used during this show trial: for a Comintern publisher, they translated the court transcript into German. In the suffocating climate of suspicion – stoked from the top of the Soviet state – virtually anybody could be considered a potential enemy. In the case of a senior figure like Heinz Neumann, who had already been sidelined, the Communist

---

[4] Quotes in Reinhard Müller, *Herbert Wehner – Moskau 1937* (Hamburg, 2004), p. 34; Ivo Banac (ed.), *The Diary of Georgi Dimitrov 1933–1949* (New Haven, 2003), p. 19. See also Reinhard Müller, 'Stalinistischer Glaubenvirtuose', in *Apropos Margarete Buber-Neumann* (Frankfurt am Main, 2001), pp. 105–12, here esp. pp. 107–10; Buber-Neumann, *Potsdam*, pp. 283–392.

dialectic of fear seemed to demand both confessions and denunciations.

Thus, Neumann 'repented' his political 'sins' (contrary to his wife's belief in her memoir that he had refused to do so), continuing the political self-flagellation for his 'errors' he had begun back in Switzerland. At the same time he reported some comrades to the authorities for 'deviation', including guests in the Hotel Lux. Neumann himself was also denounced, of course, and in September 1936 his name appeared on a secret Comintern list of 'bad elements among the KPD activists in Moscow'. The noose round his neck was tightening all the time. In this period of collective anxiety, Neumann rarely left his room, spending almost all his time with his wife. Many years later, Margarete Buber-Neumann recalled that during these last months together their love had grown stronger than ever. But even marriages were not safe from the Soviet Inquisition. In a document requested by the Soviet authorities and written shortly after the first show trial, Margarete Buber-Neumann really had no choice but to distance herself politically from her husband. While she admitted that she, too, had subscribed to some of his 'false views', she claimed that in other areas she had disagreed with him, following the 'correct' views of the party instead. She added, 'In discussions with Comrade Heinz Neumann in spring 1933, I tried to persuade him to correct his deviations and return completely to the party line.'[5]

Over the following months Soviet terror escalated further, and more and more occupants of the Hotel Lux disappeared into police custody, never to be seen again. The all-out attack on state and society engulfed the Comintern and foreign Communists – fuelled by Stalin's obsession with the supposed threat posed by saboteurs and spies from abroad. German Communists in exile were hit particularly hard, following a secret order in mid-February 1937 by Nikolai Yezhov, the fanatical head of the police and terror apparatus (NKVD), to hunt down German 'Trotskyists' and 'Counter-revolutionaries'. Thousands of German Communists were arrested in 1937–8. Having escaped Nazi Germany, they now fell victim to Soviet terror instead. Leading party figures were especially vulnerable: more representatives of the KPD Politburo died under Stalin than under Hitler.

As a former Party leader and self-confessed 'deviationist', Heinz Neumann

---

[5] Quotes in Buber-Neumann's curriculum vitae (dated 22 September 1936), reprinted in Müller, 'Linie', p. 69; idem., *Wehner*, p. 110. See also idem., 'Glaubenvirtuose', pp. 110–11; idem, *Menschenfalle Moskau. Exil und Stalinistische Verfolgung* (Hamburg, 2001), p. 290; Buber-Neumann, *Potsdam*, pp. 393–444; Robert Service, *A History of Twentieth-Century Russia* (London, 1998), pp. 210–18. Margarete Buber-Neumann's daughter Judith recalls her mother telling her that she used to complete official Soviet documents in collaboration with Heinz Neumann.

stood no chance. Arrested in April 1937, he was crammed into a prison cell in the Lubyanka, the central Moscow prison, with over a hundred others. Inevitably, the charges against him were a wild concoction of lies and fabrications. Conspiracy theories were all the rage and the Soviet leaders had convinced themselves that terrorists had infiltrated the Comintern; Neumann was one of the suspects. After months of abuse and torture – interrogators could use extreme violence to extract 'confessions' – Heinz Neumann was a broken man. On 1 November 1937 he made a last desperate bid to save his life. In a handwritten note to the NKVD he expressed his enthusiasm for Stalin's 'cleansing operation' against 'all counter-revolutionary criminals and traitors'. But his fate had long been sealed. By then, the Great Terror was in full swing – claiming the lives of an estimated one million or more persons in 1937–8 – and Neumann had no hope of escape. When he was hauled before a military tribunal on 26 November 1937, he admitted his 'guilt' to the absurd charges put to him and after only fifteen minutes he was sentenced to death. He was shot the same day. This was the reason why, when Margarete Buber-Neumann turned up at the Lubyanka in December 1937, to pay in some money for her husband, as she had done for the last few months, she was told that he was 'not here'. What she was not told was that he was already dead. Only in 1961 did the Russian Red Cross inform her that her husband was no longer alive. But she never learnt how and when he had died.[6]

Buber-Neumann herself was arrested on 19 June 1938, a few months after her husband was killed. For the Soviet secret police she was an obvious target. Even though she had only been a foot soldier in the Communist movement, her marriage to Heinz Neumann turned her into a suspect, too: following NKVD orders, wives of 'traitors' were locked up and sent to the camps. In January 1939 she was sentenced to five years' imprisonment and taken to the Gulag, the Soviet system of labour camps. By this time the Gulag was a vast landscape of detention, spread across the whole of the Soviet Union. Camps had been part of Bolshevik rule from the start, but it was only in the 1930s – during the manic push for collectivisation and industrialisation, and the explosion of state terror – that the Gulag developed its full repressive potential. A huge number of men and women were locked up, confined in settlements, camps and

---

[6] Quote in Müller, 'Glaubenvirtuose', p. 112. See also ibid.; Yezhov directive, 14 February 1937, reprinted in idem., *Wehner*, pp. 362–8; Banac (ed.), *Diary*, pp. 61–70; Service, *Russia*, pp. 218–35; Michaela Wunderle, 'Zwischen den Fronten', in *Apropos Margarete Buber-Neumann*, pp. 7–48, here p. 25; Hermann Weber, *'Weiße Flecken' in der Geschichte* (Frankfurt am Main, 1990), 2nd edition, pp. 17–35; Kevin McDermott, 'Stalinist Terror in the Comintern: New Perspectives', *Journal of Contemporary History* 30 (1995), pp. 111–30.

prisons. Among the worst were the fifty or so corrective labour camps, which by early 1939 held around 1.3 million prisoners, overwhelmingly men. One of the biggest was the Karaganda complex (Karlag) – hundreds of miles south-east of Moscow in the middle of the Kazakh steppe – where Margarete Buber-Neumann arrived in early 1939. She was one of around 35,000 prisoners confined in the camp at this point. Inmates were divided into political prisoners and common criminals, though these labels tell us little. Many political prisoners were ordinary citizens wrongly accused of opposition: in a society where paranoia ruled, any behaviour could be branded as politically deviant. Equally, those classified as hardened criminals were often not, but had been caught up in the web of terror because of trivial offences or infractions of labour discipline.

Forced labour stood at the centre of Gulag life. Unlike other Soviet labour camps, which focused on mining or construction, Karlag was above all an agricultural camp. Established in September 1931, during Stalin's murderous collectivisation campaign, its impossible mission was to turn the barren steppe into fertile fields for crops and grazing. To this end, sub-camps were spread across a great distance. Even though Buber-Neumann was moved to several different locations, she gained no clear sense how big this camp really was: the main area was the size of a medium-sized European country, substantially bigger than Denmark or the Netherlands. Everywhere in this vast territory, prisoners faced appalling conditions. Filth, hunger and disease were rampant in Karlag and there were shortages of everything. The only commodity the camp authorities possessed in abundance was callous disregard for the prisoners.

But Margarete Buber-Neumann managed to survive. One factor that may have saved her was timing. She arrived in the Gulag just after the Great Terror: mass shootings, which had characterised the camps over the previous months, had stopped and the number of deaths among prisoners fell sharply. Death rates shot up again a few years later during the war against Nazi Germany (1941–5), killing an unprecedented number of prisoners and turning the Gulag into a gigantic mass grave. But by this time Margarete Buber-Neumann was no longer in Soviet captivity. She was now fighting for survival in the Nazi concentration camp in Ravensbrück.[7]

The moment when Margarete Buber-Neumann was turned over by the Soviets to the SS is among the most poignant in her memoirs. The Soviet

[7] See Anne Applebaum, *Gulag. A History of the Soviet Camps* (London, 2003); Oleg V. Khlevniuk, *The History of the Gulag* (New Haven, 2004); M. B. Smirnov (ed.), *Das System der Besserungsarbeitslager in der Sowjetunion 1923–1960* (Berlin, 2003), pp. 51, 302 for figures; Steven A. Barnes, 'Soviet Society Confined: The Gulag in the Karaganda Region of Kazakhstan, 1930s–1950s', Ph.D. dissertation (Stanford, 2003), pp. 44, 140 for figures.

authorities, whom she had once revered, delivered her straight into the hands of the Nazis. On a cold winter day in February 1940 she was marched across the bridge over the Bug river in Brest-Litovsk, from the Soviet to the German side, one of around 350 prisoners handed over to the German authorities between November 1939 and May 1941. Some historians (and indeed Buber-Neumann herself) have suggested that this prisoner transfer was the direct result of the Hitler–Stalin pact of August 1939, which briefly turned Fascists and Communists into allies. In a goodwill gesture, it is said, Stalin handed over hardened anti-Fascists imprisoned in the USSR to the Nazis.

In this reading, Buber-Neumann's fate becomes a symbol for the collusion and unique criminal likeness of Nazi Germany and the Soviet Union. However, the historical background was more complex. To start with, the initiative for the extraditions had come from the German authorities, not the Soviets, and built on well-established precedents (expulsions of Germans detained in the Soviet Union had already taken place before the Hitler–Stalin pact). Also, the Soviet Union was not alone in colluding with the Third Reich. Other countries – friendly with Germany, or dependent on it – did the same. In 1940, for example, the Vichy authorities agreed to leave some prisoners – under their control in the unoccupied French zone – on request to the Germans (two years later, this collaboration intensified dramatically, with the involvement of Vichy France in deportations of Jews to the Nazi death camps). Finally, the extraditions from the USSR did not specifically target long-standing enemies of Nazism. Initial selections by the Soviets, picking out individual prisoners in the Gulag, were rather arbitrary: prominent anti-Fascists and political ingénues alike were sent to the extradition cells in Moscow. As for the German authorities, they actually blocked the entry of some unwanted critics of the Nazi regime. For instance, they vetoed the return of Carola Neher, the famous actress whom Buber-Neumann met in prison, on the grounds that Neher had publicly attacked Germany after she had emigrated (Neher was left behind in the USSR and perished in the Gulag). And not all prisoners who were deported to Germany were seen as threats by the Nazis. Many were quickly released, after they had been pumped for intelligence about Soviet economic and military capabilities.[8]

---

[8] Hans Schafranek, *Zwischen NKWD und Gestapo. Die Auslieferung deutscher und österreichischer Antifaschisten aus der Sowjetunion an Nazideutschland 1937–1941* (Frankfurt am Main, 1990); Carola Tischler, *Flucht in die Verfolgung: Deutsche Emigranten im sowjetischen Exil* (Kassel, 1996), pp. 119–38; Wilhelm Mensing, 'Eine "Morgengabe" Stalins an den Paktfreund Hitler?', *Zeitschrift des Forschungsverbundes SED-Staat* 20 (2006), pp. 57–84; Regina M. Delacor, '"Auslieferung auf Verlangen"? Der deutsch-französische Waffenstillstandsvertrag 1940 und das Schicksal der sozialdemokratischen Exilpolitiker Rudolf Breitscheid and Rudolf Hilferding', *Vierteljahrshefte für Zeitgeschichte* 47 (1999), pp. 217–41; Müller, *Menschenfalle*, p. 334.

Margarete Buber-Neumann, by contrast, was not set free by the German authorities. On 24 July 1940, after several months of imprisonment in Berlin, the Gestapo took her into 'protective custody' – a typically euphemistic term in the Nazi vocabulary, which generally meant indefinite confinement under brutal conditions in a concentration camp without trial or appeal. The official grounds for her detention, as recorded in her Gestapo file, were no less spurious than the ones previously used by the Soviet authorities: she was supposedly under 'suspicion of attempted high treason'.[9] On 2 August 1940 she was taken out of her police cell and transported by train to the SS concentration camp in Ravensbrück, about fifty miles north of Berlin.

Even at first sight, Margarete Buber-Neumann saw some glaring differences from the Gulag. Ravensbrück was a new purpose-built camp (opened in May 1939) and she was struck by its drill and outward order. Also, Ravensbrück was a Nazi camp for women only – the sole one at this time – as there was strict gender separation in the SS camp system. And Ravensbrück was much, much smaller than Karlag: in the summer of 1940 Buber-Neumann was one of around 3,200 prisoners, held in less than two dozen barracks, on a plot of land surrounded by a high wall with electrified barbed wire. Among the eight SS concentration camps in operation at this point, Ravensbrück was one of the smaller ones. The first of these Nazi camps had been set up during Hitler's capture of power in 1933, to terrorise (real and suspected) political opponents. But by the time Buber-Neumann came to Ravensbrück the inmate population had changed. After the political resistance inside Germany had largely been broken, the police – led by SS Chief Heinrich Himmler – set its sights on social outsiders, sending more and more beggars, vagrants and other outcasts to the camps. In Ravensbrück, women classified as 'asocial', most of them arrested as prostitutes, made up the single largest inmate group in summer 1940.

In her book, Margarete Buber-Neumann painted a sometimes rather crude portrait of the 'asocials', expressing negative feelings held by many other German political prisoners as well. This serves as a reminder that memoirs are always shaped by the author's own values. Buber-Neumann was no exception. After all, she wrote a personal account, not a systematic history of the camp. This also means that her experience should not be taken as representative of all prisoners. She escaped some of the worst labour commandos, working mostly in sought-after positions as a prisoner functionary, which was less

[9] Quote in Wunderlich, 'Fronten', p. 31. See also ibid., p. 30.

punishing and brought certain privileges, such as slightly better rations. One of her positions was as block senior with the Jehovah's Witnesses, who consequently figure prominently in her account – even though they represented only a fraction (less than one per cent) of the total Ravensbrück prisoner population. By contrast, she had little direct contact with Polish women, even though they made up about one-third of all the estimated 120,000 female prisoners who went through Ravensbrück. Inevitably, she also gained little detailed knowledge of the Holocaust – though she heard about killings in Auschwitz – as the mass murder of European Jews largely took place further east.[10]

But Margarete Buber-Neumann remains one of the most important witnesses of Ravensbrück, surviving many changes in its short history. The camp, like the SS camp system as a whole, expanded dramatically during the Second World War, turning into a large complex with factories, workshops and sub-camps (a separate camp for men was added in April 1941). Most important was the spread of satellite camps all over Germany: by August 1944, there were thirty-seven such outposts attached to Ravensbrück. This expansion was linked to the enormous growth in prisoner numbers, especially towards the end of the war. By August 1943 there were already over 14,000 female prisoners in Ravensbrück and its satellite camps. Figures had more than doubled by summer 1944 and reached their peak in early 1945, when there were more than 45,000 women (and some 7,800 men) registered as Ravensbrück prisoners. The camp was hopelessly overcrowded, like all the remaining SS camps (some had already been evacuated in the face of the advancing Allies): in January 1945 the SS concentration camps held well over 700,000 prisoners in total.

By this time life inside Ravensbrück had reached the last circle of hell. Over the previous years, prisoners like Buber-Neumann had already suffered greatly under the deteriorating conditions, which claimed more and more lives, as did the increasingly regular SS executions and killings. But the final stages of the Second World War were by far the worst: over half of the 25,000 or more deaths of women registered as Ravensbrück prisoners occurred in the last four months of the camp's existence. Many died from mass starvation and illness. Others were murdered by lethal injection and shooting, or in a provisional gas chamber, set up in early 1945.

On 21 April 1945, towards the very end of the war, Margarete Buber-Neumann escaped from this inferno. Together with around sixty other

---

[10] Bernhard Strebel, *Das KZ Ravensbrück. Geschichte eines Lagerkomplexes* (Paderborn, 2003), pp. 121, 138, 179–80 for figures. Specifically for 'asocial' prisoners, see also Christa Schikorra, *Kontinuitäten der Ausgrenzung. 'Asoziale' Häftlinge im Frauen-Konzentrationslager Ravensbrück* (Berlin, 2001).

long-term political prisoners she was suddenly released. The exact circumstances remain unclear, though other prisoners, too, were freed in the chaotic last days of the Third Reich (thanks to interventions by Red Cross officials, some 7,800 or more foreign women were allowed to leave Ravensbrück in April 1945). Buber-Neumann was fortunate to be set free. Just days after her release, most of the prisoners remaining in Ravensbrück – some 20,000 women and men – were forced by the SS on brutal evacuation marches, which claimed even more lives. Left behind were some 2,000 ill and dying inmates, who were reached by Allied troops on 30 April 1945. In one of history's pathetic twists, it was the Red Army that liberated the camp – soldiers of the very state that had handed Margarete Buber-Neumann over to the Nazis five years earlier. But she was spared another encounter with the Soviet forces. She was already on her odyssey through the ruins of Germany to reach the house of her grandparents in Bavaria, the first stop on her long journey to reclaim her life.[11]

The first year after the Second World War was particularly hard for Buber-Neumann. Some thirteen years had passed since she had last lived in Germany as a free woman. Since then, she had lost almost everything. Most of her social and professional life had revolved around the Communist movement, which she now feared and despised. In a letter to her daughter Judith, whom she had not seen for a decade, Buber-Neumann wrote in summer 1946 that 'my life is now very lonely. The people to whom I belonged until 1933 and in the years of emigration, are dead, missing or still abroad.' And her new friends and comrades from Ravensbrück had either died in the camp or returned to their own homes across Europe after liberation. Looking back on this period many years later, she wrote that 'my life had lost its meaning'. Her feelings only started to change with her move to Sweden, where she took her first tentative steps towards a new life as a writer.[12]

A decisive moment, which catapulted her almost overnight into the public limelight, came in early 1949. Three years before, Victor Kravchenko, a middle-ranking Soviet official who had defected to the USA, published a scathing exposé of life in the USSR entitled *I Chose Freedom*, which became an international best-seller translated into over

---

[11] Strebel, *Ravensbrück*, pp. 182, 459, 501–2, 509–12 for figures. See also Simone Erpel, *Zwischen Vernichtung und Befreiung. Das Frauen-Konzentrationslager Ravensbrück in der letzten Kriegsphase* (Berlin, 2005), figures on pp. 148–50.

[12] Quotes in Buber-Neumann to her daughter Judith, 30 June 1946, reprinted in *Apropos Margarete Buber-Neumann*, here p. 77; Buber-Neumann, *'Freiheit'*, p. 144. See also ibid., pp. 67–144.

twenty languages. Sober critics, while impressed by its attack on Soviet terror, also pointed to some shortcomings, but such subtle judgements often got lost in the frenzied atmosphere of the Cold War: most readers were either with Kravchenko or against him. The book became a cause célèbre, with Soviet sympathisers going all out to destroy its author. In France, the press campaign was particularly vitriolic, led by the Communist weekly *Les Lettres Françaises*, which branded Kravchenko a bankrupt, alcoholic and lying stooge of the US secret service. Kravchenko sued for libel and the ten-week trial, which began in Paris in January 1949, was a political sensation, quickly turning into a trial of the Soviet Union. The stakes were high, and with both Soviet and US authorities involved behind the scenes, it became a battle between East and West. The daily court sessions, played out in front of the national and foreign press corps, were an extraordinary spectacle, with constant mud-slinging, heckling and tantrums. At one stage the verbal attacks nearly turned physical, and a policeman had to prevent a fight between Kravchenko and one of the defence lawyers.

It was into this cauldron that Margarete Buber-Neumann stepped on 23 February 1949, called as a witness by Kravchenko. She was no friend of his – she met him for the first time in Paris and disliked his authoritarian manner – but her appearance left a huge impression on the court. Speaking clearly and calmly about her suffering under Soviet terror, her testimony contrasted sharply with the usual antics during the trial. She was not even ruffled by the machinations of the defence lawyers, with their absurd attacks – trying to blame Heinz Neumann for Hitler's reign – and desperate semantic games, insisting that Karaganda should not be called a 'camp' because it was not surrounded by a high defensive wall. Her day in court made headline news. Reflecting on the trial, which Kravchenko eventually won, the liberal German weekly *Der Spiegel* was in no doubt that Buber-Neumann's appearance had been decisive, overshadowing all other witnesses: 'In its simplicity, the testimony by Mrs Buber-Neumann was the most devastating judgement on the Bolshevik regime made during the trial.'[13]

The trial turned Buber-Neumann into a public figure and focused attention on her memoir, which was published in 1949 in Great Britain

---

[13] Quote in 'In vielen schönen Worten', *Der Spiegel* (9 April 1949), p. 12. See also *Le Procès Kravchenko contre Les Lettres Françaises* (Paris, no date), esp. pp. 550–65; 'Wenn meine Großmutter Räder hätte', *Der Spiegel* (26 February 1949), pp. 9–10; Buber-Neumann, *'Freiheit'*, pp. 231–64; Victor Kravchenko, *I Chose Freedom. The personal and political life of a Soviet official* (New York, 1946). For a measured contemporary appraisal of Kravchenko's book, see Waldemar Gurian's review in the *Journal of Modern History* 19 (1947), pp. 71–2.

(as *Under Two Dictators*) and partially in France, where it was also seri-
alised in *Le Figaro*. An edition in the US followed soon after. Her
sudden prominence gave her a platform for political campaigning in
the early 1950s. She returned to Germany and threw herself into various
projects. From her perspective, the battle against Soviet terror was the
most pressing one. The other totalitarian regime she had survived, the
Third Reich, was already receding into history, with leading officials
from the camp SS (in contrast to many other Nazi perpetrators) punished
for their crimes: several senior Ravensbrück officials mentioned in
Buber-Neumann's memoir – Commandant Suhren, Doctor
Schiedlausky, police and SS officer Ramdohr, supervisor Binz – were
sentenced to death and executed. By contrast, the Gulag still existed
– it never held more prisoners than in the early 1950s – and Soviet
influence now spread across large parts of Europe and beyond. The
Cold War provided the arena for the political engagement of Margarete
Buber-Neumann, who did not hesitate to take sides. For example, she
participated in the Congress for Cultural Freedom, an influential anti-
Communist pressure group, which brought together European intellectuals and politicians (although not directly controlled by the US, it
did receive covert funding from the CIA, subverting its message that
freedom of mind had to be exempt from political interference). This
was just one of the projects in which Buber-Neumann was involved.
In addition, she briefly ran the Institute for Political Education (also
financed by the US) and a nationwide campaign for victims of repression in Communist East Germany. On top of this she edited a monthly
magazine (*Aktion*), which she pitched as the voice of the independent
democratic left (only many years later did she gravitate towards the
German Conservatives, joining Helmut Kohl's CDU in the mid
1970s).[14]

However, Margarete Buber-Neumann's life as a front-line activist was
brief: short on funds and support, her various projects quickly folded.But
this did not overshadow her career as a writer. *Under Two Dictators*
became an international success, with six more translations in the 1950s
alone. And Buber-Neumann published several other books. Some were
autobiographical, complementing her first work. Others mixed personal
recollections with wider historical reflections and research, such as in her

---

[14] Anja Wissmann, 'Erinnerung und Neuanfang', in *Apropos Margarete Buber-
Neumann*, pp. 92–8. See also Strebel, *Ravensbrück*, pp. 60, 72, 568–9; Smirnov
et al., 'System', p. 59; Giles Scott-Smith, *The Politics of Apolitical Culture*
(London, 2002); Buber-Neumann, *'Freiheit'*, p. 266. In France, only the first
part of Buber-Neumann's memoir was published (as *Deportée en Sibérie*). The
second part did not appear until 1988.

tender biography of her fellow Ravensbrück prisoner Milena Jesenska, her only other book to be translated into English.[15]

The unflagging attacks by Margarete Buber-Neumann on the Soviet Union and its followers made her a red rag for Communists, who always saved their greatest venom for 'renegades'. Back in Ravensbrück, she had already clashed with imprisoned Communist hardliners who could not bear the truth about the Gulag. Such bitter conflicts continued after the war. Some of her public speeches were disrupted and she was vilified in the Communist press, which categorically denied that any comrades had been turned over by Stalin to Hitler. Foreign Communists had always 'enjoyed the hospitality of the USSR', a German hack called Emil Carlebach wrote in 1950. But Buber-Neumann, he added, had not been a 'real emigrant' and was rightly kicked out of the USSR in 1940 as a 'Trotskyist' and Nazi sympathiser. Buber-Neumann sued for defamation (Carlebach had also alleged that she was a US agent). She won, but not before the case had gone through the whole German court system, all the way to the Supreme Court (Bundesgerichtshof).[16]

Most disturbing were betrayals by close friends and survivors. During the Kravchenko trial, Margarete Buber-Neumann was dumbfounded when she heard that Inka Katnarova, the prisoner who had saved her life in Ravensbrück, had denounced her as an SS collaborator in an orchestrated effort to discredit her testimony (Katnarova lived in Communist Czechoslovakia and had been put under pressure to lie; apparently, she regretted it for the rest of her life). This was the first of many stabs in the back. Another Ravenbrück friend, Lotte Henschel, was recruited by the Stasi (the East German secret police) in the 1950s, as one of five secret informants who kept Buber-Neumann under surveillance. Among them was also Kurt Rittwagen – codenamed 'Fritz' – a former prisoner in Karaganda who like Buber-Neumann had been handed over to the Nazis and who gained her confidence after the war. But he was not all he seemed. A dangerous and unscrupulous man, he spied on her life and in 1955 even suggested to his Stasi handlers that Buber-Neumann should be 'liquidated' as a 'dangerous agent'.[17] But she was not intimidated. Until the end of

---

[15] Margarete Buber-Neumann, *Mistress to Kafka: the life and death of Milena* (London, 1966).

[16] Emil Carlebach, 'Trotzkisten und Unternehmervertreter', *Sozialistische Volkszeitung*, 25 May 1950, reprinted in Schafranek, *NKWD*, pp. 194–6. See also ibid., pp. 110–23.

[17] Cited in 'GM "Fritz"', in *Apropos Margarete Buber-Neumann*, pp. 101–4, here p. 102. See also Wunderle, 'Fronten', pp. 42–5; Buber-Neumann, *'Freiheit'*, pp. 269–70; Tzvetan Todorov, *Hope and Memory* (London, 2005), pp. 108–9.

her career she continued to speak out against Communism, past and present.

Margarete Buber-Neumann would have felt vindicated by the collapse of Communism at the end of the 'Short Twentieth Century' (Eric Hobsbawm). But she did not live to see it. After a long illness, which had forced her into public silence, she died in Frankfurt on 6 November 1989 – just days before the fall of the Berlin wall, the concrete symbol of Germany's division by the Iron Curtain. She left behind an impressive body of work, which still demands to be read and discussed. At its heart stands *Under Two Dictators*, the remarkably perceptive and humane account of her imprisonment. Historians have long recognised it as a standard work on the Nazi camps and the Gulag, with its unique perspective on repression in the Soviet Union and the Third Reich, Europe's two most destructive modern dictatorships. But among a general readership in the English-speaking world, the book is virtually unknown, having been out of print for over fifty years. This edition finally allows a new audience to discover a modern classic: one of the most important survivor memoirs of totalitarian terror. Back in the summer of 1947, working feverishly to complete her manuscript, Margarete Buber-Neumann explained why she felt compelled to write it: her book, she said to her daughter, told 'the tragedy of my generation'.[18]

Nikolaus Wachsmann

---

[18] Buber-Neumann to her daughter, 26 August 1947, reprinted in Bircken, Liebs (eds), *Potsdam*, p. 227.

NOTE ON THE TEXT

In 1949 Edward Fitzgerald translated the first version of this book by my mother, Margarete Buber-Neumann, from the German original into English. His translation was then published by Victor Gollancz in Great Britain and by Dodd Mead in the USA. Since then the book has appeared in more than ten other languages in many editions. In the 1960s Margarete Buber-Neumann added about 50 pages, describing her journey from the women's concentration camp Ravensbrück to the village of her grandparents in Bavaria, after she had crossed the American lines at Bad Kleinem in Spring 1945. She removed a few short passages from the earlier version to avoid repetition. At the time of this revision she also divided the text into ten chapters with subheadings – between four and ten to each chapter. In the first version the names of many individuals were not fully spelt out – so as not to endanger them. Wherever this had ceased to be relevant, she now spelt them out.

From then on, until her death in 1989, she made no further changes. The book was thus published from then on only in this revised form. I therefore decided that it is appropriate to update the English edition accordingly. I have introduced into the text of Edward Fitzgerald's translation all these changes, adding my translation of the last fifty-three pages from the revised German original.

I also added indices of names, places and subjects.

Judith Buber Agassi,
Herzliya, Tuesday, August 07, 2007

PREAMBLE TO TRAGEDY

'One Lives More Cheerfully'

It was 30 April 1937. Moscow was busily preparing for the May Day celebrations. The strong sunlight of a Russian spring day flooded the Ulitza Gorkovo. With my parcel gripped tightly under my arm, I pushed my way as rapidly as possible through the slowly moving masses of people on the streets. Loudspeakers put up for the great day were being tested. The Triumphal March from *Aida* blared over the street. I was anxious to get away into a side street and escape it all, but a great crowd of men and women, most of them still in their grey winter coats padded with wadding, had collected right across the street to watch a gigantic picture of Stalin being hoisted into position. How I would have liked to get away from that face, but wherever you looked, there it was again: in shop windows, on walls and at the entrances to cinemas – always the same face with the drooping moustache. And as I finally succeeded in making my escape through a small side street leading to the Petrovka a gay Viennese waltz pursued me.

My heart was beating hard as I hurried along. I had let two days go past, two days whilst I was struck numb with the catastrophe, two days whilst he sat in a cell at the Lubianka. How could I have been so neglectful!

As I crossed the square before the Grand Opera House, I saw that a gigantic wooden statue of Stalin striding out in a long Red Army great-coat had been erected in the middle and decorated with innumerable red flags.

Would they let me leave my packet with food and a change of linen for him? And above all my letter?

I whispered the Russian words to myself as I went along in order to be word perfect when I got to the prison: 'My husband, Heinz Neumann, was arrested by the NKVD on 27 April. Can you tell me where he is? Can I visit him? Can I leave this package and a letter for him?'

The information centre for relatives and dependants of those arrested by the GPU was diagonally opposite the Lubianka. I found the place full of people lined up in a great queue which twisted and turned because it was far too long to remain straight, waiting patiently for their turn to get to a little window like a station booking office. Those who were waiting no longer dared to speak above a whisper. The atmosphere was already that of a prison. An armed and uniformed GPU man stood on guard at the entrance. There was a continual opening and closing of doors as men carrying papers came and went. They all had the light blue or deep red stripes of various GPU formations on their caps. They were the only human beings who spoke out loud and moved freely and noisily here.

Gradually, but terribly slowly, the queue moved forward. I glanced around at the people in it. They all had the same frightened, anxious, depressed look on their faces. In front of me was a tall woman in an elegant fur coat; behind me was an old woman with a shawl over her head drawn so close that only her eyes, nose and lined mouth were visible. By far the majority of the people waiting were women, but there were some men. All ages and all conditions were represented; some of them were well dressed, whilst others wore shabby, padded coats. They spoke to each other in whispers: 'Have you found your husband yet?' 'Can you leave any money for them?' 'How long has yours been in?' And the same story was told again and again: 'They came at about one. Asked if we had any weapons, and searched the place. He wasn't allowed to take anything at all apart from the clothes he stood up in. I know he hadn't done anything.'

Then there were only three people in front of me. My heart beat hard and my mouth was dry and I had to keep swallowing. I tried to understand what the others said when their turn came, and, above all, what answers they got. But all the Russian I had ever known had deserted me. My turn came. I stood before the window. It was so high I could only just reach it. On the other side there was a man with an impassive face wearing a pair of pince-nez glasses. I began to stammer the Russian sentences I had learnt by heart, and held out the letter for him to take – the package was too big to go through that small window. But he cut me short with a gruff '*Nyet*' and turned to the next applicant, who pushed me away from the window.

I stood outside in the street helplessly, tears in my eyes, still clutching the letter in one hand and the package under my arm.

'You must go to the Butirka. Perhaps you'll find him there.' It was the old woman in the shawl. She had taken pity on me and followed me out. 'Mine isn't here either. You come with me. I'll show you how you have to do it.'

We walked together through the decorated streets of Moscow, and all around there were red streamers with slogans on them. A very popular one was: 'We are now living better and more happily – Stalin.' As we went along, the old woman told me her story. They had come a few days before and taken away her youngest, Kolka. 'They keep on saying you ought to criticise,' she said; 'and when my Kolka's had a drop he criticises, and there you are. So now they've taken him. He's a building worker and a good boy.' Although taken up with my own troubles, I tried to offer a word or two of consolation: 'Well, that doesn't sound too bad; I expect they'll soon let him out again.' But the old woman looked at me with the amiable contempt of someone who knows better: 'Don't you believe it, my dear. Once they've got their claws into you, you don't get away so easily.'

We arrived at the Butirka and went through a little door in a very high wall. Inside was a small courtyard. A few steps led up to the information office of the Butirka remand prison for political offenders. Here too the place was full of people. They stood in the yard and they waited on the steps to go in. There were children playing around whilst their mothers waited. You had to go inside, show your passport to an official, obtain a number and then wait till your turn came.

'I haven't got a passport,' I explained to the man. 'I'm a foreigner. My permission to stay is still in the Comintern.'

'Go and get it,' he said. 'Bring it here and you will be given a number.'

I took counsel with the friendly old woman, but she couldn't help me either. 'They're the regulations,' she sighed. 'And there you are.' There was nothing left for me but to give up the battle for the moment, and we parted with a friendly but sinister '*Dosvidaniya*' – *Au revoir*.

My room at the Hotel Lux, which is inhabited exclusively by employees and officials of the Comintern and similar institutions, still showed signs of the thorough and ruthless search it had sustained when my husband was arrested. That was already three days ago. Books and discarded papers were still on the floor where they had been thrown. Three days of enforced idleness lay before me. The information offices would be closed for the May Day celebrations and I could do nothing to find him. Do what I would, I kept thinking of the night from 27 April to 28 April. At about one o'clock we were woken up by a loud banging at the door. I sprang out of bed and switched on the light. The banging started again. I was frightened. 'Get up, Heinz,' I said. 'Get up, for heaven's sake.' But he only smiled and turned over in his sleep. Trembling I went to the door and opened it. There was the manager of the Lux – the Commandant, as he was called – and three uniformed officials of the GPU. They said something I didn't catch. My head was swimming and I couldn't get a word out.

They tramped into our room and went over to Heinz, who was still sleeping, peacefully oblivious to it all. They shook him roughly by the shoulder. 'Get up, Neumann.' He started up in bed at that and I saw his face. For a moment it was a study, then as he realised what had happened it grew grey and determined. 'I protest against my arrest,' he said firmly. 'You can do that later,' replied the leader of the three GPU men contemptuously. He wore rimless glasses which gave him the appearance of an intellectual.

'Have you any weapons?' was the next question, and then: 'Get up and get dressed.' He went over to the window and carefully drew the curtains. Gurevitch, the Manager of the Lux, sprawled in an armchair whilst the other three began to search the room.

Heinz began to console me as he dressed. 'Don't look so frightened,' he said. He himself showed no signs of fear or distress. The leader of the three interrupted him: 'It's forbidden to talk in German,' he snapped.

One of the three GPU men, a fat little man, was occupied in searching through the thousand-odd volumes of our library. He flicked over the pages of each book separately, and from time to time he gleefully carried some interesting find over to his superior. Books by Trotsky, Zinoviev, Radek and Bukharin began to pile up on the floor. Excitedly, he brought over a letter from Stalin to Heinz written in 1926 and stuck away in one of the books. It was a letter asking him to launch a campaign against Zinoviev in the *Rote Fahne*, the central organ of the German Communist Party. The man with the rimless glasses read it carefully and then commented briefly: 'So much the worse for him.' The air was already full of dust. The leader of the three sat at our writing desk and carefully examined everything in it. Everything, every photo, even the letters of my children, were confiscated.

Heinz and I sat opposite each other and I tried to stop the trembling of my body. He spoke unimportant Russian phrases, but from time to time he interpolated a sentence in German: 'If you can manage to get abroad, go to Friedrich Adler.' And then words of consolation for me: 'Don't be so depressed and miserable. We shall see each other again at some time or other.'

The first light of dawn came through the curtains, and then the usual noises of a big hotel coming to life in the morning began to make themselves heard. But the daylight and the normal bustle were not for us. Our last hours together had come. I knew it, and I was as though numbed. I was unable to speak.

The leader of the search commando then began to draw up the protocol of the operation: 'Sixty books of Trotskyite, Zinovievite, Kamenevite and Bukharinite content confiscated, together with a trunk full of manuscripts, letters and other documents.'

Heinz put on his hat and coat. I leaned against the bookcase for support, clenched my fists, dug my nails into my flesh and pressed my lips tightly together in order not to cry. But when we embraced the tears flowed. 'Don't cry,' he said. 'Don't cry.'

'That's enough. Get a move on, now,' ordered the leader. At the door Heinz turned and strode back, took me in his arms again and kissed me. 'Cry then,' he said. 'There's enough to cry about.'

He was gone. The room was empty; the light still on; books and papers were scattered over the floor. Then, as though it could do any good, I hurried down to the room of the Director of the Cadre Department of the Comintern, Alichanov, an old friend of ours. His wife opened the door. Alichanov was sitting up in bed. I noticed he was sweating. When I told him what had happened, he nodded and mopped his face with a handkerchief. In a trembling voice, hardly able to contain my sobbing, I asked him whether he could do anything to help us. He looked blank, but promised that anything he could do he would. Of course, there was nothing he could do, and a few months later they came for him too.

The first day after the May Day holidays the telephone rang. It was the nanny of my friend, Hilda Duty, and she asked me to come down to the vestibule at once. I could tell from her voice that something was wrong. I went down and found her waiting there with Hilda's little daughter, Svietlana. In an undertone, she told me excitedly that Hilda had been arrested in the night. The tears ran helplessly down her chubby, wrinkled, peasant face. 'My God!' she said. 'What shall I do. You must help me, Grete.' And whilst we stood in the corner with anxious faces whispering to each other the employees of the Comintern went off to work through the vestibule with its ornate pomp of huge mirrors and gilded whorls of another age. They were the 'Just', and they hoped to escape a similar fate by 'Bolshevist watchfulness'. To save themselves, many of them did not hesitate to denounce their comrades to the GPU.

'Don't cry, Zhura,' I begged, and there were tears in my own voice. 'I'll do everything I can to help you.' Little Svietlana looked up at us both suspiciously. 'When is my mummy coming back?' she asked. Zhura wiped her eyes with the end of her shawl. 'Soon. Very soon, my sweet,' she said.

I watched them go through the revolving doors out into the street. On the way back to my room, I met the old Polish revolutionary, Veletski. He had never passed me without a friendly greeting and perhaps a word or two. I smiled and nodded, but he looked away deliberately and there was an embarrassed and rather guilty expression on his face. So I was already an outcast? The dependant of one of the arrested couldn't be recognised. And it was the same with the others. They eyed

me contemptuously and curiously as they passed. It is not easy to keep
a good countenance with a lump in your throat.

Five days had passed and I was still not arrested. I hadn't yet dared
to get into touch with any of our good friends, for I was unwilling to
endanger them. Every time the telephone bell rang I lifted the receiver
hesitantly and rather anxiously. I knew that all my calls were listened
to. Joseph Lengyel, one of our friends, rang up. 'What's the matter
with you? Why don't we hear anything of you? Is anything wrong?' I
heard the well-known click on the line. The control had switched in.
'Why, nothing at all. Everything's in order.' 'Can you meet me tomorrow
in the usual place?' 'Yes, of course.' The 'usual place' was the Café
Sport. But what would happen if I were followed. No; I couldn't take
the responsibility. But in the end I went. The urge to see a friendly
face, to have someone to pour out my heart to, drove me to the
rendezvous.

Those Left Behind

During the two years we were in Moscow Heinz and I had very few
real friends. We were regarded as 'politically unreliable' and therefore
friendship had to be stronger than the fear of being compromised. The
few friends we did have remained loyal to me even after my husband's
arrest. We used to meet secretly somewhere in the suburbs, and we lived
in fear between such meetings in case we should not see each other
again. And all of them met the same fate. They were all arrested, one
after the other, before my turn came. I suffered the anxiety of being left
behind again and again, until after about a year I was arrested too.

A few days after the GPU had taken Heinz away the manager of the
Lux informed me that I was to be transferred to the so-called NEP wing
of the hotel. This was an old building on the other side of the courtyard,
and it was now used to quarter the families of those who had been arrested
from the Lux. I had to share a room with Michailina, the sixty-year-old
sister of Gorski, a Polish employee of the Comintern who had been arrested
a little while before. Before coming to Moscow for political work, Gorski
had spent almost ten years in Polish prisons. Michailina had been only a
short time in Moscow; she had come from Warsaw to visit her brother
after his long term of imprisonment. She had never been politically active
herself, and had always concerned herself exclusively with her household
affairs. 'And now in Moscow they arrest my brother!' she exclaimed. 'In
the Soviet Union, the land of his dreams.' She almost drove herself crazy
trying to imagine what he could have done to make them arrest him. After

all, he had devoted himself wholeheartedly to the cause of Communism and spent ten of the best years of his life in prison for it. Michailina told me that shortly before he was arrested she had applied to the Comintern for an exit permit to go home. 'They wouldn't even listen to me,' she said indignantly. 'They just hung up the receiver and left me there. And then came Gurevitch and told me I had to get out of my room, and they put me in this gloomy hole. Isn't it enough to drive you mad?'

Every room in this wing held a similar tragedy. Mothers and wives spent their days going from one prison to the other in the hope of finding out the whereabouts of husband or son. They were forced to sell their little possessions one after the other, for there was neither support nor work for those 'left behind'. And at night they waited for their own arrest. For weeks and months the bag which was to accompany them to Siberia stood ready packed in a corner.

From our window we could see into the vestibule of the hotel. When the light went on in the hall after midnight we knew that the GPU was in the place again, and with beating hearts we listened for the tramp of heavy boots. Whose turn would it be next? No one any longer asked why she should be arrested at all or why they had arrested our menfolk. Only very few were capable of understanding what was happening.

The morning gossip of those 'left behind' – and of many others all over Russia at that time – was: 'Did you hear who they came for last night? Comrade X.' One Polish Communist resisted arrest with a revolver in his hand and shot down several GPU men. That was talked about for days. But not only men were arrested, and there were heart-rending scenes when mothers were taken away from their children. The children were then sent to children's homes which were so overcrowded that they received scant attention and care.

As very few families in Moscow ever have more than one room to live and sleep in, the children experienced all the terrors of arrests and searches. I can still hear the more and more anxious questions of little Svietlana, the four-year-old daughter of my friend Hilda: 'Why did my mother have to go away to Prague in the middle of the night?' Her mother had told her that when she was arrested, and promised to come back soon. 'Who were those men who came to take her away?' 'Why did Nanny cry so much when Mummy had gone?'

On one occasion I overheard the children of the unfortunates in the NEP wing talking to each other. 'Is your daddy arrested, too?' 'No; my daddy's on holiday in the Caucasus.' And then the eleven-year-old daughter of one of the arrested comrades destroyed the child's illusion. 'Oh, he's in the Caucasus, is he? Well, why does your mother pay money into the prison, then? A fine Caucasus, that is!'

At that time a joke went the rounds in Moscow. 'They've taken Teruel. Have you heard?' It was the time of the Spanish Civil War. 'You don't say so. And his wife as well?' 'No, no. Teruel's a town.' 'Good heavens! They've started arresting whole towns?' A joke – with many bitter tragedies behind it.

Amongst our neighbours in the NEP wing were many Polish women, some of them over sixty, whose husbands had been arrested during the past few months. These men had all been old Bolshevists or they wouldn't have been in Moscow at all, and most of their wives had been staunch Communists – often for many years. One of these women had spent her childhood in Siberia as the daughter of a political exile under the Czar. Hardly a soul was left from the Polish section of the Comintern. Even the seventy-year-old Varski, who had been a personal friend of Lenin, was not spared. The Old Bolshevists Homes both in Moscow and Leningrad were closed for lack of inmates. In those days GPU cars drove through the streets of Moscow from all quarters taking new prisoners to the Lubianka. The foreigners represented only a very small contingent, relatively speaking, but naturally we heard about them and their fate first. Amongst the arrested were Germans, Poles, Lithuanians, Latvians, Finns, Bulgars and even representatives of the Eastern peoples, including Chinese and Japanese. The British, French and Americans were hardly touched.

On one occasion Michailina said drily: 'You get used to arrests gradually. I wonder if it'll be the same with executions.'

It was now two weeks since Heinz had been arrested and I had spent most of the time going from prison to prison: from the Lubianka to Sokolniki, from Sokolniki to the Butirka, from the Butirka to the military prison at Lefortorgo, and back again. Standing in queues for hours only to hear when my turn came: '*Nyet*. Not here.' It was the same everywhere I went. Hundreds of women besieged the prisons daily looking for their men or, if they had been lucky enough to find them, paying in their fifty roubles a month – for that was the only privilege granted to political prisoners not yet convicted. I deliberately do not say 'awaiting trial', because they got no trial. I had thought that they could receive parcels and letters, and that sooner or later their relatives would be allowed to visit them, just as relatives of prisoners can in all other countries, even in Nazi Germany, but no, not in Soviet Russia. Once when I was standing in line again at the Butirka Prison there was a little girl lining up with us. She was about ten years old and she clutched a dirty little wad of rouble notes in her hand. 'Who are you paying in for, dear?' someone asked her. 'Daddy and Mummy,' she replied in a voice hardly above a whisper.

And then at last my search came to an end. I found out where he was and was allowed to pay in my fifty roubles. He was in the Lubianka, and had probably been there all the time, all the many times I had been there and been sent away. In my excitement I paid in the whole fifty roubles at once, forgetting the advice of the other women that I should pay it in, as was permissible, twice a month, twenty-five roubles at a time, because then I should have to wait only a fortnight to find out whether he was still there instead of a month. I wrote my name on the form and I was told by the other women that this form was presented to the prisoner for his signature. In this way Heinz would know soon that I was still free and was doing my best for him. I was almost happy when I went out.

I stood in the great square and looked up at the Lubianka Prison, a great grey brick building with the red flag flying on top. Day and night it is guarded by GPU soldiers with fixed bayonets, and after dark it is floodlit. My eye travelled over the long lines of cell windows, each one so covered that no one could look out. I wondered if he was in one of them I could see, and which one. If only I could see him! But at least he was alive, and as I went home I realised for the first time that summer had come.

That night I suffered a nightmare. I saw him high up on the roof of the Lubianka. Paralysed with fright, I realised he was about to jump. With arms outspread, he held a great red flag behind him and as I shrieked he plunged down. His body hit the roadway in front of me and a great pool of blood began to spread.

One day I saw the wife of the German Comrade Schubert coming towards me. And as I didn't know whether she would greet me or not, I looked away. But she caught me by the arm. 'What's the matter with you?' she asked. 'Why don't you ever come to see us now?'

'But you know what's happened,' I replied. 'How could I dare to endanger you and your husband?' But she pressed me, nevertheless, to go and see them, and I did. X had been unemployed for months. He told me that he was expecting to be arrested any night and that they had destroyed all letters – in fact, every written word. 'Of course,' he said, 'Heinz is as innocent as I am, as innocent as all the arrested are, and all those who will be arrested. We're victims of Russian foreign policy. They don't need us any longer and they want to get rid of us. We're a nuisance to them.' His face was drawn and almost yellow and his hands trembled. When I first knew him he was strong and robust. 'Do your best for my wife and kiddie if they arrest me. She can't speak any Russian at all.'

A week later his wife and child moved into our NEP wing, and the same day many others came too. Apparently the GPU had organised a 'German Night'.

One evening, much earlier than usual, the frightening report spread through the NEP wing: 'They're here.' We were in the communal kitchen at the time preparing our evening meal. A number of German women fled out of the kitchen, leaving their pots and pans, and huddled together in an adjoining room like animals seeking safety from an approaching storm. We listened anxiously to the sound of footsteps, trying to make out which door they would knock at.

That same evening I took a bus out along the Leningrad Road on my way to a rendezvous with our friend, Heinrich Kurella. Unobtrusively, I carefully watched everyone who had got on to the bus with me to see whether any of them got out at the same stop as I did. I might be followed, but apparently I was not, and I waited in a park on the outskirts for Kurella. Would he come? Perhaps they had come for him already. They would sooner or later; they were not likely to forget him.

Kurella, the brother of the later Culture Functionary of the SED, Alfred Kurella, had worked in the Comintern until the end of 1936. At one of the usual party meetings at the time of the purge a Communist woman from Hamburg asked him publicly: 'Why do you go so often to Room 175 in the Lux?' That was the number of our room. 'Heinz Neumann is an old friend of mine,' he answered, 'and I go to see him occasionally.' That was enough. Shortly after that he was out of work and out of his room. Now he was waiting for the end.

But this time he did come, and I had real news for him. We met near the park gates. 'I've found Heinz,' I whispered excitedly. 'He's in the Lubianka and I was able to pay in fifty roubles for him.'

'Do you know what has happened in the past few days?' he asked me sombrely. 'It's the Red Army's turn now. Tukhachevsky, Yakir, Blücher, Samarnitz – all the old officers from the days of the Civil War have been arrested. Somehow I don't think they'll bring them to trial publicly. They wouldn't be docile enough.'

We talked anxiously and it grew dark. The park gates were closed and we walked together through the streets. 'Is there no chance at all of getting away? Must we wait and let ourselves be slaughtered like sheep?' How could we have suffered everything all those years without criticism? What came out of Moscow was accepted as gospel, and we suppressed all our doubts. We wanted to believe. The alternative was grim. But now we had to pay for our credulity.

That was the last time I saw Kurella. The next time I went to the rendezvous I waited vainly for two hours. He didn't come. Afterwards I learnt that he had been arrested on his way to the railway station. He wanted to get down to the Crimea in the hope of being able to escape across the Black Sea.

Foreign Communists in Russia, political emigrants or Comintern workers, were provided with a document similar to the French *permis de séjour*. Their own passport, if they had one, was always taken away and kept in the Comintern until such time as they should need it again – if ever. My German passport was held in this way. Shortly before Heinz was arrested, my permission to stay expired and they should have seen to its extension. I telephoned the department of the Comintern in charge of such matters and I was told that from now on I came under the Registration Office for Foreigners and had nothing to do with the Comintern. My work for the Foreign Workers' Publishing House was at an end, and in order to get a new job I needed some valid document or other. I therefore went to the Registration Office for Foreigners and joined the tail of another long queue. When I finally got to the official, I was informed that my permit to stay could be extended only if I produced my German passport. I tried to explain my situation, but the only answer I got was: 'Bring your passport; without that we can do nothing.' However, for the time being they handed me a little pink slip which gave me permission to exist in the Soviet Union for five days. With that I couldn't get work.

I rang up the Comintern again. They denied all knowledge of the whereabouts of my German passport and they refused to get into touch with the officials at the Registration Office. Almost all those 'left behind' suffered a similar experience, with the result that we were all compelled to go to the Registration Office every five days to have our wretched pink slips extended, which also meant that we could get no work. We were gradually being driven into a corner. The dependants of the arrested were not entitled to any assistance, and yet amongst them were many women with young children to feed somehow. In their desperation and helplessness, some of them decided to go to the German Embassy in Moscow, which was, of course, now in Nazi hands. Some of those who did that were arrested on the street afterwards by the GPU. A considerable number of the dependants of the arrested members of the Austrian Schutzbund decided to take the same course. The Nazis gave them sanctuary in a building adjoining the German Embassy, and the next day they all went to the Registration Office for Foreigners escorted by an official of the Embassy to protect them from molestation by the GPU and to obtain permission to return to Austria. It was at this time that we heard of the first deportations of dependants to Hitler Germany.

In order to exist at all, we were compelled gradually to sell all we possessed. First of all came the so-called valuables, such as gramophones, records, cameras and wireless sets, then books, and after that clothes. These we had to offer on the free market and because few of us spoke Russian fluently we were swindled right and left.

There was another of our friends who remained loyal after the GPU had arrested Heinz; that was the Hungarian comrade, Joseph Lengyel, the one I had met a day or so afterwards in the Café Sport. He was married to a Russian girl, and they invited me to visit them. Despite lively doubts about the advisability of going, and after taking innumerable precautions against being followed, I went. They had one room in a typical Russian dwelling which consisted of six rooms. At one time it had been occupied by one family; now each room was occupied by a family. The kitchen and the bathroom were used in common. As may be imagined, there was fruitful opportunity for endless squabbles, particularly in the kitchen. Each family had a small space allotted to it there to prepare its meals. And the trouble! Each accused the other of untidiness and uncleanliness. And the talk and the backbiting! When I was there we had to speak in whispers, for no one was to know that we were speaking German. My friend tried to get me some copying work, though he had been without work himself for months. He had been a contributor to a magazine, but he had written an article which had been condemned as 'deviating from the Party line' and now he was out of work. He was still a member of the Party, but he had received 'a stern reprimand with final warning'. He had also written a novel describing the experiences of a foreign worker in the Soviet Union, but unfortunately it mentioned the hunger years of 1930–1, and although it had already been accepted by the State Publishing House it was soon afterwards sent back to him with the remark: 'There was never any hunger period in the Soviet Union.'

The wife of Joseph told me about her sister, who was a poster artist. She was a talented woman and until her husband's arrest she had never lacked work. Now she was finding it increasingly difficult. On one occasion she submitted a sketch for a poster for the November celebrations. The subject was 'Stalin amongst the Children'. The sketch was returned with the observation, 'The face of Comrade Stalin is not sufficiently benevolent.' She then sketched a smiling Stalin, but again it came back, this time with the observation, 'Still not sufficiently benevolent.' Only at the third attempt with a Stalin smiling from ear to ear and surrounded by enthusiastically happy children was she successful.

Amongst the wives of the arrested men were some who did not stand by their unfortunate husbands and run from prison to prison until they had found them and then pay in the fifty roubles for them every month. These women declared themselves 'Stalinist Communists' and publicly denounced their husbands, dissociating themselves from their men's 'political deviations', proclaiming their own 'undying loyalty to the Party' and promising 'to maintain greater Bolshevist watchfulness in the future'.

Not that such an attitude always prevented their subsequent arrest, but there was a chance that it might.

The Outlaws

Before Heinz was arrested, he had been under pressure for a long time to persuade him to make a 'satisfactory' public declaration 'criticising his errors' and proclaiming the absolute correctness of the Comintern policy. He was to go down on bended knees, confess his sins and ask for pardon. He steadfastly refused. Our fate in the Soviet Union in those years was the fate of many others. The fate of the German Communists was the fate of a whole generation of former revolutionaries.

We had come to Moscow in May 1935. Heinz had been held in the Swiss prison of Regensdorf for seven months under the constant threat of being handed over to Nazi Germany, until the Swiss Government at last decided that there was no formal justification for the extradition request of the German Government. He was then escorted to a Russian steamer docked in Le Havre and placed on board. We were under no illusions about our probable reception. 'I may be arrested as soon as we get to Leningrad,' Heinz said to me. But he was wrong as far as that was concerned. We were sent on to Moscow and on our arrival we were even given a room in the Lux. But that turned out to have been a mistake, for no sooner had we settled in than Wilhelm Pieck, who was then Secretary of the German Communist Party, phoned us up and demanded that we should leave the Lux immediately and take up our quarters in a special hotel for emigrants in another part of the town. This Heinz firmly refused to do. The matter was finally dropped and we stayed temporary victors in the Lux.

The atmosphere in Moscow when we arrived was already stifling. Former political friends no longer dared visit each other. No one could enter or leave the Lux without a special pass, and the name and particulars of everyone who did so were carefully noted down. All the telephones in the hotel were controlled by the GPU from the central switchboard and we could regularly hear the tell-tale click as the control switched in. The fear of being spied on and listened to became so great that good friends would ask: 'Have you carefully examined your room to make sure there isn't a microphone in it somewhere?' and have to be reassured before they would consent to visit you. On one occasion one of our visitors insisted on searching the room himself, looking in the lamp, under the telephone and inside all the electric-light plugs.

There was hardly one of the political emigrants living in Moscow at the time who had not been guilty of some 'deviation from the Comintern

line' during the previous ten years, and in consequence the International
Control Commission or the Cadre Department of the Comintern had
every one of them under its thumb. Communists who had been guilty
of 'deviations' were told to sign 'a satisfactory declaration' admitting
their political errors and underlining the infallibility of the Comintern
line. After that they were to practise 'Bolshevist watchfulness' and
denounce any instance of criticism they noted amongst the people with
whom they associated, filing signed statements concerning any utterance
in their circle which smacked of 'deviation'. Only if they did all this
would the control authorities believe their protestations of loyalty and
be prepared to use them for political work.

During the two years we were in Moscow before his arrest hardly a
month passed during which Heinz was not called before one or other of
these control commissions: one day it would be the International Control
Commission, the next time it would be the Cadre Department of the
Comintern, and on a third occasion the Cadre Department of the publishing
organisation for which we both worked as translators. They either wanted
to urge him once again to make 'a satisfactory declaration' and admit his
political errors, or they called him to account for this, that or the other
observation hostile to the Party he was supposed to have made.

The following is a characteristic example of the sort of thing that was
constantly happening. A 'Comradely Evening' was held for all the employees
of the Foreign Workers' Publishing House, for which we both worked.
Attendance was obligatory, and the atmosphere at these affairs was one of
strained cordiality and simulated cheerfulness. They were the most stupid
and depressing social occasions imaginable. We all had to be gay by order,
just as we had to demonstrate by order. On this particular evening we had
a foreign visitor, the publisher, Wieland Herzfelde, who had come from
Prague on a visit. He and Heinz knew each other very well, and they sat
together and chatted. Heinz was delighted to find someone he could talk
to without restraint. We had not been sitting together for long when a girl
called Hilde from Prenzlau came up to our table, greeted both Herzfelde
and Heinz and sat down with us. She had married a Russian named Kamarov,
and she now spoke her mother tongue with a stressed Russian accent, and
never let even the faintest opportunity slip of informing all and sundry that
she was a '*Komsomolka*' (a member of the Russian Communist Youth League).

It was perfectly clear to us why she had chosen to sit down uninvited
at our table. I touched Heinz with my foot under the table and used
some phrase or other in which the expression 'all the same' occurred.
It was our signal that danger threatened. The conversation at our table
was interrupted. We went on talking in order that it should not be
obvious that it had been broken off on the arrival of 'Kamarova', as she

always called herself, but it grew more and more tiresome and I got up, feigned tiredness, and went back to the hotel. Heinz stayed on with Herzfelde for a while. When he came in I asked him anxiously whether he had been careful. 'Of course I have,' he replied. 'Do you think I don't know what that disgusting creature was after?'

But a week later he was called to the Cadre, or Control, Department of the publishing house. On the desk in front of the chairman of the department were two handwritten sheets of paper to which he referred from time to time – presumably Kamarova's effort. When you were talking to Comrade Herzfelde did you say this? . . . Did you say that? . . . Did you say the other? Heinz stoutly denied having said any of it, or anything like it. It was ridiculous rubbish, consisting chiefly of contemptuous and rather vulgarly formulated references to the Tchistka.

This Tchistka, or purge, was a regular institution in the Russian Communist Party. In the early days it may have had some sensible purpose, but then it must have been operated very differently; a vigorously active political party needs to get rid of some of its useless ballast from time to time. But now it had developed into a constant threat held over the heads of the Party members to keep them in fear and trembling. The operations of this Tchistka were always public. At the Party meetings, when it was in swing, any member had the right to get up and denounce any other member, or to ask him pointed questions concerning his political past or his present activities, questions which had to be publicly answered on the spot. And if the member questioned had been guilty of some deviation or other, then he had to do penance publicly and morally scourge himself if he was to avoid punishment, involving perhaps expulsion from the Party. Very often an attack of this nature at a Tchistka was the preliminary to subsequent arrest by the GPU. It can be imagined what an opportunity all this offered of paying off old scores.

Like all other political emigrants in the Soviet Union at that time, Heinz and I were prisoners at large. None of us could leave the country unless we were sent abroad by the Comintern on some mission or other. For instance, the German author, Alfred Kurella, lived in Moscow. Henri Barbusse had requested in his will that Kurella should edit his literary estate and generally manage his literary affairs after his death. For this, of course, Kurella would have had to go to Paris, but when Barbusse died the Comintern refused to let him leave the country. The highest body in the Comintern, the International Control Commission, which was elected by the World Congress, was in reality nothing but a subordinate department of the GPU. That was made very obvious to me after my arrest when my examiners used word for word the same phrases as the International Control Commission had previously used towards Heinz when he was still at liberty, living from one summons to the next as the atmosphere grew more and more hostile and the charges more and more serious.

At first they continued to appeal to him, 'as a Bolshevist', to confess his heresies and admit that he had organised 'fractional activities hostile to the German Communist Party' in the years 1931–2. He firmly denied the charge and refused to make the declaration. In the end they lost all patience with him and declared that he was responsible for the victory of German Fascism.

At the end of 1936 he was called to Dimitrov, who was at that time General Secretary of the Comintern. 'I am speaking to you at the express request of Comrade Stalin,' Dimitrov began. 'He has asked me to try and make you into the new type of Bolshevist. First of all, I propose that you should write a book on the Seventh World Congress of the Comintern showing the correctness of its decisions and admitting and sincerely condemning your own serious political errors.'

Heinz never wrote this book, and the result was his arrest.

One night in September Michailina, who had been poorly of late, and I were awakened by a hammering at our door. We knew. It was the GPU. Two men in uniform. 'Have you any weapons?' was the routine preliminary. No. I was certain they had come for me, and I told them my name. But it was not my turn yet. It was Michailina they had come for. She was so upset she could hardly dress and she begged them to be patient, but they urged her all the time to hasten, and when she was dressed they even tried to prevent her taking her case with her. There was nothing I could say to console her. 'Goodbye, Michailina,' I said. 'It won't be long before I come after you.'

It was 'Polish Night' for the GPU. All the Polish women left were taken that night. There was a bus waiting for them down below. Years later I learnt by accident that the unfortunate Michailina had been sentenced to eight years in a concentration camp.

At the end of September I received an official intimation that I had been expelled from the German Communist Party, of which until then I had still been a member. No reason was given. A few days later the management of the Lux gave me and about ten other women notice to vacate our rooms within three days, as we were no longer employees of the Comintern. Naturally, we took, and could take, no notice of it, and so the hotel management took us to court. The court was full and there were many cases to be dealt with, chiefly paternity disputes. There were the mothers with the babies in their arms, flanked by their witnesses, and the unwilling fathers with theirs. The proceedings were conducted by a friendly old gentleman, a lay magistrate, who did his best to persuade the parties to come to an agreement.

When our turn – there were ten of us – came we found that the Secretary of the hotel management was there as interpreter. I refused to accept her services and insisted on putting my own case. In broken Russian, I explained that we had all come to Russia as political emigrants, but that the GPU had arrested our husbands so that we were all without work and without support. In order not to starve, we were selling our few possessions, even our books and our clothes. If we were now turned out of our rooms, we should be on the streets with nowhere to go at all, and no one could be expected to take us in. We hadn't even got valid papers. The old man listened carefully to all this and then asked only one question: had I any relatives in the Soviet Union. Apart from my arrested husband, none. To my relief, he then decided that the hotel could not evict me and that as long as the circumstances remained as they were I need pay no rent. A similar decision was made in respect of the other nine, and we all trooped out happily. At least we still had a roof over our heads, but I knew that Gurevitch, the manager of the Lux, now had his knife deep into me for good.

Gradually I sold all our books. Finally, I was reduced to the political ones, and one day I went to a bookshop in the Ulitza Gorkovo with a case full of Hegel and Lenin. There was an assistant there I had never seen before, and it was very obvious that he was out of place. I offered him my books. 'Hegel and Lenin?' he said with a smile. 'We don't get much call for that sort of thing nowadays. Detective stories go better.' He looked through the books, noted the many marginal comments, nodded with understanding, and said: 'Of course we'll buy them.' And he mentioned an unusually high price. I was delighted, but the next time I went to the shop he had gone, and I did not do so well with my books at all. I told this story to my friend, Joseph Lengyel, and he laughed. 'I'm not surprised,' he said. 'Do you know who that was? Béla Illes. They put him there as a punishment. He was arrested a few days ago.'

Béla Illes was a well-known Hungarian writer and the author of many best-sellers. His latest novel had been written around the building of the famous Moscow Underground. The chief character was the political leader of the work. The MS had passed the censor, and the first edition was already printed when the actual political leader committed suicide. The book was then pulped and Béla Illes was severely reprimanded and sent off to the bookshop in the Ulitza Gorkovo as a punishment.

Life on Recall

The early Russian winter had already begun when Gurevitch found an opportunity of dealing with me. He turned me and Charlotte Eberlein, the wife of the well-known German Communist, Hugo Eberlein, out of the NEP wing of the Lux and gave us 'accommodation' in a room over a disused workshop. The windows didn't close properly and the stove was in disrepair – and the winter was on us. The NEP wing of the Lux had been centrally heated. Now we were to use some of our few precious roubles on fuel. Money was getting more and more scarce, so to economise as far as possible, Charlotte, Eberlein's seventeen-year-old son, Werner, Julius Gebhardt, whose wife had also been arrested, and I formed a communal household for cooking purposes. The only one of our little community still working was Werner. After his father was arrested, he was expelled from the Karl Liebknecht School, where he had been studying, and he then got a job as a transport worker. Naturally, he did not earn much – between 100 and 110 roubles a month, just about enough for him to keep body and soul together. A kilogram (just over two pounds) of beef cost between nine and ten roubles in the State butchers at the time. Pork, obtainable only on the free market, cost seventeen roubles for the same quantity, butter between sixteen and twenty-two roubles, whilst the cheapest bread was just under a rouble – ninety copecks to be precise. Presumably a worker earning Werner's wages wasn't supposed to buy himself any clothes at all. I remember that at the time women's shoes cost between 100 and 250 roubles a pair.

Next to our room lived a Russian who had formerly been employed by the Comintern, but was now working in a foundry. He had been an active revolutionary in 1917. His wife and we cooked on our *kyrasinkas*, a sort of primus stove, in the corridor. Each knew what the other was cooking, and it wasn't long before they realised just how badly off we were. She was a friendly, helpful soul and she soon discovered we were the dependants of arrested men and forced to sell our few belongings in order to exist.

'Where do you sell them?' she asked.

'On the market and in the commission shops.'

'With your Russian, they'll see you coming,' she said. 'I have to take a few things to the market almost every month before pay day. You'd better come with me next time.'

So the next time we went with her and she helped us as best she could. A Russian woman, a stranger to us, dared to be seen with us on the streets and did her best to help us, whilst our own comrades hadn't even got courage enough to greet us when we passed them in the street. The Tchistka regime of 'Bolshevist watchfulness' and 'public declarations' had removed their backbones and robbed them of all civic courage.

The woman's husband earned 300 roubles a month, which was not bad as wages went. She had four children; the eldest was in the Red

Army, the second boy was still a pupil, the third child, a girl of fifteen, was at a secondary school, and then there was an eight-year-old who had just started school: 300 roubles didn't go far with things so expensive. It was just about this time that the girl left school on her own, declaring that she wanted to be able to buy herself a new dress occasionally like the other girls did; so she went to work.

We learnt that they too had been given notice to quit because the husband no longer worked for the Comintern. 'They can't get us out,' the wife explained, 'because we've got a son in the Red Army. And as soon as he comes out, the younger one will go in, so we're safe for a few years.'

When I first went into their room I noticed with some surprise that there was an ikon in one corner. An ikon in the room of a revolutionary worker in a building belonging to the Comintern? One day the man was sitting reading the *Pravda*. It was at the time of the Spanish Civil War. 'They're burning down churches again,' he growled. 'The Godless pack.' 'Do you mean the Republicans?' I asked, a little bewildered. 'Of course I do,' he replied indignantly. Disappointed and embittered by conditions in the Soviet Union, this former revolutionary worker had returned to the beliefs of his fathers. The fact that the *Pravda* supported the Spanish Republicans was quite enough to make him oppose them. A little later the wife told me that her husband had allowed her to put the ikon back only quite recently.

Two days before the celebration of the anniversary of the November Revolution, workmen appeared and bricked in the communication corridor between the NEP wing and the main part of the hotel. Henceforth we had to go in and out over the courtyard and were not allowed access to the baths, which were in the main building. We might have been lepers.

Various workshops gave on to the courtyard through which we had to pass. One of them was a carpenters' and joiners' where furniture was made and repaired for the various buildings of the Comintern, including the Lux, whose rooms were all furnished. Almost every day through the windows of the workshop, we could see Wilhelm Pieck, the leader of the German Communist Party, choosing the timber and superintending the execution of his new furniture. At that time members of his Party were being arrested and sent to concentration camps both in Nazi Germany and Soviet Russia.

In December 1937, I was once again at the Lubianka to pay in my twenty-five roubles, but this time the official snapped '*Ewo nyeto*' – 'Not here'. And then the hunt started all over again. I went from prison to prison, from the Lubianka to the Butirka, from the Butirka to Lefortorgo,

from Lefortorgo to Sokolniki and back to the Lubianka again – in vain.
There was an institution in Moscow, the Secretariat of Public Prosecutions.
There one was supposed to be able to obtain information concerning
proceedings or judgments. When I arrived there the waiting room was
packed with hundreds of people trying to find out something about their
vanished relatives. Women who came out of the information room were
often sobbing, and they were almost all pale and distraught. 'Ten years,'
I heard on one occasion, and 'Sent to an Isolator, with prohibition of
letters' on another. But most of them could find out nothing at all. Each
department had its own information office and I went to one after the
other. Everywhere I got the same reply: 'Your husband's case is not in
our hands.'

After some hesitation, I went to the information office of the Supreme
Military Court. Here I found not more than a dozen or so women
waiting. They were all well dressed, and an almost friendly atmosphere
prevailed. These women were the wives of high officials of the Party or
high officers who had been arrested. An officer of the GPU in uniform
provided the information. He was very smartly uniformed and most
polite and helpful. He listened considerately to what I had to say; then
I had to go out again into the waiting room. About half an hour later
he called me in again. I could see at once that his attitude had changed.
'No information whatever will be given about the Neumann case,' he
said coldly. There was nothing more I could do, and I went away in
deep depression. Soon after that I heard a rumour that Heinz had been
shot. Without a trial and without a word to his wife about his fate? It
depressed me terribly, but I didn't really believe it.

One afternoon in January 1938, there was a knock at our door. I
opened it. Two uniformed GPU officials stood there. Well, here it is at
last, I thought. But no; instead they handed me a document authorising
them to confiscate the property of Heinz Neumann. Once again the
cupboards were opened. There were things that obviously belonged to
him: a couple of shirts, some underwear and a suit I had kept in the
hope that he would come out and need them again. They took them,
and then they saw the typewriter. I fought despairingly to retain it, saying
that it was mine; it was the tool of my trade; without it I couldn't work
and earn enough to eat. It was no use, and they took that too. The official confiscation of a man's belongings means that he has received a
severe sentence, a minimum of ten years' imprisonment. The same day
the belongings of R. F. were confiscated in the same way. Apparently
they had suffered the same fate, probably in the same affair.

But I still made the rounds of the prisons and stood in the queues
in the faint hope of finding him, or hearing something or other about

him. So long as I knew that he was in the Lubianka, my anxious thoughts had a point on which they could concentrate. But now? How many people did I question in the hope of finding out some new way to try, some line that had escaped me perhaps! But none of them could help me. I had come up against the final brick wall. During my enquiries, I learnt a good deal about life in Soviet prisons. The prisoners slept on boards; they had no warm blankets; all they got to eat was soup. And everyone urgently advised me to keep a case ready packed with warm things to accompany me to prison when I was arrested.

Towards the end of 1937 a good deal of excitement was caused by the report, afterwards substantiated, that Yezhov, the chief of the GPU, had shot himself when they came to arrest him. At Stalin's instructions, Yezhov had arrested hundreds of thousands and murdered hecatombs of victims. And now his turn had come. What could have been the reason for his arrest? And all we could think of, distrustful and despairing as we were, was that he had been made a scapegoat, that the people were to think that he had overstepped his authority, that he alone was responsible for the terror. Perhaps a milder course was now to be adopted?

But no, the arrests continued. Béla Kun and most of the Hungarian political emigrants were taken. In February my friend H was arrested, and his wife came to stand with me day after day in the queues at one prison after the other.

In May 1937, shortly after Heinz was arrested, I sent a postcard to my sister, who was living in Paris, telling her what had happened and asking her to write *poste restante*. In this way we managed to keep in touch for a whole year, until I too was arrested. Between unimportant observations, I slipped in everything of importance, and so my sister was kept informed of my desperate situation and able to take steps on my behalf. One day I was called to the Customs Office in Moscow and there I found a parcel containing two silk dresses which had been sent from Prague by an unknown consignor. Such things were as rare as rubies in Moscow and almost as expensive. I sold them on the market and had enough to eat for a month. On another occasion someone sent me 200 roubles. The name of the sender was given as Ivan Buber, from an address in Moscow. I hurried off to the address given, but I found it was the address of the People's Commissariat for Defence. Then in 1938 I received a postcard: 'Be patient a little while longer. Help is coming.'

A week after that I got a letter from the French Consulate in Moscow asking me to come there on a certain day. Before I went, I said goodbye to all my friends, and then I went off with my prison case already packed and all the money I possessed in my pocket, for in those days people coming out of a foreign consulate were as likely to be arrested as not.

I went by a devious route, trying to discover whether I was being followed – apparently not. Before the French Consulate were police, and one or two men in civilian clothes who looked suspicious to me. I stood there at some distance, not knowing what to do and trying to make up my mind. Perhaps it would mean my salvation. Perhaps they would offer me asylum there and then. Perhaps I should be arrested when I came out. Perhaps I should be sent to Siberia.

I summoned up my courage and went in. The French Consul informed me that the French Government was prepared to give me a *sauf conduit* for the journey to Paris and to grant me permission to stay for a period of three months. I was overjoyed, but I knew there was much more to it than that. 'Can you help me to get an exit permit from the Russian authorities?' I asked. He shrugged his shoulders. 'I'm afraid that as you're not a French citizen there is nothing we can do for you in that respect,' he replied. 'And the less we have to do with the Russkies the better we're pleased.' I explained my situation to him, the arrest of my husband, the danger of my own arrest, and all the difficulties. He remained beautifully polite to the end, but unhelpful. Very well, I'd try what I could do myself, and I left the Consulate clutching the *sauf conduit* around which all my hopes were now centred.

To my relief, no attempt was made to interfere with me, and I then went to the Passport Office to apply for permission to leave the country. They were more than a little astonished to find a German in possession of a French document, but they took my application and then gave me a twelve-day permit to stay. Twelve whole days! As a German, they had never given me more than five days at a time. The next few days I spent in alternate fear and hope. Should I now be arrested? Or would they really give me an exit permit? It took a few weeks before I was finally prepared to admit that all hope was gone. The Russians refused to let me leave the country. One more reason for the GPU to arrest me.

The old life of waiting to be arrested and standing in one queue after the other went on as though it had never been interrupted by a thin ray of hope. My prison case was no longer so heavy; one thing after another had been taken out and sold on the market. And everywhere I went looking for Heinz I got the same reply: '*Ewo nyeto*' – 'Not here.' And still I was not arrested, and outside – outside me – it was spring again. Had they forgotten me?

No; it came at last; and when they showed me the order for my arrest it was dated 15 October 1937. It was not executed until 19 June 1938. Michailina was right. You got used to arrests. When they came into my room with the usual question, 'Have you any weapons?' and began their

search I was perfectly calm and not in the least frightened – I had known
for so long now that it was inevitable.

Arrested

I was taken in a Ford between two GPU men, my prison case at my feet,
and as we drove through the streets of Moscow in the first grey of the
morning I looked around me with interest. It will be a long time before
you see streets and people in freedom again, I thought. It was – seven
long years. We drove into the courtyard of the Lubianka and the Ford
stopped. I was taken through a side door into the building and put in a
small cell with a table and a chair. Soon afterwards they brought me a
long questionnaire and pen and ink. I filled it in. After that I was put into
a so-called *sobatchnik*, or dog kennel, a very small cell without a window
and with one narrow bench to sit down on. When you are seated your
knees almost touch the door. Just in front of you is a spy-hole. Every few
minutes it was opened to reveal an unwinking and inhuman-looking eye.
The cell was lighted, and from time to time a fan was turned on somewhere and a current of air with an indefinable smell went through the
cell. After a while, I went to sleep huddled up on the bench and when
the cell door was finally opened and I got up I almost fell out head first.
   A uniformed GPU man led me along a stone corridor which made
our footsteps echo, and took me into a room where I was handed over
to a woman in a white apron whose appearance was vaguely discon-
certing. She had coarse black hair, high cheekbones and a very red
complexion, and she at once proceeded to search me. It was a very thorough and very humiliating operation.
   For many months I had got used to the idea of going to prison, but
what that really means you learn when you sit for the first time behind
a locked door without a handle. And a bodily search at the Lubianka is
the thing to let you know to the full what being a prisoner means; not
even the most intimate parts of your body are any longer decently your
own; you are no longer a human being; you are a thing, an object to
be mauled unceremoniously by such creatures as the woman with the
coarse black hair and the florid features.
   Full of the desire for revenge, I accompanied the warder up a flight of
stairs and along another corridor with many doors until finally he paused
before one of them, unlocked it and ushered me in. The door slammed
into place behind me. It was a cell with three mattresses and a number of
stools. Light came in from a barred window high up in the opposite wall.
A middle-aged woman sat on one of the stools delving into a sack she

had brought with her. She nodded to me silently and continued what she was doing. Out of the sack she produced various other sacks. I must have looked like a child watching a conjurer, for she began to explain:

'This big sack is for my clothes, so that they can't steal them so easily in Siberia. This one's for bread. This one's for stale bread, and this little one here's for salt. Yes; you live and learn, my dear. I'm better equipped this time than I was last. I was in prison then because I was my husband's wife. After a while they let me go, and then I prepared myself to go to prison on my own account.'

It was no news to me that women were sent to prison in Soviet Russia as *zhena*, as wives or mothers of male offenders, and for no other reason. The nearest relatives of a man, wife or grown-up children, were held responsible for his misdeeds with him. Before we had time to go into any further details the door was unlocked and another woman was pushed in. She was in tears and protesting her innocence – as though innocence mattered in such a place.

Soon after that the door was again opened and I was called out 'with things'. This time I was put in a smaller cell for two prisoners. Before the window was a metal covering to prevent prisoners from looking out, so that it was probably facing the street. I sat there miserably wondering what was going to happen next, my eyes fixed on the door and my ears strained to catch every sound in the corridor. Footsteps sounded. They came to a halt outside the door, the lock clicked and when the door opened a girl in a yellow summer dress came in. She had dark brown curls and a fresh, healthy complexion. She seemed tremendously amused about something. She sat down with a flop on the free stool and burst out laughing.

'How right my mother was!' she exclaimed. 'When I put this new dress on for the first time this morning she said: "You never know, a new life may start for you now." And it has.' And she shook with laughter.

It appeared that as she had left the university, where she was studying medicine, two men had arrested her, put her in a car and brought her to the Lubianka. She declared that she hadn't the faintest idea why.

The spy-hole in this cell kept going all the time too. To make it still more uncanny, it was painted on the inside in the form of a human eye. Neither of us had had any experience of prison life and when the mealtime came round I ate for the first time out of a metal bowl. It was a brown tin like a dog's dish, and in it was lentil soup which smelt quite good, but I couldn't get it down. With it was a crust of Russian black bread. Normally, I quite like that bread, but the Lubianka had robbed me of all appetite.

The door opened again and my companion was told to come 'without things' – she had none. She patted her hair, stroked her dress straight and went out with a smile. I sat behind waiting for my turn. Did they know anything about my secret meetings with Heinrich Kurella or Joseph Lengyel? Or had someone denounced me for something I had said? Or was it just my routine arrest? If only I could speak Russian better! What did they know? And in my restlessness I sprang up and took my first walk in a prison cell – five paces forward, five paces back, up and down, up and down. It was perhaps two hours when my fellow prisoner came back. This time she was not laughing and there was a look of fear on her face. I couldn't get a word out of her and she stared anxiously at the spy-hole.

Again the door was opened and this time an old peasant woman came in. She was about seventy years old with a wrinkled face brown with age and the sun. She put down her bundle, looked around for a seat, sat down and sighed contentedly.

'Thank God that I was able to come to Moscow for once in my life,' she said at last. 'I always wanted to. How nice it is here, and warm, and there's electric light, and they bring you your food. And how clean it is! There's nothing at all to worry about.'

And then she told us that many years before she had been sent to Siberia as a 'prisoner at large' because she had been a Social Revolutionary. She had lived in a mud hut, and but for the kindness of the peasants she would have starved. And how lonely it had been! Her only companion was a cat. And the trouble to get fuel during the long winter!

'Here at least you're amongst fellow human beings. I count myself lucky.'

I listened to her with astonishment. It was a new point of view to me. Whilst she was talking the door opened again. It was for the girl 'without things'. Again she was away for an hour or so and then back in the cell for perhaps ten or fifteen minutes. And so it went on through the night. Each time she flung herself down on to the mattress and tried to sleep, and each time she was called out again. I knew from the stories of others that this was a favourite GPU method – chain questioning, designed to break a suspect's spirit.

The light was on all night. I sat on a stool and leant against the wall. There were only two mattresses in the cell. The old Social Revolutionary slept as peacefully as a child on one of them.

The first thin light of morning began to come through the sides of the window cover when the young girl came back again. This time she sat huddled up on the other stool and began to talk in a frightened voice trembling with tears.

'They've arrested my boyfriend as well,' she said. 'He's a student too. They say he was preparing an attempt on Stalin's life and that I knew all about it. It's madness. My God! My God! What shall I do?'

She looked very different from the fresh, cheerful girl who had come in the day before. Her eyes were now swollen with weeping, her face was smeared, her hair was in disorder and her nice new summer dress was all creased. The old woman woke up and tried to console her, but without effect. I sat on the edge of the old girl's mattress and had to tell her about life abroad and in Moscow, and about everything that had happened in recent years. She was a real personality, and she radiated a calm and philosophical confidence which almost made me forget where I was. I shared a cell with her for two days and grew greatly attached to her in that short time. When we parted she patted me on the shoulder and paid me perhaps the highest compliment of my life: 'Don't worry, my dear,' she said. 'You're not the sort to go under in Siberia.'

On the second day she went off to be examined. When she came back she was smiling, and she chuckled as she told me about it.

'When I went in there was a young fellow, about twenty he was, sitting there solemnly. "What?" I said. "I suppose you're the oldest they've got here?" "Sit down, citizen," he said severely. "Speak when you're spoken to." And then he read out a long rigmarole. "Anna Pavlovna . . . charged with preparation for terror." "Preparation for terror?" I said. "No, batushka; that means you, not me." He didn't like that, and here I am again.'

On the third day I said goodbye to my companions and was taken away. They took me through the spick-and-span corridors of the Lubianka, where everything smells of carbolic and disinfectant – an efficient destruction machine which filled me with fear. Before I knew what was happening, I found myself in a courtyard in which there were two prison cars. One of them was the typical Russian version of the 'Black Maria', but the other was painted white and camouflaged as a baker's delivery van, with the words 'Bread, Rolls and Cakes' painted on it in gold letters – 'Maria' in disguise. So I was leaving the Lubianka without even being questioned. Perhaps they already knew all they wanted to know about me. I was the wife of Heinz Neumann. That was enough.

I was put into a little compartment about the size of a small wardrobe, with just enough room to perch on a narrow bench, and then off we went through the Moscow streets. I could hear the horns of motors and the bells of tramcars. Life in Moscow was going on as usual without me.

Cell 31

After a while the car began to slow down, and finally it stopped. My wardrobe door was opened and I tumbled out to find myself in another courtyard with about a dozen other women, both old and young, carrying bundles and cases. Uniformed officials herded us together and hurried us off into a room something like a station waiting room. It turned out that we were in the Butirka. I was placed in a small cell alone, and then the reception formalities began. My case was taken away, but I was left with a blanket, a pillow and some underwear. After a while a uniformed wardress took me to have a bath. The air was humid and disagreeable. Whilst I washed myself, an eye looked at me all the time through the spy-hole. Then the same wardress took me through corridor after corridor, and as she walked along she hammered at regular intervals with a large key on the metal buckle of her belt. This, I learnt, was to warn other warders who might be accompanying prisoners. Prisoners in the Butirka were not supposed to see any other prisoner, apart from their cell mates. It was all very well organised.

She came to a halt at Cell 31 and unlocked it. When she opened the door for me to go in, I stood on the threshold petrified and wondering whether my eyes were deceiving me. But a push between the shoulders soon shoved me in and the door clanged behind me. My first thought was that I was being put away in a lunatic asylum. There were scores of half-naked women in the cell, lying down on boards, sitting, leaning against each other and the walls. It was like a heap of worms and the air was hardly breathable. There was a constant undertone of noise as they all talked to each other in whispers. No one took the least notice of me. I was obviously just another one. I stood there with my bundle hesitantly and then I sat down with some embarrassment on the edge of the boards. A girl came up to me. It was Käthe Schulz. She had beautiful red-blonde hair and delicate features, and she spoke in authentic Berlin dialect.

'You're German, aren't you?' she whispered. 'Anyone can see that. You're not allowed to speak above a whisper here, by the way. What a hole. The cell's supposed to be for twenty-five. With you, we're a hundred and ten. I'll tell the Cell Senior. Perhaps she can find you a place somehow.'

The Cell Senior was a Georgian woman named Tasso Salpeter. She welcomed me amiably.

'It's difficult to find any more room,' she said. 'You'll have to stick it next to the lavatory pails for a while until I can find you a better place.'

And so I took my place next to the *parasha*, as the institution is called in Russian prison slang – *parasha* is the diminutive of Praskovya, a Russian girl's Christian name. My neighbour proved to be an epileptic, who had been put there on account of her 'bad behaviour'. Then there were a number of women who had neither blankets nor coats, and who could find no one to share a blanket with them. It was too cold for them near the window, so they had to put up with the smell. In order to provide sleeping accommodation for the 110 inmates, all the wall beds were turned down and planks were placed across them. These were the notorious *naris*

I had already heard of. But in order to make room for everybody, it was
not only the beds that were covered in this way, but also the spaces
between them, so that almost the whole cell was covered over with this
floor of planks. All that was left uncovered was a part of the centre
gangway near the door, and in that part was a table with many compartments which held food tins and bread. Close to the door and at my feet
were two gigantic pails whose contents stank to high heaven.

Even so, despite the ingenuity of the Russian prison authorities with
their *naris*, there was not enough room and it was impossible for the
prisoners to lie down on their backs. We all had to lie on our sides, literally like sardines, and when one hip was so tired that a move was essen-
tial negotiations had first to be conducted with the prisoner on either
side so that they could all turn together. The more experienced prisoners, old Muscovites, pointed out the marks in the walls where rings
had once been to which prisoners had been chained in pre-revolutionary
days. Things had progressed since then, but at least those prisoners of
former days had had more room than we had.

The first days in Cell 31 were like a nightmare. The two windows of
the cell had thick, opaque glass – the cell was on the ground floor –
and in consequence it was never really light. At first it was almost impossible to tell one woman from the other. No one spoke out loud and
some of them made themselves understood by signs. A group of women
huddled together at the windows were obviously intent on some work
or other. The half-exposed bodies of most of the women were of a peculiar greyish-blue tinge from long confinement without light and air. Every
time the lid of the *parasha* was lifted, which was often, my stomach
turned over. And in that atomosphere we had to eat and sleep.

My epileptic neighbour had an attractive face with eyes set strangely
wide apart, but she treated me with reserve and even hostility. The very
first day, after a whispered set-to with her neighbour on the other side,
she had a fit. Her body contorted violently in a terrifying fashion and
she rolled around in the soiled space around the *parasha*. It was as much
as I could do not to scream.

All the faces around me were glistening with sweat and swollen with the
heat. Opposite me was a woman with an old body and a young face. She
leaned against the wall and looked listless and ill. I noticed that always after
she had eaten she was sick. Her worn-out body was half naked, and I
wondered why she did not cover herself up with something or other. I
hadn't yet learnt how quickly a woman loses any sort of feeling for privacy
and intimacy in such circumstances. Another woman was wearing only a
pair of black silk knickers, and she sat dolefully staring at nothing and plucking
hairs out of her chin. Another lay with her head in the lap of a friend, who

systematically went over her scalp for lice. Some just lay inert all day. Others were in constant movement, particularly a very gross woman, who slid her fat bottom over the boards like some great crab. She went from group to group and seemed to be directing certain mysterious operations.

In one corner was the place occupied by our Cell Senior, Tasso. I often found myself looking at her. She had a lovely face with dark, shining eyes, fine eyebrows, an aquiline nose and an expressive mouth. The white of her teeth when she smiled was intense. But the most beautiful thing about her, I thought, were her movements. She was as lithe and graceful as a cat. She was the only one who was allowed to walk over the *naris*, and from time to time she would have to negotiate with the *korpusnoi*, or leading warder, of our wing, or with the ordinary wardress. By her tact and diplomacy she saved us from many a punishment. She had a rather gleeful sense of humour. When we got better acquainted, she would take one of her pigtails and squeeze it in between nose and upper lip so that it hung down on either side like a certain moustache we had all very good reason to be acquainted with.

At first I thought I should go mad, but Michailina was right: in the end you get used to anything. Käthe Schulz, the Berlin Cockney, did much to keep me sane. Her real name was Käthe Schmidt, but the GPU had registered her under the name in her false passport, so Käthe Schulz she remained. That was the general custom, and there was method in it; where foreign prisoners were concerned, it made enquiries into their whereabouts from abroad more difficult. Käthe was a working-class girl, and in Berlin she had been a member of the Communist Youth League. After the murder of the Nazi, Horst Wessel, in 1931, she was arrested by the police for no other reason than that the murderer happened to be a member of the same branch as she was. However, she was acquitted at the trial, but when the Nazis came to power in 1933 and staged a new trial she was helped to flee the country. She went first to Prague and then on to Moscow, where she worked as a stenotypist in the OMS Department of the Comintern, which dealt with all foreign matters.

During the course of 1937 the head of this department, Abramov-Mirov, was arrested by the GPU, which then made a clean sweep and arrested all his staff, including Käthe. Abramov-Mirov was accused of having spied for no less than fifteen foreign countries. The charge against Käthe was that she was his accomplice. 'You know, Grete,' she said. 'I'm not in the least frightened. The Party will get me out. They know I'm innocent.'

'Which Party do you mean?' I asked.

'Why, the German Party, of course,' she replied in wonderment. 'Wilhelm Pieck knows me very well.'

She really thought that Pieck, a notorious toady of the GPU, would help her. He was more likely to push her under still further to make his own skin more secure. I said nothing further. Why attempt to rob her of her illusions and her hope? She certainly was innocent, poor child. Much later, in 1940, when I was deported to Nazi Germany, I learnt from a German who had come from Central Siberia that he had met her at Kotlas on her way to Eastern Siberia to serve a sentence of ten years' forced labour. I can see her still. After we settled down for the night, she would pick her way carefully over the innumerable bodies with a matchbox in each hand. In one was menthol ointment and in the other vaseline, and she would offer them around in a *sotto-voce* imitation of someone selling cigarettes and chocolate at a cinema. Even when I knew her, which was more or less at the beginning of her imprisonment, she would often faint. She is hardly likely to have survived.

There was another German with us in Cell 31: Grete Sonntag from Mannheim. Her real name was Änne Krüger. She had been in the Butirka eight months when I arrived. She and her husband had worked together in a leather factory somewhere in the provinces, and they had both been arrested on the eve of the November celebrations in 1937. She was charged with counter-revolutionary agitation. She hardly said a word all day, and her face was lined with bitterness. Her dark brown hair was tied negligently in the nape of the neck with a piece of string. She took great care of the few things she had, and it was only what she stood up in. At night she would carefully examine everything and repair the least damage at once. Her great pride were the leather top boots she had been awarded in her factory for exemplary work. She spoke no Russian, and she had an idea that the Russian prisoners took advantage of her and talked about her. She grew more and more morose and hostile every day, and it was a long time before she consented to talk to me.

'I was always a good Communist,' she said to me bitterly one day. 'I always worked hard in the factory and I never did anything wrong. What do they want with me?'

It appeared that when the Russians began to deport German specialists in 1936–7 there was some excitement and indignation amongst the Germans in the leather factory where she worked. During the course of one such discussion she had said to a young German worker: 'Well, it really doesn't matter much to you if they send you back to Germany. You were never in the Communist Party, and the Nazis have got nothing against you.' This remark was overheard by a good Communist, who denounced her to the GPU. Hence her arrest and the charge. She got five years' forced labour for it at the same time as I was sentenced.

The day in the Butirka began early. At half-past four in the morning we were woken up with a rattling at the hatch and the shout: 'Wake up. Get ready.' Everything had to be done in a mad rush, and the shout '*Davai! Davai!*' – 'Quick! Quick!' – was the one most frequently heard. The effect on us was much as though an antheap were suddenly turned over. Everyone grabbed her wash things in order to be first, if possible, because, of course, the washing accommodation was not remotely sufficient for all of us. In the room where we washed there were five lavatories and ten water taps. I say 'lavatories', but they were in reality five holes in the ground and nothing else. Queues immediately formed in front of all five holes and all ten taps. Imagine if you can going to the lavatory in the morning with at least a dozen pairs of eyes watching you, and being shouted at and urged on by others waiting impatiently for their turn. And woe betide you if you couldn't hurry! And the same thing afterwards at the taps. Naturally, it was quite impossible to keep yourself properly clean. The whole business for 110 of us had to be over in forty minutes, and if it wasn't the last ones were unlucky; they were hurried back to the cell with the rest.

That was our life, whether we were there for weeks, months or years. And whatever you did, whether you went out to exercise, or were called out in the middle of the night for questioning, it all had to be done at the double: '*Davai! Davai!*'

Until you got used to it, the night was worse than the day. Try to sleep at night under strong electric light – prisoners are not allowed to cover their faces – on bare planks without even a straw sack or a pillow, and perhaps without even a blanket, pressed against your fellow prisoners on either side.

Questionings usually took place at night. The procedure would begin just after ten, and sometimes went on all night. The cell door would open with a rattle which woke us all up, a name would be shouted: 'Get ready. Without things.' The unfortunate would scrabble around hastily for a few things to put on. Perhaps one shoe was missing, and she took a little longer to find it. At once a harsh voice would begin to bawl: '*Davai! Davai!*' Most of the other prisoners would sit up. It took a really hard-boiled prisoner to turn over on the other side and go on sleeping. Sleep, blessed sleep – our one escape from all this misery.

And it was even worse in the early hours when the women came back one by one from their examination, upset and each giving vent to her feelings in her own way. Some of them crawled listlessly to their places and sat rocking backwards and forwards, sobbing noiselessly. Others would fling themselves down in a loud fit of weeping. Others used frightful language and cursed the examining officials. One of the women there was a cook. She had gone after a job which had been advertised in the *Vechernaya Moskwa*. It turned out to be cook at the Japanese Embassy. She got the job, but before she had time to start, the GPU arrested her and she was now charged with espionage. When she returned from questioning at night she would scream and rave, hammering on the walls with her fists and cursing God and the world. A storm of protest would then arise from the other prisoners, whose precious night's rest was being disturbed. They would abuse her with all the names they could lay their tongues to, until at last, intimidated, she fell silent.

There was a gradual coming and going in the Butirka, and after a while I worked my way from the *parasha* towards the windows, where I had Käthe Schulz for my neighbour on one side and a Russian gymnastic teacher on the other. This woman's favourite pastime was a game with matches which foretold whether you were going free or being sent to Siberia. It was forbidden, of course – everything which might amuse or console a prisoner was forbidden – and on one or two occasions she was seen at it by the wardress through the spy-hole. She would deny it vigorously, but the imperturbable wardress would carefully count the matches and if there were exactly forty-one, the number you needed for the game, there was punishment.

Most of the prisoners passed their time in this, that or the other prohibited activity, because everything was wrong except sitting still and doing nothing. Speaking, singing, standing up and walking around – it was all forbidden. The favourite occupation was sewing, but there was only one needle and a very limited amount of thread officially provided for all of us, and as that had to be used solely for repairs, much ingenuity was needed. If anyone was caught making a garment then there were punishments, and not punishments merely for the offender, but for everyone. The women engaged on this work would crouch at the window and others would sit between them and the door in order to unsight the wardress when she looked through the spy-hole. Quite useful needles were fashioned out of matchsticks. This type was suitable for embroidery. Another type of needle was made by sacrificing a tooth from a comb and boring a hole through one end with the sacred communal needle which belonged to the whole cell and had to be produced for inspection every morning. Everyone was punished if this needle could not be produced. It was made red hot in the flame of a match for the delicate boring operation. One thing at least was allowed – smoking. Hence the possession of matches. Naturally, we had to buy our own cigarettes; there was no ration.

A whole dress was manufactured in our cell. One of the women had been arrested on the street just as she was, and she had been in prison so long that her light dress was falling off her in rags. No one held on political remand in Moscow was permitted to receive things from home, and the prison authorities provided no clothing, no underwear and no covering of any sort. However, prisoners could buy towels and men's vests. Some of the prisoners who had a little money decided to help the unfortunate woman to a new dress, so they clubbed together and bought half a dozen towels of rough, unbleached Russian linen. But how was the dress to be cut out without a pair of scissors? A little ingenuity solved the problem. The 'cut' was marked with the burnt ends of matches, the material was folded along the marked lines and a lighted match was run backwards and forwards for a moment or two along the fold, then the material was unfolded again and the line was burnt through. The cotton for sewing was obtained by carefully withdrawing threads from other clothing. Anyone who came into our cell with a woollen vest certainly never had enough of it left to cover her nakedness after about six months; it was unravelled from the bottom up. In this way we also obtained wool for darning. Threads from coloured pullovers and so on were in particular demand. They were used for embroidery. Amongst the Russian women there were one or two who were really artists at this kind of work. The towel dress – it was made for a fat Lettish woman – went from hand to hand and was beautifully embroidered at the neck, the sleeves and round the bottom of the skirt. When it was finally finished it was damped down and carefully folded and the fortunate possessor slept on it all night. Believe it or not, but when it was produced in the morning it was really delightful; it would not have disgraced the window of a fashionable dress shop.

The illegal manufacture of this dress was carried out from beginning to end without a hitch, but our affairs did not always prosper so well, and hardly a week passed in which our cell was not punished for something or other – all of us, on the principle of collective responsibility beloved by the Russian authorities. One of the punishments was the withdrawal of the right to have books from the library, and in consequence I received only two books all the time I was there.

At first I found it very difficult to eat the prison food and I had to force it down. One day there would be cabbage soup; the next day fish soup; and the day after that cabbage soup again, and so on. In comparison with what was to come, the food in the Butirka was reasonably good, but in comparison even with the short commons we had suffered in the period after the arrest of Heinz it was almost uneatable. With the soup there was about a pound of Russian black bread a day, and in the evening there was a pappy meal of lentils, barley or groats.

Gradually I found myself getting used to prison life and its rhythm: in the mornings we all tumbled out to make our toilets as well as we were able; at midday there was *balanda*, the prison soup, and in the evening there was *kasha*. One of the rare joys of the prison day was exercise. For twenty whole minutes, sometimes during the day and sometimes at night, we were taken out into the yard, where we could stretch our legs and breathe in the fresh air. It was too great a pleasure, and therefore every-thing possible was done to spoil it for us. We had to walk round in pairs with our hands behind our backs and our eyes on the ground whilst two wardresses carefully watched our every movement, and if one of us forgot herself sufficiently to lift her head in a deep breath or to swing her arms in time to our walk there were immediate shouts. On one occasion a crow perched high up on the prison wall. I saw him out of the corner of my eye. God, I thought, he can fly away just where he pleases! There was nothing for him behind these walls. Not a blade of grass. Not a scrap of living green anywhere. Should I ever walk on grass again? Ever be in a field with trees around and the blue sky above me?

In the distance we could hear the noise of traffic, and once an aero-plane flew over our prison through our patch of sky. It was too much for discipline. All our heads lifted and our eyes went up. But immedi-ately the wardresses began to bawl at us and we lowered them again.

The Butirka was so overcrowded that it was impossible to get the twenty minutes' exercise provided for in the rules done in the day, so exercising went on all night as well.

The Deluded

Gradually I got to know the Russian prisoners. We were all supposed to be political offenders, but they were strange political prisoners. Apart from Tasso, I never heard a word of criticism of the Soviet regime from a Russian prisoner the whole time I was in the Butirka. If they had kept quiet for fear of denunciation, it would have been understandable, but there were one or two cliques in our cell who vied with each other in proclaiming their devotion to the Soviet regime and their loyalty to the Party. A woman named Katia Semionova was typical – typical not only of these women in the Butirka, but typical of the present Russian generation of women. She was a thick-set woman of about thirty, with straight hair cut short and combed back over her head. She was always dressed in a man's woollen sweater and shorts, and all her movements were deliberately masculine. She had a habit of pulling her shorts into place as though she were doing up a belt, and when we exercised she usually marched along in front with her chest stuck out as though she was marching in a demonstration. I was treated with some mistrust by these cliques: first of all, because I was a foreigner, and secondly, because no doubt my critical remarks had been reported. But one day I got into conversation with Katia.

'What on earth are you here for?' I asked.

'I'm the victim of a Trotskyite slander,' she declared, sticking out her chest virtuously. 'But you just wait: I'll pay them back for it, the scoundrels.'

'Oh, so you're innocent, like everyone else here,' I said.

'I don't know about that,' she replied. 'I only know my own case and that of one or two of my friends. You must remember that I come from a family in which there are nine Stakhanovites and in my factory I was known as the non-Party Bolshevist.'

'But, Katia,' I continued, 'you've talked with the others here just as I have; haven't you got the impression that they're really all innocent; that they really haven't done anything against the Soviet Government?'

She looked at me with fanatical hatred in her eyes. She didn't want them to be innocent. 'They haven't arrested half enough yet,' she spat. 'We must protect ourselves from the traitors. And what if there are a few really innocent ones amongst them? You can't make omelettes without breaking eggs.'

Women's Fates

I remember in particular the women who came in after me; after I had got more or less used to the life and had my wits about me again. There was a student of mathematics brought from a prison in the provinces. No sooner had she flung herself down on the boards than she was asleep. The next morning she had to be dragged out with us to the washing room. She seemed drunk with lack of sleep. But when she washed herself we saw that her body was heavily marked with dull stripes that ran criss-cross over her buttocks and thighs. The fat Lettish woman for whom the dress had been made had also been beaten black and blue during her questioning.

A few days after me came a woman of about thirty-five. Her eyes were distraught, but there were no tears in them. She refused to eat or say a word. That was nothing unusual at first, but she persisted. In the end we learnt that she had left three small children at home with no one to look after them. When she finally did talk she spoke wildly and without much sense. After a fortnight she was taken away because her brain was unhinged. Towards the end of my time in the Butirka she was brought back again. This time she ate, but she still spoke very little. She was there when I left.

The Russian prisoners told me that you could always tell as soon as a new prisoner came in whether she had been arrested on her own account or as *zhenia*, because the wives of arrested men knew they were going to be arrested and had everything ready to take with them.

The reactions of the prisoners were very varied. One day a mother of three young children was put into our cell. 'Thank God I've been arrested at last,' she said. 'Now at least my children will get something to eat.

Since my husband was arrested, I've been out of work and we've had nothing to eat.'

My close friendship with Tasso dated from the time, soon after I arrived, when she came to me and warned me.

'You must be more careful what you say. Don't discuss politics so openly here. There are spies around.'

Tasso was the wife of the commander of Stalin's bodyguard, a Lett. After the arrest of Yagoda, the Chief of the GPU, the Salpeters were given his flat. It was fully equipped, and Tasso and her husband and a friend went over it together. One of the rooms was furnished in the Asiatic style, with carpets on the walls, divans and thick rugs on the floor. Over a divan hung a large picture of Stalin. Pointing to it, Tasso said lightly: 'This has to be moved.' Shortly afterwards both Tasso and her husband were arrested. At her questioning, she was told that this was the reason for her arrest, but in all probability her husband was arrested with all the others at the time the old officers corps of the Red Army was liquidated and the Soviet marshals executed. Tasso would have been arrested as his wife in any case. However, in my experience, the GPU is always anxious to have some pretext to justify or at least explain an arrest. The charges against political prisoners were much the same: 'counter-revolutionary agitation', 'counter-revolutionary organisation' – sometimes both together – 'preparation for armed insurrection', 'preparation for terrorism', 'espionage'. I even heard of an indictment which charged the accused with 'espionage for some other country'. Amongst the 110 women in our cell there were only these five variants – one more fantastic than the other.

Tasso stoutly denied ever having made the observation with which she was charged but they seemed intent on securing a confession. Whilst we were together in the Butirka, she was not often taken away for questioning, but later on we were separated, and I did not meet her until a year later in Karaganda, where she told me the rest of the story. One night she was taken out of her cell and put into a dark cell. This, she knew, was a measure ordered by the examining judge when it was desired to extract a confession. There was no window in the cell and nowhere to sit down except on the floor. She was held in constant darkness on nothing but bread and water. There was a round hole in the door – as she thought, for air – but one day a cinema projection apparatus was set up on the other side and a film was thrown on to the opposite wall. It was a film largely of Russian and Caucasian landscapes, and the accompanying music was composed of Caucasian folk songs. Then came a picture of children playing – and then suddenly a picture of children's corpses. At that the film was switched off and a voice sounded: 'Tasso Salpeter, you are lying.'

A little while after that she was taken out of the cell for questioning.

The examining judge called upon her to confess, but she still insisted that she had never said anything of the sort. 'Very well,' he declared. 'We'll soon see.' And at that moment the door opened and her husband was brought in.

'He was in a terrible state,' said Tasso. 'His face was pale and worn and his eyes looked everywhere but at me. There were marks round his wrists as though he had been constantly in handcuffs. "Well," said my examiner with a grin, "will you confess now?" "I've nothing to confess," I replied. "Then your husband will give you the lie," he went on, and, turning to him, he asked: "What did your wife say when you saw the picture of Comrade Stalin in your new flat?" For the first time my husband looked at me. It was a frightened, pitiful look. Then he turned to my examiner and said as though he were reciting a piece: "She said: 'Well, we'll get rid of that.'" Then they took him away and after that I got eight years.'

On the wall in our cell hanging up between the two windows were the prison rules and regulations. I hadn't been there long, or bothered to go over and read their innumerable clauses, when one day they were removed. We wondered why, and the general opinion was that new and even stricter rules were about to be enforced. But they came back a day or so later with no change except a new signature. The old prison governor had apparently followed his chief, Yezhov, to prison. Whilst I was there the prison commandant of the Butirka changed twice.

A much-feared institution in the Butirka was the *obysk*, or general search. This took place at least once a month and quite unexpectedly. In the middle of the night the cell door would be flung open and a wardress would shout: 'Everyone get ready. With things. *Obysk*.' In the greatest haste we would all grab our things and stick them in whatever receptacle we had, all of us hounded by the same idea: get rid of anything forbidden. And it was astonishing how many forbidden things prisoners could amass. The women mobbed each other round the *parasha* to throw them away. We each had a mess tin, but some of the women wanted something better, so they made bowls out of black bread, moistening it, kneading it into shape and then letting it dry hard. Chess sets made in the same way were very popular, one set being made white with tooth-powder. Of course, it was forbidden to play chess, or, indeed, anything at all.

A few minutes later the wardress would herd us all out into the corridor, still half asleep, and shepherd us off to a special room, where we were searched, whilst in our absence the cell was searched from top to bottom. First of all we had to strip; particular attention was paid to all our bodily openings, and a torch was used to look into our mouths and under our tongues. They were looking in particular for pieces of

glass or metal, knives, mirrors, and, of course, pieces of paper on which
messages might be written. After that humiliating experience – yes, you
get used to that too – our things were carefully examined. My clothes
were all foreign made, and the trade marks, etc., seemed to arouse the
suspicion of the wardress, for she carefully removed them all, and where
they were not removable she cut them out with a pair of scissors. Our
shoes came in for special attention. Some of the more callous and brutal
wardresses would just tear off the soles, and women could find themselves in Siberia with flapping soles to their shoes. This wretched business
lasted a very long time and robbed us of several hours' sleep.

Naturally, quarrelling sometimes broke out amongst the prisoners, and
then the whispered hum would swell up into hysterical shouting and
screaming. A wardress would soon be hammering at the door threatening
dire punishments for the whole cell and then the hubbub would subside.
This banging on doors was usually all we heard from the world outside
our cell, but one morning we were paralysed with fright when we heard
blood-curdling shrieking, as though scores of women were being brutally
murdered or fiendishly tortured. Then the shouting of wardresses gradually rose above the infernal din and a hush descended. We were used to
a good deal, but we looked at each other in fear and trembling and our
faces were even paler than usual. What had happened? Had there been a
mutiny? Had prisoners been tortured? But in the end we ceased to think
about it any longer. The prison regime at the Butirka functioned excellently and we could discover nothing. We never got word from another
cell and we never saw another prisoner. However, some time later a cell
community had to be broken up for some reason or the other, and some
of the women were put in with us and then we heard the solution of the
mystery: whilst the women of this cell were in the washing room, a rat
had sprung out from behind the piping and run across the floor amongst
all the naked women. And at the sight, all these hardened terrorists,
counter-revolutionaries and wreckers had just gone off into hysterics.

Amongst the eight women who came into our cell in this way was a
German girl from Danzig named Franciska Levent-Levith. Her father had
been a bandmaster there and she had married a Russian named Levent-
Levith. Her husband was in the Russian Information Service, and for a
time they had been in England. In 1937 they were recalled to Moscow.
They stayed one night in the Hotel Metropole and the next day they
were both arrested. Thus poor Franciska had come into the Butirka without
any knowledge of Russian life and without being able to speak a word
of Russian. She had been there six months and it had had a terrible effect
on her. Her eyes were enough to warn you that her mind was unhinged,
and to talk to her was merely to confirm it. She was quite mad. She had

come to believe that she had been sent to the Butirka to take a course in espionage and that she had failed to pass the test. As she talked her confused nonsense, her eyes would wander backwards and forwards as though she were watching a game of tennis. Before long everyone in our cell who could speak German knew what was wrong with her. They would smile pityingly and tap their heads as she turned away, and soon no one was willing to listen to her gibberish any longer. But in her saner moments she told us that she was clever with her needle, and we got the idea of giving her something to do. The only thing we could buy apart from the towels I have mentioned were men's vests, of all things. Most of us Germans wore so-called polo blouses. They were very simple garments, but they were the envy of the Russian women. Franciska thought she could make such a blouse out of two men's vests, so we clubbed together and bought four of them. Protected from the prying eyes of the wardresses, she sat near the window and worked away. The result was remarkable. Not only did she produce two excellent polo blouses, but the concentration literally restored her sanity. She spoke less and less of the mysterious things which she alleged were going on, and before long she seemed quite normal again. Then one evening at about ten o'clock she was taken away with a number of other women, and we never saw her again. 'She's off to get her sentence,' was the opinion of the old hands.

A Birthday

I had been a month in prison now and I was still left in ignorance of the formal reason for my arrest. Apart from leaving the cell with the others for exercise and so on, I had not been outside it except to have my fingerprints taken and to be photographed, but every day from the stories of others I extended my knowledge of the procedure at the questionings, of the charges and the likely sentences. My friends in the cell told me to make up my mind to a charge of espionage at least, and perhaps counter-revolutionary organisation as well. 'But don't be alarmed,' they said consolingly. 'Everyone gets that. When they question you you must insist that you don't know anything at all, that you never occupied yourself with political affairs – don't understand politics – were never anything but a housewife doing the cooking and the washing up and making the beds. Stick by that through thick and thin. And, above all, don't sign anything. It doesn't matter how long they keep you here; it's still better than Siberia.'

Gradually the nights were not quite so terrible or uncomfortable as they had been. I got used to sleeping on my side on bare boards, until

on each hip I had skin as hard as leather, like a poor carthorse constantly
chafed by the shafts, and from long crouching down instead of standing,
the muscles in calves and thighs began to disappear.

The Butirka had a canteen. It was in this that the prisoners could
spend the fifty roubles a month they were allowed to receive if they
had anyone outside to pay it in for them. Canteen day was a high day
and holiday in Cell 31. Everyone who had money took part in the
shopping. When the cell was not suffering from collective punishment,
which included the withdrawal of the privilege of using the canteen,
the great day came round about once a month. In the way of food
there was bread, herrings, boiled sweets and sugar, and sometimes even
sausage and cheese. A number of us were chosen to go to the canteen
to collect the purchases. On that day the atmosphere was so cheerful
you could almost forget you were in the Butirka. Each prisoner who
had money had to contribute to providing the *neimushtchi*, or 'have-
nots', with food, and their share was always carefully put to one side.
After that the treasures were spread out on the table and the process
of distribution began.

The first birthday I spent in prison came round whilst I was still in
the Butirka. Tasso had made a note of the date. After *balanda* at midday
I had sat back against the wall and gone to sleep as usual. When I woke
up there was a touching little birthday spread set out at my feet. The
'tablecloth' was made of several embroidered handkerchiefs, and in a tin
bowl, which was also laid out with a handkerchief, there were presents from
the last canteen purchase, and in another tin there were special 'sandwiches'. The black bread had been carefully cut into thin slices with a
piece of thread, and covered with 'salad'. This salad consisted of pieces
of cabbage fished out of the soup, cut up small, mixed with onion and
flavoured with salt. It was regarded as a great delicacy. The words 'Happy
Birthday' were made out of pieces of bread in a semicircle around the
'birthday table'. In addition, there were various little knick-knacks made
out of kneaded bread, and a 'rose' artistically formed out of an onion
in a vase made of bread.

I was deeply touched, and we gathered round, drank tea and were
almost happy. Unfortunately, the birthday party was interrupted by the
sudden arrival of the wardress, who spotted the 'table'. We did our best
to whisk the things away, but she caught us. Everything was confiscated.
The whole cell got a bad mark and everyone was deprived of exercise
for a week. Another disagreeable result of my birthday was that the clique
led by Katia Semionova began to make a dead set against Tasso as Cell
Senior on the ground that she lacked discipline and favoured a foreigner
at the expense of the cell.

Grete Sonntag was taken off for questioning. She came back about two hours later in great despair. She was so upset that the next day she even neglected to do her hair. I crawled over to console her.

'They brought a worker from our factory yesterday,' she said dolefully, 'and he repeated what I told you about. And all the time I've denied ever having said it. What a disgusting person!'

We had a number of officers' wives in our cell whose preliminary examinations were at an end and who were now expecting their sentences. Our cell was on the ground floor, and between the metal covering of our cell window and the wall we could just see part of the steps that led down into the yard. We arranged with these women that when they were taken out after receiving their sentences they should let us know how many years they had received by spreading out their fingers behind their backs as they went down the steps. The arrangement worked very well and we saw that five fingers were invariably spread out. The joy amongst the Russian prisoners was great. 'Only five years!' they exclaimed. 'That's the new policy under Beria; you never got less than ten under Yezhov.'

One day there was a new arrival in our cell, a woman in camp clothes, a dark grey, padded jacket, a round hat and knee boots. She had a pale, Madonna-like face with straight hair combed down at either side and fastened in a knot at the back. The other prisoners whispered to each other: 'She's from Siberia.' It took a long time before she would consent to talk. The first thing she asked for was a book. After a while we learnt all about her. She was thirty-two and by profession a teacher. As the daughter of a priest, she had received ten years for 'counter-revolutionary activity'. For good conduct, she had been remitted one year and released at the end of the ninth year. She had served her term in the Kolyma Camp, which lies in northern Siberia in the Arctic Circle. Her release papers specified that she should return to her home town, but on her release she had gone straight to Moscow and presented herself just as she was with her padded jacket, round convict's cap and top boots to the British Consulate to ask for a visa to England, where she had an aunt. At the Consulate they promised to make the necessary enquiries and told her to return, but when she left the Consulate building she was immediately arrested by the GPU. I saw her body in the washing room; it was like a corpse with all the signs of scurvy – nine years in a concentration camp.

Shortly afterwards she was taken away and after a while we forgot all about her. Several weeks later there was another interesting new arrival. We all knelt on the boards to look at her. At first we thought it was a Negress. Her hair stood up like a bush on her head and her face was dark. She lay down on the boards exhausted. 'Water,' she said. And then we recognised the teacher from Siberia. She had been kept in solitary confinement in the dark for forty days in order to force her to reveal what dangerous things she had said at the British Consulate, and during that time she had not been allowed to wash or comb her hair. We did our best with her hair, but in the end it had to be cut off it was so matted with dirt. Before long she was taken away again and that was the last we saw of her.

The Damned of this Earth

Interrogations

One night the door of our cell opened. 'Margarita Genrichovna Buber-Nejman,' called the wardress. 'Without things.' I was asleep and it was not until my neighbours shook me back into life that I realised that I was meant. With my hair in disarray and my shoes not done up properly, I crawled over the sleeping bodies and staggered out into the corridor, where I found a uniformed man waiting for me. He seized me by the arm and hustled me along the corridor as though I were a tough criminal likely to offer resistance. We came to a staircase. The banisters were extended by a wire netting to prevent those who were tired of life from throwing themselves over. We went down and along a corridor which was carpeted so that our footsteps made no sound. The doors along this corridor had handles and it was all more like a corridor in some business house rather than in a prison. We came to a halt before a door, which the soldier opened. Releasing my arm, he piloted me in. Again the room was reminiscent of an office. The windows were wide open and there was a sweet, fresh smell of wet leaves and grass. There was a picture of Stalin on the wall and behind a desk sat a robust young man in his shirtsleeves with the self-confidence of a limited intelligence.

'Sit down,' he ordered. 'What's your name?'

He spoke German and from his accent I recognised the Volga German. I was unable to speak for a while. My tongue seemed stuck to the roof of my mouth. I had expected this for so long, but now it had come too suddenly. If only I had a cigarette to soothe my nerves! There was an open packet on the table. It was a minute or two before I was able to speak, and it seemed like hours. After a while he read the indictment against me. I was charged with 'counter-revolutionary organisation and agitation against the Soviet State'.

'What have you got to say?' he demanded.

What on earth did he expect me to say in reply to that senseless rigmarole? There was nothing I could think of to say. What was the use of saying anything?

'Do you hear?' he insisted. 'What have you got to say? Where did you conduct this counter-revolutionary organisation and agitation, and how did you do it?'

'I never did anything of the sort,' I replied at last. 'If you charge me with it, you ought to know.'

'You're an insolent liar,' he said angrily. 'You'd better think it over. Stand up.'

I stood up and he lit himself a cigarette and paid no further attention to me. I stood there and wondered how long he would keep me standing. I knew that it was a favourite method. Sometimes a prisoner stood for hours every day. Through the open window I could see the wet leaves of a tree.

'Well?' he asked after a while. 'Have you thought better of it? Your memory isn't too good, is it?'

'I have never committed any act hostile to the Soviet Union,' I insisted.

'Still lying,' he snarled. 'We know better.'

I looked at his face. It was odious. 'When and where and how am I supposed to have conducted this counter-revolutionary activity?' I asked.

'I'm asking the questions, not you,' he said. 'Don't be impudent. Don't think we haven't got ways and means of making you talk. If you don't come round to reason, you'll stay where you are for months – years if necessary.' And with that he pressed a button and the GPU soldier came and took me back to my cell. How it stank after the fresh air through that window! You got so used to it you didn't notice it any more. I crawled over to Käthe's side. She was awake and waiting anxiously to hear what had happened. How much good that did me! A human being who cared about my fate. I could have kissed her.

A few days later I was taken out to be questioned again. It was just the same. He wanted me to confess and I wanted to know just what it was I was supposed to have done. One thing really did frighten me: did the GPU know anything about my conversations with friends? The only difference between the first examination and the second was that my examiner smoked two cigarettes before he became aggressive and threatening. Finally he despatched me back to my cell with the threat that I would turn grey before he let me out again unless I confessed. On the principle of where there's smoke there's fire of some sort, I racked my brains to discover what could possibly be the basis of the charges against me, but I came to no satisfactory conclusion.

At the third examination my examiner seemed to have got tired of the game. 'Very well, then,' he said. 'I'll tell you when and where you carried on counter-revolutionary agitation against the Soviet State. You won't dare to deny that you were in the opposition in the German Communist Party in the years 1931–2?'

'I certainly do deny it,' I replied, and then I made a bad mistake: 'But in any case, what has being in the opposition in the German Communist Party got to do with counter-revolutionary agitation and organisation against the Soviet State?'

At that my Volga German almost had a fit. 'What?' he ejaculated. 'You're not only a counter-revolutionary; you're a Trotskyite.'

The next questions after he had calmed down a bit showed me that the charge against me was the same as against my husband. 'Now tell me all you know about the fractional activity of Heinz Neumann.'

I did my best to convince him that as an ordinary rank-and-file member of the Party I had naturally known nothing of the discussions which took place in the Central Committee and in the Political Bureau of the Party. He got no further with me, and as the questioning went on I could see that he did not attach much importance to my case and was anxious to get it over and done with. Certain of the questions he wrote down as a protocol of the examination: Did you take part in the frac- tional work of Heinz Neumann in the German Communist Party? Were you a member of the opposition? Who were your friends and acquain- tances in Moscow? What political discussions took place in your room in the Lux? Who came to see your husband?

I answered all these questions as well as I could. Of course, I had never heard any political discussions in the Lux, and all the people who had come to see us were only those who were now safely outside the Soviet Union. My examiner made no further attempt to force me to give the answers he wanted. When he had finished with his precious protocol, I read it through carefully. It was a pitiful document, but there seemed nothing particularly dangerous in it, so that when he asked me to sign it I almost did so, but then I remembered Tasso's warning, and I refused. This time he was really angry and cursed me furiously, but still I refused and so he sent me back to my cell in great disfavour.

A fortnight later at night I was called out for my fourth examination. It was a different room and a different examiner, a man who spoke only Russian. He handed me a document on which was written: 'The exam- ination has established the guilt of the prisoner, Margarita Genrichovna Buber-Nejman, who conducted counter-revolutionary agitation and organisation against the Soviet State.' At first I thought perhaps I misun- derstood what was written there, but he confirmed that there was no mistake: the examination had established my guilt.

'May I write my comment in German on the back?' I asked. He nodded and I wrote: 'I protest against this examination which establishes my guilt without a shadow of proof. I demand the reopening of the inquiry.'

Three days later – for Russian conditions, an incredibly swift reaction – I was again taken off to an examination. This time the Volga German was there again and with him was an older man of perhaps sixty, with white hair and rosy cheeks. The older man addressed me in a friendly tone and told me to sit down. The Volga German stood by his desk very respect- fully. 'Were you unfairly treated during the examination?' he asked. 'Why do you protest against it?' From the way he spoke, I realised that he thought I was protesting against ill-treatment on the part of the examiner.

'It is true that he called me a liar and threatened to keep me in prison indefinitely if I didn't confess,' I said, 'but that's not what I'm complaining about. I protest against being found guilty of counter-revolutionary agita- tion and organisation against the Soviet State without the slightest shred of proof of any kind having been brought forward. The examiner took no notice of the fact that as a simple member of the Party I could hardly be expected to know what went on in the Political Bureau of the Party. He made no attempt even to prove that I was a member of the oppo- sition in Germany, and he certainly made none to prove that I had ever been guilty of counter-revolutionary agitation or organisation. How can I be convicted without even being tried? How can I be found guilty without the slightest proof against me?'

The white-haired man heard all I had to say patiently. 'Perhaps there has been some mistake in your case,' he said finally, 'and everything will be cleared up.' He spoke in a friendly, almost paternal tone, and I was very favourably impressed. Then he drew up a new protocol and passed it over to me for my signature. I hesitated. All my old doubts and suspicions crowded to the fore again, and I refused to sign.

'Why not?' he asked, as though it were the most harmless affair in the world.

'Because I don't trust you,' I said bluntly.

The Volga German turned red in the face and shouted: 'How dare you talk in such a fashion to a Soviet Prosecutor!' The older man was not disturbed. He quietened the Volga German with a gesture, and, making no further attempt to obtain my signature, he pressed a button. A soldier entered and took me back through the well-known corridors to my cell.

Autumn came with cold weather and rain, and day after day it was sunless and gloomy, and the rain trickled down through the fine mesh which covered our cell windows. When library-book day came round again I asked Tasso to get a German book if she could, because there were two of us who couldn't read Russian. We were lucky enough to get a volume of Brentano's poems. Käthe Schulz and I read it together, learning the poems we liked best by heart.

Winter came, and there was more and more talk about Siberia. Soon after the first snow had fallen our cell was broken up. We were woken up in the night: 'All out. With things.' At first we thought it was one of the regular searches, and we flung all our illegal possessions into the *parasha*. But it was much worse than that: it was the parting from all good friends we had come to know and learnt to value. Such partings are very painful, and more tears are shed over them than over the subsequent sentences. Good friends embraced each other sadly. We all knew we should never see each other again, and that each of us must now expect a terrible fate. How much easier things are if there is an understanding friend to share them!

This time I came into Cell 23. There were about 100 prisoners there too, and the atmosphere was very different. There was no intelligent, friendly Tasso to smooth things over. It was in this cell that I met Gertrude Tiefenau, a German girl who had been arrested in the summer of 1937 on the street, just as she was in a thin summer blouse and skirt, with sandals and socks. She had been held now for eighteen months with absolutely nothing beyond the clothes she had worn at the time. She had no stockings, no coat, not even a jacket, and, of course, no blanket. Unless she could find some sympathising soul to share a blanket with her at night, she had to sleep uncovered on the bare boards. When it was cold she was unable to go out to exercise, and when she went out into the air for the first time when the weather got a little warmer she fainted.

She was disliked by almost everyone because she 'made a nuisance of herself', which meant in fact that she never ceased to protest vigorously at the treatment accorded to her. She wrote letters of protest to the Prison Commandant as often as she had the chance, and she demanded to speak to the *korpusnoi*, or head warder of the wing, every morning. All that she asked him for was the clothing, underwear, etc., which was in her room at the time of her arrest. This refusal to give in and accept the inevitable had naturally put her on the prison black list, and because she constantly condemned the Soviet prison regime she was known amongst the Russian prisoners as 'the German Fascist'.

She was always in trouble, because when she came into contact with the prison authorities she invariably lost her temper and denounced them as every bit as bad as, if not worse than, the German Nazis, because they claimed to be Socialists. Her battle led her repeatedly into the dark cell on bread and water, and the prison authorities revenged themselves on her by refusing to hand over a stitch of her clothing. Being on the official black list meant that every time the May Day or November celebrations came round she spent the holy days in the dark cell on bread and water. She told me that on one occasion she had been stripped naked and kept in a bare cell for hours. It was impossible not to admire her unbroken spirit, but unfortunately her excitability led to constant clashes with her cell mates, and she was often in the wrong.

She had been arrested because one day in a discussion she had said that the only Nazi with any brains was Goebbels – a thing that most German Communists recognised and had said at some time or other. This observation was denounced to the GPU, which based a charge of 'counter-revolutionary agitation' on it.

Judgment

I did not stay long in Cell 23. I suppose the slightest vestige of hope in such circumstances becomes greatly exaggerated, and after my interview with the Soviet Prosecutor I began to imagine myself almost free. I could even see myself in Paris on the sunny boulevards, and I banished all thoughts of Siberia. Then one evening at about ten o'clock the hatch window of the cell door slammed down: 'Stefanie Brun and Margarete Genrichovna Buber-Neumann. With things.' Always this ridiculous 'Genrichovna' because my father's name was Heinrich. I made my farewells and for the first and last time I saw Gertrude Tiefenau in tears. Then Stefanie Brun, a Russian girl and the sister of the former People's Commissar Unschlicht, and I went out into the corridor, where we found six other women prisoners standing waiting with their bundles. There was little doubt left; we were going to hear our sentences. We fell in and marched two by two behind the wardress hammering with a key on the metal buckle of her belt. We were all put into an empty cell and there we sat waiting with our bundles beside us, each occupied with her own thoughts and unwilling to talk, each wondering what her fate would be.

Stefanie Brun was called first. She got up slowly and as she left the cell she leant for support for a moment against the door jamb. I saw her yellow, heavily veined hand as it sought support against the door and her terrible legs, fat and the same size all the way down. The cell door closed behind her. One of the women began to sob softly. Within a few minutes Stefanie was back again. 'Eight years,' she said slowly.

'Margarita Genrichovna Buber-Nejman.'

It was my turn. I was taken into a fairly large room quite close to the cell. Placed across the far corner was a desk behind which sat a freshly shaved and rosy-cheeked GPU officer with a light-brown highly polished shoulder strap and a well-fitting, spick-and-span uniform. The desk was covered with a red cloth and on the walls were pictures of Stalin and the latest chief of the GPU, Beria. I went up to the desk and the officer handed me a typewritten sheet of paper. 'Can you read Russian?' he asked. I nodded. 'Good enough to read this.'

There was the ridiculous name again: 'Margarita Genrichovna Buber-Nejman'. And my social status: 'Socially dangerous element'. And the sentence: 'Five years' reformatory labour in a camp'.

The officer handed me a pencil. Apparently I was expected to sign it. 'What!' I exclaimed in indignation. 'I'm to sign that? Give me pen and paper and I'll make a written protest against this sentence. I am innocent. I demand a proper trial.'

'You can have pen and paper when you're back in your cell,' the officer said, and he motioned to the soldier to remove me. Within two minutes I was sitting next to Stefanie Brun again and the next unfortunate was called out. Grete Sonntag, who was with us, got five years, Nadia Bereskina five years, a woman who was a cousin of Marshal Yakir got ten years, the tailoress Rebecca Sagoria got eight years, a Russian woman who had worked for many years in the Comintern got ten years, and so on. No one cried; no one protested; no one spoke a word. The sentences were passed by a Special Commission. When it was all over the eight of us were taken out and marched along a corridor past the mouldy-smelling washing room, where a cricket chirped monotonously, and out of a small door into a court-yard brilliantly lit by an arc light. Then we went through a Gothic archway into the old building. This was the so-called 'Pugatcheff Tower'. It was here that the peasant revolutionary leader Pugatcheff lay in chains waiting to be quartered in the Middle Ages.

The room we were put in was semicircular in shape, with an arched ceiling supported by one powerful pillar. High up was a small Gothic window covered with wire meshing. The same *naris* were here as in the other cells of the Butirka. Central heating pipes went through the place and all night there was an interrupted gurgling. We sat down on the boards and no one took off coat or shoes. There we sat awake the whole night with our bundles beside us and no one spoke. Only once Stefanie Brun whispered to me: 'Shall we survive it?' It was a question I was unable to answer. Grete Sonntag sat leaning against the pillar, her sad eyes staring blankly at the opposite wall.

In the morning the hatch in the door was let down and eight rations of bread and a jug of weak tea were handed in. No one wanted either to eat or drink. When it was lighter someone noticed that there was a tap in one corner and went over and washed face and hands. It brought movement into all of us, and soon the eight of us were gathered around the tap washing in turn. We were delighted at the opportunity and, much refreshed, we faced the world again. Chatter began. Everyone was in agreement that it was a wonderful cell in which there was actually running water. You would have thought that we had all forgotten our future in Siberia.

We settled down in our new cell and took full advantage of its washing facilities. Days passed. Every morning we asked for pen and paper to write formal protests against our sentences, and every day they put us off to the next. Life went on as it had done before and there was no difference in the routine. Every day – sometimes at night – we exercised for twenty minutes in the courtyard. On one occasion we exercised at midnight and there was snow on the ground. In front of me walked Rebecca Sagoria in thin summer shoes and an elegant fur coat. In the light of the lamp I could see the snow on her blonde hair and the flakes twisting and turning slowly as they fell noiselessly to the ground. Once we heard a sharp challenge, '*Stoi!*' from a guard, but otherwise it was silent and our footsteps made no sound in the snow.

And then suddenly we clearly heard the cry of a new-born baby. Thin, piercing and unmistakable on the silent air. We stopped in astonishment and looked around, wondering how we could possibly hear such a sound in such a place. It came from the Pugatcheff Tower and we stood listening, deeply moved. Even our wardress forgot to snarl at us for stopping and raising our eyes. Above us in the Pugatcheff Tower arrested women with young babies were held.

Transport

We began to prepare ourselves as well as we could for our transport to Siberia. We dried bread on the central heating pipes and we sewed together sacks of various sizes out of odds and ends of material. We rarely spoke about the future. The favourite topic of conversation of the mothers was about their children. Those whose children were still small had less to worry about than those who had grown-up children. Stefanie Brun was very anxious about her sixteen-year-old daughter, for fear she had been arrested too, for in Soviet law, which applies the principle of vicarious responsibility, grown-up children can be made responsible for the offences of their parents.

And then the day of our departure from the Butirka arrived. We were placed with our bundles in a special cell and our cases and bags were given back to us. Everything of value had been removed, but receipts were there instead. Drinking vessels and pannikins were taken away and we were all once again subjected to a thorough bodily search for concealed weapons, instruments, and any other forbidden article. Late in the afternoon we trooped out into the prison yard and climbed into the 'Black Maria'. I was the last to get in and all the compartments were full so I had to stand in the narrow gangway. Through a gauze-covered window in a door which separated the car into two compartments I could see that there were male prisoners in the other half. I learnt that there were two Germans amongst them and they came up to the window. They were wearing padded jackets and round hats with ear covers, the standard camp uniform. Their names were Lüschen and Gerschinsky, and they had been teachers at the Karl Liebknecht School in Moscow. They had both already done two and a half years in camp. After a new period of enquiries which had lasted seven months, they were now on their way back to the camp to do another two and a half years to complete their sentences.

The women in the cells wanted to know whether the men knew anything about their husbands. Only Grete Sonntag learnt that her husband had been sentenced to five years in camp and had already gone on transport.

We came to our destination and got out. It was a goods station. We lined up, the women in front and the men behind, and soldiers with fixed bayonets scuttled around busily. It was a dank, misty evening. Yakir's cousin, whose name I have forgotten, was sick with excitement and anxiety. At the end of a street down which I could see there was a couple walking arm in arm. At that moment a terrible feeling of depression and sadness overcame me. The two unknowns walking arm in arm seemed to symbolise my lost freedom. But then with many shouts of '*Davai! Davai!*' we were herded off across a set of railway lines. Suddenly a new command I had never heard before was shouted. I didn't know what to do, but when I saw everyone else sit down in the dirt I did the same. Nadia Bereskina was next to me. 'What's this for?' I asked. 'I expect there's someone or other around who oughtn't to see us,' she replied.

After a while, the order came for us to get up and go on. We came to a fixed railway carriage without wheels, the so-called Peresylny Wagon, in which prisoners are kept until the transports can be put together. Before we went in, Nadia, who was more experienced than me, whispered: 'You mustn't say you're a Political; say you're a prostitute or a thief.' I had no time to ask why, and we were hustled through the door into a long compartment separated down the middle lengthwise by wire netting which reached to the ceiling. The place stank of petroleum, tobacco and sweaty bodies. A babel of voices and shouts welcomed us. On one side were bunks up to the ceiling and human beings lay in them like animals in a pet shop, each with his face towards the wire. One after the other of us squeezed our way along the narrow gangway between the wire and the bunks. To my surprise, I could see scores of shaved heads and the naked torsos of men. Questions came from all sides. 'How many years?' 'What for?' 'Are you from the Butirka?'

Suddenly amongst the deeper men's voices there was the high, clear voice of a child. As my eyes gradually got used to the gloom, I saw the laughing face of a boy amongst all those men. 'How old are you?' I asked in horror. 'Thirteen,' he replied. 'And whatever are you here for?' 'Stealing,' he said proudly.

That was the first imprisoned child I had ever seen in my life, but he didn't seem to mind in the least.

We stood around helplessly. There seemed no room for us anywhere. Only Nadia Bereskina had managed to find a place. Now I understood her whispered advice. For a prostitute, they were prepared to move up, but not for a Political. At last I managed to find room in one of the upper shelves. Next to me snored a drunk. The air was thicker up above and it was difficult to breathe. Every now and again you forgot where you were and bumped your head on the roof. 'We'll get our first lice here,' said Stefanie. It was the confident prophecy of the expert. 'Let's hope that drunken sot next to you behaves himself decently. He seems full up to the brim. Where on earth do they get the vodka from, I wonder. Bribe the guards, I expect. Never mind, Grete. Don't let it get you down. Come. We'll smoke a *mahorka*.' And with trembling fingers she rolled two cigarettes of the coarse, strong tobacco known as *mahorka*. I had to learn how to do it.

'Where's the German?' someone called from the gangway. 'Here I am,' I said. It was Lüschen, and I slid down to him in the gangway. 'Have you got a place?' he asked. 'Of a sort,' I said. 'Get up with us,' he invited. 'There's room for one.' I did so and we crouched together and talked. Both he and Gerschinsky were bound for the Polar camp, Kolyma. They had lived in the Soviet Union as political emigrants, teaching at the Karl Liebknecht School in Moscow. In 1936 they were both arrested by the GPU and charged with being 'Trotskyites'. The documentary proof against them consisted of circulars from a number of publishing houses abroad which they had had sent to them. As these foreign publishing houses had issued books banned in the Soviet Union as Trotskyite, their circulars counted as Trotskyite material and their possessors as 'Trotskyites'. On this account, they had both received five years in Kolyma, where they worked in the gold mines. He talked on of the Polar night, the prevalence of scurvy amongst the prisoners, the high death rate.

'The worst thing that can happen is that you get injured in the mines, because when you lie down your legs swell as though you had dropsy.'

Kolyma, it appears, lies on a high plateau several hundred metres above sea level. The polar air there is rarefied, with the result that the hard work imposes a great strain on the heart, and many prisoners die of heart failure, a cause of death which looks very respectable on a death certificate.

'Apart from the gold mines, there's also an experimental farm,' he went on. 'Chiefly women prisoners work there. And there are about 400 children of various ages, all born in Kolyma. They seem comparatively healthy. The best time is during the harvesting in the very short summer you get there. Everyone has to lend a hand. It's then that marriages are arranged and after that new citizens of Kolyma get born.'

A guard walked up and down on the other side of the netting. We sat there in the dark and talked in whispers. Snoring was going on all around us and the atmosphere was foetid. Men and women made love in this hole. For many months, sometimes for years, men and women were together again for the first time.

'Why did they take you back to Moscow?' asked Stefanie.

'That's a depressing chapter,' he said. 'The former Director of the Karl Liebknecht School, who was also with us in Kolyma, denounced us to the camp GPU. He said that we weren't only Trotskyites, but spies for a foreign Power. He hoped, of course, to earn a remission of his own sentence for being such a loyal prisoner. We were taken back to Moscow for enquiries and kept for seven months in the Butirka. We were both beaten up during the interrogations. They sat Gerschinsky on hot pipes until he burnt his behind badly. But we both refused to sign their protocol, and in the end they gave up trying, so now we're going back to serve the rest of our sentence. I'm afraid the seven months in the Butirka doesn't count. Listen. I don't know whether we shall survive the next two and a half years or what will happen to us afterwards even if we do, but if you ever get out, my father lives in No. 5 Bergstrasse, in Berlin; let him know what's happened to me.'

I promised, but with very little hope that I should ever be able to keep my promise. Lüschen was twenty-seven then, and when I saw his face in the light the next morning I realised that he had given up all hope.

The next day they began to sort out the various transports. Some went off to Central Siberia, some to Eastern Siberia and some to the north. Lüschen and Gerschinsky went with the northern transport. We shook hands with them when they left us and Lüschen turned his head away, but I had already seen the tears in his eyes. Two of our small group went with them to the north, the cousin of Marshal Yakir and the Russian woman who had worked for the Comintern.

At about midday they put together a group of fifteen women, including Stefanie Brun, Grete Sonntag, Rebecca Sagorje, Nadia Bereskina, an eighteen-year-old Polish girl and me, and a much larger number of men.

With our sacks slung over our shoulders, we were hurried along the lines until we came to a prison wagon, the so-called Stolypinsky Wagon. Here we were halted and for the third time in an hour there was a roll-call and we all had to answer, giving our numbers, names, offences and the length of our terms. My litany was: 'Prisoner No. 174,475 Margarete Genrichovna Buber-Neumann, socially dangerous element, five years.' At first I stammered and stuttered over this mouthful, but before long and with much practice I could reel it off word perfect.

When we were outside the guards and officials all seemed tremendously anxious that we should get back out of sight as quickly as possible, and they bullied and pushed and shoved us up into the high wagon. It was an ordinary Russian coach which had been converted to its present use by iron gates between the compartments and the corridor. There were four sleeping berths in each compartment, six if you count the luggage shelves, but they pushed all fifteen of us women into one compartment. The windows were covered over and there was no light. In the roof was a ventilator which was jammed and couldn't be opened properly. All the other compartments were equally crowded. There was no question of whispering here, and the hubbub was tremendous. The guards cursed and the prisoners cursed back.

When we were served with bread and tea, it was discovered there were no mugs to drink out of. Everything of that nature had been taken away from us when we left the Butirka. In the end we found an old and rusty tin and we all drank out of it in turns. Our food during this transport, which lasted several weeks, consisted of about a pound and a half of black bread and a piece of dried salt fish about the size of a herring daily and tea three times, each time with a small piece of sugar. That was all we ever got. The fish was hard and dark red from the salting. It had to be eaten because there was nothing else to eat but the bread, and after eating it we were tormented with thirst. This was our daily ration at the start, but we discovered that the further we got from Moscow the smaller our ration became. The lumps of sugar were the first to go, then the tea leaves disappeared from the tea, which was then practically hot water, and in the end the fish portion was about half the size. And the guards got lazier and more neglectful as time went on. They couldn't be bothered to give us the 'tea' three times a day, so more often than not we had to go thirsty. They even refused to give us water, despite all our pleadings. 'At the next station we'll get you some,' they'd say.

The situation with regard to our physical needs was even worse. The coach was carrying more than twice as many passengers as it was built for and there was only one lavatory. It meant that all day long someone or other wanted to be let out, and the guards soon got tired of this, so they declared that each prisoner could go out only three times a day and for not more than two minutes at a time. During these two minutes the guard would look with interest through the spy-hole of the lavatory door. The men simply peed through the bars of the corridor.

I knew only five of the women in our compartment. The rest of them came from another Moscow prison. They were all Politicals. The good spirits of most of them were difficult to understand. We were all on the way to Siberia with sentences ranging from five to ten years. At night we were all squeezed up together in great discomfort, and yet these women kept up their spirits. When they left prison they had been given back their handbags, and now they produced powder-puffs, rouge and mirrors and got to work on their faces. Having decorated themselves to the best of their ability, they proceeded to flirt with the guards. I hated my sex. How could they smile and chat with those who were robbing us of our freedom and even of our human dignity? With these men who were part and parcel of the GPU organisation? The only women who were depressed were Stefanie, Rebecca Sagorje, Grete Sonntag, myself and a twenty-two-year-old, fair-haired girl who looked as though she might have come straight out of high school. Side by side with the robust, lively Nadia Bereskina, who was about the same age, she looked sixteen. I noticed that every time she had to reel off her little litany: name, number, offence and sentence, she blushed. 'Counter-revolutionary organisation – eight years.'

We got into conversation. She had been the secretary of a factory director, and had taken no part in politics. When she was arrested they had presented her with an indictment charging her with active membership of a counter-revolutionary Trotskyite organisation together with about thirty other people, most of whom she had never even heard of. They were all alleged to have carried out acts of sabotage in the factory. Of course, she denied all knowledge about any such things, but her examiner insisted. When she refused to confess, she was left standing for two days with short interruptions, and when even after that she still maintained her denials the examiner seized her by the throat and half throttled her. That brutal violence and further threats broke her physically and mentally, and she signed a 'confession'. The GPU then arrested her chief and the thirty others.

The good spirits of the other women in our compartment gradually flagged, and after about two days we hardly knew whether it was day or night. We would crouch on the bench with our knees up and doze like sick birds. Someone said we were already on the other side of Kazan. Sometimes the train stood for a whole day on the open track. The air was almost too thick to breathe. What little water had been available for washing had long since dried up and was not renewed. Why bother to wash, anyhow? What did it matter? If one could only go to sleep and never wake up! When we had been under way about ten days, or perhaps it was a fortnight, we were roused from our lethargy by the shout: 'Get ready. With things.' We had arrived in Sisrin, the first stage of our long journey. Exhausted and dirty, we crawled out. '*Davai! Davai!*' The guards were at it again, and we were hurried along the lines like scared chickens. Two lorries were waiting in a goods siding. Bullied and urged on by the guards, we clambered up in a panic. The keen, fresh air literally made us giddy. They squashed more and more prisoners into the lorry until finally it was impossible to squeeze in even another one. Then the lorry started up and went off at a great speed through the town, which seemed to consist entirely of wooden houses. It swayed and bumped alarmingly and I held on grimly to a chain that happened to be near me. Two soldiers sat on the tailboard. When we started up, a little boy ran after us as long as he could, shouting, '*Vragi naroda. Vragi naroda*' – 'Enemies of the people.'

The prison of Sisrin was packed to capacity. We were herded into a stinking washroom for delousing and then put into a damp cell where there were plank beds knocked together out of odd bits of wood. Then we were given a meal. It consisted of lukewarm soup that had gone sour, but we swallowed it with avidity. In the night I woke up with a shock. The cell was full of rats eating up our dry bread and skipping and hopping all over the place. They were obviously quite used to human company and they paid no attention to us; all they were interested in was our bread. When it grew light we discovered that all the bread sacks had holes bitten in them. We remained in this rat paradise for three days and then our journey began again. In the meantime, our transport had been increased by the addition of a number of male political offenders, several officers' wives, five pregnant women, a seventy-year-old woman and two criminal offenders.

This time there were no lorries to take us to the station and we had to march in columns of five through the dark, snow-covered streets. The pregnant women and the old woman had at least the warm and comfortable footgear made of felt and known as *valinki*. They brought up the rear, and behind them marched a young soldier who constantly urged us on with shouts of '*Davai! Davai!*' But the women could not keep up with the men, and the column began to straggle, despite all the furious shouting of the soldiers. The men in front halted and some of them came back to us: 'Give us your bundles,' they said; 'and you go up to the front and make the pace. Let them shout. They can't do anything.' We went up to the front of the column and the men took our bundles. After that the journey was easier for us.

There was a great to-do when we got to the train, because the transport leader was at first unwilling to reserve one of the compartments for the women and wanted to bundle men and women all in together. In the end a compartment was reserved – though that word conjures up visions of comfort and privilege – and as soon as we scrambled in a fight started for places, chiefly on account of the two criminal offenders who each took as much place as had previously been occupied by two. They were brutal types and in foul language they told us that we had better keep our distance, because they had the clap and syphilis. Whether true or not, it had its effect, and the rest of us squeezed up even more closely than before.

When we were already beyond the Urals we learnt from one of the guards that we were destined for Karaganda. At the thought of how far away I was from everyone I loved, I leant against the bars of our cage and wept openly. One of the guards was moved by my despair and stopped to console me. 'Don't cry,' he said. 'It won't be as bad as all that. You'll live through it and get home again.' If only I could have believed that!

Arrival in Karaganda

It was early evening on the day we arrived in Karaganda. We were tired, exhausted and stiff when we got out. It was freezing hard, and all around wretched men and women with their bundles were slipping and falling, getting up and slipping again, and all the time the escorting soldiers kept up their bullying shouts of '*Davai! Davai!*' We were hustled over a large space towards a brilliantly lit wooden gateway with a watchtower above it. Barbed-wire fences stretched away on either side. We came to a halt in the quarantine compound of the Karaganda concentration camp and the roll was called. Each of us had to step forward and recite the usual particulars. This business lasted for hours, and we sat on our bundles and grew colder and colder until I was numbed to the bone. Then we were taken into the washroom, where all our clothing was sent off to be deloused. Everyone tried to hide what clothing he could, because the old hands knew that the clothing came back even lousier than before and often scorched in addition. Male guards were in charge of our washroom and when the women tried to get them to go out whilst they stripped they thought it a great joke. Each prisoner was given a metal disc, and on handing this over each received half a wooden bucket of hot water.

The washroom was absolutely bare. It stank, and there was not a dry spot anywhere and not enough room for all the women who were trying to wash simultaneously. A man whose job it was to fill the water containers strolled around amongst the naked women slapping the bottoms of those who happened to be bending at their task – and a task it was. The fierce protests of the women merely amused him all the more.

After that depressing experience, but at least a little fresher, we were quartered in a hut made of dried clay. The roof of such a Siberian hut comes down to the ground and the floor of stamped earth inside is below ground level. In the winter there is nothing to be seen but a heap of snow, and if there has been fresh snow in the night it means that the occupants have to dig themselves out. In our hut was a broken stove and sleeping places knocked together out of unplaned wood. The floor was filthy and scattered around were discarded items left by previous occupants. In one corner there were some large lumps of coal and an axe, but nowhere was there even a scrap of wood to start a fire. A number of us went out to see if we could find some. Here inside the camp we could at least move freely and were not confined to a cell, and we were also not watched at every step. Our quarantine was surrounded with barbed wire and at each end of the space was a watchtower, but we could walk around freely within this space and between the various huts. I found some wooden cases and, taking one, I went back to our hut and began to break it up with the axe. I hadn't got far with my efforts when a man rushed in, seized me by the arm and amidst a storm of curses accused me of stealing the case and tried to drag me out to hand me over to the *natchalnik*, or officer in charge.

Fortunately, my fellow prisoners came to the rescue and in the end he was pushed out, taking the greater part of the box with him. My first day in Karaganda almost ended up in arrest. However, we had enough wood to start a fire, and I began to break up the large lumps of coal with the back of the axe. The coal was very hard and at one particularly heavy blow the head flew off and nearly brained me. It would have saved me many years of misery. In the end we succeeded in getting a fire going, but then we were faced with the alternative of being asphyxiated or going outside to freeze, for smoke and fumes poured out of innumerable cracks in the sides of the dilapidated stove.

The food here was very bad compared with the Butirka. The bread ration was about the same, but the soup was very weak and usually sour, and we very rarely got *kasha*. There were no washing facilities. If we wanted to wash we took an old tin, went out and filled it with snow and then came back with it and waited until it thawed. The women as yet had no work to do, and so they made themselves as presentable as possible and then went out into the brilliant Siberian sunshine and flirted with the men, who had already been put to work. They were digging holes in the frozen ground and setting up posts. How wretched these poor 'cavaliers' looked! Most of them had beards so thick you could hardly see their faces. They were all miserably dressed and their movements were slow and tired, but when the women came along they perked up.

Three of the men in our transport had sentences of twenty-five years. One of them, Valerie Alexandrovitch, had been in charge of the cattle-breeding on a number of big farms. Unfortunately for him, some sort of cattle murrain broke out and several hundred of the animals perished. This brought him in an indictment for sabotage and twenty-five years' forced labour. Another man had been an assistant of Michurin, the famous fruit and wheat expert. He told us that after Michurin's death his whole scientific staff had been arrested and charged with counter-revolutionary activity against the State. Another of our prisoners was an engineer who had a French mother who lived in France. He had corresponded with her and made one or two incautious observations which the censor had construed as criticism of conditions in the Soviet Union.

On the third day a good-looking stranger with broad shoulders came into our hut. But it wasn't a stranger at all; it was Valerie Alexandrovitch, who had managed to shave off his beard and tidy himself up. He had come to see Nadia Bereskina. The first love affair in our transport was well under way.

After a day or so of inactivity, Grete Sonntag and I decided it would be much better if we could get something to do rather than pass our time being alternatively smoke-cured in the hut and frozen outside, so we went to the office and asked for work of some kind. They were startled that anyone should want to work, but they enquired what we wanted to do. 'Isn't there a sort of laundry or something here?' I asked. We had already thought that if we could get a job in the laundry we might be able to keep ourselves clean as well. There was, it appeared, and we were sent to the man in charge, who took us on, gave us a piece of soap about the size of a matchbox and seventy-five garments each, which, he declared, represented the day's labour quota.

When we came to examine the garments, which consisted of men's shirts and underpants, we found they were full of lice. We considered the matter for a moment and then decided they ought to be boiled first to kill the lice, so we got to work. When we had boiled them we began to scrub away with our bits of soap. The foreman came up and watched us. He had a really terrible face and we learnt afterwards that he had been a professional thief. However, his manner towards us was quite amiable.

'You really don't want to do it that way,' he said after a while. 'You want to do it the camp way.'

'What way's that?' we asked.

'Why, you just pocket the soap. That's valuable. You can get all sorts of things for it. Then you pitch the things into the cauldron and boil them. Just leave them in for a while, and that's it.'

We thanked him for his good advice. Who were we to introduce innovations? He continued to watch us, and then he asked in a friendly fashion: 'Would you like a piece of bread and butter and a gherkin?' Would we not! And we agreed joyfully. After a while he returned, and really and truly there were two thick pieces of bread smeared with butter and two gherkins. We fell upon them and ate with avidity. But hardly had the last mouthful disappeared than he began to make improper proposals to Grete Sonntag. She spoke no Russian and couldn't understand him, so he turned to me, jerking his thumb towards the other room. 'Come on,' he said. 'Let's have a bunk up in there. Plenty more bread and butter and gherkins where they came from,' and he accompanied his words, whose purport I gathered, though the expression was new to me, with gestures that made his meaning quite clear. Even Grete realised that he wanted to be rewarded for his liberality.

The situation was far from reassuring. We were alone with him in the wash-house, and we had eaten his food. I did my best to persuade him to forgo his price just for this once, explaining that we were Germans and quite unused to camp customs. Affairs of the heart weren't settled quite like that where we came from. He took it all in fairly good part and in the end he burst out laughing. 'So,' he said, 'you're Germans, are you? Well, you're prisoners in Karaganda now, anyway, and if you don't learn it quick you'll starve.' Thankfully we made our escape.

In our quarantine there was a special hut which was isolated from the rest and constantly guarded. Inside were prisoners who had served their time and were due to be returned to freedom. We heard that there were two Polish women amongst them. Each of them had done her five-year term, but now suddenly each was to go back to the camp 'until further notice' and with no reason being given. On one occasion we saw a transport leave with such prisoners. They were all clad in the same old camp rags and each carried his poor little bundle of things. They wearily plodded their way through the snow to freedom and we watched them from a distance with heavy hearts. Would we all one day be in a column like that on our way back to freedom after serving our sentences of five, eight or ten years' forced labour? Should we ever again live outside the barbed wire, away from the fixed bayonets and out of earshot of the constant bellowing of *'Davai! Davai!'*?

After we had spent a fortnight in quarantine, our transport was sent off to the reception centre of the camp proper. The life there was very different. There were great wooden, barrack-like structures each housing several hundred prisoners, all waiting to be sent to various parts of the vast Karaganda labour camp. In the women's barracks we found a great room which ran from end to end of the building. Round the walls were two tiers of planks to sleep on and more planks in the middle. The place was heated by an oven, but the temperature was not very high. It was completely infested with bedbugs. They lived in swarms under the planks and at night they came out to feed on the recumbent prisoners. At least there was no shortage of fuel, for the camp area reached well into the Karaganda coal basin, where many of the prisoners worked. Here for the first time I saw criminal and asocial elements in large numbers. Clothed in rags, most of them were in a dreadful condition.

The first night fell in the reception centre. We had been warned to take good care of our things, as these criminal and Asocial elements stole everything they could lay their hands on. The best thing to do, we were told, was to sleep on our things and use the sack with the remainder as a pillow. But you had to protect yourself from the bugs as well as from the thieves. You slept completely dressed, with gloves fastened at the wrists, a scarf over your head and a cloth over your face, with two eyeholes. But the bugs were clever and some of them found a way in, despite all our precautions. They even crawled inside our nostrils.

The first night I lay against a small window. Outside a snowstorm was raging. I got off to sleep, but before long I awoke from the cold and found snow falling on me through the window. Someone had opened it and stolen my sack from under my head. The thieves in Karaganda were experts. The next morning I reported my loss to the Hut Senior and asked whether anything could be done to get the things back. 'No hope at all,' she said, shaking her head. 'In any case, one of the guards may have had a hand in it.'

'But', I protested, 'all my documents were in the blouse pocket, the receipts for the things which were kept back in prison – all the papers I possess, in fact.'

'Well, we might try it,' she said doubtfully. 'We could send someone over to the men's barracks and say the foreigner gave up all claim to the things, but would like the papers back. That's the best you can hope for.'

I agreed. What else could I do. The negotiator was then sent and a little while later a quite elegantly dressed young man with a modern overcoat padded excessively at the shoulders and a smart fur hat perched on one side of his head came over to me. 'Are you the foreigner who lost her papers in the night?' he asked with a smile. I nodded. 'Here they are,' he said, and handed them over. 'We managed to get them back for you.' Something told me that this smart young man was also the smart thief who had taken my sack and things in the first place.

That was my first lesson, but despite my experience and all the precautions I took, before long I possessed only the things I stood up in, and

the others who had come with me were not in a much better state. In
the Siberian camps criminals are a favoured category. They occupy all the
minor posts in the camps and they lead what might even be called a social
life. Unlike the political prisoners, their life in the camp did not represent
any very great break with their normal lives. One might almost say they
were strictly organised. They had their leaders whose word was law, and
if one of them decided for some reason or other that there was to be no
work the next day not a single criminal would dare to disobey, although
after refusal to work on twenty-five occasions the penalty in Karaganda
was death. These criminal elements regarded the political prisoners with
the greatest contempt. We were enemies of the people, whilst they, although
they might be criminals, were loyal Soviet citizens. There were class divi-
sions amongst them, too, and the big thieves regarded the little sneak
thieves, or *kusotchniki*, with the contempt of the expert for the bungler.

A real criminal gang-romanticism prevailed in this reception centre in
Karaganda. The big hut was dimly lighted by a paraffin lamp and men
and women sat on the upper stage of the planks in the centre and played
cards. Although the temperature was by no means comfortable, these
women wore only knickers and bras, apart from the coloured scarves they
wore neatly turbaned round their heads, one end hanging decoratively
down at the side. These women, it appeared, often staked their clothes,
and when they had lost them they had to steal others. They were never
short of vodka and they always seemed to have plenty of food.

The camp rules forbade men to enter the women's quarters and vice
versa, and when the patrol went through the barracks at night with their
lamps and found a man in the women's quarters he was carted off to the
cells at once, but certain of the criminals seemed to be exempt from this
rule, and when the guards found them with the women they were not
interfered with. I often saw criminals sleeping with women, and so did
the guards. There seemed to be a firm understanding between criminals
and guards.

At the End of the World

It was in the reception centre that all prisoners were medically examined
to discover what work they were suited for. On examination day the queue
was endless. When at last your turn came, the doctor asked name, number,
offence and sentence. After that all he said was: 'Put your leg up on here.'
Then he would examine the leg and note down whether you were in category one, two or three – hard, medium or light work. Unfortunately, my
leg satisfied him and I was noted down for category one, hard work.

A lively trade with garments went on, and nothing was too dilapidated to find a purchaser. It appeared that some of the prisons gave prisoners their money back, so that quite a number were in funds. Up to fifty roubles was paid for a worn pullover. Many of these prisoners were insufficiently clad and so had to buy themselves clothes.

The food in the reception centre was even worse than in quarantine. We received a smaller bread ration and one helping of watery soup a day. At last our turn came to be organised into a column. Eighty of us, both men and women, including Grete Sonntag, Stefanie Brun, Rebecca Sagorje, Nadia Bereskina and myself, were to go to the Birma district of Karaganda. Before we went we were thoroughly searched once more, and anyone who had been fortuante enough to find some little thing to make life a bit easier, such as an old tin can or a pannikin for soup, had to part with it. I had managed to get hold of a wooden spoon, but this I concealed successfully in the top of my stocking. The search took place in the club room for employees of the reception centre. To my secret amusement, I saw there was a large picture of Yezhov still in a place of honour on the wall, surrounded by red bunting. Yezhov had been arrested and shot some time before, and Beria's portrait should have been there now. It was easy to see we were a long way from Moscow.

We travelled three stations with the train steaming through the camp area all the time, and finally we halted in Sharik. From there we had to walk about six or seven miles. The land was flat and bare, typical steppe country, and there was hardly a tree or a bush. Far away on the horizon there were mountains. Karaganda lies in the Kazakhstan steppes. This area used to be called the hunger lands, and it was very well named. Until the twenties there were hardly any settlements at all. The natives of Kazakhstan lived a nomadic life, wandering from water hole to water hole with their cattle and horses, for grass does grow there in the summer. It was not until about 1932 that the Soviet Government decided to use prisoners to bring the area into cultivation. Experiments were made with the cultivation of sunflowers for their oil-bearing seeds, and certain kinds of wheat and barley. If there was enough rain in the spring, they cropped very well on this virgin soil, but if there was not then the sun burnt up everything remorselessly. In the years 1938 and 1939 the harvests were very poor. As the Karaganda camp was unable to feed itself, supplies had to be sent in from outside. They were not overgenerous, and so in those years our nourishment was particularly bad. Karaganda was regarded as a camp for light agricultural labour. It was tremendous in area, though I had no means of judging just how far it extended. I know of five different areas which lay about twenty-five to thirty miles apart, and each of these areas was subdivided into smaller districts, some of which consisted of little more than a settlement of mud huts for the prisoners, both male and female, and sheds for the cattle.

The first visit we paid in Birma was to the washroom. It was just the same as all the others: inefficient delousing arrangements, men in the women's washroom, severely rationed hot water, not a dry spot to put clothes down and nothing to hang a thing on. It turned out that Birma was so overcrowded that there was no room for us anywhere, so we had to spend the first night in the washroom. The next day we were let out and we strolled around to survey our new home. The washroom was a little off the beaten track. Incidentally, that expression is literally correct: there were no proper roads or pavements, but just beaten tracks between the various barracks, and when the weather was wet the mud was churned up by lorries and ox-carts.

There was only one decent-looking building in the place, and that was the hospital. The main street of the camp was about a mile in length, and it was flanked on either side by large and small buildings, mostly made of clay. Only two of the houses had proper windows and curtains. Camp officials, including the Commandant, Serikov, lived in these. There were also barracks for the guards, administration buildings and so on, and even a cinema to which sometimes, we were told, prisoners were allowed to go to. Around the kitchens was a great collection of leavings and debris of all sorts. Built on to one of these kitchens was a large room, apparently originally intended as a storeroom. It was now full of heaps of dirt and human excrement. Then there was a special barracks for women containing rooms made to house fifteen each, but they were already so overcrowded that there was no room for us. There were two other similar places, one of them on top of a small hill above a pond. There was a barracks for men on the main street of the camp and behind it was a stud farm with well-built stables for the horses. Altogether, the cattle sheds and stables were much better than the accommodation for human beings, at least for those who were prisoners. On the other side of the street were grain barns, a repair workshop for agricultural machinery, a smithy and sheds for tractors, and so on. Before these sheds all sorts of agricultural machinery stood out in the open: tractors, combines, ploughs and so on, all modern implements. At the far end of the street there was a canteen for the employees and officials of the camp and one for the prisoners. Next door to this there had been a camp library, but this was long since disused and closed down. A little way from the street was a mill driven by machinery and next to it a huge barn. There was a dynamo here which generated electricity, but only for the administration buildings and the homes of the officials. All the living huts were lighted by oil lamps. On the other side of the pond were solidly built sheds for cows and sheep. Railway lines ran through the camp, and beyond them were a number of huts and the prison compound, surrounded by barbed wire. On this first day the sun shone brilliantly and sparkled in the snow, and over our heads was a great sky of lovely blue, but we were all very depressed, fully convinced that we should never leave the place alive.

We were surprised to find that the camp was not surrounded by barbed wire or a wall. Prisoners, we were told, were allowed to move freely up to within half a mile of the camp; after that the guards shot without warning. The registration of newcomers did not begin until the second day, and then it was discovered that some of us, including Rebecca Sagorje and the eighteen-year-old Polish girl, had a note, 'Keep under special surveillance', on their papers, and so they were taken off to the prison compound. The same day groups were organised to go off to various sub-districts of the camp, and in the end, of the foreigners, only Grete Sonntag and I were left. Towards evening we went from barracks to barracks trying to find a place to sleep, but they were filled to over-flowing with Russians and no one would let us in.

After three nights spent in the washroom, we got to know the camp barber, a young Georgian prisoner. For sixty copecks, he cut off prisoners' hair. 'Don't you want your hair cut?' he asked us. 'It's much better, because of the lice.' We told him we had no money to pay him and he agreed to cut our hair off on credit. He could speak a few German words – one in particular – and he liked talking to us. In this way we learnt quite a lot about the camp. We were always hungry, and he told us that there were four different kitchens in the camp and four different ration scales. It appeared that we were in the fourth and worst category – field workers and prisoners in the punishment compound. The third category was for men working in the repair shops and in the offices; the second for workers engaged in transport and building; and the first and best for skilled agricultural workers. Only prisoners in this first category were fairly well fed.

Once again we decided that we might be able to better our lot by working, so we asked our friendly barber if he knew of anything. He told us we could probably get work unloading lorries. We went in a lorry with three men and a guard to Sharik railway station. Here we found three railway trucks full of coal and were told to start unloading them. Then I did something I might not have done later. I refused to work.

'You can't expect us to unload coal in our own clothes,' I said indignantly. 'They're all we've got. And in any case, it's men's work.' The man laughed in astonishment and told the guard what we had said, but nothing happened. After a while one of the men came up and asked us if we'd care to unload sacks. He was quite polite about it. 'If they're not too heavy,' I replied. 'Oh no,' he assured me. 'They're quite small sacks.'

They turned out to be half-hundredweight sugar sacks. We set to work willingly, together with the men, and when the lorry was full we were told to sit at the back and see that no one stole anything. Then the lorry started off. Grete and I had one idea: how to get at the sugar. We had not gone far when the lorry stopped and the guard and the men went off to some clay huts. One of them turned back to us and winked. 'Look after the sugar,' he said. 'See that no one steals it whilst we're gone.'

Whilst they were away, we turned our attention to the sacks, and soon we had lumps of sugar concealed all over us. We were newcomers and therefore we stole far too modestly. When we got back we were afraid that we should be searched, but no one bothered about us, and we scuttled off with our booty. We didn't even have to unload the sacks – there was a rush of volunteers to do the unloading; they all wanted a chance to steal some sugar. Safely back in the washroom, we began to munch our booty.

It was another two days before we could find anywhere to sleep, and then an old door was laid over two blocks of wood, and that was the bed for Grete and me. One side was uncomfortable because of the iron lock, so we took it in turns, change and change about. Then we were instructed to report to the clerk in charge of the finance department for work. I have forgotten the man's name, but not his humanity. He was a political prisoner – quite rightly regarded as more reliable for such a job than a criminal. 'What sort of work would you like to do?' he asked. We were rather vague about that. 'I don't know,' I said. 'You see, Grete doesn't speak any Russian at all and I don't speak it too well.' 'All the same,' he replied, 'you're educated people; you can't go around doing hard, manual labour. I don't think I've got anything you could do here, but I'll send you over to Konstantin Konstantinovitch. He's in charge of the repair-shop office. You can start with him as learners.'

We set off to find Konstantin Konstantinovitch. Grete was grumbling. 'It's all very well for you,' she said, 'but I don't want to go into an office. I'm a skilled leather worker. It would be ridiculous if there were no work for me here with all these cattle. They must tan the leather and work it, surely?' 'Don't be a fool,' I replied. 'Be satisfied if you can get into an office. It will be warmer, and you'll soon learn Russian.'

When we made the acquaintance of Konstantin Konstaninovitch our welcome was not so friendly. He was a political offender, too. When we explained to him that we had been sent from the finance office to work for him he made a sour face. 'I've got enough here already who don't do any work,' he said. 'What should I want with you when you don't even speak Russian properly?' But I was anxious to get the job and I assured him that we at least would work, and, after all, we were to start as beginners. He got pencil and paper and dictated a Russian sentence which I wrote down carefully. Grete angrily refused to try. 'All right,' he said to me. 'You can start here, but I can't use your friend.'

On the way back we nearly quarrelled. Our friend the clerk in charge of the finance department didn't know what to do with Grete. We explained that she was a skilled leather worker; surely there must be something or other in that line here? Yes, there was, of course, but a dangerous cattle disease was rampant, and anyone who worked with skins inevitably fell ill. No; he couldn't take the responsibility for that. The skin-workers died or were ruined in health for life. I translated this to Grete.

'What typical rubbish,' she exclaimed angrily. 'The Russians catch things because they're dirty pigs with no idea of cleanliness. Tell him I can look after myself. I'll see that I don't catch anything. Tell him not to bother about his responsibility. It's mine.'

I translated as much of this as I thought suitable. He was still doubtful, but we persuaded him, and so Grete got work in the tannery. The prisoner in charge was a Jew from White Russia who 'couldn't speak German, but could understand it', which meant he spoke Yiddish, so they were able to make themselves understood. When we went into his workshop there was hardly room to put a foot down. There were skins all over the place. The disorder was almost indescribable, and the stink nearly choked you when you came in from outside. Grete made a few disagreeable remarks about the state of the place and got the job. The foreman also found her a corner to live in attached to the hut. When I went to visit her a few days later the workshop was almost unrecognisable. The skins were all sorted and stacked into neat piles. In one corner were specially valuable skins from new-born sheep. Each skin was ticketed and the skins themselves sorted out into three categories according to their quality. Although she spoke no Russian, Grete had managed to obtain a bottle of carbolic from the camp hospital and a pair of rubber gloves. The place was clean and there was room to move about easily, and even the stink had largely disappeared. A touch of German efficiency had worked wonders. A little while later, when I was already in the punishment compound, I heard that a special commission of investigation had been sent to Birma from the central administration in Dolinki to report on Grete's miracle.

First Work

In the meantime I began my own work under Konstantin Konstantinovitch. I was made very welcome by my new colleagues:

Clement Nikifrevitch, a former school director of Novosibirsk; Semion Semionovitch, a former Party employee in White Russia; Grigory Ilyitch, an agricultural expert from Kazakhstan; and Maslov, a former cashier on the Caucasian Railways, who suffered badly from malaria and had a face like Nicholas II. They were all political offenders, and this made the atmosphere much more pleasant. They all spoke some German, and they were very kind to me, helping me with my work as well as they could. Clement Nikifrevitch, in particular, was quite a cultured man, and he could quote by heart from the German classics. The others, too, were educated men. They had all served from three to five years of varying sentences and it had left its mark on them. They were thin and emaciated; their cheeks had fallen in and their eyes were unnaturally bright, and almost all of them had gaps in their teeth, for there was no such thing as dental treatment in Karaganda. When a tooth went bad, it just rotted until finally it had to be extracted. And what a pitiful sight they were in their camp clothing, with their grey, padded, much-worn jackets and their coolie trousers and close-cropped hair! But their faces come back to me as amongst the finest and kindest I ever saw.

My work was to keep a statistical record of the daily performance of the tractors, noting down carefully how many hours were lost and the reason, whether it was the fault of the prisoner driver, or lack of petrol or breakdowns. In the circumstances which existed in the camp, such a record was grotesque. The repair shop was always short of spare parts and in consequence many of the tractors were always lying idle. But if an hour was lost by the fault of the driver it had to be carefully noted down.

Konstantin Konstantinovitch was a Hungarian, and my first impression of him had not been wrong. He was a little bureaucrat by nature and he fitted perfectly into his job. The man in charge of the repair shop itself was a Czech, German Germanovitch. You could see that at one time he had had a paunch, but now his poor belly hung down in sad folds. He spoke German fluently, but he was so scared that it was never possible to get any further than: 'Good morning. It's a lovely day, isn't it?' He was efficient and good at his job, and his ideas of how a repair shop should be run were Western European. The tractors were garaged in neat lines and the floor space was kept free and swept. No valuable machinery was ever allowed to stand outside his workshop to deteriorate, and in this respect it differed greatly from the usual run of Russian factories and workshops.

In the harvest periods the office employees were formed into 'shock brigades' to lend a hand – 'voluntarily', of course. Not only that, but they were even expected to take up 'State loans' from their pitiful earnings, and there were many who hadn't enough courage to refuse. During the harvest we worked from sunup to midday in the fields and from one o'clock to eight o'clock in the office after our return. In the fields we had to perform a certain labour quota. At that time I still had enough strength to do the work required without much trouble and even to help Clement Nikifrevitch finish his. He had already been five years in the camp and it was a great effort for him to get his quota done in time. This work in the fields was paid at a little higher rate than the work in the camp, though as a beginner in the office I got no pay at all. From the summer of 1939 on, the work in the field was paid at the rate of twenty copecks a day, provided the quota was performed. If you failed to complete the quota, you got nothing at all. In a month in which you reached the target every working day you could earn no more than six roubles. A pound of herrings in the canteen cost about three roubles and a pound of bread about fifty copecks. Really skilled work in the fields was much better paid. I was told that a combine driver and mechanic could earn up to 100 roubles in a month. In the summer of 1939 an order came out that the better-paid categories, who were also in the first and best food category, had to pay for their food from their earnings.

Whilst I was working in the office I belonged to the third category, the one above the worst, and I lived in a hut on the other side of the pond I have mentioned. I had to cross over a dam in order to get there. The dam had been built by prisoners in order to create a water reservoir for the kitchen garden, which was on the other side of the dam, with artificially irrigated potato fields, tomato plantations, rows and rows of all kinds of vegetables and many hothouses. Things grew very well on the steppe soil, provided there was sufficient water. Needless to say, the produce of this kitchen garden was never used for the prisoners' food, and I cannot remember ever having seen even a potato in the soup of the lowest food category, not to mention tomatoes or anything of that sort.

The room in which I lived was so low that you could touch the ceiling with your hand. Both walls and ceiling were bare. The floor consisted of stamped clay, which meant that it could be swept only in dry weather. A special kind of flea, about twice as big as the fleas in Western Europe, was at home here, and it was infested with bugs. The windows were very small, and most of them were broken and the holes stopped up with anything that came to hand, so they were not much use either for ventilation or light. I still slept on the door laid across the lumps of wood, though I now had it all to myself, as Grete was quartered at her place of work. I had no straw sack to sleep on and no pillow. Only those who had brought them into the camp and had managed to secure them against the attentions of thieves had blankets.

This barracks was divided into ten large rooms. Three rooms were connected and they had a common door into the corridor. For 'security reasons', the prisoners in one room would employ a *ndevalnaya*, usually an old prisoner unfit for work and therefore not receiving any pay from the camp, and each of them would pay so much a month for her services. The one in my room was a criminal offender. She fetched the soup at midday and did various other things for those who combined to pay her, but for me, who had no money to contribute, she never did a thing, and she regarded me with great contempt as a parasite.

The *ndevalnaya* of another room was a sixty-year-old German woman from Berlin named Margarete Paulovna. She had a podgy face and untidy grey hair which hung down in wisps. She wore glasses and had bags under her eyes, and her legs were swollen with dropsy. Amidst tears she told me that she had emigrated to the Soviet Union in 1933 with her two sons, one of whom was an actor. Both had been arrested; she did not know why; and shortly afterwards she had been arrested too. When her sons were arrested the Russian Prosecutor had advised her to take Russian nationality, and she had been afraid to refuse for fear she would never see her sons again. She had, in fact, never seen them again and there was very little likelihood that she ever would. In her opinion, Nazis couldn't be worse than people who sent an innocent old woman to Siberia, and she was sorry she had lost her nationality.

There was a special room for mothers with babies in our barracks. When I went into it, it was some time before I could get used to the atmosphere, which made my eyes water. Hanging from the ceiling on string were wooden boxes containing the babies, who were wrapped up in all kinds of odd rags. However, women with babies did not stay long in Birma. Sooner or later they were sent off in an ox-wagon to another section of the Karaganda camp. Women who had comparatively short terms to serve – they were exclusively criminal and asocial elements – were allowed to have their children with them.

When I learnt that the so-called *udarnik* or 'Shock' work in the fields was paid for, I borrowed sixty copecks on account from Clement Nikifrevitch and went to pay my debt to the young Georgian barber. He was delighted to see me and, I have no doubt, greatly astonished that I should come to pay him. He asked me about my work and about my food, and so on, and as he talked I had the impression that he was steering round to some point or other. After a short pause, he asked: 'Have you got a camp husband yet?' I laughed. 'Don't laugh,' he said seriously. 'Five years is a long time.' And then, as though taking his courage in both hands, he burst out: 'Why don't you be my wife whilst you're here? I earn about twenty-five roubles a month and I've good connections in the kitchen. I get meat and all sorts of things. And I've got a room to myself; you could live in with me. Quite comfortable. And as my wife, you could use the washroom every day.'

He was a good-hearted lad, and so I explained patiently that though all the privileges he mentioned were attractive, yet they weren't sufficient to justify marriage. You needed something else: real affection, if not love.

'Oh yes,' he replied. 'I know all that, but that's outside. In here a woman just must have a good camp husband if she doesn't want to starve.'

He said he would give me time to think it over, and made me promise to tell him at the end of the week what I had decided.

One evening when I left the office a worker from the smithy spoke to me, asking me how long I had been here, how many years I had to serve, and where I came from. I told him and then he asked 'Have you got a *katylok* yet?' A *katylok* is a tin can which the prisoners use as a mess tin for their food. The camp provides nothing of the sort and no cutlery. A new prisoner has to see how he can get hold of one, or something similar to serve the purpose. I hadn't one, of course, and he asked me if I should like him to make me one. I said that would be very nice and we parted. The next day he was waiting for me in the street with a brand new *katylok* which even had a handle to it. I was very thankful for the gift and we strolled along the street chatting. I learnt that he had been a locomotive driver until one day he had had an accident, and here he was for sabotage. He was so trustful that I almost began to wonder whether he was a provocateur trying to betray me into incautious remarks. I decided that it was probably because I was a foreigner and he didn't think it necessary to be so careful with me. A day or so later he came with another present, a tin plate. That was even more beautiful than the *katylok*. But then he began to talk enthusiastically about a national resistance movement in Kazakhstan, declaring they were only waiting until war finally broke out between Russia and Germany. I was horrified and did my best to explain to him just what Hitler meant. At the very best it would mean replacing one dictatorship by another. They would all be out of the frying pan into the fire. But he was not to be persuaded, and he remained enthusiastically pro-German. He brought me one other marvellous present, a knife he had made in the workshop. It was strictly prohibited for a prisoner to possess a knife, but everyone who could possibly obtain one, or had managed to smuggle one through all the searches, had a knife, and all the others did everything possible to obtain one. This was a lovely knife with a grip of hard rubber beautifully decorated with inlaid metalwork.

In the Punishment Block

I saw very few wild animals whilst I was in Karaganda. The only natural life consisted of a very large type of vulture and a number of beautifully plumaged birds which had no song. But one day on our pond we saw two wild ducks floating around as though they had been there for ever. At midday everyone was happy at the sight and stood on the bank and watched them. In our excitement we even fed them with pieces of precious bread. Where on earth could they have come from? There was no water surface anywhere around for countless miles. And yet somehow they had flown an enormous distance to land on our pond. We were delighted. They were not in the least shy and they swam around as though the pond had always been their home.

In the evening after work my first thought was about the ducks. They were still there. Perhaps they would stay with us and have a clutch of eggs, and then there would be ducklings. I was quite moved and I went into the barracks seeing them swimming around with their mother in my imagination. A little later we heard a shot. Everyone ran out in foreboding. On the other side of the pond stood the GPU *natchalnik* with a whole group of uniformed men around him. He was shooting at our ducks. A number of male prisoners stood a respectful distance away. Oh, my God, I thought. Why don't they fly away before he hits them? But the ducks continued to swim around, though they kept together as though for protection. They obviously knew nothing about guns. A second and third shot sounded, and with the third the *natchalnik* hit one of them, and it turned over and floated breast upwards in the water. The other duck swam around anxiously quacking, but still it made no attempt to escape. The *natchalnik* was a rotten shot, but he had plenty of time and plenty of ammunition, and he fired five more times before he killed the second duck. Then one of the prisoners flung off his clothes and plunged in the water to fetch the booty like a gun dog. At that moment I hated the human race.

Clement Nikifrevitch declared that in his opinion it was perfectly useless for a prisoner to ask for the reopening of his case. Such an application had no chance of success at all unless it was made by someone outside, by a relative or friend. I was not at all convinced. 'I have the impression that you all accept your fate too resignedly,' I declared. 'I am going to appeal to the Supreme Court and lodge an application for the reopening of my case.'

They were truly horrified and from all sides they begged me to do nothing of the sort, declaring that I should only succeed in worsening my lot. People who did things of that sort were regarded as a nuisance;

their applications went into the waste-paper basket and they got into the bad books of the camp authorities. However, I was still unconvinced, and so the next day in the midday pause I went to the camp office and told the *natchalnik* what I wanted to do. To my surprise, he received me in quite a friendly fashion. 'Yes; of course you can,' he said, and in answer to my question he told me that I could even write my application in German.

'There's another thing,' I said. 'My mother lives in Potsdam in Germany. She doesn't know what's happened to me and she'll be worrying because she hasn't heard from me. Can I write her a line just to let her know I'm all right. Just greetings on a postcard would do.'

That too, it appeared, was in order. I drew up my application, wrote a postcard to my mother and left them both with the *natchalnik* and then settled down to see what would happen. I hadn't to wait very long. About two weeks later a fellow prisoner who worked in the administration came to me in my office and told me I was to finish work and go back with him to the barracks and get my things. Then I was taken to the punishment compound.

It appeared, however, that regulations would not permit my reception until six o'clock in the evening, so I had to squat down outside the barbed wire with my bundle and wait, which I did, falling deeper and deeper into dejection. My fellow prisoners had been right. Delivery into the punishment compound is like being arrested all over again. In the camp a prisoner was relatively free. He could walk about and go to and from his work without being under guard or surveillance. After work there was about an hour's free time, and I would often visit Grete Sonntag and together we would look out over the steppes and admire the wonderful sky in the evening. It was spring and about the middle of May the steppes begin to bloom. There were great patches of lovely iris and others of some yellow flower, and then there was a sort of tulip which grew freely. Now I had lost all that and was parted from my comrades in the office, whom I had grown to like so much. I was very near to tears.

The punishment compound was surrounded by barbed wire. It consisted of a block for women, another for men, a house for the *natchalnik* and a block of cells. At the gate was a small wooden hut for the guard. Prisoners entered one at a time through a narrow space. The dirt in the camp was bad enough, but in the punishment compound it was shocking. The place around the latrine pits was covered with piles of human excrement. The prisoners did not bother to use the pits. They just did their business wherever it suited them, and it was impossible to get away from the terrible stench. The block for the women was worse than anything I had yet experienced in the camp. The sleeping places were knocked together out of rough bits of wood of various sizes and thicknesses, and some of the women slept on the floor on twigs.

There were two categories of prisoner in the compound. First, those who had offended against the camp regulations. The highest sentence for this was three months. These offenders were amongst the worst types in the camp; men and women who constantly came into conflict, not only with the camp authorities, but also with their fellow prisoners. Some of them were dangerous criminals. And, secondly, there were those political prisoners who for some reason or other had '*pod konvoi*', or 'under surveillance', marked in their dossiers. The contrast between the Politicals and the criminal and Asocial elements was particularly strong in the punishment compound. Unfortunately for the Politicals, the *natchalnik* of the punishment compound was a criminal sentenced for swindling and he supported his fellow criminals against them. When criminals refused to work, he turned a blind eye to it, and if any camp clothing was distributed it was the criminals who got the pick, or, indeed, often all of it. The 'brigadiers', or those in charge of a working column, were chiefly criminals. These 'brigadiers' had to keep a check on whether the members of their columns performed their working quotas or not. The opportunity both for favouritism and chicanery was great. In addition these men distributed the work amongst the individual members of their gang. They were in fact, very much like the notorious *capos* in Nazi concentration camps – in both cases they were often more cruel and brutal than the real authorities. Prisoners in the punishment compound were deprived of the right, or privilege, to buy in the canteen. This did not apply in practice to the criminals, who had their connections, and the *natchalnik* tolerated it silently. Theft was rife and nothing whatever was done to prevent it or to punish the offenders.

Amongst the criminals were many men and women who constantly landed back in the punishment compound. Refusal to work, or refusal to obey an order was punished with up to three months in the compound. Refusal to work for the twenty-fifth time was punished by death. To live together with such criminal elements in the same block is the worst punishment imaginable, and at first the Politicals were not able to secure a special place for themselves in the block.

The number of prisoners in the punishment compound varied constantly. There were sometimes several hundred men and women there and sometimes as few as fifty. Gangs were sent out from the punishment compound to do the worst and dirtiest work. Older prisoners who could

no longer stand up to the work were sent to a special so-called invalid
department, where they were placed on 'light work' and given a ration
of only half a pound of bread a day, on which they slowly starved. There
was also a special department for prisoners suffering from venereal diseases,
and there were always very many of them.

At about three o'clock on my first morning in the punishment
compound when the first thin light of the steppes began to creep into
the huts a trumpet signal sounded the reveille. It was followed almost
immediately by a banging on the door of the women's hut and loud
shouts of 'Get up, women. Get a move on.' Thank God the night was
over, was my first thought. I had found it impossible to sleep comfortably on the uneven boards, and there was not enough room to lie on
my back. My bones ached and my skin was sore over the joints. To add
to the general discomfort, the place was swarming with bedbugs. The
air stank of them and it was impossible to put a hand down anywhere
without touching them. The first time I woke up in the night my body
itched all over. But bedbugs were not all; there were lice as well. In the
darkness any struggle against the bloodsuckers was impossible.

The women crawled out of their stinking hut, still half asleep, grumbling and swearing. Trembling with the cold of the early morning, they
made their way over towards the latrines, or just squatted down in any
convenient spot. From the men's block came a chorus of coughing and
spitting.

After that we all lined up for our soup, and the wind blew the stink
of human excrement over the whole compound. On one side of the
greasy tub in which the soup was brought up stood a line of men and
on the other side a line of women. All eyes were fixed greedily on the
ladle to make sure that it was properly filled, and the arguments and
protests of those who thought they had not been given a full ladle filled
the air with squabbling. I said 'ladle', but it was a home-made scoop
consisting of a small tin can tied on to the end of a stick. It was millet
soup, and some of the prisoners drank their share at once and hung
around afterwards in the hope that at the end they might get another
portion.

The silhouette of the far-off mountains was black against the sky. The
sun would soon be up – the sun that makes free people elated and happy.
Here it was the sign for the slave labour of the day to begin. Under
constant exhortations of 'Hurry up, women, get a move on', we formed
up for the roll-call and were then divided into gangs for the field and
garden work. I was amongst the healthy and vigorous prisoners and I
found myself told off for field work. With a sack over my shoulder and
my *katylok* in my hand, I marched with my gang out into the steppes.

The women went in front and the men brought up the rear, accompanied by an armed guard on horseback.

The sun came out and it grew warm. I breathed the fresh morning air in great gulps and my eyes turned towards the west across the endless steppes. Should I ever get out of this hell, I thought, or perish here like a mangy dog? We went along a dusty path through the fields. Most of the prisoners around me seemed to be still asleep as they plodded along, and their dragging feet stirred up the dust in clouds. After about an hour of this, we came to a vast field of sunflowers and a halt was called. This was our place of work. Our job was to hack out all the weeds and surplus plants and to leave one plant at every foot or so along the rows. Our day's quota was about 3,000 yards in all. When you had done that to the satisfaction of your 'brigadier', your daily ration of a pound and a half of bread was secure.

The lines were divided up amongst the prisoners. Some lucky people came together with those they knew and perhaps liked. They could work side by side and chat. What a difference it made to have someone you knew and liked at your side, someone you could talk to!

I began hacking up the weeds. The sunflower plants had been sown by machinery and they were not more than an inch or so high. Delicate sprouts were just appearing between the thick leaves at the base and it was not easy to distinguish them from weeds. Again and again my blows went awry, and finally I lost my patience and began to hack up the lot savagely. Why should I bother? Did they expect me to cultivate the steppes? I had not got far when an inspector on horseback came riding along my furrow. He pulled up and cursed me furiously. He was a prisoner himself, an agricultural expert. He got down from his horse, took my tool and showed me how to work.

'You're not blind,' he said angrily. 'That's a plant. Look at it. The rest are weeds. What the devil do you think you're doing?'

He bullied me in the same way as a Prussian estate inspector would bully a wretched farm labourer. It might have been his land, but in fact he was my fellow unfortunate in this slavery. After that I was kept under close watch and he kept coming back to see that I was working properly. In addition to him, the 'brigadier' and a favoured prisoner also went from furrow to furrow inspecting the work. The only one who did nothing was the guard, and he remained immobile in the middle of the field with his rifle across the pommel of his saddle, surveying his slave charges.

The sun began to get hot and burn my arms. More and more often I had to straighten my back and wipe the sweat from my forehead. The rest were far ahead of me. They were more experienced in the work, particularly one young woman, who had been a peasant. I heard afterwards that sometimes when she felt like it she would do a double quota in order to get a double ration of bread. She was a danger to the rest of us; because she could do the quota so easily the inspector used her example to raise the quota for the rest. The women talked from furrow to furrow in shrieks. They all seemed to know each other. I was the only stranger.

At about 300 yards' intervals over the fields were tubs of water. At last I reached the first one and plunged my face into it and then drank eagerly. There was no cup or drinking receptacle. There was scum on top of the water, but, no matter, it was water, even if there was grass, dust and remnants of the morning's soup floating in it, and even if the water-carrier's ox had just buried his muzzle in it. Oh, there were worse things than a dumb beast's muzzle! Women would also use this fleeting opportunity to do a bit of washing. Scooping the water out in their *katyloks* and crouching down on the other side of the tub out of sight of the guard they would hurriedly wash out some article of clothing. It was their only chance of doing any washing at all. Of course, they had no soap or washing powder, and the sun of Kazakhstan was their only bleaching agent.

I fell gradually further and further behind the others, and the 'brigadier' walked round with a flat piece of wood on which, for lack of paper, he noted the names of those who had done half of their day's quota. Would it never be midday so that we could rest a while? I had already eaten the last crumb of bread from my sack and I was beginning to feel ravenous. A bellyful of dirty water did not keep hunger away for long.

My furrow seemed a tangle of weeds. Despairingly, I hacked away and suddenly I came face to face with a mother bird, who looked up at me anxiously. Her nest was in the furrow camouflaged with weeds. She was a sandy colour and I did not know what sort of bird she was. But there she was sitting on her eggs in this God-forsaken place. I forgot my hunger and my weariness and looked at her with delight. I don't know why the sight of her engaged on her ageless task moved me so. Perhaps it was because she was so helpless, so exposed there to all the blows of Fate. I carefully skirted her nest and hoped that no one would find and destroy it. As I worked on with heightened spirits and courage an old, long-forgotten nursery rhyme about a bird in its nest came back to me.

One of the prisoners had the job of going from furrow to furrow to sharpen the hoeing tools. Finally, he came to me. He looked disdainfully at mine. 'They've switched the worst one on to you,' he declared.

'No wonder you can't get along very well. Let's see what I can do with it,' and he set to work. Happy at the interruption, I crouched by his side and watched him.

'This is the first time you've been out, isn't it?' he asked sympathetically. 'I haven't seen you before.'

'No. I only came yesterday, *pod konvoi*.'

'What have you been up to?' he asked.

I told him what I had done – merely made an application to have my case reviewed. He grinned from ear to ear. 'You're not Russian, I can see. Where do you come from?'

'I'm a German.'

'What! From the Volga?'

'No, from Germany.' And then to my surprise and delight he began to talk German in a strange, old-fashioned Swabian dialect. He was a peasant from the Volga German colony. 'What are you doing here, then?' he asked; and then with a suspicious look: 'You're a Communist, I suppose?'

'I was,' I said, 'for many years. And then Hitler came . . .'

'Yes, I know,' he said. 'But you'd have done better to stay at home, for all that. Is it as bad as they say in the papers? I always think it can't be much worse than here. Does Hitler take the land away from the peasants like they do here? That's why I'm here. I didn't want to join the *kolkhoz*, and neither did anyone else in my village. Then along came the GPU and took all the men away. Five children, I left behind; the oldest only fourteen. I'd like to know how my wife is managing to feed them, and what's happening to our fields.'

In the distance I saw the 'brigadier' coming over to us, and I got up.

'Give me it,' I said. 'He'll begin to make a row.'

'Let him,' he said. 'If they give you a lousy hoe like this, I must do the best I can with it. Sit down again. You don't want to be afraid of him.'

But I was upset and nervous. 'Tell me all about it after work,' I said.

'All right,' he replied; 'and I'll show you photos of my brats and a letter I had from the eldest.'

Before he came up to us, the 'brigadier' began to shout: 'Think you've got all day to hang about in. You don't look like getting your quota finished.'

The old Volga German turned to him deliberately. 'How d'you expect her to,' he asked, 'if you give her a hoe like this? And in any case, she's not used to it. She's never done any farm work before. She's an educated person.'

The 'brigadier' grumbled something and went away. The peasant gave me back my hoe and I began to work. He watched me in silence for a moment.

'No; you really don't know how to go about it,' he said. 'You're making hard work out of it. And nothing grows properly in this summer, anyhow, so why bother. It's much too dry for sunflowers.'

He took the hoe out of my hands. 'Here; this is how you use it. Don't strike so deep. Take shallower strokes. It's much easier.'

I watched him work for a while and then took the hoe and tried again myself. It was easier. He turned to go.

'When's it going to be midday?' I asked.

'Stand up,' he said; 'and when your shadow's only about two feet then it's near midday. It's very near now. Look! There comes the cart.'

He went off, promising to bring me a lighter and better hoe in the afternoon. I dug my hoe into the furrow and followed after the others, who were all making their way towards the ox-cart on which there was a greasy tub covered over with a dirty sack. In it was the *balanda*, the much longed-for midday soup. An old woman ladled it out. It was thin stuff with a few cabbage leaves and stumps and grains of millet. Those of us who hadn't performed our quota received only a pound of bread, and some of them began to grumble.

'What about fat Tania?' said one. 'She's got her full ration, but did you ever see her do her quota?'

'She does it at night,' interjected a man with a face like creased leather; 'and that's why she gets her full ration.'

And another man turned to the fat favourite and exhorted her in the foulest and plainest language to go about her real business and not to come eating other people's bread.

When we had drunk the soup and eaten the bread we all sprawled out exhausted to rest in the broiling sun, for there was no shade anywhere. Lying with my face between my arms and with a sack over my legs, I immediately sank into a leaden sleep.

Boris

I was woken up by someone shaking my shoulder. Bending over me was a young man with fine brown eyes and a smiling, friendly face. 'Sorry to wake you up,' he said, 'but they told me you were a German Communist. Is that right?'

'That's right,' I said, only half awake. 'Who are you?'

'I'm a Lithuanian Communist.'

We shook hands solemnly. 'How long have you been here?' I asked in order to end the silence that had fallen in which neither of us seemed to know what to say next.

'Nine months,' he replied. '*Pod konvoi* all the time.'

'What are you here for?'

'What am I here for? What do you mean? Do you want to know the invented indictment supplied by the GPU, or the real reason why they get rid of Communists?'

'Be careful,' I warned. 'If anyone hears you talking like that you can get into more trouble. And in any case, you don't even know me.'

'You're a foreign Communist, and that's enough for me.' His name, it appeared, was Boris Resnik. I told him mine, but before we could talk much further there were shouts of '*Davai! Na raboti!*' from our 'brigadier'. 'Get back to work! Get a move on.'

'Let's work together,' proposed Boris.

'That suits me,' I replied; 'but I'm miles behind.'

'All right; we'll change furrows then.'

He seemed to know everyone, and with a little bargaining the exchange was effected. After that we worked together rapidly, leaving a sunflower plant standing at the requisite distance from the next and hacking out the weeds all around.

'Let's have a smoke,' said Boris after we had worked for a while. 'I've got some *mahorka*.' We stopped work, wiped the sweat from our faces and he made a couple of cigarettes from a piece of newspaper.

'Have you been long in Russia?' I asked.

'Eighteen months under arrest and ten months free before that. Just ten months. You know, I'm gradually coming to the conclusion I'm a born jailbird. I was only nineteen when I got ten years' hard in Lithuania for Communist activity. I served seven years of that sentence. There were a whole gang of us Politicals in prison. Three of the fellows developed TB and the rest of us weren't doing too well, so outside influences got our sentences suspended until our health improved. Yes, you might well stare, but things like that did happen in Lithuania. The Red Aid was illegal, but it worked all right and it sent me to a sanatorium. Look out. Let's get down to it again; Popka's got his eye on us.'

We began to work again. 'Who's Popka?' I asked.

'Popka's Russian for scarecrow,' he said. 'That's what they call the guard because he just sits there in the middle of the field and does nothing.'

I looked at Boris. He was a nice-looking boy with bright, sparkling eyes. He noticed my look and rubbed his stubbly chin. 'Pity you can't help looking like a swine here,' he said. We went on working. Seven years' hard labour in Lithuania for Communist activity, and now he was here in Siberia. Almost all his adult life he had been in prison either there or here. It certainly hadn't broken his spirit and he did not seem embittered.

We had worked so well that we gradually caught up with the others. In the afternoon the work generally did not go forward so fast.

'Hey, Boris,' a young man called out cheerfully. 'Found a girlfriend?'

'He's a Greek,' Boris explained. 'A good enough fellow, but unfortunately he's hand in glove with the criminal elements here; mixed up in everything. That's why he's in the punishment compound.'

I was getting very tired again. 'Where does our work end?' I asked with a sigh.

'See that girl with the white scarf round her head. Where she's sitting. That's Djura. She's finished her quota already. But you sit down and have a rest if you're tired. I'll do both furrows until you've had a breather.'

Boris still wore a civilian cap which was perched jauntily on one side of his head. He had crisp, black, curly hair and his face was tanned from the sun. When he laughed he showed two rows of strong white teeth. He reminded me of a Frenchman both in appearance and manner. Whilst he worked on, I walked back to fetch his prison jacket and our two tin cans, which we had left further back along the furrow.

We finished our quotas before the end of the day and were able to sit down and rest in the late afternoon sun. Boris rolled me a *mahorka* cigarette and gallantly held it out for me to lick. Such delicacy in a place like this! We smoked contentedly. Insects were crawling around in the warm grass and there was a noise of crickets. When the steppes are in bloom they are lovely. I have never anywhere seen such a mass of flaming colour with patches of golden, red and almost black flowers, each patch sharply defined from its neighbour. A little distance away, where the ground seemed to dip, the steppe grass was very high and it moved gently to and fro in the early evening wind like reeds at the side of a lake.

'Isn't that water over there, Boris?' I asked.

It was so quiet and peaceful as the sun gradually declined – in the west. In the west – but I mustn't think about that. This was the most peaceful moment I had yet spent in the camp. Others who had also finished their quotas were lying around fast asleep.

'What happened to you after you went into the sanatorium, Boris?'

'Oh, the Party got into touch with me. It was illegal, of course, but it was easy enough whilst I was in the sanatorium. They told me that I was to make a getaway. I was very glad, of course. I had three years' hard labour in front of me and one lung wasn't too good. And then to go to the Soviet Union! It had always been my ambition. You know, Fatherland of the Toilers, and all that. I was tremendously excited. They organised everything all right and I got away. In Moscow I was taken

over by the Mopr,[1] welcomed like a hero and sent to a sanatorium in
Yalta on the Black Sea. It was really lovely there and it wasn't long before
my trouble healed up. Then I looked around for a job. I had been a
shoemaker before I was arrested. Political prisoners don't have to work
in Lithuania, and we weren't kept in solitary confinement. We had books
and studied together, organised courses, and so on. The prison was my
university. There I learnt all I'd missed before. I hadn't been able to go
to a higher school because when my father died my mother had four of
us to feed, so I had to go out to work as soon as possible. But in prison
we had good teachers, really cultured men sentenced for political offences.
In Yalta the doctors advised me to stay in the south just in case, because
of my lung, so I went to Odessa and got a job in a boot and shoe
factory. I met a girl there. She was my first, and we got married. We were
very happy for about six months, and then one night, unexpectedly, like
a bolt from the blue, the GPU came for me. It appears I was a Lithuanian
spy. The Lithuanian Okhrana had recruited me whilst I was in prison and
sent me over the Soviet frontier – and so on. That was the examining
judge's tale and I was supposed to admit it all and sign a confession. I
told him I'd had a certain amount of experience and knew how a
Communist had to behave himself in the hands of the police. Then they
started to beat me up. I bellowed like an ox to let everybody hear, so
they stopped it. We had tried that in Lithuania and found it usually
worked. In prison I got trouble with my lungs again and had a hæmorrhage, so they had to put me in the prison sick ward. When I was
discharged I found my sentence already waiting for me: eight years'
forced labour in a camp with *pod konvoi* just because I had made myself
a nuisance – and here I am. And here I've been for nine months. Seven
years and three months to go. But it's good to have met you. One of
the worst things here is not to have anyone you can talk to; not to have
anyone who speaks the same language and thinks the same way. Let's
have another cigarette before we go back. Grete, you said? Can I call
you Margaret? There's a lovely song in Lithuania about a Margaret.'

The sun was beginning to sink towards the horizon. The 'brigadier'
and the guard rounded us up and got us into marching order and off
we went, Boris and I side by side. He was dirty, ragged and unshaven,
and I was in not much better case, with my feet wrapped in rags and
wearing rubber shoes several sizes too big for me. But I was almost
happy. I had found a fellow soul I could talk to.

At night when I lay down on the hard, uneven boards which were
my bed, with the stench of bedbugs in my nostrils, my lips were smiling.

---

[1] International Red Aid.

Life had become a little easier. I dreamt of giant sunflowers and inextricable tangles of weeds stretching away far out of sight, but I woke up with the consoling thought that I should see Boris again tomorrow. He had promised to sing some Lithuanian songs for me, including 'Margareta'.

When I look back on the first two months of my stay in the Birma punishment compound, I hardly remember the laborious work in the fields, the scorching sun beating down, the constant hunger, the terrible nights with bedbugs and lice, the malice and chicanery of my fellow prisoners, and I think instead of my friendship with Boris Resnik. We met every morning before the roll-call. He would make me the morning cigarette of *mahorka* in newspaper, and together we would stand and smoke and marvel at the daily wonder: the rising of the sun over the mountains in the distance.

The first morning I met him in this way he had managed to shave. And that evening he stood behind the men's block washing out his shirt with 'organised' water which should have been devoted to some other purpose. Then he wrung it out and hung it on the barbed wire to dry, not daring to leave it out of his sight for fear it would be stolen.

He had hardly been a month in the compound when he had suffered another hæmorrhage. After a while in hospital he had been sent back to the compound, but, thanks to the good offices of the chief doctor, he received a little supplementary food. It was only a small basin of noodles or porridge, but it was something, and it helped to keep him on his feet. This small supplement aroused the envy and malice of his fellow prisoners, who would wax highly indignant.

'Him sick! Look at him! Brown as a berry. Influence, that's what it is. He's got connections.'

One day we decided to work in the kitchen garden instead of in the fields. As a TB case, Boris had the right to work there, though generally he preferred to go into the fields because he didn't like the head gardener. Of course, I had no such right, but the next morning we lined up with the garden gang and hoped for the best. The controller came around accompanied by a criminal who occupied a minor post. The criminal immediately spotted Boris.

'Get back into the field gang, you,' he snapped. 'That'd just suit you hanging about in the garden, wouldn't it?'

'You know perfectly well I'm entitled to light work,' Boris replied.

'What's entitled here?' the man enquired disagreeably. 'You're healthy enough. Do what I tell you.'

'I won't,' replied Boris firmly. 'I'm entitled to light work and you can ask the doctor if you don't believe me.'

Suddenly a leering grin came over the man's face. 'Oh!' he bellowed, 'so that's it, is it? You think I don't know what you're up to? You want to get down to it with Grete under the bushes, heh?'

His remark was greeted by a burst of sycophantic laughter, which restored his good humour. 'All right, then,' he said. 'Get on with it.' And he passed on, quite forgetting that at least I was not entitled to work in the garden.

A humiliation of that sort would be enough to make a decent woman wish the ground would open and swallow her up in normal circumstances, but when you're forced to live like a pig you soon get used to swinishness. We were delighted to think we had won the trick, and we marched off together to the garden.

Our work there consisted in weeding a patch of grass with our hands. We progressed on our knees, singing softly. A young gipsy girl was working in our row, and when the overseer, a much-feared bully, happened to be away for a while she read the future from our palms. It was a very satisfactory reading. There was nothing about a dark stranger, but there was a journey very soon – a journey into freedom and much happiness.

The kitchen garden was artificially irrigated from the pond on which our two precious ducks had met their end. The soil was good and both grass and vegetables grew well. There were even a few poplars – a rare phenomenon in the steppes. At the midday pause we sat down in their shade and chatted, telling each other about our dreams, which play a much bigger role in the life of a prisoner than they do outside.

In the short time left to us in the evening before lights out, we would sit together in the stinking compound square. One day a new transport of prisoners arrived, including one or two political prisoners from Georgia. Amongst them was the eighty-year-old husband of the wetnurse who had nursed of the GPU chief, Beria, the man who had signed my five-year-sentence. In addition, there was a Georgian Menshevist, and a teacher from the Caucasus named Dzagnidze. They would sit with us in the evenings and sing their melodious Georgian folk songs in a sad undertone. I sang them a German song or two, and then, to their surprise, I sang a Georgian song which Heinz had taught me. He had learnt it because it was the favourite song of his friend, Lominadze, who was always singing it. It was a sad song: 'For you, poor soul, no fortune beckons; for you, poor soul, no lute sings happy songs.'

We spent many evenings with these Georgians, and the eighty-year-old husband of the nurse of Beria, a typical old Georgian vintner with bright, bird-like eyes and a lined brown face, told me indignantly how he had been arrested because he had been unwilling to give up his vineyard and join the *kolkhoz*. Ten years' forced labour was his sentence. Dzagnidze had a bad heart. He too was sentenced to ten years. This was for 'counter-revolutionary agitation', unspecified. A little later Dzagnidze and the old man were removed to the invalids' compound.

We had just heard of the Russo-German Pact and we were discussing it one evening when the Georgian Menshevist declared very loudly – presumably in order that as many people as possible should hear: 'The Russo-German Friendship Pact is a work of political genius; the greatest act of our great leader, Stalin. My admiration for him is unbounded.' We fell silent in embarrassment, but we understood.

One day our *natchalnik* announced that the compound must be cleaned up at once, because a commission of inspection was on its way from the administration centre at Dolinki. Our *starosta*, the Compound Senior, ran around like a dog who had lost its tail trying to get volunteers to clean up the frightful mess he and the *natchalnik* had let the place get into, but the only one he could get to help him was his girlfriend, a Yugoslav, who said she was a Communist. Perhaps she was. She was afraid that if the Commission came and saw the state of the compound her boyfriend would be dismissed and then her privileged life would end. She never did any work and she was well fed, thanks to her far from ambiguous relation with the *starosta*.

The sum total of the cleansing action was that for the first and only time the heaps of excrement were removed. All other attempts to bring a little order into our chaos broke down owing to the sabotage of the criminal elements, who openly jeered at both the *starosta* and the *natchalnik*. The Commission arrived. It consisted of Serikov, the Camp Commandant, and a number of uniformed men. They walked through the neglected blocks, listened silently to those who had courage enough to complain and then departed. Nothing further happened, and every-thing remained as it had been before.

Soon after that a rumour spread that a transport was to be made up to go off to Central or Eastern Siberia. It threw us all into a panic, for it meant that prisoners who had become friends might be separated. Boris and me, for instance. We looked at each other in unspoken fear. And so it came. We had a few days' notice. They were terribly sad days. Boris carved me a cigarette-holder out of a piece of wood and gave me a little carved box he had made so that I should have something tangible to remember him by. I knew that Eastern Siberia meant death to him, and my heart was heavy. He promised to do his best to let me have news, and all I could do was to thank him with tears in my eyes for the two months' friendship which had brought a little happiness into my life and made me almost forget the misery of Birma.

The lorries drove up in front of the compound and the names of those who had to go were called out. They marched out of the gate and climbed into the lorries. The rest of us gathered behind the barbed wire. 'Don't forget me, Grete,' Boris called out. My throat was dry and I could only wave my hand. The prisoners began to sing:

> 'Stream over your banks, O mother Volga;
> My lover takes his leave of me.
> The sails swell grandly in the wind,
> But my heart is heavy with sorrow.
> Farewell, my love, farewell.'

The days that followed were sad and weary. I seemed to lose my strength, and more and more often I failed to perform my daily quota. But for the fact that I now had a Political as my gang leader, I should seldom have got more than a pound of bread a day, but he made false entries in his log to help his fellow Politicals. I was back in the fields again. From morning to night out there we all had only one thought; it was of bread. One afternoon I had the best part of my bread still uneaten in my sack. To give myself more freedom in working, I put it down in the furrow and went on, going back from time to time to retrieve it. But once when I did that I found the empty sack. Someone had stolen my bread. A piece of bread! Just a piece of bread! What a bagatelle! No one knows how much that means who has never gone hungry, really hungry. It meant that I had to work the rest of the day and the following morning before I got any more. But that day passed too, like all the rest.

My life was made still more miserable by the really foul language which was constantly used around me. It was bad enough in the camp, but in the punishment compound it was frightful. At first most of it passed over my head. I simply did not understand the words or their implication, but as my Russian improved it was often difficult not to blush. Russian is particularly rich in that respect, and the prisoners in the compound were virtuosi. For the criminals, who represented the majority in the compound, I was 'the German Fascist'. Soviet newspaper propaganda had brought them to equate German with Fascist. In addition, I was a Political, and for them a Political was the most contemptible creature on Russian soil. On one occasion I worked my furrow level with a criminal in the next furrow. She amused herself whenever we came near by making me the target of the foulest abuse she could think of, and it was foul. The unprovoked attack riled me to such an extent that the next time she did it I involuntarily replied with a scorching expression I had picked up. A look of respect came over her face.

Soon after Boris left I was sent out with a gang to join in the campaign against *brzlose*, a sort of cattle murrain which is terribly prevalent in that part of the world and causes heavy losses to the herds. One evening when we returned to the camp tired and exhausted we were all called together and a list of fifty names was read out, including mine. 'Report at once. With things.' An order like that causes panic amongst the prisoners affected. A prisoner is strangely conservative. Once he is settled down, even in our lousy, dirty huts, he is unwilling to move and have his life disturbed. What comes may be, and probably will be, worse. And, in any case, it is upsetting. It also means a separation from people he has got used to.

In the Heart of the Steppe

An ox-cart stood waiting outside the compound and our bundles were thrown into it, then, to the accompaniment of much shouting and bullying, we were lined up behind it and our journey into the unknown started again. At least the cool night air was better than the stench of our barracks and before long I became conscious of the vast dome of stars over my head. Such a sky can probably be seen only over steppes and deserts. It is indescribably magnificent. But soon my legs grew weary and I began to stumble over the dried-out ruts of the path we were following, almost losing my over-large rubber shoes. The dust stirred up by the trudging feet made my eyes smart and my throat sore. Tiredness was overcoming us all and soon there was no more talk. The only sound was the creaking of the ox-cart in front, the plodding and scuffling of our tired feet, and the monotonous chirping of crickets by the wayside. If one could only sleep on the march! How much longer was this going on? Behind us we could hear the familiar shouts of '*Davai! Davai!*' as the stragglers were bullied along, and for a little while hatred and resentment gave me new strength.

At last we came to an empty hut into which we were driven like cattle. There were not even *naris* and there was nowhere to sit or lie except on the straw which was scattered on the floor. We were so tired we just flung ourselves down and fell asleep. I slept like a log and not even the 'bed'bugs could keep me awake.

The next day we found that we were in Leninskoie, a sub-station of the camp. There was a hut like ours for the men, a house for the guards, a washroom, a punishment block and a number of well-built pens for sheep. In summer the sheep live in the open in the steppes. Our gang

was equipped with picks and shovels and told off to remove the top
layer of mixed earth and dung in the pens and around them, load it up
and carry it out into the steppes to be burnt. It was hard work, particularly as the ground around the pens was a matted tangle of deep-rooted
couch grass which obstinately defied our efforts.

One day a miracle happened. We did our best with the hard ground
and its tough roots, but although the sweat poured off us with our
efforts, we made little progress. There wasn't a strong, vigorous man or
woman left amongst us. A soldier told off to guard us watched our vain
efforts. Then he came over to us, put down his rifle, took a pick from one
of the prisoners, and set to work. With powerful strokes, he dug a long,
shallow trench which gave us a chance of getting under the roots. It
was the only time in all my experience I ever saw a guard help prisoners.
He was human, that Kazak soldier, and the prisoners loved him. They
chatted with him, laughed and joked with him, and when he was in
charge of us the atmosphere was almost free and happy.

Some weeks later I was with a gang sent out for grain-cleaning. There
were seven of us, all women and all Politicals, in my group, and we were
in the charge of this same Kazak soldier, who accompanied us on horseback to a so-called *tog* about five miles away from the camp. A *tog* is a
place which has been cleared and in which the grain reaped by the
combines is stacked to be cleaned by a machine. Seven women do the
various jobs in connection with such a machine.

On the way we had chattered and laughed with our escort, and told
him how hungry we were. Gradually we worked round to what we had
in mind. Our *tog* was not very far from the railway station at Sharik, and
in Sharik there was bread and sugar to be had. On horseback he could
easily ride into Sharik and buy us some. Would he? We didn't think so,
but our need made us persistent and we had nothing to lose.

'That's a fine thing,' he said when we finally asked him. 'And whilst
I'm gone you all take to your heels. Or perhaps the control comes round.
And where should I be then? In camp with you, or worse.'

Midday came and went and the ox-cart had already trundled off with
the soup barrel. We were working in a cloud of black dust cleaning the
steppe barley, fully convinced that all our wheedling had been in vain.
After all, it was a risk for him, and we bore him no malice for his refusal.
But when the ox-cart was finally out of sight he came up.

'Give me your bread bags and some money,' he said. Delightedly, we
handed them over to him with all the money we could muster, and immediately he turned his wiry little steppe pony about and galloped off. We
watched the cloud of dust churned up by the pony's hooves rapidly disappear in the distance. And then seven prisoners trembled for the safety of

their guard. Supposing a control did come? Anxiously we kept a lookout in both directions, and as the time passed we became more and more nervous and anxious. Supposing we had got our friend into trouble? Supposing he had been caught by someone in Sharik? The suspense was dreadful, but finally, to our great relief, we saw the cloud of dust on the horizon coming nearer and nearer, until up galloped our gallant Kazak, our bags dangling from his horse's neck full of bread and sugar.

Whilst we were in Leninskoie we received no soap for two months. We were entitled to one small piece a month. It was about the size of a matchbox and rather soft, which meant that it didn't last very long. This time we had either been forgotten or someone had stolen our soap. The dirt was deeply engrained in our skins and the powdered sheep-dung filled all our pores and got into our nostrils and mouths. On the wall was a poster issued by the Commissariat of Health. It read: 'Danger! To avoid infection with the deadly *brzlose*, it is forbidden to smoke or eat during working hours. Hands must be thoroughly washed before meals.'

One day the cashier, himself a political prisoner, came over to our sub-point to pay out the wages. I knew that wages were paid out months in arrears and therefore expected nothing. But to my surprise my name was called out and I received the sum of twenty-five roubles for *udarnik* work performed before I was sent to the punishment compound. Twenty-five roubles is not much, but it's a lot in a prison camp.

At about this time a new gang came out to us, including a number of newcomers to the camp. One of them was a woman named Olga. Originally German, the family had emigrated to Russia about a century and a half ago. One of her great-great-grandfathers had been bandmaster to one or other of the Czars. The family had remained steadfastly German – in fact, as often happens, they had become more German if anything. Not only did Olga look German, but she was German in all her ways, and a German of the old-fashioned sort. She was tall and very blonde, with a fair complexion which would not stand the sun, and she wore her hair in a bun at the back like our mothers had done in their young days. But Olga was only thirty. By chance, I saw the contents of her sack. There was old-fashioned underwear with lace and embroidery just as though it had come out of Grandmother's drawer.

She was a pianist and quite well known on the concert platform. Her husband, also a musician, had been arrested in the usual way; no one knew why; and shortly afterwards she had been arrested too. The charge was: 'Espionage on behalf of a foreign Power' – unnamed. As a young woman she had studied abroad and she had still written to her old friends there. That was quite enough. She had been sentenced to five years' forced labour with *pod konvoi*.

She had never done any manual work or taken part in any kind of sport. Now she had to work terribly hard. In a blouse which had once been white, with bare legs, and her hair hanging down, she ran backwards and forwards with a pail full of grain. It was her job to keep the funnel of the cleansing machine filled. The pail was too heavy for her weak muscles. With an effort, she would hoist it up to the funnel and half the grain would be spilled on the floor. She could not work fast enough, and from all sides she was driven on with shouts of '*Davai! Davai!*' So that was how the intelligentsia worked? It was about time they learnt to work properly.

After a few hours, Olga's face was as red as a turkey cock's from the sun. They changed her job and put her to turning the handle of the machine. She managed it for a while, but then she was exhausted and begged to be relieved. Unfortunately, she was just the perfect target for the brutality and callousness of both overseers and fellow prisoners. It was not long before she was in a terrible state from the scorching sun. Her arms and legs were inflamed and swollen and she could hardly stand up. In this state she begged the 'brigadier' of our gang to excuse her from work for the day and let her lie down in our hut. Immediately there was a vicious chorus from her fellow prisoners: 'Yes; that would just suit you: get off work for a little sunburn. What about us? She's just lazy. We had to work hard all our lives whilst she was taking it easy.' I turned to one of the most malicious of the harpies.

'Is that the way you treat musicians in the Soviet Union?' I asked. 'How much easier it is to do manual work than play the piano. There are millions who can serve a grain machine; how many can play the piano as she can?'

But it didn't help Olga much. And she really was very clumsy and slow. It irritated them, and made them lose their tempers. In the evenings when we plodded home as black as coal-carriers there was a big basin full of water for us to wash in. That is to say, the basin was there, but the water was gone. The oxen almost invariably drank it dry long before we got back from the fields, which we were allowed to leave only when the sun had already begun to sink below the horizon. Then we would go stealthily to a half-empty well which we were forbidden to use and lower our *katyloks* into it on the end of a piece of string, keeping an anxious lookout in all directions for fear the guards discovered us. And who was almost invariably caught? Olga. And then there was a storm of curses and things were made more difficult for the rest of us.

Hardly had we managed to get the worst of the dirt off our faces and hands when we had to rush for our food for fear of missing our share of the thin soup. And when we had eaten it was time to turn in. The twilight period was very short in Karaganda after the sun had once set. Because of the heat, and because the bedbugs had grown simply intolerable, we got permission to sleep outside the hut. One or two tough ones who were so hardened to bedbug bites that they didn't care any more still slept inside, but most of us were anxious to get out. In that hot weather they simply swarmed. When we went in in the evening to get our bundles they would drop on to us off the ceiling, whilst others ran up and down the walls like a disturbed colony of ants.

We slept on the bare ground with our heads to the wall of the hut all in a line, and about five or six yards in front of us a soldier sat on a stool with his rifle over his knees to see that no one made an attempt to escape. Olga was always late and she usually arrived after everyone else had settled down. That was bad enough, but then she would begin to talk to me about the stars: 'Look, Grete. There's Venus' or whatever star it was. And at her voice, particularly as she spoke in German, there was a combined roar of abuse from guard and fellow prisoners who wanted to sleep. She never seemed capable of conducting herself so that she did not provoke these storms of abuse.

If in the night any of us felt a pressing urge we had to go up to the guard and ask his permission. '*Davai!*' he would say and swivel round to watch you as you went out a little way into the steppes to squat and attend to your business. One night I woke up and wanted to go through this performance, but the stool was empty. No soldier. I looked around. No sign of him. What was I to do? If I went out without permission and he happened to be anywhere near and saw me going he might shoot. And then towards the end of the row I heard a certain noise. The guard was in the arms of one of his prisoners. I went up to him with determination and asked the routine question. I got a curse in return which I translated as permission and retired.

At that time we were working behind the combine, loading sacks of grain on to wagons. The newcomers still had their things with them, including coats. In the morning when we went out into the fields it was very cold and so they went out in their coats, but before long it grew warm and then hot, and so they would take off their coats and put them down at the side of the field. This worked all right for a while, but then one day when they went to fetch their things everything had gone. It is a very serious matter to lose a coat in the camp; apart from the coat itself, it means that you have lost your covering for the night, for, as I have already said, no blankets were issued. There was a tremendous weeping and wailing and wondering who could possibly be the thieves. We older hands knew perfectly well who had stolen them. The *natchalnik* was a criminal, a notorious Moscow bandit named Ivan Petrovitch. His assistant, Sosnin, was also a criminal. He was a former lawyer who had already served eight years of a ten-year sentence for murdering his wife. Hand in glove with these two were two girls who were their 'camp wives', and also an old gipsy woman who was supposed to watch over the things.

The Work Animals

Whilst I was still at Leninskoie we had two nuns working in our gang. They were women between thirty and forty serving terms for 'counter-revolutionary agitation'. They always wore a cord around their clothing which still gave them a nunlike appearance. Once out in the steppe during the midday pause the two sat on some bags of grain and sang softly. I went nearer to listen to them. They were singing Church hymns and singing very beautifully. When they saw that their singing pleased me they became friendly. Up to then they had been very reserved towards everyone. They asked me whether the Germans had such hymns and I sang them a lovely old *Marienlied* I knew.

One day there was meat in our soup and the food was altogether much better. That was because the men on the combine were working in our section and had to be fed with us. One of the nuns came to me a little hesitantly and told me that it was a fast day for them: would I like their meat. Would I? It was a long, long time since I had eaten so much meat. But what strength of character was necessary to refuse such a rarity as meat!

I was the only one of the prisoners they ever had anything to do with, and they lived in complete isolation from all the others. They accepted their fate with humility and resignation, and they never complained or asked for anything. When our column went back to Birma, there was no sleeping place for them in the hut and so they slept on the floor in the dirt without a word of complaint.

Lydia, one of the prisoners in our column, was a cretin. She was the butt of them all – guards, overseers and fellow prisoners. All the clothing she had was an old cotton dress, and that was torn in many places. Underneath she had nothing on at all. She had no front teeth, although she was still quite young. She seemed not unhappy and she would tell us with a toothless grin of her conquests with men. All she had done to land herself with us was to leave her locality without permission. Many of the Asocial elements were with us for the same offence. The men pulled her leg mercilessly: 'Lydia, where have you left your beautiful teeth? When you get them back, we'll hop into bed together.' But Lydia didn't mind. To show how strong and vigorous she was she would turn the handle of the cleansing machine for hours whilst the sweat poured off her forehead and the tip of her nose and she forgot to contain her water. She was always hungry and would beg constantly for bread just as a little child might beg. It was pitiful and depressing.

Whilst I was still in the office of the repair workshop, the camp feeding regulations had fallen into my hands. There it was in black and white, all the food we were supposed to get, including, I remember distinctly, three grammes of fat a day. It was laughable. Whether it all went into the kitchens, I don't know, but we didn't get it. It was stolen some-where on the way. And what food was cooked we got only after the friends and favourites of the cooks had been at it. What constant squab-bling and fighting there was over the distribution of food! Prisoners would fly at each other's throats over it. In one section a political prisoner had the job of ladling out the soup. On one occasion a criminal declared that he had been given less than the others and demanded some more. The Political knew perfectly well that the distribution had been fair; no one had got much; and he refused to comply. The next day he was found dead with his throat cut. The murderer was arrested and as a punish-ment he received an additional three years on his sentence.

One day was a happy day for me. My name was called and I was handed a small packet. It was from Tasso Salpeter, who had also been sent to Birma and had found out that I was there too. It contained sugar.

Soon after that I was sent out again with a gang in the anti-*brzlose* campaign. With a woman named Alexandra, who had kept a fashion shop in Moscow, and a criminal from Warsaw, I had to load the ox-carts with the dried sheep-dung. Alexandra had been plump and much given to laughter, but now she was like a scarecrow; her beautiful white teeth were beginning to decay and her black hair was going grey. She had been arrested in 1935 and had not known freedom since then. At first she had worked for others in Moscow, but then, as she was good at her job, she had made herself independent. Through someone's good offices, she obtained the custom of the ladies of the Japanese Embassy. It was her undoing, for she had to go to the Embassy from time to time for fittings. Before long she was arrested by the GPU. Her innocence must have been very obvious, but, even so, she was lucky, for instead of being sentenced to camp, she was sentenced to so-called 'free banishment'. She was given the name of a little town on the edge of the Kazakhstan steppe where she was to spend her exile, and off she went. She was married, but she did not expect her husband to accompany her. She found that a number of other 'free' exiles like herself were already living there. Most of them were almost starving because the only job available was that of water-carrier. The wells were widely separated and often outside the villages, and water-carrying was a normal occupation.

But Alexandra was ingenious. Before long she had built herself up a very good business amongst the wives of the Kazak officials. Through Alexandra, they got a chance of wearing European hats and clothing for the first time in their lives. Up to then they had gone about in Moslem garb. She was a tremendous success and she even turned her attention to the male world and designed a sort of uniform hat which became all the rage. Before long she had plenty of money and, what was more important, food. She told me that she had never lived so well in her life as she had lived in that little town on the edge of the steppes. She begged and pleaded with her husband to come and visit her at least, but he couldn't pluck up courage enough, and finally she gave up writing. Her banishment was for three years and she had already been away from Moscow for two and a half when one night in the winter of 1938–9 all the 'free exiles' were arrested and taken in sleds to the nearest GPU post.

She still had to laugh when she told me about her examination. She was dressed in everything she had, one garment on top of the other, and she looked like a ball. She had to sit on a stool much too tall for her and there she sat sweating with heat and fright. The official read the indictment. She was alleged to have planned an armed insurrection against the Soviet power with the other exiles in the town. 'What, me?' she exclaimed. 'Armed insurrection? Look at me!' And even the official had to laugh. But it had not ended humorously; she was sentenced to eight years' forced labour, and here she was in Birma. She was always hungry. It seemed to hit her harder than others. One day she stayed behind in the stall whilst we went out to load the ox-cart. After a while I wondered what had happened to her and why she didn't come out to help us. When I went back into the stall I was only just in time to save her. She had hanged herself from a beam.

In our section there was a little donkey. One day it began to bray excitedly, and the old hands all shouted: 'The *layok's* coming.' The *layok* was a small cart drawn by a donkey which was the mother of our little donkey – hence his joy – and it brought canteen goods for the men working on the tractors and combines. We were not supposed to be allowed to buy anything, but if you had money they closed one eye to the regulations, and I had some of my twenty-five roubles left. I bought two pounds of bonbons and a whole loaf of black bread. Then we stood there covered from head to foot with dust from the sheep-dung, probably heavily infected with *brzlose*, ate the bread between us and sucked the bonbons and for a while forgot our misery – even Alexandra laughed again as she had used to laugh.

From Alexandra we learnt more about the so-called 'free exiles'. The others did not strike it as lucky as she did. They were all men and women whose innocence of the charges against them was crystal clear even to the examining judges, but the authorities needed people to colonise Siberia, and so off they had to go. Apart from security measures against socially unreliable elements, or elements which are supposed to be socially unreliable, the GPU is a great slave trust. Wherever labour is needed, the GPU sends its prisoners. They fell timber in Central Siberia and Carelia, work in the heavy industries in the Urals, cultivate the steppes of Kazakhstan, mine gold in Kolyma in the Arctic Circle, build towns in the far east of Siberia, and so on. Clearly, under such circumstances the GPU is not sparing in its arrests. Many of these 'free exiles' would voluntarily report to the GPU after a while and ask to be arrested, for the alternative was starvation. Such 'free exiles' were often little more than vagabonds, sleeping under bridges and begging their bread and with no possibility of getting work. Small wonder that any change seemed preferable, and those sentenced to a concentration camp had at least some sort of a roof over their heads and their daily *balanda* and bread.

There was a gipsy girl with us in the punishment compound. Perhaps she was sixteen, but she was already a woman, and very pretty. She never bothered to work. If you were pretty enough and not overburdened with moral scruples, there was no need to work. She was with us because she had made an attempt to escape from the prison in which she had been serving a sentence for horse-stealing. Her father was a horse-thief and his father before him. And she 'loved horses' more than anything else. She showed us a scar on her neck where she had been bitten by a stallion she had broken in as quite a young girl. For her the most beautiful thing in the world was the free life in the *tabor*, or gipsy camp, and when she talked about it there was an expression on her face as though she were talking of her lover. One of the soldiers was very much interested in her, and I overheard a conversation between them:

'Have you ever been to school, Zena?'

'No,' she replied with great contempt. 'What should I want to go to school for?'

'Why, to learn something, of course; become a cultured person.'

'Go to the devil.' Though that is not really what she said. 'I know all I want to know already.'

'I don't suppose you even know what Socialism is.'

'Don't I! And I don't like it. You can go and —— your mother with your Socialism. I'm a free gipsy.'

To our surprise, this pretty gipsy fled one night with one of the Politicals, a fat, blond, equable cook from Leningrad. A more unmatched pair it

would have been difficult to imagine. We were working long hours at
the time cleansing the grain, and it was already dark when the gangs came
in from work. Between the time we arrived and the roll-call the two
disappeared. It was useless to attempt to go after them in the darkness,
but we expected they would be caught the next day, but they weren't,
and a week later they were still at liberty.

I talked to the old one-eyed gipsy woman who was supposed to look
after our things at the *tog*. Her face lit up.

'Ah, Zena!' she exclaimed. 'There's a clever child for you. She's got
an idea there's a *tabor* somewhere in the neighbourhood. If she can get
to that, she's safe. If only I were young again and had two eyes and my
looks!'

The old woman was a thief, like they all were, but she was good-
hearted. She offered me a special kind of tea she prepared from herbs.
It didn't look very appetising in the dirty old tin can she offered it to
me in, but I couldn't wound her feelings by refusing her hospitality. I
returned it by giving her a pipeful of tobacco. After that we were always
good friends and I never lost anything.

It was no easy matter to escape from Karaganda. The best time of
the year was during the harvest. We were all out in the fields and the
supervision was not so strict. Those who made an attempt at escape
always did so at night. During the day, when mounted guards patrolled
the countryside, they would hide in the sheaves until darkness fell again.
Their aim was to get beyond the mountains, about four days' journey
away, and to reach the town of Karaganda. Their difficulties were by no
means over then, of course, because the railway was closely watched.
However, whilst I was in Karaganda five prisoners did succeed in escaping.
Apart from Zena and her friend, there were two criminals and another
woman. Somehow they had got hold of horses, and that had given them
a very good start the first night. One of our Ukrainian peasant women
made the attempt, for she was consumed with homesickness, but they
caught her and she was sentenced to a further two years' concentration
camp and put into the punishment compound.

Sundays were not days of rest for us, and the only days on which we
did not have to work were during the May Day and November celebrations – unless Nature was kind to us and sent a sandstorm in the summer
or heavy snow in the winter.

There is a growth in the steppes called *karagandik*. It is prickly and
round, about the size of a football. Gangs of prisoners would go out into
the steppes to cut it down and clear the ground for the animals, which
otherwise pricked their snouts on the stuff. The *karagandik* would be piled
into great heaps to be used as fuel. When this dried *karagandik* began to

move, that was the first sign that a sandstorm was on the way. A sandstorm in the steppes is something quite fantastic. Gradually the *karagandik* would come into motion, rolling slowly here and there like hedgehogs undecided which way to go. Then as the wind freshened they would begin to roll with increasing speed, blowing first here and then there like hundreds of hedgehogs gone mad. They would blow together in heaps, split apart, rise in the air, swoop down to the ground again, twist and turn in a whirlwind, whilst above the sky grew the colour of sulphur, the horizon disappeared and everywhere the cattle, sheep and horses bolted for some sort of cover. Then the sand would come and the sky would be blotted out altogether. It was a terrifying sight. The wind roared and howled, the sand rained down and was swept up again, lashing furiously against the sides of the huts, changing colour, sometimes light, sometimes dark. But we were happy. We sat in the huts and sand was everywhere, but we didn't mind. We had no work to do. 'That's from Mongolia,' said the experts.

When I think of the miserable and depressing time I spent in Leninskoie, I always remember a decorative arch of timber which stood there. It was just an arch; it led nowhere, and there was nothing else around it. It stood out in the steppes and gradually became weather-beaten and dilapidated. On its cross-beam was written the inscription: 'Long live the November Revolution of the Workers and Peasants!'

Autumn

One evening when we came in tired and aching from our work we found an ox-wagon already waiting, and amidst loud shouts of '*Davai! Davai!*' we were ordered to get our bundles together and load them into the cart. And then, dirty, tired and hungry, we were lined up and sent off into the night behind the cart. The journey took many hours, and a number of the women just collapsed and had to be loaded on to the cart with the bundles. When the first light of dawn came we could see that we were much nearer the mountains. At last we reached our journey's end and were herded into a hut on the old familiar lines. We threw ourselves down into the straw and fell into an exhausted sleep. This was El Marje, another sub-station of the Karaganda camp.

El Marje lay bedded between hills, the foothills of the Urals. The mountains shut in the view in a semicircle and only behind us was there a clear view out over the steppes. It was autumn – a sunny Siberian autumn. The wild rose bushes growing up the sides of the hills were a mass of deep red, and a blue September sky formed a dome over the beautiful little valley in which El Marje was situated. But there was no peace for us in this lovely spot. There was an epidemic of *brzlose* in El Marje and our gang of twenty women was sent to combat it. Conditions were bad in El Marje. Our *natchalnik* was a born slave-driver, and he bullied and tormented us to get the very last ounce out of our labours. He was a free man, but they said he had been a prisoner. He was never satisfied with our work: either we had not loaded up the carts full enough, or we had not dug deep enough into the stony clay soil in and around the pens. Probably, as a former prisoner, he was particularly anxious to show himself to the authorities as a reformed character, and to get the utmost out of those under him. How we suffered from his zeal! And the *natchalnik* as usual set the key for all the others under him. The guards and the overseers bullied and shouted just as he did. '*Davai! Davai!*' The shouting went on all day long until when night came we were crushed and beaten.

Bathed in sweat, aching in every limb and covered with dust, we crawled into our hut after sundown. In this hut there were not even *naris*. We slept on the clay floor on a sprinkling of dirty straw just where we collapsed. None of us had the strength to wash. That means something for women, and particularly for Politicals, as most of us were. And we were hungrier than ever because the food was the worst we had yet encountered. I was working together with Alexandra, a poet named Tamara and little Tania, who sang such beautiful Russian folk songs – or had sung them. One morning Tamara and I had high fever. There was no such thing as a thermometer in El Marje; the *natchalnik* judged for himself who was sick and who was not. In both our cases it was too obvious, and he unwillingly decided that we really were ill. Tamara and I lay together in the hut feeling almost at death's door, but smiling. At least we were spared the brutal slavery of work in El Marje for a while. We were so happy that even the thought of the deadly *brzlose* did not frighten us. And in any case, what was death when life meant El Marje?

Tamara was only twenty-one; a dark-eyed beauty with delicate features and fine limbs. She was the daughter of a doctor and she had been studying medicine at his wish, but her heart was in literature and in particular in poetry. There was a literary circle at her university and she was one of its leading lights. At the meetings of the circle the students discussed literary problems and read aloud from their own works. It was quite a happy life, but one day Tamara read a poem she had written entitled 'Hymn to Freedom'. Shortly afterwards she was arrested by the GPU and charged with 'Preparation for terrorism'. For what tyrant other than Stalin could she possibly have been attacking? Her sentence was eight years in Karaganda, with *pod konvoi* as an aggravation.

Tamara was one of those who had lost her coat in Leninskoie, and so she had nothing to cover herself with at night. By this time she was so weak and exhausted that she had even given up delousing herself. I just have no words to describe that state of exhaustion. The fact must stand for itself. She must have been beautiful, but now she was as thin as a rake and all her bones jutted out of her skin. 'The worst thing is that they arrested my father as well, and now Mother's all alone,' she said to me one day, and there were tears in her eyes.

Three days our rest lasted, and then the *natchalnik* decided we were well enough to work. The gang needed a water-carrier. 'Who can deal with oxen?' he demanded. 'I can,' I said at once. No animal could be as bad as these human beings, and the oxen were patient, gentle-looking creatures. So, armed with halters, I went out into the steppe to catch a couple of oxen for the water-cart. There were two wells, one in our valley and another in a side valley. Water had to be drawn from them and carted to the pens where, 'the campaign against *brzlose*' being ended, the women were engaged repairing walls and roofs. For this they needed water to mix the clay mass with which they worked.

Ten oxen were peacefully chewing the cud some distance out in the steppe. With my halters in my hand, I made my way towards them a little nervously. I had never had anything to do with animals in my life, apart from the domestic cat, but I thought it would be all right. Gradually I came nearer and nearer, but just when I was close up they lumbered off. They knew perfectly well what I wanted and they were not going to be caught if they could help it. The slow hunt went on and on. Every time I got near them they would trot off again. I was beginning to get very depressed. Being a water-carrier appealed to me. It meant that I should be more or less emancipated from the constant slave-driving of the *natchalnik* and his servile underlings. I began to fear that he would realise that I had lied to him, and I grew desperate, but the more I tried to catch them the more easily they evaded me. Then I tried cunning.

I stretched myself out on the ground and pretended to have no further interest in the oxen. When they saw this they lost interest in me too and dropped down to rest. I gave them a little while to gain confidence, and then I cautiously crawled round behind them and approached a black-and-white beast from behind. I got nearer and nearer to the unsuspecting ox, and then I sprang to my feet and darted at him with the halter ready. He lumbered to his feet, but too late. I was quicker than he was and the halter was already over his horns and round his neck. My heart was in my mouth. The halter was round his neck and I held the other end. But what now? If he proved fractious, he could drag me away instead of my leading him. But fortunately, at the feel of the halter, he submitted to his fate meekly and trotted after me as I pulled him away.

But now there was another problem: how was I to catch another one without losing him? There was no tree or bush to which I could tie him in the meantime. But then, wonder of wonders, the problem solved itself. A brown ox left the others, who had got to their feet and trotted off, and followed my ox. I learnt afterwards that I had caught Vassya, and where Vassya went Mishka, that was the brown one, always followed, for they were used to pulling together in the same yoke. I easily fitted the second halter round Mishka's neck and led them both back in triumph. Then I had to yoke them to the water-cart. It was a primitive Kazak yoke and no easy matter for me. It was like trying to fill a pail full of holes. As soon as I got one ox in and turned to the other, the first one broke loose and sat down again. Fortunately, the *natchalnik* was not in sight to observe my inexperienced efforts. A Kazak yoke is a thoughtless piece of cruelty to animals. If one beast sits down he drags down the head of the other by sheer weight. And what a state the poor beasts were in! Ill-treated and neglected. Anyone who felt like beating them beat them to his heart's content. Their backs were bruised and cut with blows. The old blows were scars, the new ones were marked with crusted blood, and their poor muzzles were torn and bruised. Even in my own misery, the sight of the poor, patient, ill-treated beasts brought a lump to my throat. And how unnecessary all that thoughtless cruelty was! I never had to beat them. With Vassya and Mishka I spent the best time I had ever spent in Karaganda. When I urged them forward they went; when I cried out '*Zobi!*' they turned to the right, and when I shouted '*Zop!*' they turned to the left. That was oxen language in Russia and I was the best ox-driver the poor beasts had ever known.

After a while the nearer well became exhausted and I had to journey with them to the other well in the next valley. How lovely that was! The guards could not see into that valley and once there I was completely alone with Vassya and Mishka. As soon as we were out of sight of the armed guard perched on one of the roofs, I would shout '*Stoi!*' Immediately Mishka would go down, to be followed by Vassya, and then we were alone and unwatched. On both sides the slopes of the hills were covered with undergrowth and here and there were patches of glowing red hawthorn berries. I would scramble over the rocks and fill my bag with berries, for they were good to eat, but then I would have to hurry on again, for the *natchalnik* was supervising the repair work and woe betide me if there was any shortage of water. The biggest job was to get my two friends to get up once they had got down. They were only camp oxen, after all, and to persuade them to get up and go on with their work without beating them was a difficult problem. Beating was to them the only sign that they were expected to get on with the job until I came. However, with much shouting, tugging and a few slaps over their rumps I managed it, and then we would lumber on, clouds of birds with green, iridescent plumage rising up from the ground before us as we went. At the well I had to fill up the barrel with a pail. It was hard work, but infinitely preferable to labouring under the constant lash of the *natchalnik*'s tongue. And when it was filled up back we went to the pens. And so it went on all day long, with shouts of '*Zobi-zop!*' till sundown and rest for me and the oxen.

In the evening I would release Vassya and Mishka from their heavy yoke, patting them, stroking their muzzles and whispering friendly words into their great ears. Then off they would trot out into the steppes, free at least for the night. In the mornings I never again had any difficulty with them. All I had to do was to go out and call and they would both come trotting up, to the vast astonishment of any Russian who happened to be a witness.

On one occasion – it was a great event because of its infrequency – the *layok* came to El Marje. All it had was herrings and noodles. We decided to buy noodles. They were cheaper than herrings. But then the problem of cooking them arose. We hadn't thought of that. And then I remembered having heard that sheep's dung was excellent fuel. With my experience from many weekends out in the country with the German youth movement, I built a fire behind the huts near the latrines – which was the only place our unpleasant *natchalnik* would let us build a fire – and there we cooked the noodles in a tin can. In our anticipation we forgot our tiredness, and when the noodles were ready and the water poured away we sat down right there well within whiff of the latrines and ate our fill. I don't think I ever ate noodles that tasted better than they did. We were all in high spirits, laughing and chattering. And when the guard came along to herd us back into the stinking hut, we begged him again and again for 'just a few minutes more', and under the influence of our good spirits he left us there until a great yellow moon rose gradually over the mountains.

'Grete,' whispered Tamara, 'one of the scenes in the play I'm going to write when I get out of Karaganda is going to be in El Marje.'

One midday we were called away from our work to a waiting lorry. That meant a long journey and, unfortunately, parting from Vassya and Mishka. Our women's gang was sent out to some brick works. After the beautiful neighbourhood of El Marje, we found it bare and depressing around the brick works – nothing but dust, yellow steppe land scorched up by the sun, with hardly a blade of grass anywhere. In a hollow the clay was dug out and packed into moulds. There were no kilns; the clay forms were just laid out in the sun to bake hard.

I worked together with a young Kazak Moslem. It was our job to turn the bricks over. They were laid out in the sun in long rows, and we went along turning them over one by one. After an hour or two our hands were grazed and bleeding. The bricks were twice as big as the ones in use in Western Europe and as they dried the edges were sharp and jagged. Our good fortune was that the guard and the overseer had a wide area to control and they could not be everywhere at once. When they were away we had a chance of sitting down and taking a rest. My fellow prisoner was a practising Moslem. Round her neck on a chain she wore a medallion with a crescent and a star engraved on it. It was some sort of religious emblem which she valued highly. She had thick, shining black hair which she wore in two tightly plaited tails over her shoulders. She lived strictly in accordance with her tribal customs and she suffered much mockery on that account from the other prisoners. When she went to the latrines she always took a tin-can with water in order to make her ablutions. A Mohammedan woman is not supposed to go abroad without long trousers, which she was unable to obtain so she solved the problem by attaching her worn stockings to a short pair of knickers. Comic? But it was not comic to look into her broad, serene Mongolian face with the friendly, brown, slit eyes and the smiling lips.

'You are an educated person,' she said to me one day. 'Perhaps you can tell me whether I shall ever be free again.'

'What are you here for in the first place?' I asked.

She hesitated and seemed embarrassed.

'Unless I know that at least, I can't even guess,' I said.

'I am absolutely innocent,' she said finally, and she added a religious formula which I did not understand. 'But my husband killed a member of the Soviet in our village. And then all our family was arrested. They said we all had something to do with it. Of course, we didn't. And in any case, it wasn't planned at all; just done suddenly. I was at home all the time with my children.'

Her pleading brown eyes were directed at me. 'You're a *grammatny sheloviek* [a literate person]. Surely you can help me. Tell me what I must do to get back to my children again.'

What could I do? What could I say? I had to take refuge in vague hopefulness. 'I'm sure your case will be reopened. Have you got anyone outside who could take the matter up for you?'

'No. Not a soul. Everyone in our village was arrested at the same time.'

The situation was obviously hopeless. There was nothing she could do and nothing I could do.

One day we saw a cloud of dust approaching. The Kazak girl grew very excited. 'They're my people,' she said. 'My people.'

They were two herdsmen on horseback, and they dismounted some distance away and began to make themselves a fire to prepare their food.

The herdsmen were also prisoners, but the nature of their work left them in relative freedom, as the herds wandered for many miles seeking good grazing grounds. These men were given quantities of food to last them for a long period. And, as everyone knew, they were much better off for food than anyone else. Clearly, from time to time a sheep would meet with an accident, a fatal accident, and then they had *shashlik*.

'Go over to them,' I said. 'They'll have food, probably meat. They'll give you some.'

But she was scandalised at the suggestion. 'Never,' she replied indignantly. 'A Mohammedan woman can't approach men. It isn't right.'

'Why not forget about that here,' I said. 'You're in a concentration camp. Things are very different. Different times, different manners.'

But she was not to be persuaded. As we worked, I noticed her eyes constantly turning in the direction of the two herdsmen, who were now squatting down eating their food. Then when the guard was not in the neighbourhood she began to sing, a strange little melody of unresolved accords. Her religion would not allow her to approach the men, but she knew how to get what she wanted. The two herdsmen heard her singing and looked up. Then they began to answer with the same sort of melody. This strange, melodious communication went on for a while and then one of the men rose and came over to us. He stopped a few yards away, bowed ceremoniously and began to talk to the woman. They talked in their own tongue, of which, of course, I did not understand a word. Then he invited us with a sweep of his hand to come to their fire and eat. We both went and there was a porridge of millet prepared with pieces of mutton. For us it was a rare delicacy and we ate it hungrily. Only the fear that the guard would come up and spoil it all made me nervous.

Back to Birma

I did not stay long in the brick works. One evening when I came in from the day's work the *natchalnik* called out: 'Buber-Nejman. Get ready at once. With things.' Wondering what was going to happen now, I got my things and came back. A lorry was waiting for me. It had been sent specially from Birma to take me back. There was great excitement amongst my fellow prisoners at this to them most significant circumstance. 'Transport alone!' they cried. 'That can only mean one thing: release.' And they embraced and kissed me delightedly. 'Don't forget us when you're free, Grete. Do what you can for us.'

'*Davai! Davai!*' shouted the *natchalnik*. 'What's all this nonsense. Get out of it, all of you. Into the lorry you.'

I climbed into the lorry and it started up. I waved and kissed my
hand to my fellow unfortunates for as long as I could see them, and, as
in all partings, my heart was heavy. Release? Their optimism was kind.
I didn't believe it. I did not share it. There could be a dozen and one
explanations for the strange phenomenon. On the way I hardly wondered
what was going to happen to me. We neared Birma in the darkness and
the lights of the hospital were the first I saw. The building was lit with
oil lamps. At that moment my dearest wish was much more modest than
freedom; it was to be able to sleep just once again in a decent bed free
of bugs, lice and fleas. The lorry pulled up before the punishment
compound and I was taken in. No one bothered in the least about my
arrival. Still wondering, I went off to see the *natchalnik*.

'It's no affair of mine,' he said in answer to my question. 'I don't
know anything about it. Just wait. They'll call you if they want you.'

They never did call me, and I never learnt why I had been brought
back alone.

It was the same ex-criminal *natchalnik* – though why I say ex-criminal I don't know. But all the other faces were strange. The women's
hut was full to capacity. I flung my sack down on the slippery clay floor
in one corner of the place. Most of them around were criminal types.
For a change, the hut was nice and warm, and the stove burnt well. It
was easy to see that this gang had good connections to the coal dump.
Opposite me lay a criminal on the *naris*, her head reclining on two
embroidered cushions of exceptional vulgarity. She seemed to be the
prima donna. Her name, I discovered, was Raiza, and her wants were
attended to respectfully by a number of other criminals. On the stove
were stolen potatoes boiling in an old can, and the place was full of
steam. There was a hubbub of chatter, and in one corner a number of
women were singing in drunken voices. A sack hung in front of the
door and I was astonished at the nonchalance with which male prisoners of the criminal type went in and out. Relations with the guards
must be very good, I thought.

At first pleasant, the warmth was beginning to get oppressive. Most of
the women were dressed only in knickers and brassières, and many of them
were tattooed. A pigeon carrying a letter in its beak dived interminably
down between the breasts of one, and on the back of another was a male
head. There were messages, too: 'I love Vassya,' and so on; and one even
insisted: 'Mother, I'll never forget you.' There was one woman who never
took off her black knickers in public even in the washroom. It was said
that the tattooing on her belly was so indecent that even she was a little
embarrassed by it. The chest of one of the women was criss-crossed with
scars. 'What on earth's all that?' I asked her. 'Kolya did that with a razor,'

she said proudly. 'He loves me so much and he's so jealous.' Hardly a
sentence was spoken which did not either begin or end with a curse.

During the night I must have given sustenance to at least fifty fleas,
not counting bugs and lice. The next morning I staggered off to work
after having left my things in the keeping of an old political *ndevalnaya*
I had found. I didn't want to lose the few odds and ends I still possessed.
The place was absolutely packed and the women slept together almost
like sardines in a tin, but after a few days I found there was a place free
in the back room, the one with the sack hanging in front of the door.
The boards were so uneven that it was more like a switchback, but it
was better than the floor. There was no oil lamp in this part and I soon
discovered that it was used as an abode of love – both day and night.
And it was very busy during the day, because most of the criminals didn't
bother to go to work. Their understanding with the *natchalnik* was too
good. Anyone else who missed the gang was sure to be flung into the
arrest cells at once.

On one occasion I was working in a gang sorting out frozen potatoes.
We stood in the potato dump, a gloomy, mouldy place, and searched in
the icy mess for any potatoes which might still be eatable. Next to me
a criminal was working. Probably she was as tired and disgusted with
the work as I was, but her reactions were different. She kicked me in
the ankle irritably. At first I thought it must have been an accident, but
I couldn't see how. 'What's that for?' I asked in some astonishment. Her
only reply was to kick me again, and this time there was no doubt about
the intention. I protested angrily and immediately she struck me in the
face. Boiling with indignation, I went for her and in a moment we were
engaged in a fierce scuffle. The others pulled us apart. The 'brigadier'
of the gang was a Political. 'Grete,' he hissed in my ear, 'be careful.
Don't get into trouble with the criminals. It's dangerous.' He knew, of
course, that I could not have started the trouble, and he seized the
offender and hustled her off. She then flung herself on to the ground
and indulged in a fit of hysteria, kicking and shrieking. They pulled her to
her feet still kicking and dragged her up the cellar steps into the fresh air.

I stood there almost in tears with humiliation now that my anger had
drained out of me, but suddenly another woman came up to me, and
before I realised her intentions she had hit me between the eyes, so that
I literally saw stars. My blood rose again at this second unprovoked attack
and I gave her a blow every bit as good as she had given me, and in an
instant the second fight was on. My unknown enemy shrieked and cursed
and threatened to kill me. We were soon separated, and the other woman
was hustled off in her turn. My 'brigadier' was very upset. 'Why did that
have to happen?' he said in despair. 'That was Tania, the bosom friend

of Djura, the other one. She's one of the most dangerous furies in the camp. If she says she'll kill you, she will if we're not careful.'

I was very depressed by the whole disgusting business, but he seemed to be attaching more importance to a scuffle than it warranted. However, the Politicals decided that I was not to go out alone again; if I went to the latrines, I must always be accompanied by someone. I consented to this unwillingly and I carried it out strictly for a while, but it was a burden, and after about a week when nothing had happened and the thing seemed to have been forgotten I went out to the latrines alone. There was snow on the ground and there was only a narrow path to the latrines. When I was still a little distance away a woman came towards me, and I recognised Tania. I would not show my fear by turning round and going back, and as she came close I stepped to one side in the snow to let her pass. My legs were trembling and my whole body was on the alert for an attack. She stopped. 'Have you got a fag?' she asked. 'No,' I said. She looked at me for a moment. 'Oh! it's you, is it? Well, never mind. Forget it. I've forgotten it.' I was greatly relieved. Deadly enmities can end like that too.

One evening all the occupants of the women's hut had to parade outside. A uniformed member of the GPU then read us out a list of sentences passed in Dolinki on various prisoners for offences against the camp rules. There were two and three years extra for attempts to escape; two years for stealing skins; eighteen months for letting some sheep die; three years for the murder of a fellow prisoner; and seventy-five death sentences for repeated and wilful refusal to work. He had hardly finished and turned about than the women began to laugh and imitate his peculiar, high-pitched and cracked voice. A good deal of discussion about the sentences followed, during the course of which I learnt that in 1937 400 allegedly incorrigible prisoners in the Karaganda complex had been liquidated in this way by administrative sentence from Dolinki.

At this time there were constant batches of incoming prisoners. Amongst them was the wife of the German Communist, Hans Kiepenberger, who had received a five-year term in Karaganda. I did my best to get into touch with her, but I was unsuccessful. She was transported to another sector and I never managed to see her.

Many of the newcomers were the first victims of the new law against voluntary abortion, which was promulgated by the Soviet Government in defiance of a popular plebiscite. These women were generally received with laughter and mockery by the other prisoners – at least by the criminals and Asocials, who seemed to find something funny in their plight.

One day quite unexpectedly I was called out of the hut, and who should be standing there waiting for me but Tasso Salpeter. It appeared that she was employed in the administration, and, knowing where I was, she had got herself placed in charge of an inventory in our *natchalnik's* office. Whilst there she had left the office under some pretext or other and here she was. It was the first time we had seen each other since our stay together in the Butirka. Hastily, we told each other all that had happened to us since, and then she said: 'Here's paper and an envelope. If you want to write a letter and smuggle it out, now's our chance. I've got a dead-certain opportunity.'

I took the paper and the envelope and hurried off to write a short note to my mother. When I had finished it, I passed it to Tasso. What hopes I attached to that precious letter! It never arrived.

On one occasion my work consisted of carrying sacks of grain from a cleansing machine up into a barn along a narrow plank. The sacks were heavy and many of the women groaned and grunted under the burden. A male prisoner from the 'free camp' sat on a wall, dangled his legs and made jokes as they passed.

'You'd do better to help instead of sitting there amusing yourself,' I said indignantly.

'Hark at the German Fascist,' he mocked. 'She doesn't like carrying heavy sacks. Russian women are different. They're proud of doing the same work as the men.'

'It's a pity the men don't show them more consideration,' I retorted. 'They've got to bear the children.'

And, believe it or not, all the Russian women around sided with the man, and there was a chorus of indignation: 'We are proud of it. Women in Soviet Russia play a different role from women in the capitalist countries. We have equal rights.'

I had nothing more to say. Persistent propaganda is very powerful.

On our way to work and back we saw a new building going up in the steppe. There was much speculation as to what it could be: a bakery, someone said. No; new offices. I regarded it with some suspicion. It looked menacing and familiar to me. I was right; it was the new prison for the Birma section of the Karaganda Camp.

In the Hospital

Dzagnidze, the Georgian teacher, was back again from one of the subsections, and I worked with him and others shovelling grain. Under the low roof of the granary and in clouds of black dust so thick that you could hardly see the next man the heat was terrible and the atmosphere stifling. My lungs threatened to burst and from time to time I had to stagger to the door for air. The 'brigadier', a criminal, began to shout and bully me back to work, but Dzagnidze came to my rescue and offered the man tobacco if he would show me a little consideration. He took the tobacco and grinned: 'Your girlfriend, hey? All right.'

The next morning, when reveille came, I could hardly stand and I reported sick. The *natchalnik* took my temperature with a thermometer and decided that it was not high enough, so off to work I had to stagger. And at least in the granary there was one soul who cared a little about my well-being. One look was enough for Dzagnidze, and when I told him about the *natchalnik's* thermometer he hurried off and managed to get hold of another one from somewhere. This time I had a high enough fever to satisfy even the *natchalnik*. I seemed to be consumed inwardly with fire and I lay there on the wretched boards in the sickbay, if it could really be called that, and shivered with cold. There was no doctor, only a semi-qualified ambulance man. The next morning he diagnosed *brzlose*. The morning after that he thought it might be malaria, and on the third morning, when I began to spit blood, he decided that I must go to hospital.

At midday I was loaded on to an ox-cart, tied down so that I should not fall off, and taken to hospital. There was no need to bother any more about my few poor possessions. Whilst I was unconscious they had all been stolen. All that was left was the sack they had been in. Every new arrival in hospital was supposed to wash himself, but as I couldn't stand I was unable to and no one bothered. Here at least I had the real bed I had longed for and blankets as well – but, alas! not the immunity from bugs and lice. The blankets were all lousy. However, I didn't notice that until many days later, when I recovered consciousness properly again.

The doctor who visited me spoke German and was very friendly. 'I know Germany quite well,' he said. 'I studied in Leipzig.' He was kind to all the patients and spoke to everyone, and no doubt did what he could for them, but medicaments and instruments were scarce here as everywhere else in Russia.

Next to me lay a young woman with double pneumonia. Apparently the lice were troubling her greatly, for she never ceased to scratch and roll from side to side. Many of the other patients were suffering from *brzlose*, and they looked just like photos of people from the hunger districts during the famine – just bags of skin and bones.

The hospital was more than full and there were beds along the corridors as well as in the wards, but at least each patient had a bed. The beds even had sheets and each patient was given a shirt. Unfortunately, these garments too were lousy. Amongst the patients were also quite a large number of advanced syphilis cases. Venereal diseases were very widespread in Birma, although bad cases were usually isolated in special VD departments.

When I had sufficiently recovered to have my wits about me again, Tasso visited me in hospital. That was strictly forbidden, but she just came, and she had a way with her which got her past most things. She told me all the latest news from the 'free camp'. All the male employees of the repair office had been called out with others to rescue a flock of sheep that had got into difficulties because the bell-wether had led them into a morass in his search for water. There were over 300 of them, and men were sent to the spot in lorries and then roped together and sent in after the sheep. It was a difficult and dangerous job, and poor Grigory Ilyitch had broken his leg. Many of the sheep, of course, were lost, and the unfortunate shepherd was now awaiting his fate for wrecking activities.

As the result of the Russo-German Pact, war was, of course, now going on in Europe. It seemed a long way away from Birma. Tasso told me all she knew about it. But really we were more interested in our own fate. I despaired of ever getting out alive, but Tasso's spirits never flagged. 'Nazarenko had a fifteen-year sentence, and he's been amnestied,' she said consolingly. 'Why shouldn't you get out some day? I'm sure I shall. I'll have a bald head and no teeth by that time, but *nitchevo*: just to see Tiflis once again!' Indeed, her lovely black hair had gone thin and she waggled her teeth with finger and thumb to show me. 'They'll all fall out soon,' she said cheerfully. 'Never mind.'

After three weeks in hospital, I was discharged, but the doctor gave me a form which said that I was no longer to be used for heavy labour, that I was to have fourteen days' 'inside service' and to receive supplementary food. I was then taken back to the punishment compound, where in the meantime further changes had taken place. I received a place on the *naris* amidst all my old comrades from my working party, who had by this time come back to Birma from the outlying jobs they had been engaged on. The place was still overcrowded, but they had succeeded, after much trouble and a bitter struggle, in securing a part of the place to themselves away from the criminal elements. And there was a note waiting for me from Dzagnidze: 'Goodbye and good luck. Don't forget me. I am being sent to an invalid sector.' The one wish of all these poor unfortunates, forced out of life into this misery, was not to be forgotten; to feel that someone still thought of them with kindness.

During the fourteen days I was allowed to stay in the compound I got to know a Russian woman. She was a teacher of languages from Leningrad. She was only about thirty, but her heart was so bad that not even our *natchalnik* could send her out to work. She could walk only slowly and every now and then she had to sit down to get her breath. She spoke of her home and her little girl, but when I asked her about her sentence she grew nervous.

'It's better not to speak of such things here,' she said; and then after a while: 'Do you speak English?'

'A little,' I replied.

'Then we can speak English together. No one will understand us here. But we must never speak Russian. Someone might overhear us.'

She told me her story. It was nothing unusual. Her father had been an engineer. He had been involved in the Shachty Trial in 1928 and sentenced to five years in Siberia. After three years he had died. She thought the world of him and still carried a very small and much dilapidated photo of him with her which she had succeeded in saving through her period of examination. She herself was married to an engineer. She had never taken any part at all in politics, but professionally she had taught Russian to various English people in Leningrad. Her sentence was for 'espionage'. Her husband, to whom she had been married for five years, was still at liberty.

At the end of my fourteen days' convalescence I was told off to work in the vegetable cellar. From then on I became the chief provider for our little circle. There were wonderful things there: potatoes, carrots, beetroot and onions – things we hardly ever saw in the punishment compound and then only illegally. It was an exciting and satisfactory life. My chief problem was how to steal without being found out. All the members of the vegetable gang were searched on leaving the cellar and again on returning to the punishment compound. However, I was a Political, and Politicals were not such notorious thieves as the criminals and Asocials, with the result that Politicals were searched only very cursorily. In order to run the blockade, I made myself a bag which was fastened round my waist, and during the course of the day I would fill it with whatever came to hand: potatoes, carrots, onions, and so on. It was always a risk and it was not too easy to walk properly with the bag dangling between my legs, but I managed it, and it was worth the risk to hear the exclamations of delight when I got back into our corner and emptied out the precious contents. Our old *ndevalnaya*, she was a Tolstoyan, would then make us a vegetable soup. After a few weeks of this the appearance of all of us changed. For the first time we were getting enough food, and good food. Our spirits were higher and we were in much better condition altogether.

After some I had an accident. I had managed to 'organise' some water to wash with, and in my oversize shoes I stumbled over the doorstep and fell, breaking my metatarsal bone, though this exact information as to what happened did not come to me until six years later, when I was in freedom and was X-rayed to find out what was still troubling me. At the time all I knew was that my foot was red, blue and swollen and and that it was excruciatingly painful to put my weight on it. At any other time, and had I been engaged on any other work, this crippling accident would have been a Godsend, but now I was maintaining the health of all our company with my depredations it was a tragedy, and deep depression reigned. The medical attendant in the compound painted my foot with iodine and ordered me to stay away from work. That day I practised walking with set teeth and grim determination. It was painful, but gradually it became possible if I put most of the weight on the outside edge of the foot. The next day I reported for work with the vegetable gang. Off we went and for a while I kept up, but then I could stand the pace no longer and began to lag behind, hobbling along on my crippled foot. The guard began to curse and shout, but by this time I was becoming a hard case: I could stand a lot of shouting and abuse in a good cause, and I had good reason to persevere. Fortunately, two of my fellow prisoners took pity on me and helped me along.

Siberian Winter

It was winter in Birma and an easier time for the prisoners. We worked from sunup to sundown as usual, but in winter the days were short, which meant very much less work. In addition, it was often freezing so hard that it was impossible to work at all, or there was a snowstorm and then we were kept in our huts. The worst work which had to be done in winter was shovelling the snow and carting it to the kitchen garden to pile it up there so that when the thaw came as much water as possible would soak into the soil. Certain work also had to be done in the granary. When it was wind-still and not snowing the air was crystal clear and everything glistened marvellously in the winter sun. And endless peace seemed to lie over everything and the scene was like a picture postcard.

In the very cold weather certain prisoners were relieved from their labour obligations, primarily those who had no footwear and no proper clothes. The criminals and the Asocials took full advantage of this. I remember at one roll-call an Asocial was told off to go out with the working party. She was a big, powerful woman and she dragged her skirts up over her belly and showed the *natchalnik* that she was naked underneath. 'How do you expect me to go out and work in the cold like this?' she demanded. There was a roar of laughter and the *natchalnik* grinned and dismissed her.

During the winter the prisoners were not so exhausted and the general spirit was much better in the huts. Some sort of social life developed and there was even communal singing in the evenings. In our room we had an opera-singer from Leningrad and a concert-singer from Kharkov, and they vied with each other to gain our applause. I must say it was not an unmixed blessing when the opera-singer raised her powerful voice in our little hut. She made the rafters shake – or they would have shaken had there been any. When she sang, her eyes were closed and there was an expression of ecstasy on her face. I am sure she was in the opera house again in her imagination. But I had seen her sitting naked, her body covered with louse bites, picking lice out of the seams of her shirt in the light of our one oil lamp, an intent look on her great, moonlike face. But we were a thankful audience, and both our singers lapped up our applause.

There were also others who could sing. There was a blonde Russian girl from some small town in the provinces who sang us a long and doleful folk song about the tragic fate of a fisher-boy. I can still recall the melody. And there was a dancer too. Somewhere or other she had got hold of a fiery red shawl and she would dance exhibition Cossack dances with tremendous verve.

I heard one day that prisoners were entitled to a visit to the Camp Commandant to put forward anything relating to their case or to make complaints, so I put my name down on the list for a visit, and after a while I was escorted to his office with a group of others from the punishment block. Each applicant was heard separately. It was a tremendously long wait, but at last my turn came. Serikov, the Commandant, sat at a table, together with the GPU *natchalnik*. A number of other uniformed men stood behind them.

When I gave my name, my dossier was produced and laid in front of Serikov. He raised his round, rather friendly face to me and asked what I wanted.

'I should like to know the reason for my imprisonment in the punishment compound?' I said.

Serikov and the GPU man looked through the dossier.

'I can give you no information about that,' he said finally.

'Then can you tell me how long I'm likely to stay there?'

Again they looked through my papers. 'Throughout your sentence,' came the reply.

I went back to the compound heavy-hearted. Three years more? I should be lucky to survive that at all.

For some time we had had the uneasy feeling that there was a tale-bearer in our hut. 'It's either Nina, who was once a member of the Party, or it's Raiza from Harbin,' whispered Alexandra. 'When Poniatovska went to the Commandant's office, the GPU *natchalnik* asked her some very peculiar questions. There's something wrong.'

Nothing is more terrible for prisoners than to feel that one of their comrades is a spy. Everyone was anxiously trying to recall whether she had said anything compromising. What might I have said, for instance? I came to the conclusion that it was Nina; the other woman was just a lazy, good-for-nothing who was unlikely to bother her head much about politics. I began to watch Nina more closely. There she would sit in the evenings in her torn underskirt, her angular arms and shoulders bare, and lay down the law.

'Even here it's our duty to be watchful. Our country is in the greatest danger.'

And so on. An odious creature like that would not hesitate to twist even a harmless remark into a counter-revolutionary utterance, and whoever she denounced would be lost. I turned away in disgust. She made me want to spit.

But I did her an injustice. She was serving a fifteen-year term, and those speeches were delivered for the benefit of the real spy. It turned out to be Raiza, after all. She was found out because the authorities did not treat their spy with sufficient care. She was constantly being called away from her work and she was always present at the Commandant's office when he received the prisoners.

When the winter began, prisoners were allowed to receive parcels from outside. During the summer the authorities want them to work hard for their pound and a half of bread. If they could get food any other way, they might not work so hard. The first parcel was an event in our room. The Leningrad teacher of foreign languages received it from her husband. Not many prisoners actually received parcels, because in the majority of cases their friends and relatives were too frightened to send them; it might be construed as sympathy with the offenders and cause their own arrest. The second one to get a parcel was our old *ndevalnaya*. The name of the sender was that of her twelve-year-old grandchild. She was moved to tears. 'Look how beautifully she's packed it all,' she said. 'And see what she writes here,' and she showed us the childish handwriting: 'Dear Grannie, I've broken up the sugar small, just like you like it. Love; and I'll never forget you . . .'

The old Tolstoyan was full of stories of this child, who had lived with her until her arrest. The old woman loved her dearly.

'When the GPU took me away she ran after me crying: "Don't take my grannie away." And when they put me in the car she tried to get in too. They had to push her away. As we drove off, I saw them dragging her away.'

Each parcel that arrived caused an emotional outburst and floods of tears. We were not forgotten.

At the sight of the rare parcels, Alexandra had a bitter struggle to fight out with herself. Should she write to her husband and ask him to send her something. Finally, she decided she wouldn't. 'He's too great a coward,' she said. 'He wouldn't dare to send anything.' And then she thought of an old friend of hers, an actress. 'If she's still free, she might send me something.' She wrote to this woman and before I left Birma a parcel actually arrived for her.

And partings happened again and again. This time it was our old Tolstoyan *ndevalnaya*. Her health had been growing steadily worse, and now she was sent away to an invalid group. It hit us all hard and there were many tears. I had a lump in my throat when I saw the old lady go. When we had come in from work in the evening there had always been her welcoming smile, an account of the day's doings and a proud display of the coal, or whatever it was, she had managed to get hold of for us. It was one more step in the degeneration of our punishment block. Yes, even such a place could get worse, and ours did. For one thing, it got more and more crowded. There were about 150 newcomers, all criminal offenders. Despite the cold, many of them had to lie packed close in the entrance space, which had neither a door nor windows. The general atmosphere rapidly worsened. Vodka and food were smuggled in and noisy brawling drinking parties were held. They had their own songs and for anyone unused to criminals' slang they were very difficult to understand. They were usually a mixture of sentimentality and defiance. One of them, which was sung to the rhythm of an express train, dealt with the misadventures of poor Kolka, who had tried unsuccessfully to steal a trunk on the line from Pensa to Moscow and had been caught in the act. Others made fun of the public prosecutor, the guards and the Commandant. It was said that all these newcomers were only with us for a time until they could be formed into a transport to be sent on further.

There was another Tolstoyan in the compound, a man of about sixty who looked much older. I had already seen him outside in the 'free camp' begging for food. It was his job now to sit in front of our arrest cells and see that no one brought the prisoners food or messages. The cells were surrounded with special barbed wire, but there was no need to keep anyone away: Alexei Michailovitch performed his functions to the satisfaction of all the prisoners and their friends. If anyone wanted to send in food or messages to a prisoner, all he had to do was to give it to Alexei Michailovitch and it was as good as delivered.

He sat on the ground clothed in rags, and armed with a great cudgel as his staff of office. He had a huge beard which engulfed the greater part of his face and about all that was visible was a potato nose – and even that was hairy – and two friendly blue eyes which looked out from under bushy brows. He knew that I was a German.

'Margarete Genrichovna, come and talk to me a little,' he said one day. 'Let's talk about Boris. He was your friend and he was mine. A fine lad. I wonder where he is now.'

Under the hair on one cheek there was an open boil and the yellow matter was all stuck into the hairs. His padded jacket was torn in many places and the filling poked out. His trousers were very short and in sitting they had slipped up still further, and there he sat with his emaciated bluish legs crossed.

'Where do you come from in Germany, Margarete Genrichovna?'

'Potsdam, Alexei Michailovitch.'

'Potsdam! You don't say so, Margarete Genrichovna? I remember Potsdam very well, with the little Palace of Sans Souci, the great steps and the fountain.'

'Were you in Germany, then?' I asked in surprise.

'Oh, I know you wouldn't think so to see me sitting here in this state' – and he pointed to his feet bound up in rags – 'but when I was young I was a student in Germany, and in Paris, too. And I went back to Russia through the Mediterranean. Those were days, I can tell you. Happy days.'

He slapped with his hand at the cloud of flies which were buzzing around his suppurating boil. Gradually he told me his story. His father was a landowner, and on his death Alexei Michailovitch was supposed to inherit. Yet as a Tolstoyan he had lived the life of a simple peasant and been happy, but when the collectivisation had come he had refused to join. And as though that were not enough, he had spoken against the methods used to enforce the collectivisation.

'And when I spoke out for humanity and denounced their violence, they came for me.'

He had already been four years in the camp. One day when I returned to the compound after having been away for a while working in the brick fields, he had lost his office as watchman. The authorities had discovered how well off the prisoners were under his care. But everyone liked him and now he had another function; he was in charge of the *kipiatok*, or hot-water machine. In a little hut near the men's block there was a so-called 'Titan' which supplied the *kipiatok* for the tea without which no Russian can exist, even in a forced labour camp. There was no tea, but every month each prisoner received a small package of tea substitute made of apple pips and dried peels. Every day each prisoner was entitled to about half a tin of hot water for the purpose of brewing this mixture. My old friend sat like a little god next to the 'Titan' and dispensed the hot water justly to all the prisoners without curses and without abuse.

One day there was a heavy snowstorm and the wind howled and swept

up the snow in great clouds and lashed it against the side of the huts.
From the huts to the *kipiatok* a rope had been spanned on which the prisoners could pull themselves along against the storm. It was long past
midday, but we had received neither bread nor soup because the ox-cart
was unable to make headway against the storm. With our 'tea' we lay on
the *naris* in the huts and were happy, because we had not to go out to
work in such weather; and Tamara told us Pushkin's story 'The Snowstorm'.

From time to time someone went to the door to see if it was possible
to go out. The snow was beginning to lie in deep drifts against the side
of the huts and it was impossible to see more than a few yards through
the driving snow. Inside we sat and sang. A favourite song was one about
the *bezprizorni*, the orphaned children of the Civil War. It was a sad and
sentimental little ditty which we sang with great feeling. It ended with
the death of the little orphan and his burial in an unknown grave.

We learnt from a newcomer that there was a special section for these
bezprizorni in the Karaganda Camp. The world was given to understand
that they were picked up with love and care and put into comfortable
children's homes and taught a trade – reclaimed as citizens, in short, as
described in the famous Russian film, *The Way into Life*. Whatever may
have been the truth in the beginning, the new *bezprizorni* produced by
the enforced collectivisation and the famine ended in Karaganda. The
woman who told us about them had come from a section where these
waifs and strays were kept. Condtions were terrible, and the children
were completely out of hand; nothing was done to reclaim them. It was
almost impossible to go from the place where the soup was ladled out
back to the huts without being fallen upon by these little devils and
robbed of it. 'Thank God I'm amongst civilised people again,' she
concluded.

A Turning Point

One day in December 1939 I was called out of the hut after work. An
official from the administration stood there. When I told him my name,
he said: 'Would you like to work in the district administration?'

'Yes,' I said, trying to conceal my joy. 'But would I be released from
the punishment compound then?'

'You won't be in the main administration,' he said. 'You'll work in
the camp clothing office under surveillance. Tomorrow morning you'll
be taken there.'

I worked at a table in the corner of a large room. A guard was always
marching up and down in the corridor. Five other women, all from the

'free camp', worked there, including Tasso. So that was the solution of the mystery. I was not supposed to speak to the others or they to me, but no sooner was the guard far enough away than we talked nineteen to the dozen. My guess was wrong.

'What on earth are they up to with you, Grete?' Tasso said. 'Is Serikov your boyfriend by any chance?'

I gave up wondering why; it was sufficient that I was here in this warm, comfortable room and could speak to Tasso. I kept the card index of the prisoners who had received camp jackets, trousers and caps, noting the date of issue and so on. Tasso gave me a piece of bread, some sugar and a mug of *ersatz* tea. The guard saw it, but as he seemed doubtful about what he was supposed to do he did nothing and said nothing.

Soon after that the door was opened, and who should come in but Grete Sonntag. Tasso made a sign to her to look in my direction and her lined face with its constant expression of bitterness lit up and she smiled. Tasso whispered to her, and she nodded and went out again. About half an hour later she returned carrying a *katylok* covered over with a piece of paper. My own empty *katylok* was under the table. She came up to me wordlessly, put her own down and picked up the empty one and went off. At a convenient moment, I lifted the paper and a delicious smell of baked food filled my nostrils: baked potatoes and even some meat. That was the torture of Tantalus. I couldn't eat it with the guard walking up and down and I had to wait. And there in the *katylok* waited the finest meal I had had in years.

Grete Sonntag not only managed the tannery, but she also superintended the slaughtering, and when the meat was cut up there was always a share for her.

It was Paradise in that office, but it was not eternal bliss; it lasted just two weeks. In that time all my old friends and acquaintances from the 'free camp' came to visit me – the guard had given up everything except just seeing that I didn't run away. Stefanie Brun, who worked in the main administrative office, brought me some *mahorka* and some sweets from the first parcel she had received from her daughter. I think we both got a shock when we saw each other. Stefanie's cheeks had fallen in and there were deep bags under her eyes, and her ankles and legs were still very swollen. 'And where are your round cheeks?' she asked.

And my old colleagues from the repair workshop's office all suddenly found things which had to be settled in our office. Grigory Ilyitch hobbled in with the aid of a stick. His broken leg had not been splinted properly and the bone had knitted badly. 'I'll soon be ready for the invalid sector,' he said jokingly. And Clement Nikifrevitch smiled all over his face at the sight of me. 'What a piece of luck!' he said enthusiastically. 'You'll see, you'll be home before any of us.'

Grete Sonntag came every day with her *katylok* of food, and if it had gone on much longer I am sure I would soon have been back to normal again. There was always an opportunity for unwatched conversation behind the latrine.

'Do you think we'll ever get out of here now that Stalin's got this pact of friendship with Hitler?' she asked. 'We Communists are a bigger nuisance to him than ever now.' Her eyes filled with tears. 'I keep dreaming of my mother,' she said. 'I'm sure she's dead.'

At the end of the second week of this heaven in Birma, I was called during working hours to the *natchalnik*, who sat in a nearby room. I stood before his desk and churned out the usual formula: 'No. 174,475. Margarete Genrichovna Buber-Neumann. Socially dangerous element. Five years.'

'A wireless message has just come through from Dolinki,' he said. 'You are to go to the reception point of the Karaganda Camp. That's all.'

I turned round and went back into the office. My feet were not very secure under me, but I felt no pleasure, no upwelling of hope. Tasso and the others were tremendously excited. 'What's the matter with you?' they cried. 'Why aren't you dancing for joy. That means release. Aren't you lucky.' And Tasso embraced me heartily in full view of the guard. 'Grete, that's wonderful. Perhaps you'll soon see your Heinz again.'

'Do you think so?' I was loth to believe. 'Strange, I can't feel any pleasure. I don't believe it – yet.'

'Well, you needn't work here any more. Go back to the compound and pack your things all ready. Perhaps you'll go off this evening.'

The guard made a feeble attempt to interfere, but Tasso sent him – one might almost say ordered him – to go to the *natchalnik* and find out for himself. He went and came back a few minutes later.

'Right,' he said. 'It's in order. Let's get going.' And, slinging his rifle over his shoulder, he made as though to go. '*Davai!*'

But he had made a mistake in his timing. 'Not so fast,' said Tasso. There were farewells to be said and embraces to be exchanged and tears to be shed. They sent for Grete Sonntag. She embraced and kissed me too. 'Goodbye,' she said. 'We shall never see each other again. I know it. You are going to be released now, and I must stay on here.'

When I finally went off with my guard she accompanied me part of the way, sobbing, hopeless, despairing. It is always an ordeal to see someone else go.

In the evening the Politicals returned from their work and heard the news. Opinions were divided. Some were sure I was going to be released. Others were not so sure.

'It is just possible that Grete is being sent to a special section for foreigners,' said Poniatovska. 'There's one in Central Siberia. She'd have to go to the reception centre in that case.'

'But why only Grete, then?' said someone. 'There are plenty of other foreigners here.'

And so the discussion went on. They were more interested in it than I was. My mood was one of resignation: just wait and see. It was useless to speculate.

In case I might be on my way to Central Siberia, the Politicals in the compound began to collect for me as a *neimushtchi*, or 'have-not', which I was since all my things had been stolen. The transport from Karaganda to another camp could last weeks and mean hunger and cold. They collected a sack of bread, another sack of dried fish – and sixty roubles. That was a small fortune, for a prisoner in the punishment compound could earn only five or six roubles a month even if he completed his labour quota every day.

We sat together on the *naris* on my last evening in Birma, and the concert-singer told my fortune from a pack of home-made cards. Of course, it turned out well:

'After much suffering comes peace. A journey. You will return to your homeland at last and to your father's house. And henceforth you will enjoy much happiness.'

And whilst she pored over the cards a fat louse appeared on her neckerchief intent on a journey too. Politely, I removed it without disturbing her at her deliberations and brought its journey to an end with the precision of long practice.

I did not leave that night and I lay between Tamara and Alexandra unable to sleep, wondering what the fates held in store for me now. The next day I learnt that, apart from me, an Uzbek officer was to be taken to the reception centre as well. We had not seen each other before, but a common fate made us talkative. He was serving a sentence of fifteen years, of which he had so far served only two years. We stood there waiting for the lorry to take us away and chatted like old friends, whilst the sun shone down on the glistening snow and the air was crisp and invigorating. Once or twice whilst we were waiting, Grete Sonntag passed by and waved to me. Her face was downcast. It seemed to depress her terribly that I was going away from the camp – she was convinced I was going out into freedom – whilst she had to remain behind. They did not come to fetch us until the evening, and then all my comrades from the hut accompanied us down to the gates and a chorus of good wishes followed us as we plodded through the snow with our bundles. In the corridor of the main office we sat down on our bundles to wait. Three old men were already there. They were to be transferred to an invalid sector. We were kept waiting for hours and at about ten o'clock the door opened and Stefanie Brun came into the corridor.

'Grete,' she whispered anxiously, 'I had to come and say goodbye to you.'

'Steffie!' I exclaimed in horror. 'You don't mean that you've gone out of the hut after dark!'

The tears came to my eyes as we embraced. 'Go back quickly now or you'll be caught.'

'Goodbye,' she whispered; 'and don't forget me.'

'Don't forget me!' Always the same refrain.

BETWEEN FEAR AND HOPE

Back To The Collection Point

At eleven o'clock our names were called and who should turn out to be our escort but the smiling, friendly Kazak soldier who had ridden into Sharik for us. My spirits rose at once at the sight of him. His face was pink and shining with the cold and his eyes danced merrily. There was no lorry for us, but a low Siberian sledge drawn by two ponies. The five of us lay down in it and the Kazak guard squatted with his rifle at the end. Then the driver whipped up his ponies and away we went. It was a beautiful night, cold but dry, and there were myriads of stars above us and from time to time one would shoot across the sky like a comet. The ponies went at a good pace, galloping along, their bells jangling merrily in the still night. We arrived at the railway station at Sharik with freezing faces, cold hands and feet, and we were very glad to be able to get out and stamp around to restore the circulation.

'Can we go to the station buffet and get tea and bread?' I asked.

'Why not?' said our Kazak, and off we ran. In the buffet we bought bread and real hot tea and sat on the floor drinking it. The Uzbek officer was a young man, and he began to tell me about his life. He had married at the age of fourteen and he now had two children. He did not doubt that he was going to be released. As he sat there in the badly lighted buffet he looked like a Persian prince with his olive-coloured skin and his almond-shaped brown eyes. He wore a white scarf round his neck and the contrast to his olive skin suited him well. He was a handsome lad. Otherwise he was not dressed in the least like a prince. It appeared that he had given almost everything he possessed to his fellow prisoners who had to stay behind, even his high boots, and his feet were now bound up in rags.

Our train did not leave until the morning, so we spent the night on the floor of the buffet. I had a fur jacket and a blanket, and, using our bundles as pillows, we settled down for the night under my blanket, lying on the jacket. That was warmer for both of us and a perfectly natural and normal thing to do.

We slept well, but we were cold and stiff when we woke. We climbed into the train. Neither of us spoke. The happy expectation of the day before had gone and we were just tired, hungry and ragged prisoners on another stage of an interminable journey.

When we arrived at the Karaganda reception centre, we found that nothing had changed. In the women's block I was the centre of a great deal of attention. For one thing, I was German, and for another I was an old hand, and almost all the women here were newcomers, in the camp for the first time. I learnt that there was another German there, and they took me to her. A pale-faced woman with dark rings under her eyes lay apathetically on the boards in an upper bunk. I didn't recognise her, and was surprised when at the sight of me she showed signs of animation and welcomed me by name:

'Grete! What are you doing here?'

It was some time before I realised who she was – Klara Vater, the wife of well-known German Communist Kreuzberg. We had met on a number of occasions in Moscow, but then she had been a healthy, happy woman. Her appearance had changed terribly. Thanks to the good food I had had in the last few weeks in the camp, I was probably looking very much better – easily recognisable, obviously. She had been two years in prison on remand and it had ruined her health and her looks. She had been in the clearing centre now for several weeks, waiting for transport into one of the sectors. Other women had come with her, but they had all been sent on. She had been separated from the rest and was still here. Two days before my arrival a Russian woman who had already served three and a half years in the camp had been sent back to the clearing centre in the same way as I had. She was the wife of the German composer, Fon, and therefore a German national. Frau Fon and Klara Vater were called out together, and obviously their fate, whatever it was, was going to be the same. They both made me welcome, and we slept huddled up together for warmth.

Frau Fon came from a sector of the camp I had never heard of. She had been suddenly taken away before the end of her sentence just as I had. Comparing notes, not only with her, but with many others, I can only conclude that the Karaganda complex was vast in extent. Frau Fon told us that in the few weeks before she had left her sector her life had been a little easier. It had not done much to improve her appearance though; she was still painfully thin and looked about forty. Her eyes were like those of a beaten dog. She was not at all happy about the future:

'Why didn't they leave me where I was?' she would ask hopelessly. 'I was just getting on all right. It's so difficult to settle down in new places again.'

I had given up wondering what Fate held in store for me now, and I was resigned to waiting. In the meantime, I enjoyed the unaccustomed freedom of the clearing centre and strolled around on a tour of inspection. Nothing had changed except that there was a lot more barbed wire than before, and a special arrest block for prisoners who had offended against the regulations and now awaited their transport to Dolinki for sentence. Around this block there was a space enclosed with barbed wire in which they exercised.

One face I saw was familiar to me, and its owner greeted me by name. It was the young Ukrainian who had been so homesick that she had made an attempt to escape. They had caught her and now she was on her way back from Dolinki, where she had received a further two and a half years on her sentence, with *pod konvoi*. I went over to the men's hut to see if I could find out anything about the young Uzbek officer. On the other side of the barbed wire were a number of pale-faced, unshaven men. They came up, and when I spoke they obviously recognised my accent as German.

'Are you a German?' one of them asked. I nodded. 'Do you know Comrade Schubert, by any chance?'

'Yes; quite well. We were in the Butirka together. He was arrested in July 1937.'

I asked them about various people. The well-known German Communist leader, Hermann Remmele, had lost his reason, they said. He was always coming to blows both with the guards and his fellow prisoners. The man who had first spoken to me had received a fifteen-year sentence. 'An amnesty,' he said. 'That's the only hope. No one survives fifteen years.' From someone who came out of the hut I learnt that my Uzbek officer had already been sent on to Dolinki.

There was an old man there the Ukrainian girl knew. He was on his way to Dolinki to get his sentence. It appeared that he had been a shepherd and some of his sheep had died. 'He'll be lucky if he only gets two years,' she said.

At midday a miserable *balanda* of soya beans – and not too many of them – was ladled out in the open, despite the great cold. What did I want with *balanda* when I had bread and fish? My two comrades and I organised *kipiatok*, made ourselves some tea and had a wonderful meal of black bread and salt fish. Frau Fon had a small sack of millet her fellow prisoners had given her on the way. That, too, went into the common store. 'If only they'd left me there,' she sighed again.

In the afternoon the three of us were called out together, so apparently whatever their fate was to be I was to share it. We were taken to the photo and fingerprint department and went through the whole procedure all over again. We were annoyed about the fingerprinting – it was the whole of both hands – because they just turned you loose with the black ink over your hands and no means of getting it off properly. However, we were quite certain now. We were leaving Camp Karaganda. That was the usual farewell ceremony. Our conclusion was confirmed a little later when we were called one by one to the *natchalnik*. He had a large sheet of paper before him with various questions on it. First the usual litany. Then:

'Has your health suffered in any way during your stay in the reformatory labour camp?'

That was an easy one: 'Good heavens, no,' I ejaculated in mock surprise. 'What a question!'

He gave me an old-fashioned look but made no comment.

'What kind of work did you perform whilst in the camp?'

I gave him a description of all my various occupations.

'Have you any complaints to make about your treatment in the camp?'

'No,' I said firmly. What had happened to me before was quite enough. I knew better than to complain now.

'Sign here, then,' he said.

I signed. 'When am I to be released?' I asked.

'As to that I can give you no information,' he replied.

I went out into the corridor and waited for the other two. I was interested in my fate again now. Obviously we were leaving Karaganda, but was it to go to another camp? And would they make so much fuss if that were all? Was there any connection between it and the arrangement with the Germans? Were all Germans now to be gathered into a special camp, perhaps? And if so, why?

There were a lot of prisoners waiting in the corridor to see the *natchalnik*. They were the newcomers who had not yet lost faith in the efficacy of petitions and complaints, and did not yet know what happened to prisoners who dared to file the one or make the other. There were two youngsters waiting together, about fifteen or sixteen years old. They did not look like *bezprizorni*. 'Are you newcomers?' I asked. They nodded. 'What do you want to see the *natchalnik* for?'

'To see if we can find out what happened to our father.'

'Were you arrested as members of the family?'

'Yes; we were all arrested together.'

'How long have you got?'

'Three years each.'

Back in the hut the news had spread that the three Germans were going on transport, and our case was discussed with interest. Some were sure we were going to be released, but there are always one or two people who know everything, the 'experts'; they said releases were always made from Dolinki, therefore it was unlikely that we were going to be released. However, they were prepared to admit that perhaps it would be different with foreigners.

'Did you have to sign an undertaking not to say a word to anyone about what you saw in the camp?' one of them asked.

'No; we didn't.'

'That settles it: you're not going to be released then.'

A little later a woman I didn't know came up to me and asked me to take a turn round the block with her; she wanted to talk to me. I did so and she told me that she was a *zhenia*, or a prisoner who had been arrested merely as the wife of her husband. She had been held in Akmolensk for a while and now she was waiting here for transport further on.

'I wanted to ask you if you'd do something for me,' she said. 'I know it's a lot. You see, I left a daughter behind in Moscow. She doesn't know what's happened to me. Would you take a letter for her? You might get a chance to slip it through. Try for me, will you? It means such a lot to me and her.'

I agreed to try and she gave me a letter, which I tucked away in my brassière. It was a risk, but what did anything matter?

At about five in the afternoon our names were called and a woman member of the GPU in uniform came into the hut. I had never seen one in Karaganda before. She was fresh and young, perhaps twenty, and her face was agreeable.

'Get ready. With things,' she said, and her tone was very different from the one we had gradually become used to.

We were ready very quickly, and we followed her out whilst the others looked after us enviously. Whether it was certain or not, they strongly suspected that we were going to be released. We walked across the camp compound with our bundles and at the guardroom we were stopped.

'Come inside. Search,' said the girl. My heart sank. How could I get rid of the letter? We went inside and opened our bundles. Two soldiers rummaged about in them. Perhaps they would not search us bodily? But when the two soldiers had finished they went out.

'Undress,' said the girl.

We undressed, and surreptitiously I took the letter and put it on the floor and placed one foot over it. Fortunately, she was not very experienced in the wiles of prisoners and after a fairly cursory search we were allowed to dress again. I found little difficulty in putting the letter back into my brassière. Then we took our bundles and made our way towards the main gates.

Taking Leave of Karaganda

We passed through the gates and found ourselves outside the reformatory labour camp, Karaganda. Two soldiers were waiting for us, as escort. They took us to the Karaganda railway station; not to the goods depot where prisoners usually go, but to the waiting room. It was a properly built house, not a hut or a wooden shed. On the wall were timetables. So this was freedom. There were very few people at the station. Apart from us, there was only one other passenger in the waiting room, a man. We put down our bundles in a corner. 'It looks as though we're going to travel in a real passenger train,' I whispered to Klara. 'Shall I ask the GPU girl?' Klara nodded, and I went up to the girl who was standing with our escort.

'Can I ask where we are going?' I said.

'Of course you may. You're going to Moscow with the six o'clock train.'

Moscow! Moscow! And she said it as though it was nothing at all; just part of a routine. But for us it meant leaving, not only Karaganda behind, but Siberia. Back to Europe! I almost jumped for joy and hurried back to Klara and Frau Fon. 'We're going to Moscow,' I burst out. 'Just think of it! Moscow!'

It was not long before the train drew in. One of the soldiers came up to us. He was apparently the senior.

'You are not to get into conversation with other passengers in the compartment,' he said, 'and you're not to answer any questions they may ask you. The best thing is to pretend you don't understand Russian.'

We followed the soldiers out on to the platform and trotted after them down the length of the train until they found the compartment they were looking for. We got in. It was an empty carriage with full-length places reserved for us. Each of us stowed her bundle away and then lay down. This time I was excited. I wanted to sing, laugh, whistle, do anything to express my feelings. The train was clean and well-heated. We had not been so comfortably installed for a very long time. When it finally moved out, even Frau Fon began to smile.

Our escort occupied the compartment next to ours and it was not immediately visible that we were their prisoners. Travellers passing down the corridor looked in at us curiously. Now, people in padded jackets and rags carrying bundles are nothing unusual in the Soviet Union, but we were certainly a bit out of the ordinary. We had rubber boots much too big for us, our legs were wrapped in rags to keep out the cold, and we wore padded jackets and the typical camp caps with ear warmers. And in all probability our faces betrayed us. The camp creates a physiognomy all its own and we had been there quite long enough to develop it. One friendly woman paused at the door of our compartment.

'Where are you bound for?' she asked.

We made no answer. She repeated her question and again we said nothing, and then a look of fear came over her face. She had understood. She nodded in a friendly fashion and went away at once. We looked at each other and laughed. At about midday the next day the train stopped in what was apparently a fair-sized town. The GPU girl came into our compartment.

'What would you like to eat?' she asked.

What should we like to eat? It was a long time since any of us had heard that question. We looked at each other. 'We've still got some bread and fish left,' I said hesitantly. The question embarrassed us. The girl smiled, said nothing more and went out, leaving us wondering. After a while, she came back with white bread and three tins, one for each of us.

'Here are two-pound tins of canned pork,' she said. 'With that and the bread, you ought to be all right for a while.'

We thanked her as though in a dream. White bread and canned pork! What had happened that they began to treat us like this. We borrowed a tin-opener from the guard and set to work. We had neither knives nor forks, but we managed quite well with our fingers and made a good meal. Later on the other two had stomach-ache. They were not used to that sort of thing. Thanks to Grete Sonntag, I had eaten meat for the past few weeks before I left Birma. But better still was to come: at another station where the train stopped we were actually taken out of our compartment into the station restaurant and given a proper hot meal.

The landscape through which we passed began to change. We saw the first clumps of trees and welcomed them like long-lost friends. The steppes, Asia, Siberia – they were all behind us. Then we passed through a chain of mountains with snow-loaded fir trees. That was the Urals. On the other side was Europe.

Our escort hardly spoke to us at all, but kept to their own compartment, smoking and playing game after game of dominoes. The warmth in our compartment seemed to make our lice more lively, and sitting with our backs to the door we organised a great hunt, killing them by the score. I was sorry for the passengers who occupied this compartment after us.

At every station I looked for an opportunity to get rid of the letter I still had in my brassière, but our young guard kept her eyes open and walked behind us if we left the carriage, so I found no chance of passing it on. When the train stopped in Kazan, I asked her to let me go to the toilet to wash. Fortunately, at that moment there was a group of circus people who attracted her attention and I managed to close the door behind me. Carefully, I opened the window and looked out. A man in

working clothes was approaching. I threw the letter out at his feet. It
was the best I could do. I saw him bend down and pick it up and then
I closed the window. When I went back to our compartment, I looked
out of the window. The man was nowhere to be seen.

The coming and going in general was of tremendous interest to us.
Here were free people, men, women and children, standing, walking,
running – doing just whatever they wanted to do. I realised how long
it was since I had seen a child. At the sight of the children, Klara began
to talk sadly about her little daughter. Two years old, and both father
and mother arrested on the same day, and not a relative in the country
to look after her. 'I wonder what they've done with her,' she said fearfully. The news she had of her husband was not heartening. He had
been so ill-treated during the preliminary examination because he refused
to say what they wanted him to say that several of his ribs had been
broken. And Frau Fon was down in the dumps again: 'We've got nothing
good to look forward to,' she said dolefully. 'What the GPU once gets
its claws into isn't let go in a hurry.'

'I don't call this in a hurry, anyhow,' I said obstinately.

Gradually, we approached Moscow. Our bundles were ready. All we
had to do was to pick them up and get out. We breathed on the window
panes and rubbed the ice away so that we could look out. In a very
short space of time now our fate would be decided. At last the train
slowed down; slower and slower; and then it came to a halt. Our escort
appeared and we got out. We walked along the platform with them,
carrying our bundles, and all the busy life of a big railway station went
on around us. Moscow! At least Moscow. It had to be the first stage,
whatever befell. I was so happy I felt as though I were walking on air.

They took us into the waiting room and we sat down amongst the
ordinary public. The place was overheated and our faces glowed. On the
wall was a loudspeaker, and a plummy tenor sang a patriotic song:
'Motherland, great Motherland; land of the free and the brave'. A discussion was going on between the GPU girl and the two soldiers; then they
went off and she came over to us.

'I've never been in Moscow before,' she said naïvely. 'Isn't it wonderful.
So many people and such a great place! Look, there's ice-cream over
there. Would you like some?'

There's always a *morozhnie* seller in Moscow, no matter what time of
the year it is. We readily agreed and she went over and bought four
portions. We ate it greedily. It was very good. The Muscovite ice-men
haven't got the technique of making frozen fluff like their confrères do in
the West; owing to their backwardness, they still have to make it in the
good old-fashioned way. And when we had finished, the brave lass bought

us *pirozhnie*, the famous Russian pancakes filled with cabbage, or seasoned rice or meat, and fried in deep fat. They were good, too, and we ate them gratefully. By this time we were all beginning to feel very happy.

Butirka Again

All Moscow railway stations are always full of people day and night, and many of them are not much better clad than we were. They come in from the villages in the hope of getting work in Moscow, and as they have nowhere to stay, they spend hours in the waiting rooms, where it is usually warm in winter. As long as we remained sitting on our bench, no one took much notice of us or thought us anything out of the ordinary, but when the two soldiers came back, as they did after about half an hour, and we had to get up and make our way to the door we became the centre of attention. Everyone realised what we were, and there were many curious and not a few sympathetic looks.

We went out into the station yard and my heart sank suddenly. There stood the Black Maria. I don't know quite what I expected; I hadn't thought about it. But after that pleasant journey it was a shock. And we had almost felt ourselves free.

Silently we climbed in. There was no one else inside and they didn't trouble to put us in the cells. We sat on a bench in the corridor in semi-darkness and once again the journey went through the streets of Moscow with all the noise of motors, buses, trams and carts. After a while it stopped and we got out. I recognised the courtyard at once. We were in the Butirka. Back to where the whole long train of misery had first started.

It was 1940, and air-raid preparations were already in swing in Moscow. In the corridors of the Butirka the lamps had been half obscured with blue paint and the atmosphere was ghostly. Human faces looked like the faces of corpses. Once again we passed through the *vogsal*, the hall where you enter when you first lose your freedom, and the hall you pass through on your way to five, ten, fifteen years in Siberia.

There was normal light in the reception room and we filled in the usual forms with the help of an official.

'Smoker or non-smoker?' he asked.

'What?' I ejaculated in surprise.

'Smoker or non-smoker?' he repeated.

I recovered my wits first. 'Oh, smokers,' I said. 'All three.'

He made the necessary note on each form. Things seemed to have changed. Since when did the GPU interest itself in our harmless vices?

After that we were taken to be washed and deloused, but not to the

ordinary common washroom I already knew so well. We were each put
into a separate bathroom. In addition to the bath, there was a wash-
basin with hot and cold water and the walls were tiled. It was all very
neat and clean. I stripped, and a woman attendant took away my lousy
clothes and gave me a bottle of disinfectant for my head. Then I proceeded
to enjoy myself. The hot water was unlimited and there was a large piece
of soap. At last the Siberian dirt of months was off and I was clean.
How often in Birma had I longed to be back in the Butirka again! And
here I was – and in a different, much better Butirka.

After a while the bath-attendant opened the door. No shouts of '*Davai!*
Davai!' No bullying. With a smile, she handed in a clean shirt and underwear. It was men's clothing, to be sure, but it was clean. Since when
did they issue clean clothing in the Butirka? How things had changed.

It was about ten o'clock when the three of us, clean and fresh, wearing
our own deloused clothes still warm from the delousing oven, walked
through the old familiar corridors behind a wardress banging on her belt
buckle with her iron key. That custom at least had not changed. Many
doors and gates were opened and closed behind us until at last, in the
same old corridor as in 1938, she opened a cell door and showed us in.
We could hardly believe our eyes.

Where over a hundred women had huddled together on *naris* were
now rows of properly made beds with white sheets neatly turned down
over white pillows. It was incredible.

The occupants of the cell came forward to greet us.

'Where do you come from?' one of them asked in broken Russian.

'Siberia,' we replied.

'Are you Germans?'

'Yes.'

'That makes us all Germans here, then. Who are you?'

We told them our names. The lamp in the cell was also half obscured
by the wretched blue paint and it was difficult to see properly until you
got used to it. Some of the women had been asleep. We soon recognised old friends and acquaintances. There was Roberta Gropper, Hilde
Löwen, Zensl Mühsam, Carola Neher, Valy Adler, Betty Olberg, and
others we had not met before. There were twenty-three of us, and we
had all been brought back to the Butirka from camps and prisons all
over Russia. We three were the first to come from a Siberian concentration camp.

'What on earth's happened here in the Butirka?' I asked in wonderment. 'Proper beds; proper bed linen; nobody bothers to speak in whispers; here you are all prancing around in the night and there's no one
to interfere; no one lets down the hatch and bellows. What's it all about?'

No one knew any more than I did. They were just happy that it was so, and left it at that. Zensl Mühsam was the Cell Senior and she gave us each a bed. We were dog-tired, but it was very late before I got to sleep. This was what I had dreamt of: a bed with a real mattress and proper bedclothes. And now I couldn't sleep in it. In the end I did, of course.

We were woken up at six o'clock instead of the usual half-past four, but there were no loud shouts of 'Women, get up' and no banging; no '*Davai!*' and no one urged us on to ever greater haste. We lay there in clean sheets. The cell was light and airy and its walls had been freshly whitewashed. And throughout the night not a bedbug, not a louse and not a flea had fed on us. All around the others were sitting up, stretching, yawning lazily. No one rushed around and searched desperately for the other shoe. One or two of them had turned over and gone to sleep again. Others were already up and about in their linen trousers. 'Good mornings' sounded from all sides when you sat up. This was civilisation. It was difficult to believe that only a week ago I had slept on bare boards, bone sore, weary and bitten all over, in a dirty clay hut in Siberia, fully convinced that I should never get out of it alive.

Gradually most of us got up and dressed. One or two who were not well, or who felt lazy, stayed on in bed. The wardress opened the cell and led us to the washroom, where we were left to our own devices for the best part of an hour. No one bothered us. Then we went back to the cell and a little while afterwards breakfast was served. I say deliberately: breakfast was served. It was handed in on separate clean enamel plates for each of us. There was both black and white bread, butter, two boiled eggs each and China tea.

Zensl Mühsam saw the look on my face. 'That shakes you, doesn't it?' she enquired. 'We must be important prisoners of State. You needn't pinch yourself; you're awake. But don't ask me what's happened.'

I forgot to say that there was a large table with a stool for each of us, and we sat round it eating our breakfast like a big, happy family. Naturally, the astounding treatment we were receiving and the possible reasons for it were a constant subject of discussion, but it was all speculation. No one knew anything definite.

'They're going to put us over the frontier into one or other of the Baltic States.'

'What? After all we've seen? Not likely.'

'Well, what then?'

And there we were again: we just didn't know. In the meantime we were well content to have escaped what lay behind us. It had been worse for some than for others, but it had been unenviable for all. And one way or another, we were now optimistic and hopeful. The good food and the good treatment saw to that.

During the day we did what we liked. Chattered, joked, laughed freely, played chess – this time there were real chessboards and real chessmen – and sewed. In the beginning someone had asked for a needle and cotton, and the wardress had immediately brought a work-basket with needles, reels of cotton, a pair of scissors and darning material. I don't think any cell in the Butirka ever held such a merry company.

Carola Neher was in prison garb. Compared with our camp rags, it was almost elegant, and the elegant Carola wore it with an air. It consisted of a blue flannel blouse with red lapels, a dark blue skirt and a short jacket. As she had been doing a hard labour term, her lovely hair had been shaven off, but it was just long enough again now to stay down.

At midday dinner was served. There was very little variety about it, they said, but it was very good always. First of all there was a good *borshch* with a slice of meat in it and a piece of bread. Then there was *goulash* with mashed potatoes, followed by either *kissel* or stewed apples.

We had plenty of time to exchange our stories. Carola had been longest in prison, having been arrested in the autumn of 1936. She had been a top-line star in Germany and tremendously popular with her public. However, she had always been anti-Nazi, had worked with Bert Brecht and when the Nazis came to power in 1933 she had, like so many others, gone first to Prague. In Prague she had met and married a German engineer from Romania. He was a Communist and burning to go to the Soviet Union and help in the building up of Socialism. As soon as things could be arranged, they had left for Moscow, where Carola had begun to work in films and on the wireless.

She and Zensl Mühsam were mixed up in the same 'case'. They both came from Munich, and whilst they were in Prague they had met an old Munich acquaintance, Erich Wollenberg, who had held a high command in the Red Army, but who by that time had broken with the Soviet Union and the Communist Party. Neither Carola nor Zensl belonged to the Party, so they were not subject to the Party discipline, which would have prevented their associating with Wollenberg. Wollenberg gave Carola the address of a friend of his in Moscow, and Carola got in touch with the man when she arrived. That and her association with Wollenberg was the cause of her arrest. The GPU indictment turned her into a secret courier of the 'Trotskyite' Wollenberg, and she had been sentenced to ten years' hard labour. During the period she spent on remand in the Lubianka, she had attempted to take her life by slashing her wrists with a piece of metal she had got hold of. Her husband had also been arrested; why she did not know. But her greatest sorrow was that she had never been allowed to see her little son again. He was a year old at the time of her arrest.

Carola showed me a photo of him and a letter from the woman in charge of the children's home in Kazan where he was being kept. It showed a sturdy little fellow quite naked and hugging a teddy bear. The letter was charming and Carola would read it again and again. It described the child's character and his ways, and said he was very intelligent and lovable. It was the letter of a woman with a heart and it greatly consoled Carola. She described the long and wearisome struggle she had had with the prison authorities before she had succeeded in finding out anything about him and getting permission to receive this letter and photo.

The only trouble in our cell was the children. Quite a number of our cell mates had left young children behind, and many of them were not so fortunate as Carola, who at least knew where her little son was. Hilde Löwen had a three-year-old daughter of whose fate and whereabouts she was totally ignorant; and it was the same with Klara Vater.

Zensl Mühsam had the darkest forebodings. 'Who knows what the GPU has in mind with us. It's quite possible they intend to make some sort of a bargain with Hitler and hand us all over. I'll throw myself under the train first. I won't let them take me back to Nazi Germany alive.'

Zensl's husband, the famous anarchist, Erich Mühsam, was murdered by the Nazis in Oranienburg concentration camp in 1934. He was slowly tortured to death. Zensl had left Germany the same year to lecture abroad about the horrors of Nazi concentration camps and prisons. She had made it her mission to tell the world the truth about National Socialism it was so unwilling to hear. In Prague she had worked together with the Communist Red Aid, which had assisted her to get her material published. The leader of the International Red Aid, Stassova, then invited her to go to Moscow. Zensl, who had joined the Communist Party, had not been spoiled by it. She was an upright character who spoke her own mind once she had made it up. She lived in Moscow as Stassova's guest and had a room in the Hotel Novaya Moskaya. She had not been in Moscow long before many things became clear to her, and then she did not hesitate to criticise openly. The end, of course, was inevitable. From being an honoured guest, she became a prisoner. Before the examining magistrate, she found herself faced with the same indictment as Carola: allegedly she was a secret courier of the 'Trotskyite' Wollenberg. Then after a few months in prison she was suddenly released. The news of her arrest and imprisonment had become known abroad and caused a disagreeable amount of publicity and a great number of protests.

Zensl was even allowed to return to her room in the Novaya Moskaya. By this time she had only one thought: how to get out. She wrote to her sister in the United States, and they succeeded in getting an entrance permit for her. Whilst she was still waiting for a Russian permit to leave, the GPU arrested her a second time. They were more expeditious on this occasion, and within a week or so she had been sentenced by a Special Commission to eight years' forced labour in a camp. She was sent to a camp in European Russia, where, according to her account, conditions must have been better than in Karaganda. The women were chiefly engaged in sewing.

Zensl was about sixty, but she was slim and upright and she moved like a young woman. Her grey hair was worn in a neat plait round her head. Her spirit was completely unaffected by her experiences and she never complained about her fate. Her calm bearing was an example and a strength to us all. Her husband still played a tremendous part in her life, and his name was constantly on her lips: 'Even then Erich said . . .' 'If Erich were still alive . . .' And she told us calmly of his sufferings in Oranienburg and of her constant attempts to secure his release which had ended only on the day they had led her in to see his dead body.

Roberta Gropper, a former Communist Member of the German Reichstag, was another one I knew from Germany. She had been in prison awaiting sentence – there were no trials – for two years. She had never been sentenced and now she was here with us waiting for what came next. The charge against her was that she had belonged to 'the Neumann group'. Her face had that deadly pallor which a long time spent in prison gives, and there were deep rings under her eyes. She tortured herself trying to arrive at some satisfactory explanation for all that had happened, including her own fate. One day she asked me whether, if I got free, I would make public everything I knew about the Soviet Union, and when I said I certainly should because we had kept silent too long and to keep silent any longer meant connivance with the GPU terror, she was shocked.

'You shouldn't do that,' she said anxiously. 'If you deprive them of their illusions, you rob them of their last hope.'

'I don't agree,' I said. 'Illusions of that sort are dangerous.'

After a while the machine began to work. Three women from our cell were called away with their things and never returned. A few days later three others went, and again we knew nothing of their fate. Then two newcomers joined us. They were from a concentration camp in Central Siberia. One of them was a Jewess named Fischmann, and the other was a German girl who had worked as a typist in the Comintern headquarters. When I listened to them, I was astounded at how quickly I had discarded concentration camp habits and the camp outlook. Karaganda seemed years ago. They told us that on their way back they had travelled for days on a sledge together with two Germans: Hugo Eberlein, who was suffering from asthma, and a younger man who had an unhealed wound in his leg. They also said they had met Käthe Schulz in Kotlas on her way to a concentration camp in Eastern Siberia. Later I heard a report that Eberlein had died.

In the meantime, the life of those who were left went on in the same pleasant lines. We received books from the prison library, could buy things freely from the prison canteen and we had an hour's exercise each day. One of us, a fresh-air fanatic who had stayed out too long in the yard, got frostbite in both cheeks. It was a hard winter. The glass of our windows was frozen over, and every morning there were icicles on the *pfortutchka*, the little window which could still be opened in severe weather. The wardresses undoubtedly had special instructions for dealing with us for we never heard the word *Davai!* or the word *schtraf* (punishment), and when we exercised we could look around us to our hearts' content; no more: 'Hands behind your back!' 'Eyes down!'

After about a week of this wonderful life most of us had a touch of gastric trouble. We had probably eaten too much and the food was too rich compared with what we had been accustomed to. Zensl, as Cell Senior, asked the wardress for some medicine. Instead of that, a white-robed doctor appeared, flanked by two nurses. We were all put to bed and examined with great thoroughness. Then we were told to stay in bed for a day or two on medicine and diet. The doctor visited us three times a day for several days until he finally pronounced us fit and well again. We lay in bed and laughed and joked. In Siberia a woman could have bloody diarrhœa for weeks and not a soul bothered his head about her, but here when we had a slight gastric indisposition of no consequence all the resources of medical science were mobilised to cure us. Why had our lives and well-being suddenly become so valuable to the GPU?

What Will Become of Us?

There were one or two women in our cell who recovered from their experiences only very slowly. The worst was perhaps Betty Olberg, who weighed only about seventy pounds. Valy Adler was also very pale and still weak. She had been very roughly handled during the examinations. According to the indictment, her parents had been associated with Trotsky abroad, and through them she was supposed to be in touch with him. That was a very serious matter and they exerted a great deal of pressure on her to make her 'confess'.

Once on our way to the washroom we saw a number of clean enamel plates and dishes outside a cell door. So there were other magic cells in the Butirka, and other privileged prisoners in them? We discussed the matter excitedly in the washroom and arranged that when we passed the cell on our way back we would scuffle with our feet and shout out something in German. Let the wardress make a report if she liked.

The stratagem worked perfectly. The wardress did her best to keep us quiet and hurry us on, but a voice had shouted to us from the other side of the cell door in German. They were perhaps the women they had taken out of our cell. But why? What had happened to them in the meantime? Why weren't they sent back to us? There was plenty of room in our cell. We arranged that the next ones who were taken away should leave us a message in the washroom. We found a suitable place in a corner where, we discovered, we could write on the wall in soap. The very next day three more were taken away, including Carola. The day after that, when we went to the washroom, we looked anxiously for a message. There was none. Had the wardress seen it perhaps and wiped it away?

We had to contain our curiosity as best we could, and indeed, our life had many distractions. The only non-German amongst us was Frau Fekete, a Hungarian. She was a hairdresser and beauty expert by profession, and she gave us the benefit of all her arts. She washed our hair, cut it, set it, massaged our faces and generally transformed our appearance. Old, long-forgotten female vanities came to life again, as we prepared ourselves for freedom. One of our fellow prisoners had been a teacher of gymnastics and she began exercises with those of us who were interested. I remember Carola, who, like most of us, was beginning to put on weight, looking over her shoulder at her haunches and sighing: 'A woman with a fat bottom can never be a convincing tragédienne.'

About ten days after Carola had been taken out with two others, Betty Olberg, Klara and I had to go. We were all in much better spirits, and this parting was not so sad as the others had been. We all felt fairly confident that we should see each other in freedom again.

'Don't forget,' said Zensl. 'If you really do get out of this country, get into touch with the chemist de Witt in Eindhuizen and let him know all about me.'

I promised and then we went out with the wardress. We were taken into another wing of the prison and then each shut up in a separate rabbit-hutch, the almost forgotten *sobatchnik*. After our recent treatment, this seemed an unnecessary indignity and it irritated me. However, perhaps we were getting overconfident. I was not kept in this confined space for long, and a soldier then took me off to a door before which I had to deposit my bundle. In the room two GPU officers were sitting at a table, and they invited me in a friendly tone to take a seat. I did so.

'How is your health? Do you feel quite well? Have you made a good recovery?'

Apparently, despite the *sobatchnik*, there was to be no relapse. Their attitude was comforting. They ran through the papers on the desk before them.

'Have you relatives abroad?' one asked.

'Yes,' I replied eagerly. This was it, then. 'I have a sister in Paris and I have permission to go to France from the French Consulate . . .'

He interrupted me: 'No; I mean in Germany.'

That was a shock. 'What is to happen to me?' I blurted out. 'Where are you going to send me?'

'I am not allowed to give you any information on that score,' he replied. 'You will learn in good time. That's all.'

My escort was already behind me, and I got up and went out, my head in a whirl and my heart in my boots. I quite forgot my bundle and the soldier picked it up and carried it. I was locked up again in the *sobatchnik* and tried to sort out my impressions. What were they going to do with me? It looked very much as though . . . It hardly bore thinking about. After about ten minutes I was taken out of the *sobatchnik* and led off with the other two to the cell before which we had seen the clean enamel plates. The door was unlocked and we went in. The cell had only one occupant. It was Carola. She was delighted to see us, but then she began to sob. Gradually we discovered what had happened. She had already been before the same commission and they had asked her more or less the same questions, but then suddenly one of the officers had said:

'Would you like to work for us? For the NKVD, I mean.'

At first Carola had hardly been able to believe her ears. She had been sentenced to ten years' hard labour as a 'Trotskyite' courier and had already served three years, and now they were suggesting that she should spy for the GPU! She refused in great excitement. Become a Russian spy? Never.

'Calm yourself, Citizen Neher,' the officer had replied. 'Calm yourself. We'll give you time to think it over. Perhaps that will make a difference.'

She had then been taken to a part of the Butirka she had never been in before and placed in a single cell. The central heating had been cut off; there was no bed, not even a mattress and no blanket. There she had stayed for three days without food. On the fourth day the heating was turned on and they gave her a mattress, a pillow and blankets and meals. This went on for a number of days and then she was taken before the two GPU officials again, and the same question was asked. Again she had refused: 'I should be no use at all for that sort of work.'

She had then been placed in the cell we were now in. We were shocked at her story. We certainly had been overconfident ever to forget that we were still in the hands of the GPU.

Carola sat on the edge of her bed despondently.

'It's all up with me,' she said. 'Now I've refused to spy for them, they'll never let me go. And they certainly won't let me get out of the country.'

We tried to console her. 'But why not, Carola? After all, I don't suppose they want anybody who's unwilling. They just tried it, and now they've seen it didn't work they've put you back with us. That looks as though we're all going to be treated the same way, doesn't it? Otherwise they'd have left you in solitary.'

Gradually Carola calmed down. Our life went on as before. There was *goulash* with mashed potatoes for midday and noodles with meat in the evening. When we went out to the washroom I remembered our arrangement. 'We must leave a message. What shall we say?'

We took a piece of soap. Finally, I wrote the following whilst the others listened at the door for the wardress:

'Been before commission. Were asked about relatives in Germany. No reply to question: what is to happen to us? Carola with us. All well. Reply.'

The next day when we were taken to the washroom we hurried over to the corner as soon as the wardress had gone, and there was our answer:

'Thanks. Know anything about the future? Where was Carola? Regards.'

We answered the questions as well as we could, and then filled up the rest of the space with odds and ends, just like you do on a postcard when there's still some space left. The next day the answer was always waiting for us.

Carola was our Cell Senior. One morning the door of the cell opened and there stood the *korpusnoi*, whom we seldom saw.

'Cell Senior, forward,' he said, and his voice was stern. Carola went forward. 'Your cell has constantly written up messages in German on the wall of the washroom,' he said. 'That means severe punishment.'

Carola had on her best air of innocence. 'But that's quite impossible,' she said amiably. 'There must be some mistake, I'm sure.'

'Be quiet,' he ordered. 'There's no mistake. We know perfectly well you did it.'

The cell door closed with a bang. We looked at each other. What would happen now?

'Forbidden messages mean solitary at least,' said Carola. 'They needn't even bother to find out who actually wrote it; all four of us will get it.'

'So what?' I said. 'They've got their reasons for treating us as they've been doing, and they won't change just on that account.'

I was right. The day passed and the next day and the day after that, and nothing happened – at least nothing happened in connection with our offence, but something else happened, something extraordinary. We were taken out of our cell and led to a room equipped as a hairdresser's, with washbasins and mirrors, and there we sat and had our hair trimmed, washed and set.

When we were back in our cell we discussed the implications. We came to the conclusion that our release must be very near now; they would not attend to our hair and make us look as decent as possible in order to send us to Siberia again. Even Carola was convinced, and our spirits rose. A great deal of our time was spent wrapped up in blankets playing chess. The cell was heated, but obviously the temperature reckoned with supplementary heat from a full complement of prisoners, and the four of us were not enough to keep it up to a comfortable level. However, it was not bad enough to cause us any great inconvenience.

Another pleasant surprise was in store for us. One day we were taken out of our cell into a room full of women's clothing of all sorts, and there we were equipped with clothing, shoes, hats, coats, gloves. The things were second-hand and rather old-fashioned, but they were far better than anything we possessed. In addition, they were another proof, almost indisputable, that we were a step nearer to freedom.

At this time I became very good friends with Carola. I had often seen her on the stage, as Haitang in the *Chalk Circle* of Klabund and later in Brecht and Weil's version of *The Beggar's Opera*, but I had not known her personally. She seemed to me even more beautiful now than then. She had recovered her confidence sufficiently to think of plans for the future.

Journey into Uncertainty

This went on for about twelve days, and then one morning the cell hatch opened. 'Klara Vater, Betty Olberg and Buber-Nejman: get ready. With things.' The hatch slammed to. We stood there motionless. Carola's name was not included. No one could find a word to say. Carola walked over to her bed and sat down. Mechanically, we collected our things. The cell door opened and the wardress appeared.

'Come along,' she said. 'Don't hang around. There's no time to lose.'

We embraced Carola. She put her arms round me and hugged me tight. 'Good luck,' she sobbed. 'Goodbye and good luck.'

I never saw her again and I have never been able to find out what happened to her.

This time we were taken direct to the office of the Governor and were not first put into the *sobatchnik*. I went inside first whilst the other two waited outside in the corridor. There were five GPU officials at a long table. One of them handed me a paper: 'Can you read Russian?' he asked. I nodded and took it from him. It was a printed form, but in one place had been typed: 'The sentence of five years' reformatory labour passed on Margarita Genrichovna Buber-Nejman is commuted into immediate expulsion from the territory of the Soviet Union.'

'Sign it,' he said and handed me a pen.

'Where am I being sent to?' I asked.

'I can give you no information about that,' he said. 'Sign it. You'll find out that in good time.'

Whilst I still hesitated about signing anything at all in this country, Klara was led in. She couldn't speak or read Russian, and so I had to translate it for her. The text was in essence the same as on my form. 'Sign it,' said the official. Suddenly everyone seemed in a great hurry.

'I won't sign it until you give me back my child,' declared Klara. Her voice trembled, but her face showed desperate determination. 'Give me back my child and then I'll go at once.'

I translated what she said. The official was furious. 'Sign it,' he insisted. 'We've got no time for that now. Your child will be sent after you. Sign it now, quickly.'

'I won't. I won't,' she said desperately. 'Not without my child. I won't go.'

The officials looked at each other doubtfully.

'Very well, then,' the one said finally. 'Write an application at once.'

They put us both in a cell and gave us paper and ink and I wrote the application in Russian: 'I, Klara Vater, etc., am prepared to leave the territory of the Soviet Union as soon as my child . . . who was taken away from me on the day of my arrest in Samara, etc.' And she signed it.

Klara remained behind in the cell. I learnt after the war that Klara Vater and Roberta Gropper (alias Langer) returned to East Berlin. Betty Olberg and I were hurried along the corridors and through the *vogsal* out to the prison gates, where a Black Maria was waiting. We climbed in and were immediately locked in two cells. There were other prisoners in the wagon and we heard men's voices. 'Who are you?' someone called out. 'German?'

We told them our names and they immediately began to ask about this, that and the other woman; their wives, apparently, but we could tell them nothing. The Black Maria had started up immediately we got inside, and once again we heard the sounds of Moscow's traffic. After a while it stopped and Betty Olberg and I got out first and were taken through a goods yard to where an ordinary prison coach of the Stolypin type stood on the rails. I recognised the White Russian Station in the distance. It was from here that the trains went to Poland and the West. Betty had difficulty in keeping up. 'They're sending us to Germany,' I whispered. 'You can go nowhere else from this station.'

We clambered into the prison coach. As we went along the corridor, I saw that there were already many prisoners in the compartments. They seemed to be all men. Indistinguishable faces were pressed against the bars as we passed. Was Heinz there? My heart beat high with hope. He might be! We were taken down to the last compartment and locked in together. There was a confusion of voices as the men asked for information, chiefly about their wives. 'Has anyone of you seen Heinz Neumann or heard anything about him?' I called. Not one of them had seen him, or knew where he was, or what had happened to him.

There were a number of uniformed GPU officials and one woman in the corridor, but they made no attempt to interfere with us or to prevent our shouting from compartment to compartment. Gradually the talk ceased. We had not been able to give them any information about their wives, and they knew nothing about Heinz. There was nothing Betty wanted to find out. Her husband had been sentenced to death and executed in the first big Moscow trial in 1936, and she had been sentenced to hard labour. She was very ailing, and she had not made a good recovery even during our pleasant weeks in the Butirka. She lay on the bunk and breathed heavily from the excitement and exertion of the past few hours. Her hair had been shaven off in prison and it had not grown sufficiently in the Butirka to lie down. It was thick, wiry hair and it stood out from her head like a golliwog's. Her face was grey and her eyes sunken. In prison she had made an attempt to commit suicide by throwing herself over some banisters. Betty was Jewish and had worked until 1933 as a kindergarten teacher in Berlin.

After a while our coach was shunted on to the end of a train. There was no window in our compartment, but we could see a little of the outside world through a barred window on the other side of the corridor. Our journey started. It was a fast train apparently and it stopped at very few stations. The rattling made it impossible to talk from compartment to compartment and the only chance was at stops or when we went to the lavatory.

There were seven men in each of the other compartments. Only one face was familiar to me. It was Bloch, a Jewish-Hungarian emigrant who had been Chief Editor of the Communist daily, *Ruhr Echo*. He seemed to have forgotten me. We could only spend a minute or two at the bars talking to them. I found it strange that they all seemed so certain that we were not being handed over to the Nazis. According to them, we would change trains at Minsk and then go north to be put over the Lithuanian frontier. The idea that the Soviet Government would hand us over, all anti-Nazis, to the Nazi authorities was one they refused to accept.

During the journey we were well treated and well fed. There was bread and butter, cheese and tinned meat, and tea to drink, and each smoker received a packet of cigarettes a day. The guards were friendly and obliging, but they refused to tell us anything about where we were going. Our men began to sing. A favourite song was the 'Solovski Lied', text and music by a young German actor named Drach. There were three or four former members of the Austrian Schutzbund with us, and they sang their song: 'We comrades of the mountains'. Betty and I made ourselves a chess set out of bread and we sat and played for hours, chatting and listening with pleasure to the men singing.

And then we passed through Minsk and the train continued on its way towards Poland. At last the men believed. There was no more singing. They refused the next meal. It was tinned peas and meat. The escort tried to persuade them to eat. 'Eat whilst you can,' they said. 'You may not get the chance to eat so well for a long time.'

Although I had thought we were to be sent back to Germany, I now realised how strongly I had clung to the faint hope that after all we should branch off at Minsk . . .

EXTRADITED

The Bridge of Brest-Litovsk

At last the train came to a halt, and for the last time we heard the familiar shout: 'Get ready. With things.' The compartment doors were unlocked and we left the coach, got down the steep iron rungs to the permanent way and stood around shivering in the cold air. A little distance away was a station. We could just see the name on a nearby signal box: 'Brest-Litovsk'.

There were twenty-eight men and Betty and I in our group. Betty and I, an old professor and a prisoner with a wounded leg were taken on in a lorry. The men had to walk. We got out on the Russian side of the Brest-Litovsk bridge and waited for them to come up, looking across the bridge into occupied Poland. The men arrived and then a group of GPU men crossed the bridge. We saw them returning after a while, and the group was larger. There were SS officers with them. The SS commandant and the GPU chief saluted each other. The Russian was a good head taller than the German. He took some papers from a bright leather case and began to read out a list of names. The only one I heard was 'Margarete Genrichovna Buber-Neumann'. Some of our group began to protest and to argue with the GPU. One of them was a Jewish emigrant from Hungary, another was a young worker from Dresden, who had been mixed up in a clash with Nazis in 1933 as a result of which a Nazi had been killed. He had succeeded in escaping to Soviet Russia. At the trial the others had put all the blame on to him, knowing, or, rather, thinking, him safe in the Soviet Union. His fate was certain.

We went over the bridge. The three who had protested were hustled along with the rest. Further resistance was useless and they resigned themselves to their fate. When we were halfway across the bridge I looked back. The GPU officials still stood there in a group watching us go. Behind them was Soviet Russia. Bitterly I recalled the Communist litany: Fatherland of the Toilers; Bulwark of Socialism; Haven of the Persecuted . . .

From Brest-Litovsk we were sent on in cattle-trucks to Bialas. There we were lined up and then marched through the streets under SS guard. Two of the men supported Betty, who was unable to walk alone. We came to a halt before what looked like a church door. An SS man pulled a chain, and somewhere far away a friendly bell jangled. This was the prison of Bialas. The door opened and we went inside. A man in civilian clothes was apparently the Governor. After various formalities had been complied with, he looked at Betty and me doubtfully.

'What can I do with them?' he said. 'I can't put them in with the women here, criminals and suchlike. Perhaps they had better go in with their menfolk.'

We were all put together in a large room with real windows. It was so cold that there was ice on the walls. It was a strange sort of prison. There were no meals and no heating. Prisoners who had money could buy food and fuel. Those who had none went without. Prisoners from the town had their food brought into the prison by their relatives and friends. We had no money, of course, but we had something just as good – cigarettes. It was here we first discovered the important role of the cigarette as currency. After a little bargaining, a youth who served as messenger brought along loads of fuel and got the stove going in our room which soon became comfortably warm.

Along one side of the room ran a wooden bench with sleeping places for fifteen. The rest had to lie on the floor on straw. Betty and I had the warmest places nearest the stove. The door to the room was left open in order to permit Betty and me to go to the lavatory, which was in the corridor. When we were in the corridor and unwatched, we could not resist the temptation to lift up the spy-hole covers and look into the cells. Most of the men inside were Chinese pedlars who had been arrested by the Germans. Some of them were marching up and down swinging their arms to keep warm. One of the cells was more like a furnished room. A Polish aristocrat occupied this. He had a manservant to wait on him and the priest came to visit him regularly. He had his own food brought in and always a bottle of wine. This was a very Christian and Catholic prison. In the main hall was a huge crucifix, and on Sundays there was a religious service, and then they all knelt down together: the hungry and the well-fed, the shivering and those who had wine with their meals.

In our cell we shared what we had and obtained more by bargaining with the cigarettes we had left. We were soon talking about our experiences. Most of the men had had a very bad time. Many of them had been beaten up when they refused to 'confess' and admit the truth of the fantastic charges against them. One of them told us how his friend had been beaten until he could stand it no longer and had committed suicide by throwing himself out of the window of the GPU investigator's room. Several of them had been imprisoned in the notorious Solovki Prison, an old monastery in the Arctic regions, and most of them had been sentenced to between ten and fifteen years. Out of the twenty-eight, only one or two were not members of either the German or Austrian Communist Party, but now they all hated the Stalinist regime, which was not surprising. Some of them were even beginning to discover favourable points in National Socialism: progressive elements in the methods of government and Socialist elements in the economic system and the labour laws. And almost all of them were sure that Germany would win and that National Socialism was due, if not exactly for a thousand years' reign, at least for a long term of existence. I found it depressing to listen to them. They had suffered; they had been deceived and betrayed; and now they despaired.

From Thomas Migsch, one of the men I had known in Berlin, where he had worked for some years in the Western European Bureau, I obtained the only reliable information I had had about Heinz. Thomas Migsch had shared a cell in Solovki Prison with an Englishman named Hamilton Gold. From Gold he had heard that Heinz had been his cell mate in the Butirka in the summer of 1938. That was eighteen months after his arrest. His spirit then was still unbroken and he had not signed anything. All the others could only repeat what they had heard indirectly: that he had been sentenced to death, that he had been sentenced to hard labour; that he was still in an Isolator, and so on.

Incidentally, the story of Hamilton Gold was interesting. In about 1935, this young man – he was about twenty-five then – had come to Russia with an Intourist party. He was an enthusiastic Communist and Russia was the land of promise for him. Whilst he was in Moscow he made the acquaintance of a Russian who suggested that he should stay in the Soviet Union and work at his job – he was a wireless mechanic. He agreed with alacrity. Then came the Spanish Civil War and the Russians sent him to Spain as a wireless technician. Towards the end of 1937, or beginning of 1938, when the Russians suddenly pulled out with bag and baggage, Hamilton Gold was in Barcelona. Whilst there, he was invited to go on board a Russian ship in the harbour to examine a new type of wireless apparatus. He went on board and was then prevented from leaving. He was taken off at Odessa as a prisoner. From there he was taken to Moscow and brought before the examining judge on a charge of espionage. His sentence was ten years' hard labour. In case that sounds fantastic, be it added that something of the same sort happened to almost all those who were in Russian service in Spain. They probably knew too much.

At midday on the second day we were taken out of the prison of Bialas to a kitchen of the National Socialist Welfare organisation, where we were

given pea soup, a day's bread ration and some marmalade. One of the prisoners, a former member of the Red Seamen's Union, greeted the SS men
with upraised arm and 'Heil Hitler'. Willi Beier, who was walking next to
me, winked. 'Some of them are getting their hands in quickly,' he said.

During our stay in Bialas many new illusions were born. 'They're
treating us quite decently, I must say.' 'Perhaps there'll be an amnesty
for returning Politicals.' Many of the men thought they would be called
up for military service immediately. 'Anything's better than a Russian
prison.' After about a week we were all put into an ordinary passenger
train and sent off in the direction of Warsaw. The train was unheated
and without lights, and very few lights were burning in the stations
through which we passed. The main topic of conversation was still our
possible fate. Perhaps we were going straight through to Berlin? Would
we get a chance of informing our relatives?

I got talking with the Hungarian emigrant. 'At least I've got no illusions,' he said. 'I'm a Hungarian citizen, and I think there's little doubt
about my fate. They'll hand me over to the Hungarian authorities for
certain. I left Hungary after the collapse of the Soviet Republic in 1919.
If you do get free, let my wife's relatives know what has happened to
me.' And he gave me the name and address. As far as he knew, his wife
was still under arrest in Russia.

In the Hands of the Gestapo

The next morning our train stopped in Lublin and we all had to get out.
We marched through the streets. Betty still had to be helped along. It
was here that I saw bomb damage for the first time. The general atmosphere was depressing. There were few people on the streets, but from
doorways and windows I saw curious faces looking at our little column
as we passed. We were taken into the Ghetto, to a great square building
which turned out to be the prison of Lublin, where we stayed for the
next two weeks. Here for the first time we came into the hands of the
Gestapo. An official in civilian clothes gave us each a form to fill in,
requiring name, date of birth, date of joining the Communist Party, positions held in it, date of emigration, position occupied in Russia, date of
arrest by the GPU, sentence, and so on. It was here that Betty and I
parted from the men to go into the women's wing. We were placed in
a cell with six other women, including Frau Fon and Frau Fekete, the
Hungarian, who had also been deported from Russia. Apparently Lublin
was the clearing station at which transports of prisoners were put together
to go further inland. Seventeen women and 130 men were waiting for

transport. They had all been deported from Russia and handed over to the Nazis.

'Are you Gretchen?' a young, fair-haired girl asked me. I was astonished. There were only two people who ever called me Gretchen, and they were Heinz and Hilde D. 'I am,' I said, 'but how did you come to know that name?'

'I was in prison in Kazan with Hilde Duty,' she replied. 'She told me to keep my eyes open for you and to tell you what had happened to her if ever I met you.'

Hilde, it appeared, had received ten years' hard labour for her alleged membership of the 'Neumann group', and she had received a letter from her little daughter, Svietlana.

'You wouldn't know her now,' the girl said. 'Her hair's gone quite white, though she isn't more than thirty, as you know.'

Hilde was a Czech citizen, and we discussed what we could do for her if we got free. At least we could let her parents know what had happened to her.

After about half an hour in this cell, the door opened and my name was called. A Gestapo man took me along a corridor. 'You're not as clever as you think,' he said sarcastically. 'Don't think you can get by with us on an assumed name. We know who you are.'

He led me into a room in which a fattish young man sat at a desk. Behind him stood the neatly dressed civilian, who had handed out the forms.

'What's your name?' asked the young man at the desk.

'Margarete Buber,' I replied.

At that the civilian waved a form he held in his hand.

'Don't try any funny business with us,' he snapped. 'It won't pay. You're the wife of Heinz Neumann.'

'That's perfectly true,' I replied. 'But as I was not officially married to him, my name is still Buber.'

'Oh, I see: his girlfriend.'

'No. His wife.'

'Have it your own way. So you were arrested in Moscow and sent to Siberia?'

'Yes.'

'What happened to your – friend – Heinz Neumann?'

'My husband was arrested by the GPU in 1937, and I haven't seen him since.'

'You can tell that to the Marines. He's in Paris; working for the Comintern. And so are you; you're an agent of the Comintern and the GPU. You don't think we're fools enough to believe the Russians would hand over Heinz Neumann's wife without some very good reason, do you?'

I was then subjected to a long examination, and from some of the questions asked – for instance, what I had talked about to Thomas Migsch – I realised that someone in our group must have given them information. Afterwards, on the way to Berlin, the men told me that the former member of the Red Seamen's Union had told the Gestapo about everything that had been said and done on the journey from Moscow to Lublin. Naturally, I admitted to no more than I had to, and when we had got, as I thought, to the end, my examiner asked:

'So you've told us everything you know?'

'Yes; I have.'

'What about your sister Babette in Paris? What's she up to?'

And then followed a series of long and detailed questions, from which I could see that he was very well informed. There must certainly have been a spy in my sister's office. He knew everyone who worked there, and he referred to them by their Christian names or nicknames.

After this examination, I felt sure that I would be brought to trial on some charge or other, and I resigned myself to a long period of remand for enquiries.

The atmosphere in Lublin Prison was strange owing to the presence of both Gestapo and Polish prison personnel. The common enemy of both the prisoners and the Polish prison staff was the Gestapo, with the result that the Poles treated us as well as they could. There was a Polish doctor in the prison sick ward who smuggled letters in and out for prisoners, and wardresses would leave the cell doors unlocked so that prisoners could visit each other. We heard of executions and escapes. In the men's part of the prison there were said to be over 100 Polish priests. Almost every night we heard the sounds of lorries and motorcycles, and shouted commands in German. The old hands told us that there were constant raids on the Polish and Jewish population, and new prisoners were being brought in every night.

There was a woman with her daughter and nine other women in one of the cells. She did not know who we were or where we came from, and she told us with shining eyes that in a few days she hoped to cross the frontier into the Soviet Union, and then all their sufferings would be at an end. All those in her cell had opted for Soviet citizenship. They were Polish Communists.

At first we didn't know what to do or say, but then we decided that it was our duty to tell them of our own experiences. We explained that we, too, had gone to Russia as Communist political emigrants, and we told them what had happened to us and all the others, including the Polish Communists who were already there. We might have saved ourselves the trouble. Their faces turned to stone, and from that time on they avoided any contact with us, as though we were lepers.

Every day we waited with impatience for the next transport from Moscow in the hope of meeting new friends and obtaining more information, but a week passed and none arrived. All seventeen of us women had now been before the Gestapo.

The food was very poor in both quality and quantity. We received only about a pound of bread a day and a ladle of the usual German prison soup, made of barley. There was a Russian woman in our cell who spoke hardly a word of German. She had married a German technician in the Soviet Union and now she was deported with us as a German national. She accepted her fate with extraordinary indifference and her good spirits declined only when cigarettes grew short. To get cigarettes, we each contributed a little from our small bread ration and exchanged it with the criminal occupants for *mahorka*.

A second week passed and still no further transport came from Moscow. I was taken out for examination twice more, but on neither occasion was the questioning anything like so detailed as on the first occasion. Then my fingerprints were taken and I was photographed. All the other women had vague hopes that they would be released. I had none; which, as it turned out, was just as well.

The men informed us through the Polish doctor that the SS man in charge of their section had given permission for husbands to meet their wives if their wives were in our section. That applied to only one man, but about fifteen of the men all declared that their wives were with us and gave some name or other. The SS man saw through the game, but apparently he had a sense of humour.

'All right,' he said; 'but when I take you over and unlock the door to the women's cell if you don't all recognise your wives at once and embrace and kiss them there'll be trouble, I can tell you,' and off he marched them.

We knew nothing about this arrangement and suddenly in the afternoon the door of our cell was unlocked and a swarm of men dashed in. Each of them seized the first woman to hand, whispering in her ear: 'Pretend you're my wife or there'll be the devil to pay.' We hadn't laughed so much for a long time and the SS man stood looking on, roaring with laughter at his little joke.

That sort of thing was still possible in Lublin, but it wasn't always to be as amusing as that.

At the end of the second week in Lublin, all our women were taken one by one to the Gestapo – except me. They each returned with a form on which it said that they were to return at once to their home town, wherever it was, and report there to the Gestapo within three days of their arrival. The form served as a railway warrant. Frau Fekete, the wife of a doctor, was a Hungarian Jewess, and she was released in Lublin and sent into the Ghetto. They all said goodbye to me and tried to cheer me up with words of consolation which I knew to have no substance. And then they went off, leaving me alone in the cell feeling terribly downhearted and abandoned. My only hope was that a new transport would soon come from Moscow with some of my friends in it – perhaps Carola Neher and Zensl Mühsam and the others – but the next day my cell door was unlocked and I was told to take my things. I was going on transport.

I stood with my bundle and waited in the prison yard, filled with uncertainty and anxiety. After a while there was the sound of many feet and a group of forty men arrived and lined up. Amongst them were many of those who had come with us from Moscow. Out of the 150 who had been handed over by the Russians, the Gestapo had detained forty men and myself. We were to go to the Police Presidium in Berlin under Gestapo escort.

A very different tone prevailed on this transport, and we were correspondingly depressed. At the station there was a special coach reserved for us with 'Hospital Train' painted on the side. Women of the German Red Cross, who had no idea what sort of patients we were, treated us kindly and gave us mugs of hot *ersatz* coffee. On the journey we received Army rations and were therefore much better fed than we had been in Lublin. In Warsaw our coach was attached to the rear of another train and we had to wait for some time. The town had already been badly knocked about even then, but the thing that struck me most was that all the women wore hats. I hadn't seen women in hats for a long time.

On this journey everyone avoided political subjects. Some of the men talked about their families, and the members of the Schutzbund enthusiastically described ski tours they had made in the Austrian mountains. No one spoke of what might possibly await him when we got to Berlin, and behind all the talk was a terrible homesickness.

At Neu-Bentschen we had to get out and line up on the platform. Allegedly, we were to spend the night in the local prison, but after waiting around for a long time we were ordered back into the coach again. It was said that the prison at Neu-Bentschen was too full to accommodate us. The next stop was Schwiebus, and there we got out again and the train went on without us. Silently we marched through the darkened streets to the prison, but it was an odd prison when we got there. In the half-light it looked like a big peasant house, and when we went inside we found a large hall with curtains at the windows and tables and chairs around as though in a restaurant. Either there was no proper prison in Schwiebus, or, what was more likely, it was too full to take us. The place was a sort of hostel, and the man and his wife who were running it looked curiously at this mob which had invaded them, dressed in old-fashioned and rather comic clothes – the kit the GPU had thought suitable for Europe. The Gestapo gave instructions to the landlord and we heard ourselves referred to as 'returned emigrants'. We all sat down at the tables and were served with an evening meal as though we were paying guests.

We spent five comparatively happy days in this place, and after a while our spirits revived and we began to sing and laugh again as only prisoners can for whom a few happy days can always be the last for a long time or for ever.

On the third day the door opened. Someone shouted, '*Achtung!*' and we all got to our feet. A crowd of uniformed SS officers and Gestapo men came in and inspected us. They were the local lights of Schwiebus. One of them, apparently the Commandant, made a short speech:

'You have experienced the blessings of Communism at first hand and we should like to regard you as cured. You are returning to a very different Germany. Naturally, you will have to go through a course of preparatory training before you can have the honour of assisting in the building up of the Greater German Reich. We will now sing the German National Anthem.'

And the SS and Gestapo men thrust their hands into the air in the Hitler salute and began to sing '*Deutschland, Deutschland über Alles*'. Hesitantly, our men followed suit, and there were very few who did not raise their arms and join in the singing. Amongst these latter was the Jew from Hungary.

For a long time after they had gone we sat there with hanging heads hardly daring to look at each other. 'What did he mean by preparatory training?' someone said at last. 'Oh, a few months in a camp, I expect,' replied an optimist; 'and then we shall be able to go home.' At the thought they brightened up, and before long they began to sing folk songs, led by Wilhelm König, a former German Communist Deputy from Central Germany. Again and again one heard: 'When I once get out of this I'm finished with politics for good. I've had my bellyful.' On the whole, they were optimistic, except the young workman from Leipzig who had tried to resist at the Brest-Litovsk bridge. As the days went by, he grew more and more restless. He was unable to sit still for more than a few minutes together, and then he would get up and wander off somewhere else. He remembered 1933 and he was frightened. We tried to establish contact with the outside world and perhaps get messages out, but it was impossible. The hostel was closely guarded day and night.

Berlin: Alexanderplatz, 1940

On the morning of the sixth day two covered police lorries drew up before the hostel. Commands were shouted and suddenly everyone had the face of a prisoner again. The men stood to attention with their thumbs to the seams of their trousers, and in their eyes was fear, submission or silent resentment. Everything had to be done in a rush again and the men tumbled into the lorries to the accompaniment of the usual bellowing from the guards.

I was taken to the front of one of the lorries and sat between the driver and a Gestapo man. It was a dull, cold, miserable day. Snow and slush were on the streets. We passed through Frankfort-on-Oder and then drove along the Reich's Motor Road. We were apparently going the whole way by lorry. The whole time I was wondering what the Gestapo in Berlin would ask me, and how much they knew. The lorries travelled at a high speed and my only impression of the journey was of fir woods on either side and then flat, open country. Then we approached the eastern outskirts of Berlin. Berlin! It had been a far-off dream in Siberia: once again to be back in Berlin. But now there was no joy in my heart. I sat there huddled up and I was afraid. These streets were not the old, familiar streets I had longed for. They were stark and hostile. As we turned into Alexander Platz all I noticed was that the Nazis had put the great, clumsy statue of 'Berolina' back into its place.

We got out in front of the Police Presidium, the 'Alex', and lined up. Passers-by stopped and looked curiously at us. We must have presented an odd sight with our old-fashioned Russian clothes. We were taken into the building, up some stairs, along a corridor and into a large room in which sat a good-natured official of the old school. His thermos flask and his packet of sandwiches were on the desk beside him. He was Herr Krohn, a former traffic policeman and now a minor official with the Gestapo. He read out our names, and addressed us all as '*Du*', which was an improper familiarity, and to me he said in particular: 'I expect you're glad to be home.' It sounded quite honest and I didn't know whether he was really sympathising with me or being sarcastic at my expense. I produced a wan smile in answer.

We waited for a while and then other officials came along and took the men away. Not one of them thought to say a word of farewell. It was as though we had all ceased to be individuals with individual fates. Then Krohn took me on a long journey up and down steps and along corridors, until at last we came to a door with an enamel plate on it with the words, 'Women's Department'. He rang and the door was opened by a very tall, very thin woman of advanced years in a white

overall. Her hair was done in a bun on top of her head, which made
her even taller. To my surprise, the voice of this strange apparition was
a deep bass. It was, I subsequently discovered, 'Aunt Annie', the head
of the Women's Department in the Police Prison, Alexander Platz. Krohne
had handed her over a paper together with me, and I stood beside her
as she wrote all my details in a large book. I had a shock when under
the heading 'Charge' she wrote the words 'High Treason'.

'Aunt Anna' was a fixture at the 'Alex'. The Nazis had 'taken her
over' from the Weimar Republic and under her rule the Women's
Department of the 'Alex' was an idyllic little oasis. Like master, like man;
and all the wardresses under Aunt Anna were friendly and considerate.
One hardly ever heard a snapped order. It was very different from the
Butirka here – I mean the real Butirka, of course, and not the comedy
that was put on specially for us at the end. When we went out into the
yard for exercise, it was just as bare and depressing, but there were no
shouts of 'Hands behind your back!' 'Eyes down.' Most of the women
were prostitutes, and as they went round and round, detectives and
Gestapo men looked down on them from the windows with an expert
eye, and from below more than one mocking remark went up. The
women were on the best of terms with those who had arrested them.

The prison of the Police Presidium was a clearing centre which received
prisoners arrested by ordinary detectives and by the Gestapo. After a
preliminary examination, prisoners would then usually be transferred to
Moabit Prison or released. Long-term lodgers, as I proved to be, were
rare. Every night groups of prostitutes picked up during raids were
brought in for some offence or other, and their loud protests and jibes
echoed down the silent corridors.

I came into Cell No. 17. It was supposed to be for four prisoners,
but sometimes there were as many as ten of us in it. We were all given
mattresses and blankets at least. The place was moderately lousy, but
after the Butirka a few bugs meant nothing to me. Unfortunately, the
food was poor and there was very little of it. The cell had a large window
of opaque glass which gave it the appearance of a classroom rather than
a cell, and in one corner there was a proper water-closet. For a prisoner
from Soviet Russia that was a great luxury.

The door was of wood and it was covered with inscriptions scratched
into it by former inmates. There was a representation of a clenched fist,
with the words 'Red Front!' underneath. Many of the inscriptions were
of a revolutionary nature, but others were pious little mottoes and quota-
tions. One read: 'Everything comes to an end at last – even a "lifer."'

I spent four months in Cell No. 17 and I saw very many prisoners
pass through, including some of the accused in the 'Adlershof Trial'. A

representative of the Comintern had come illegally into Germany from
Denmark and begun to organise anti-war propaganda and the distribution of leaflets from Adlershof, near Berlin. One of these women was
Frieda. She was put into our cell after a period in solitary. For a day or
two she wouldn't speak, and she sat there reading the Nazi *Völkischer
Beobachter*. Gradually she thawed and then we learnt her story. Her husband
was a Communist who had been badly beaten up by the Gestapo in the
notorious 'Columbia House' after his arrest and then sent to a concentration camp. After his release, he had promised Frieda to have nothing
further to do with politics, and for a long time everything had gone well.
He had good work and she was expecting a baby. Then he met an old
comrade on the street, and after that she began to notice that he was
taking up his old connections again. She knew what that meant. When
he was not to be dissuaded, she joined in with him. And now they were
both under arrest again, and she had had a stillborn child. She was in
great despair. 'Everything was all right,' she would say again and again,
'and then this happened; and now we're both unhappy. Why, oh why?'
She reminded me strongly of Grete Sonntag. The one pined away in
Siberia under the GPU and the other in Germany under the Gestapo.
One might well ask: Why?

Her morale was quite broken. She insisted again and again that
Germany must win the war. Didn't I think so? I doubted it, and she
sought to persuade me. 'And then,' she said on another occasion, 'there's
no denying that the Führer has done a lot for us. After all, without him
my husband would never have got work. The Gestapo official dealing
with my case is sure the war will be over by Christmas. And then there
might be an amnesty for political prisoners. Do you think I'll get more
than five years? If only my husband hadn't . . .'

Frieda was finally transferred to Moabit to await her trial and some time
afterwards another of the Adlershof defendants was put into our cell. This
was Melitta, who had been brought from Moabit to the 'Alex' for a
confrontation. She was quite a different type, cheerful and confident. She
had lived with her husband and three small children in Adlershof. Before
1933 they had both been members of the Communist Youth Movement.
The Communist representative had got into touch with them and persuaded
them to take part in the illegal anti-war work. Melitta had typed the propaganda material on stencils and they had been pulled off in the cellar of
a grocer's shop. They had all been arrested, including the grocer and his
wife. Melitta had admitted everything, and she now hoped to get off at
the trial with a light sentence. She, too, had now come to a different
opinion about National Socialism. 'When I get free, I promised the Gestapo
I would do everything I could for National Socialism. What a fool Erich

is not to admit everything. It would make it so much easier for him.'

'Who's Erich?' I asked.

'Oh, that's the Communist representative who came in illegally from Denmark. I'm here for a confrontation with him.'

After the confrontation, of which she said little, she seemed not quite so cheerful, but before long she was doing up her hair, earnestly discussing summer clothes, and trying on things her mother had sent her. In this National Socialist prison the inmates were allowed to receive packets, money, letters, and visits from their relatives.

The day after the confrontation Melitta was taken back to Moabit, but before long another of the Adlershof defendants arrived. This was Lisa, a young woman with beautiful auburn hair who wore a green dress which suited her excellently. She had a beautiful voice, and when we sang softly in the evenings we discovered that we knew all the same old songs. But sometimes depression would overtake her and then she would be in tears. She had not long been married . . . 'And the worst of it is that my husband knew nothing about it all. I didn't tell him, because I didn't want to involve him. I worked in the Post Office, and from there I despatched the illegal material. Someone gave me away. The Gestapo won't get anything out of me – if only my husband doesn't leave me . . .' That was her chief worry.

From her I learnt that Melitta had given way first. She had only been a few days under arrest when she began to talk. It appeared that she had had a love affair with the Communist official, Erich, and through him she knew all the details of the illegal work. They confronted her with Erich and her husband, who both stoutly denied what she had said, but then they put the grocer's wife into the same cell with her and Melitta had soon persuaded the woman to talk as well.

Very much later, when I was already in Ravensbrück concentration camp, I met another Adlershof defendant. By that time the trial was over. She told me that Erich had been decapitated and that Melitta, for all her willingness to help the prosecution, had got fifteen years. Most of the other defendants had got five years. I never learnt anything about brave Lisa.

Sentenced to a Concentration Camp

At that time there were very many political prisoners in the 'Alex'. There were several women in solitary confinement who were supposed to be spies, but I never had a chance of making their acquaintance and comparing the Gestapo 'spies' with those of the GPU. Under both Gestapo and

GPU, suspicion of a political offence was enough to deprive the suspected person of freedom for years; no ordinary legal proof was required.

One day the door of our cell opened – Lisa was still with me at the time – and a wardress ushered in a middle-aged woman with the words: 'Now, just keep calm. You're not the only one here, you know. Take it easy.'

The newcomer was a woman of perhaps fifty, with hair going grey and collected into a Grecian bun in the nape of the neck. Apart from the fact that they had taken away her belt, in case she might hang herself with it, which made her dress look something like a nightgown, she was typical Potsdam. She was obviously overcome with indignation and for a moment or two I don't think she even saw us.

'Who do they think they are?' she enquired of high heaven. 'Are decent citizens helpless in their hands? Is there no justice left in Germany? The woman was sent to spy on me. Are we no longer safe within our own four walls?'

When this outburst was over, she saw us.

'I beg your pardon,' she said formally. Her voice, too, was classic Potsdam. 'Allow me to introduce myself: Frau von Gehrke. Forgive me if perhaps my nerves ran away with me. But consider what I have experienced. I was invited to go to the Gestapo, and there a young lout with neither education nor manners informed me that I had insulted Hitler and other members of the Reich's Government. That was that woman, you must know. She must have been sent into my house to spy on me. Apparently one may not express one's opinions within one's own home now. What times we are living in, to be sure!'

When she grew calmer we heard the story. She had been denounced to the Gestapo by her charwoman. She had, it appeared, given the woman a newspaper to line the garbage bucket with, but on that particular paper was a photo of Hitler surrounded by his chief henchmen. And now she was here.

'Just as I was,' she insisted, as though that made the enormity greater. 'Without anything except what I stand up in.'

In our situation, her misfortune seemed funny, but we consoled her as best we could. It cost her fourteen days with us, but as she had influential friends and relations the Gestapo let her go in the end.

She counted amongst the Politicals, and there were quite a lot like her. More serious was the case of those who had listened to foreign broadcasts and been unable to keep what they had heard to themselves. Not only had they listened, which was an offence, but they had 'propagated' what they had heard, which was much worse. At that time the punishment was a term of hard labour, and later on there were even executions. Other 'Politicals' were people who had bought 'pointed' goods without surrendering points, or committed some such offence against the rationing system. Hardly a week passed without one or two of these people coming to us on their way to Moabit.

One of our prisoners, plump Frau Globig, who was so tightly laced into her corsets that her generous bosom almost met her chin and she could hardly breathe, kept a stand in the Central Market. She sold fruit. She had exchanged her goods with another market woman who sold meat. 'You know, oranges for a bit of liver now and again,' and she had been denounced by another stallholder who had observed the transactions. Frau Globig was really comic in her distress. She bemoaned the bad luck she was having. Only a little while before, her 'Lorchen' had died. She was so upset when she talked about 'Lorchen' that we thought it was her daughter, but it turned out to have been her pet canary. She had its heart, specially embalmed, in a locket which she wore round her neck. They kept her in for ten days and then she was discharged with a caution.

Apart from these 'Politicals' and the real ones like Lisa and myself, there were quite a number of prisoners who had been arrested on racial grounds. A Jewess from Leipzig, named Frau Kroch was in our cell for some weeks. She had been caught trying to cross the frontier into Holland to follow her husband and her four children. She was a motherly soul and she took her fate philosophically.

'At least I know they're safe,' she said. 'I stayed behind and let myself be seen every day until I knew they were well out of it.'

When she spoke of her children, her beautiful brown eyes glowed with tenderness. I met her again in Ravensbrück. They had cut off her hair and she went about in bare feet. I shall never forget the sad look she gave me. She perished in the gas chamber in 1942.

In the first few months of my stay in the 'Alex' I was taken out for examination after examination. I can't remember how many different examiners tried to make me confess that I was an agent of the GPU sent to Germany on behalf of the Comintern. On several occasions I was taken to the Headquarters of the Gestapo in the Prinz Albrechtstrasse. Often during the examinations the wireless would blare out some new Nazi victory, and then all the officials would forget me for the time being and rush over to a great wall map to shift lots of little flags to new positions. That depressed me more than anything. My personal fate was already settled: obviously, it would be either prison or concentration camp – but what was going to happen to Europe if Hitler won?

Even in the dull, drab life of prison there are ups and downs. Sometimes I was kept in solitary confinement, and then I saw the sun only through fluted glass, and as I sat there I dreamt of summer, swimming, green meadows and trees. It was May, but I hadn't seen so much as a green leaf of the spring. But on another occasion, when I was escorted to Krohn to have my fingerprints and photograph taken, he asked me whether I had any relatives in Berlin.

'My younger sister,' I said, 'but I don't know her address.'

He found her address and telephone number and whilst I sat there he brought her to the phone and then handed me the receiver. And on another occasion he arranged a meeting between us in one of the corridors. Visits were not supposed to last more than twenty minutes, but he let us stay together over an hour. He watched us all the time, but at least we hadn't to talk in a crowded room. And one day I had toothache. There were no arrangements for dealing with dental cases in the 'Alex', so Krohn took me to the police dental surgery – not in the Black Maria, but through the streets and by Underground like an ordinary citizen. That was a tremendous experience, but I went through it as though in a dream; I had so long lost the habit of walking freely amongst fellow human beings.

Needless to say, the Gestapo men were not all like Krohn, and many of them were brutes and bullies comparable with the worst types of GPU men, but their methods of examination were different from those of the GPU – or perhaps I should say, rather: the object of their examination was different. The GPU examiners aimed from the beginning, not at finding out whether there was any factual basis for their suspicions against their prisoners, but at establishing their 'guilt' and securing sufficient 'proof' for a heavy sentence without all the preliminary bother of bringing them to trial. The Gestapo men, on the other hand, were still bound, if ever so loosely, to the judicial traditions of a civilised country, in which, in the ordinary way, an offender had to be formally charged and brought up for trial. They were certainly prejudiced parties, and it was not truth as such they were striving to establish, but facts at least, in so far as they spoke against the prisoner and seemed to warrant a charge and a trial. When they were unable to secure sufficient evidence there was even some hope that a prisoner might be released.

In my case, unfortunately, there appeared to be none. They certainly did their best to cajole or intimidate me into giving them sufficient evidence to justify a charge, but in the end they had to content themselves with branding me as a 'suspected person', and in July 1940, after four months, an order was issued for my 'preventive arrest'. As I subsequently discovered, it read: 'The past life of Margarete Buber provides every reason for assuming that if she were set at liberty she would engage in activity on behalf of the illegal Communist Party. Her transfer to a concentration camp is thereby indicated.'

Although I had expected it, the moment when the order for my preventive arrest and transfer to a concentration camp was read to me was a bad one. My strength seemed at an end. I had only just escaped from certain death in Siberia and now a concentration camp was my future again. It is easier, I think, to face an uncertain future. I knew only too well what a concentration camp meant. Those around me talked of 'three months' reformation period' and were almost happy in their optimism. I had no such hopes of early release. There was no settled term to a concentration-camp sentence in Germany. It could mean three or six months, or it could mean three or six years, or even longer for political prisoners – as long as the Nazi regime lasted, perhaps, and in those days it looked like lasting out our lifetime.

With that I left Cell No. 17 at last and came into a much larger cell in which there were about 100 other women all awaiting their transfer to a concentration camp. Some of them were real Politicals who had already served five or six years' hard labour and were now being sent to a camp at the end of their sentences instead of being released. Others were Jewesses; Bible Students, known as 'Jehovah's Witnesses'; 'race-defilers', girls who had had affairs with Jews, Poles and other sub-humans – 'bed Politicals', they were called – prostitutes, vagabonds and criminals.

The atmosphere here was depressing and rumours of what it was like in a concentration camp formed the chief subject of discussion: the beatings, the police dogs, the constant standing to attention, and above all, the story that any woman found with vermin in her hair had it shaved off at once. They seemed more afraid of that than of anything else, and many of them spent hours going through each other's hair looking for lice and nits. But newcomers were brought in almost daily, and with them came reinforcements of vermin, so that for all their efforts many of the women lost their hair as soon as they arrived in Ravensbrück.

Every Saturday a transport of about fifty women went off to a concentration camp. On Friday evenings the names of those to go the next day were read out. There was a Jewish doctor named Jacoby with us. She had already served a term of hard labour. One Friday her name was on the list. The lavatory in the cell was screened off from the rest of the room. That night she hanged herself from the water cistern, but she was discovered and cut down in time to save her life. In Ravensbrück she developed tuberculosis and in 1942 was sent off in a 'Sick Transport' to the gas chamber. We meant well, but was it really humane to cut her down?

Amongst the real Politicals, I made the acquaintance of Lotte Henschel. At the age of twenty-three she had been a member of the Socialist Workers' Party, or SAP, an independent organisation formed from oppositional Communists and left-wing Social-Democrats. She had been arrested together with her whole group and sentenced to the comparatively mild term of eighteen months' hard labour. Whilst in prison she had come under the influence of Communist prisoners. One of them had given her a written message to pass on, and she had been caught with it. Unfortunately, it contained a whole programme of Communist political instructions. With that she had come into the hands of the Gestapo again, but she had resolutely refused to say who had given it to her, and she had been brought to trial again and sentenced to another three years' hard labour. She had now served the four and a half years and was to go to a concentration camp.

She knew I had come from Soviet Russia, and for her that was the land of hope. Eagerly she asked me about my experiences, and when I told her she was horrified. She sat on the mattress beside me and wept.

'All those years in prison I was consoled and strengthened by what the Communists told me about Soviet Russia. It made it all seem worth while. It was my only hope. And now . . . I wish I could disbelieve you, but I can't. All this suffering seems so useless. What have we got to live for now?'

RAVENSBRÜCK

A New Hell

On Saturday, 2 August 1941, we started off for Ravensbrück. There were fifty women in the group and we went by prison coach from Stettiner Railway Station in Berlin. My anxiety and depression, and my fear of what was to come, were so great that I hardly remember any of the women who shared the narrow compartment of the prison coach with me. The only two I can vaguely remember were a woman from East Prussia, who had the appearance of a schoolteacher and who was a member of that strange religious sect whose members called themselves Bible Students or Witnesses of Jehovah, and a prostitute from Hamburg. And I remember the prostitute only because of the insistence with which she assured us all that she would only be about three months in the camp 'for re-education'.

The train stopped in Fürstenberg in Mecklenburg. There was a loud and fierce barking of dogs and a shouting of orders even before the doors were unlocked. 'All out. Line up in fives. Hands to the side. Get a move on.' We tumbled out. Two uniformed women concentration camp guards stood there with two great Alsatians. Obviously the dogs had been trained to savagery, and the two guards took a delight in letting them growl and snap near the legs of the frightened women as they hurried out of the coach.

Outside the station were two covered-in lorries, and we were rushed along to them and herded in as though the loss of a single minute would be fatal. The shouting and the bullying were obviously part of a deliberate plan to frighten and intimidate us. Our 're-education' had begun. After a short drive, we came to a gate. The woman in charge handed a list to the guard, who counted us, and then the gate was swung back and we were hustled through into concentration camp Ravensbrück.

We lined up in fives in front of a newly painted wooden hut before which was a neat garden plot. A woman guard with jackboots, a field-grey skirt and tunic and a sort of forage cap set at an angle over one ear stood watching us, shouting from time to time: 'Quiet! Hands by the side. Stand to attention!' I was astonished at what I saw: neat plots of grass with beds in which flowers were blooming. A road leading away from the entrance square was lined with young trees, and before the wooden huts which extended away on either side were more flower beds. The square and the street were obviously most carefully kept and even the gravel paths had been freshly raked over. To the left of us, towards the watchtower, there was a large timber barracks painted white, and next to it was a great aviary as though in a zoological garden. Peacocks were strutting slowly around and monkeys sprang from branch to branch, whilst a parrot was squawking something that sounded like 'Mother'.

Opposite this aviary, on the other side of the entrance square, was a big, well-kept lawn with silver firs which partly hid the only building in the camp which was built with stone, as far as we could see. This, we had very good cause to learn later, was the camp prison; in its basement were the notorious Bunkers – it was the inner sanctum of hell. From outside everything looked beautiful – more like a neat holiday camp than a concentration camp. But behind the aviary we could see part of the barbed-wire fencing which surrounded the camp and served to remind us where we were.

A diffused sun shone over the camp. Apart from us one might have thought the place was deserted; no one was in sight. And there was no sound but the squawking of the parrot and the regular shouts of our guard. But whilst we were waiting a column of prisoners came by and I saw German camp inmates for the first time. They marched in orderly ranks. Each woman wore a clean white kerchief bound round her head and fastened at the back, a broad-striped dress and a dark-blue apron. They were all barefooted, but at their side went a woman in clogs, shouting from time to time. Their faces were impassive as they passed. One looked just like the other. My heart fell as I realised that this was how I was going to live: regimented, drilled and shouted at day in, day out, for year after year: 'Left, right. Left, right. Heads up. Arms by the side. Line up!'

Suddenly a siren began to howl quite close to us. How we were to hate it! It was the midday siren, and now the scene changed. From all sides came marching women, all in columns of five, some of them with spades on their shoulders, arms swinging exaggeratedly in time with their step. And what astonished me most – they sang. Some silly marching song or other. And all the while the dogs bayed and growled and the guards bawled out orders.

We were marched up to an office and then taken in one after the other to have our particulars registered. A woman official assisted by two prisoners made out a card for each of us. Later it would have a photo attached and be filed away in the 'Political Section'. Our dossiers were also kept in this 'Political Section' so that the Camp Commandant or his officials could consult them at any time. What was in them none of us was ever privileged to know.

Everything at Ravensbrück was done with typical Prussian thoroughness. A prisoner was passed from hand to hand until every detail was complete and she had become a permanent inmate, registered, photographed, listed and uniformed. After we had gone through all this, we were taken to the washroom, which was fitted with showers. We had to undress and wash ourselves under the showers, and all our things were taken away. The attendants here were in white. They were also prisoners and on their arms they wore a small patch of triangular cloth whose colour indicated their status: red for Politicals; lilac for Bible Students; red and yellow in the shape of a star for political Jews; black and yellow for Jews who had been guilty of 'racial offences'; black triangles for Asocials; and green for criminals.

After our clothing had been taken away, the long-feared procedure of looking for head lice began. This was carried out by two prisoners whose lilac triangles showed them to be Bible Students. One of them was called Emmy. She performed her office with a certain grim pleasure. She would give a woman a sickly-sweet smile and beckon her to take a seat, then she would search her head with extreme care, and if she found the least sign of lice or nits, off would come the wretched woman's hair. No begging and pleading were of any avail. Ruthlessly, Bible Student Emmy would brandish her clippers and turn an attractive head of hair into a pitiful bald egg. I came into her hands, but to my astonishment, search as she would, she could find nothing and, greatly relieved, I was allowed to retain my hair. With the same meticulous thoroughness another prisoner attendant searched the women for that particularly odious type of louse which fastens itself into the skin under the pubic hairs.

At least there was hot water and soap and a towel for each woman. This procedure was supervised by a prisoner attendant, whose loud shouting and bullying was in no way different from that of the guards. When it was all over we were left sitting around the room on benches, naked and shivering with cold, waiting for the next procedure. It was the medical examination, and a pitiful travesty it was.

The SS medical chief, Dr Sonntag, was a giant. We lined up before him, fifty naked women, many of them without a hair left, some of them trying to cover themselves like Venus. He stood there slapping his jackbooted leg with a riding whip and looking along the line. 'Hands to the side,' he snapped. 'Stand to attention.' And the feeble attempts at modesty had to be abandoned. One by one we were called out for examination, which consisted chiefly of a glance into the wide-open mouth with the aid of a torch.

'Why are you here?' he asked when my turn came.

'Political,' I replied.

'I see,' he said. 'The usual Bolshevist shrew. Get back to the ranks,' and he gave me a flick with his riding whip on the bare leg.

After this 'entrance examination' we were given prison clothes: a shift of coarse material, ridiculously long knickers, the striped dress we had seen, a blue apron and a white cloth to bind round our heads. In this rig-out we were then marched barefoot to the accompaniment of much shouting to Block 16, which was the block for new arrivals.

The blocks were situated in rows down the long road we had seen, each at right angles to it so that between each hut there was a gangway. In these gangways were the doors to the huts, opposite each other. There were 500 women prisoners in Blocks 14 and 16, which were side by side; in charge was a Block Senior, a prisoner, and two Hut Seniors. In addition there was an SS woman overseer for each block, the so-called Block Leader. But for the moment this camp hierarchy was a mystery to us. We fifty newcomers stood waiting in front of the hut and I rubbed the soles of my feet in turn against my calves in an effort to get rid of the sharp flints which were pricking me. None of us was as yet used to walking barefoot on gravel. The Block Senior appeared. Her name we learnt subsequently was Minna Rupp. In coarse Swabian dialect, she read out our names and we answered. We each then received a dish, a plate and a cup made of aluminium, a knife, a fork, a spoon, a tooth-glass, a towel and a tea-cloth. And although we were henceforth always to go barefooted we were each given shoe-cleaning materials. With our treasures under our arms, we were then ushered into the day room, in which there were ten highly scrubbed tables at which long lines of women in striped dresses sat, some of them with hair and some without. They were all knitting field-grey socks. A faintly mouldy smell of scrubbed and undried wood filled the place. As we came in, silence fell, but after the women had looked us up and down, a hum of conversation began, until, in a voice which would not have disgraced a barracks square, the Block Senior bellowed, 'Silence!' and deep silence fell again at once. The Hut Senior then gave each two of us a narrow locker for our things, and instructed us exactly how they were to be put away. The dish, plate, cup, etc., had to be placed in a certain order; the towels had to be hung on hooks, folded in a certain fashion something like a man's tie. After this first lesson in Prussian thoroughness we were given places at one of the tables.

Before long the door opened and metal food containers were brought in and set up on stools at the window near the door. Brandishing a large ladle, the Block Senior shouted: 'Silence. Line up for food.' Everyone hurried over to the lockers to get her things, and then we lined up in a queue which wound round and round the tables. My first German camp meal consisted of a sort of sweet porridge with stewed dried fruit. But in addition each of us received a large piece of white bread, a piece of sausage, a portion of margarine and a portion of lard. I turned to one of the old hands:

'Is there an inspection or something, or is this some sort of special occasion?'

She shook her head and looked at me to see, I think, if I looked quite right in the head.

'Do you always get as much to eat as this, then?' I went on.

'Well, yes, but it isn't as much as all that, is it?'

'No,' I replied, 'but I thought perhaps . . .' And left it at that. Anyone who has been in a Russian concentration camp has quite different views about what constitutes quality and quantity in foodstuffs.

After we had eaten, the camp siren sounded again, and immediately everyone in any sort of authority began to shout 'Roll-call!' We put our stools upside down on the tables to clear the hut for sweeping and then we all hurried outside and lined up between the huts. Even when we were already in line the shouting still went on. I was on the end of a line and beyond the huts I could see the high camp wall and the five-fold lines of barbed wire. On a grass bank below the wall was a large black board on which a skull and crossbones were painted in yellow.

'What does that mean?' I asked my neighbour in the line.

'Don't you know that the barbed wire is charged with high-tension current?' she whispered. 'Didn't you hear what happened today with the gipsy girl?'

A thunderous shout of 'Quiet there!' stopped our whispered conversation. And then we stood there and waited, and waited. Again and again we went through the motions of 'lining up'. The Hut Senior would march along the lines and inspect. This woman's headdress wasn't bound properly, that woman wasn't standing properly to attention. Then there was a loud shout of 'Attention!' and a uniformed guard accompanied by the Block Senior went along the lines counting us. And after that we still waited. My bare feet were very sore and my legs began to ache. For months we had not been used to walking and standing. I put my weight first on one foot and then on the other, and wiggled my toes to get them warm. This endless waiting around was a torture. At last, after an hour and a half, the siren sounded again and a relieved gasp went up on all sides. This was my first roll-call in Ravensbrück, and the same thing happened twice a day, morning and evening, day after day, all the time I was there, no matter what the weather, in rain and broiling sun, in the bitter cold and in snow in winter.

The woman who had stood next to me in the line now told me of the gipsy incident. A gipsy woman, mother of several children, had flung herself into the live wire that morning after hearing that her husband had 'fallen on the field of honour'.

'When we take the dirty things to the washroom in the morning you'll see the place,' she said. 'Her fingers are still stuck on to the wire. They were torn off when they pulled the body away.' Horror and lust for sensation were mingled in her voice.

The newcomers received two woollen blankets and a white sheet, a pillowcase and a long blue-and-white striped nightdress. And then we had to learn 'bed-building', which is a typically Prussian piece of chicanery. All the huts had two wings, an 'A' wing and a 'B' wing. Each wing had a day room and a dormitory. Originally built to hold 100 prisoners, each wing held 250 in 1940, and later on the number was even increased to 500. In addition each hut had a washroom with basins and foot baths, a lavatory, and an office for the SS Block Leader, which, however, she occupied only for a short time mornings and evenings. During the rest of the day it was the privilege of the Block Senior to use this room, which was more like an ordinary living room.

The Ravensbrück hut seemed a palace to me after the wretched clay huts of Birma. And the equipment: a proper lavatory, a washroom with proper basins, tables, stools and lockers! There was not a table or a stool for any of the prisoners throughout the whole of Karaganda. And then there were the rows of neat, double-tiered beds, and every prisoner had her own bed and her own straw sack to sleep on. My bed was in the upper tier. My neighbour, a nineteen-year-old girl with a face like a child, was a 'bed Political'. She was in Ravensbrück because she had had a Polish lover – 'race defilement'.

However, there are disadvantages to everything. In this case, one of them was 'bed-building' and the other was the tyrannical attitude of the Block Senior. In a zealous desire to keep in with the SS Block Leader and show herself well suited to her high office, she never lost an opportunity of shouting, bullying and chivvying us around until she made our lives a misery. But for that it might have been quite tolerable in our wing. Most of the inmates were Poles, schoolteachers, civil servants and intellectuals of all sorts. On the whole they were good comrades and I got along very well with them.

But back to the 'bed-buildings'. The straw sack had to be punched, shaken, pushed and smoothed into a mattress-like shape, flat across the top, with flat sides and clearly defined edges. And when the job was finished it had to pass muster first with the Hut Senior, then with the Block Senior, and then with the SS Block Leader. There is a knack about it which has to be learnt. When the straw sack is finally ready the blankets have to be folded in a particular fashion and laid on top of it as though they were boards. And then the pillow! That has to have a strictly rectangular shape as though it were a wooden box, its edges also clearly defined. Words fail me to describe the miseries and frustrations of this Prussian 'bed-building'. Its difficulty is increased if you happen to occupy the second tier, as I did. Fortunately, one of the older prisoners, a Polish music teacher, came to my assistance and initiated me into the use of the 'tools' for the job. They consisted of a stick to chivvy the straw around with, and two flat pieces of board to get the right shape.

Woe betide you if your 'bed-building' failed to meet with approval. At first the newcomers were merely shouted at and bullied, but after a day or two, during which time you were supposed to have mastered the art, one or other of the inspecting authorities would pull down the whole laboriously constructed bed and you would have to start all over again, devoting your precious leisure time at the midday pause to the job. Once you failed to satisfy an inspection it was more difficult than ever to pass muster subsequently. If it happened more than once you were liable to get a 'report'. A 'report' was the constant threat which hovered over our unfortunate heads. It was invariably followed by punishment. The first stage was 'punishment standing without food'; the second was 'solitary confinement in a dark cell'; and the third, most terrible of all, was 'twenty-five lashes'.

Unsatisfactory 'bed-building' was usually punished with eight days' loss of either the morning or evening meal. The delinquents, who had, of course, worked hard during the day, assembled on the camp square and stood to attention facing the Punishment Block. There they would stand for hours until the siren went for lights out at nine o'clock, and then, hungry, tired and with aching feet and legs, they could crawl into their beds.

But even in bed after lights out we were not certain of our rest. Our clothes had to be laid out on stools in the day room folded in a particular fashion so that the coloured triangle with the prisoner's number was uppermost – and neatly folded at that. When we were in bed the night watch would carefully examine all the piles, usually soon after nine o'clock, and if anything was wrong, if a pile was not folded neatly enough, or if a garment was missing – perhaps one of the prisoners had dared to go to bed with her woollen stockings on for warmth – then there was an immediate uproar. The night watch, always accompanied by a great snarling police dog, would fling open the door of the sleeping quarters and wake up everybody with her noise, drag the offender out of bed, usually boxing her ears, and shoo her out into the day room to rearrange her pile. Or sometimes, if she felt like it, the fury would suddenly drag the clothes off some unfortunate for a fancied offence. We were often frightened out of our sleep in this way.

As long as prisoners were kept in the reception block they had no work to do. All in all the formalities lasted about a week, during which we were led off 'in column of five' to one office after the other by the Block Senior, always to the accompaniment of the same military shouting of orders. And in each office we were asked the same questions: 'When were you arrested? Where were you arrested? Why were you arrested?' Thanks to standing waiting around for hours, and marching again and again over the gravel paths in our bare feet, the soles were sore and swollen like cushions. Every step soon became painful.

When we had finally gone through the long and complicated process of registration, I received the triangular piece of red stuff with a number which stamped me as Political and a regular inmate. The Block Senior then instructed us in the way to show proper respect to the SS officials. As soon as addressed, we had to spring to attention with our arms close to our sides and say smartly: 'Protective Custody Prisoner X . . . Y . . . No. . . .' My number was 4,208.

Four thousand two hundred women lived in sixteen huts in 1940. At that time Ravensbrück had only one street of huts; later there were three. In addition to the living huts, there were huts for clothing and utensils, two tailors' workshops, two sickbays and a large laundry. The camp square was surrounded by the kitchen huts, the offices of the SS Commandant, the baths, an SS canteen, the aviary and the prison block.

As an inmate of the reception block, I was cut off by railings from the camp street, and I looked with astonishment through the bars at the thousands of women in their striped dresses who walked up and down in their bare feet during the exercise hour. One of the highest functions ordinary prisoners could attain was 'Camp Messenger', and these privileged ones wore a red armlet as insignia. There were also other prisoners wearing coloured armlets whose job was very much like that of the so-called 'brigadiers' in Karaganda.

After I had been about a week in Ravensbrück I was sitting at my table one day knitting grey Army socks. The Hut Senior had ordered silence, and not a whisper of conversation was to be heard. Then a voice sounded: 'Is a Margarete Buber here?' In the doorway stood a Camp Messenger named Betty Wiedmann, together with our Block Senior

Minna Rupp and a third I didn't know. I replied and they called me out. The Camp Messenger examined the number on my arm. Then the three led me into the sleeping quarters, into which we were strictly forbidden to go during the day, and a new and this time unofficial examination began.

'You were arrested in Moscow?'

'Yes.'

'Why?'

I realised that these three had been sent by the Communist group to subject me to a political examination. When I had finished answering their questions, which I did very frankly, the three looked at each other.

'All right,' said Minna Rupp finally in her execrable Swabian dialect. 'You're a Trotskyite, that's what you are.'

And I realised that, just as once before in Moscow, I had been branded as a counter-revolutionary and enemy of the people. I went back to my knitting without altogether understanding the full consequences of the incident: even before my entry into the camp life proper I had been branded as an outlaw.

Among Prostitutes and Criminals

As I have already mentioned, I was on very good terms with the Poles, and in the second week the friendly music teacher came to me with another Pole and declared in the name of all the Polish prisoners that they wanted to propose me as Block Senior. They were sick and tired of the brutal and stupid tyranny of Minna Rupp. I was a Political and a German and I had had camp experience.

I refused in horror. 'Whatever do you think of me?' I asked. 'I couldn't be a Block Senior. "Quiet. Hold your tongue. Attention! Hands to your sides." And shouting *Achtung!* when the SS comes. That wouldn't suit me at all. I'm only too glad if I'm left in peace, and I certainly don't want to bully and chivvy others around.'

But they were prepared for my objections. 'You'd be with us,' they said, 'and you wouldn't have to bully us. We're all intelligent women, and we'd help you. You certainly wouldn't have any trouble with us, and you'd do us a favour because we wouldn't have any trouble with you. This other woman's impossible.'

I went hot at the thought of being a Block Senior and I used every argument I could think of, particularly that a Block Senior had to make 'reports', but they replied patiently to them all, pointing out that it was primarily in their interests; Minna Rupp was driving them mad. Gradually

I let myself be convinced and at last I consented. I don't know what channels the Poles used, but they were supreme in the camp in their ability to use 'connections' and obtain 'positions'.

In any case, shortly after this discussion I was called out to see the Senior SS Overseer. I was taken out by the Hut Senior and lined up with half a dozen other women in the square, and there we waited, standing to attention. Waiting is one of the chief occupations of the concentration camp inmate. After we had waited there for a very long time and were already very tired, the Senior SS Overseer Langefeld came along and subjected us to a detailed inspection, asking one after the other where, when and why they had been arrested, and how long they had been in the camp. And then she picked out a number of us, including me.

'Take your things and go to Block 2,' she said to me. 'You are Hut Senior there.'

I went back to my waiting Poles. They had arranged it all and it was therefore presumably all right, but their faces when I told them that I was now Hut Senior in Block 2 showed me that something must have gone wrong. 'Great God!' they ejaculated. 'Block 2. But that's the Asocials' Block! That's not what we wanted at all.'

However, there was nothing further to be done about it, and so, filled with anxiety, I went off carrying my belongings to Block 2, where I reported to the Block Senior, Liesl Müller. When I entered the hut there was a tremendous noise going on and the place stank like a monkey's cage. Liesl Müller was a Lorrainer. Together with her husband, she had been convicted under the Weimar Republic for espionage. On the outbreak of war the Nazis had put them both in 'preventive arrest', meaning concentration camp. She pulled a face when she heard that I had been in Ravensbrück only fourteen days. She was a woman of rather limited outlook. On the one hand, she tried to keep in with the authorities by seeing that all the regulations were strictly carried out and by a markedly servile attitude to the SS, but on the other she had not sufficient strength of character to avoid the temptations and corruptions of camp life. In the end she got into the criminal set. She was an ideal Block Senior for the SS. She ruled with a rod of iron and bullied and shouted. She constantly threatened those under her with 'reports' and she had no scruples about making them. At the same time she fawned on the SS Block Leader Drechsel, who was one of the best-hated and most-feared shrews in Ravensbrück at that time.

Together with her, I entered 'A' wing of Block 2, where henceforth I was to be Hut Senior. Only after she had picked up a piece of iron and banged it violently against a metal container did the hubbub subside.

'Quiet!' she shouted. 'This is your new Hut Senior.' And all eyes turned to me. I felt as though I were naked in a cage of wild animals.

Amongst the privileges of my new office were a locker all to myself, a new dress which really fitted, a better quality linen apron and wooden clogs. And, above all, a green armlet, my insignia of office, which permitted me to move about at will throughout the whole camp. But in the first week I had no time to use my new freedom. The instruction in the duties of my office took about ten minutes, and at the end of it I went off with reeling head to perform my first duty, the distribution of the midday meal.

I stood there with a ladle in my hand feeling, and probably looking, absolutely helpless amidst the seething mass of women who surrounded me, shouting and gesticulating: 'Table 3 starts off today. Table 5 gets the extra portion today. It's my turn to scrape out the tubs today.' And so on and so on. And all the time greedy eyes were fixed on the two iron tubs in front of me, the one filled with vegetables, the other with potatoes in their jackets.

'Absolute silence must be maintained during mealtimes,' I said, as I had been instructed. Only those right close to me could have heard, and it had no effect whatever. And all the time I was thinking anxiously that whatever I did I must be absolutely fair in the distribution; each must get just the same portion. Some of them were dancing on the stools. 'Get on with it,' someone shouted. 'The siren will go if you don't, and then nobody'll get anything. Get on with it. Buck up.'

By this time I was almost in a panic and hardly knew where to start first, but then a powerful woman with lively brown eyes and a determined chin jumped on to a stool and bellowed in a voice worthy of any sergeant-major: 'If you don't line up in an orderly manner at once and stop mobbing the new Hut Senior the tubs will go back to the kitchen and then no one will get anything.' This was Else Krug, a 'sadistic' prostitute from Düsseldorf.

It worked like a charm, and, to my relief, after that I had no further trouble – for the moment. There were 150 of these so-called Asocials, and for the next two months I spent my days and nights in their company, and, I must confess, I never entirely managed to control them. When I had been there for a while and got more or less settled down into my new job I did my best to establish human relations with them and to introduce some sort of social decency into our joint existence despite concentration camp and SS, but with one or two exceptions I met with disappointment after disappointment. After my experiences with the Siberian Asocials I ought not to have had any illusions; the type is fundamentally the same everywhere. However, for me these women were victims of society in one way or another, and in a certain respect their lot in German concentration camps was more onerous than that of their colleagues in the concentration camps of the GPU.

In the chaotic conditions which existed in Russian concentration camps a prostitute was at a distinct advantage; she was, in fact, in her element, and the continued practice of her profession greatly improved her lot. But in Germany the situation was very different. A prostitute, often suffering from venereal disease, and often mentally defective, her health undermined, used to late hours and no regular work, came into a German concentration camp to be 're-educated', to be 'broken in to regular work' and 'taught discipline'. Her lot was an unenviable one. Needless to say, all this talk of 're-education' was hypocrisy. Society now brutalised them in a different fashion, that was all – and not always in a different fashion either, as the following incident illustrates:

In 1942 a 'Commission' of SS officers arrived from Mauthausen. They inspected the human flesh available in Block 2 and made a preliminary choice. All the women picked out were then led off to the washroom, where they had to strip and be examined by the 'Commission'. Those with firm breasts, sound limbs and general physical attractions were shortlisted, so to speak, and from their 're-education' in the camp they were sent to replenish the SS brothel in Mauthausen. After six months of this activity they were promised their freedom – to return to the world of free citizens 're-educated' and cleansed.

It is quite understandable that no inmate of a concentration camp is willing to do more work that he is obliged to do, and that he dodges it when he can, but the situation becomes quite different when the work he dodges falls on the shoulders of others, or when its non-performance means trouble for others, reports, and punishments. 'Reports' were a much more serious matter with Asocials because all of them had some hope of being released at some time or other, and each punishment imposed for infractions of camp discipline automatically meant three months extra on the term. I did my best to make this clear to them and I appealed to their common sense and self-interest, for I hated shouted orders or threats of 'reports'. But it was no use. They seemed to regard 'bed-building' and my insistence on neat and clean lockers, and so on, as my private passion to be frustrated whenever possible. Although hardly one of them had succeeded in avoiding punishments, which meant an increase in their terms, they were like naughty schoolchildren and took a delight in dodging their obligations whenever they got the chance.

In order to avoid the necessity of 'reports', I mobilised one or two of the better characters, particularly those who, for this, that or the other reason, did not go out to work during the day, or those who belonged to the so-called 'Emergency Labour Pool', whose duty it was to be ready for any special work at all times. With these I would go round rebuilding the worst beds and tidying up the lockers. But after a while this stratagem became known and then the situation grew worse than before, because they said to themselves: 'Why should we bother? The Hut Senior does it anyway.' And, in addition, I found that some of my helpers were secretly blackmailing those whose beds and lockers we found in disorder to extort food from them. Some of them even told tales to the Block Senior, Liesl Müller, and to the SS Block Leader.

Denunciation was the worst characteristic of these Asocials. It was pitiful and heartbreaking. Friendship and comradeship in prison and concentration camp play an even more important role than they do outside in freedom. I had always thought that the common misery and common dangers of a concentration camp would strengthen such feelings, but it was certainly not the case with these types. Friendship, of course, can never be higher than the character of the friends, and here sworn friendships were sealed one day and broken in hatred and enmity the next, perhaps because one of the partners had managed to get hold of something a little better than the other. The subsequent squabble would often end in one of the 'friends' running off to the Block Senior or to the SS Block Leader to denounce the other for stealing a carrot or a reel of cotton, or for some other offence she knew of by virtue of the fact that her 'friend' had opened her heart to her the day before. It was sickening, and profoundly depressing.

And all these personal squabbles were conducted in full public. In the sleeping quarters at night, when I would have given anything to sleep – just to sleep and get away from it all – the squabbles of the day would burst out again, and the vilest insults would be hurled around, based invariably on the confidences told under the seal of secrecy whilst the 'friendship' lasted. One of the most wounding types of insult touched on their professional honour, the accusation that they had charged low rates: 'Hark who's talking!' was a typical opening: 'Took drunks in a doorway for a tanner a time.' And then the fur would fly.

And the amount of petty thieving that went on amongst these women was unbelievable, despite the fact that 'stealing from a comrade' as the SS regulations virtuously called it, was punishable with 'twenty-five lashes', and solitary confinement in a dark cell up to a period of forty days, and even, in bad cases, with the Punishment Block. Thieving, mutual accusations and denunciations were everyday affairs, and my chief anxiety was to prevent anything coming to the ears of the SS Block Leader Drechsler, for then punishments rained down on the wretched women.

And Again – Camp Life

When I first came to Ravensbrück the roll-call seemed to me a sort of Chinese torture, but whilst I was in Block 2 with the Asocials it became something of a relief. Twice a day to stand in silence in the fresh air: no shouting, no squabbling, no tale-bearing, no denunciations, and no stench. The Asocials stood with their backs to Block 2 during the roll-call. Opposite us were the Politicals of Block 1. Next to us were the gipsies of Block 4, and diagonally opposite were the Bible Students of Block 3. All the other blocks were lined up on both sides of the camp street. Silent and motionless we stood there in our striped dresses, each line as straight as frequent 'line-ups' could make it, each prisoner at exactly the same distance from the next one.

From time to time the silence was broken by a shouted order, and above the black pines which could be seen beyond the camp confines rose the sun. In Birma I had thought that the steppe sky was the most beautiful I had ever seen, but it seemed just as lovely in Ravensbrück. For a prisoner the sky takes on a particular importance and beauty. It is the only thing he is not cut off from by walls and barbed wire, or bars. The moving clouds, the bright stars and the passing birds are the only things left of his freedom. The other freedom – the woods, the fields, the streets, the houses – gradually fades away and even the strong desire for it becomes weaker in time. But the sky remains. At the morning roll-calls the clouds would scurry along or perhaps roll over the sky majestically, tinged with the first golden sun of the day, and at the evening roll-calls they would turn pink and then red as the sun sank behind the horizon. The sky was the only thing which changed continuously in our life. The rest was like a stage background, rigid and changeless, the same scenery for the same monotonous play. Behind the camp wall to the east there were great dark fir trees; to the west, above the roof of the Punishment Block, there was a large friendly willow tree, and behind Block 2 there was a wood of spindling young pines growing out of parched and sandy soil. Month after month, year after year, everything remained the same, a bare, poverty-stricken drop cloth to our miserable lives.

When the morning roll-call was at an end none of the prisoners was allowed to return to the huts, and the Block Seniors stood at the doors to see that no one slipped in and dodged work for the day. The formation of the labour gangs took place immediately afterwards. On winter mornings legs, hands and noses were blue with cold by the time the waiting was over and the women were ordered to their gangs. Many of the Asocials were employed in the garment workshops or the laundry.

Most of them had learnt these trades during the various terms they had spent in prison as a result of their profession. Others did heavier work, such as digging, carting coal or unloading barges. Some of them were in the Emergency Labour Pool, and from day to day new gangs were formed from amongst its members for this or that particular task. The advantage of belonging to this Labour Pool was that on some days there was nothing to do, and the women were then permitted to return to the warmth of the huts, where, however, they were supposed to occupy their time by scrubbing floors, tables and stools, or knitting socks. At such times they were constantly bullied and chivvied by the Block Senior, but they had got so used to this that it seemed to have no effect on them whatever.

The 'Labour Roll-Call' was carried out on strictly military lines. An SS official sat at a table in the centre of the square and the various gangs marched past in strict military formation to be counted. Each gang was inspected, counted and entered into a book. In the early years this procedure was merely another piece of chicanery, and it was not until 1941 that a change came about. At first work was regarded merely as part and parcel of the 'process of re-education' and labour productivity had nothing whatever to do with it. If there was nothing else to do, piles of sand would be carted from one place to another and then back again. It was work for work's sake. But as the war went on the shortage of labour became more and more acute, and concentration camp labour began to play an important economic role. In 1941, when the 'KZ' prisoner had begun to play a role in Germany's war economy, concentration camp Ravensbrück sent out gangs at so much a head to help build airfields, repair roads, work in various factories, and help till the surrounding Mecklenburg farms. At the end of 1942 the well-known German electrical firm Siemens-Halske built workshops just outside the camp, and prisoners were employed there for ten and afterwards eleven hours a day manufacturing various electrical and wireless apparatus. But all that, and further developments such as a garment workshop for SS and Army uniforms, a furriers' workshop and so on, came later. In 1940 the women worked an eight-hour day and returned to the camp for two hours at midday, but in that eight hours they were kept constantly at it and the last ounce was squeezed out of them.

At that time, too, concentration camp staffs were recruited along National Socialist lines, and the guards were all impassioned Nazi types, like Drechsel, Lehmann, Hase and Fräser, who treated the prisoners badly on their own initiative, and took a delight in tormenting them and making their lives a misery. Later on there was a great shortage of labour, and concentration camp personnel had to be recruited wherever it could be obtained. The result of this was that on the whole the types recruited were not so brutal.

When the others had gone off to work, the remaining Labour Pool prisoners went back into the huts. They had been standing around for three hours, but they were seldom left in peace for long: 'Line up to fetch bread. Line up to get fresh linen.' And so on. In 1940 there was still fresh personal linen once a week and fresh bed linen once a month. And when the Labour Pool prisoners had a moment or two to spare someone would start them scrubbing; scrubbing the floors, the tables, the stools, the lockers – everything that could possibly be scrubbed, whether it needed it or not. This was done so often that the wood really had no chance of drying out properly before it was scrubbed again. The result was that the huts always smelt of wet wood. It was worst in the sleeping quarters, which were never heated. On one occasion when a visit from Himmler was expected the order came to scrub everything both inside and out.

Prisoners were allowed to receive money from outside, and this could be spent in the canteen. In 1940–1 they could buy bread, cake bread, jam, syrup, fish paste and various brands of toilet articles. This canteen was a special source of profit to the SS, which ran it and charged whatever prices it liked. Block 2 could use the canteen once a week according to a strict procedure. When it came round there was great joy amongst those who received money from friends and relatives outside, and great jealousy and resentment amongst those who had none. There was no sharing out amongst the 'have-nots' in Block 2.

Prisoners could write and receive one letter a month. However, they were never allowed to write to more than one person, whose name and address had to be registered on arrival at the camp. In the first years there was a strict censorship of all letters both incoming and outgoing, but later, when conditions in the camp began to deteriorate, that regulation, like many others, was much less strictly observed. All outgoing letters had to be written on special camp paper with a printed heading, 'Ravensbrück Concentration Camp for Women', and underneath the censorship rules. Politicals who had been arrested before the outbreak of war had paper on which the heading, etc., was printed in red. They were allowed to write two pages twice a month. The paper on which the Bible Students wrote was printed in green, and had, in addition, the words: 'I am still a Witness of Jehovah.' They were allowed to write only five lines at a time. All those arrested during the war had paper printed in black, and they were allowed to write sixteen lines.

As Hut Senior it was part of my duties to go through the letters of the women in my hut to see that they did not offend against the regulations, a sort of preliminary censorship. The letters written by the Asocials to their relatives were often heart-rending:

> DEAR MOTHER, – I know I've been a great shame to you, but do write me just a word. I'm so unhappy. When I come out I will make a fresh start; really I will. I will work very hard and make up for everything. Send me a mark . . .'

Or the father, a sister or an aunt would be asked for a letter – and a mark. Very few of them ever got an answer. Most of them had been turned out by their families. But sometimes on a Saturday – that was the day on which post was delivered – there would be an unexpected answer for one or other of them. Some mother's heart had been touched – and then the tears would flow in streams. But by Sunday all remorse had been forgotten.

Apart from the roll-call, Sunday was a holiday, and for years there was even a special Sunday meal: *goulash*, red cabbage, and potatoes in their jackets. The prisoners were allowed to turn the camp street into a *corso*. Loudspeakers were fixed at intervals along it, and if the SS man on duty happened to remember it we could listen to a Sunday broadcast concert from the Berlin Rundfunk. The concerts were often very good and it was always a delight for me to stroll along and listen, for I had not heard good music for years. I gladly put up with the numerous military marches and the dreadful 'soldiers' songs' in return for Schubert, Mozart and Beethoven from time to time.

A thousand women in striped dresses, all wearing the same white headdress in exactly the same way, showing just the same amount of hair, promenaded up and down the street singly or in twos and threes to the strains of the music. It was an uncanny parade. And we were not left entirely in peace. From time to time wardresses with police dogs on the leash would stride through the throng, roughly pushing to one side any prisoner who didn't get out of the way quickly enough. And if she noticed any of the women daring to walk along arm in arm she would box their ears and perhaps report them. There were many other 'offences' against good conduct: putting the hands under the apron, for instance; an improperly fastened headdress; a skirt that was too short or too narrow at the waist. Many of the prisoners were young; they were still women even in concentration camp, and they wanted to look their best, and they were constantly being reported for attempts to make the camp clothing look a little smarter. The women would work on their clothing with needles and cotton stolen from the workshop. And woe betide the prisoner whose numbered triangle wasn't in just the right place. The

chicanery of all these pettifogging rules and regulations was designed to
make our lives a misery.

One Sunday I was walking along alone and dying to talk to someone
with whom one could hold a reasonable conversation when a small,
stocky woman with piercing eyes and a red triangle suddenly addressed
me in Russian. In the autumn of 1940 there were as yet no Russians in
Ravensbrück and I looked at her in surprise. However, she seemed to
attach no importance to talking Russian and she immediately began a
conversation in German. She had heard that I had lived in Moscow, she
said, and wondered whether I knew any of her friends there. Where had
I lived in Moscow? 'In the Lux,' I told her.

'Oh, you'll certainly know Comrade Tchernin then?'

I nodded. 'Quite well,' I replied.

'What was the number of his room?'

At once I was on my guard. This was another Communist examination.

'I don't see why the number should interest you,' I replied, 'but if I
remember rightly it was No.—. But Tchernin was arrested by the GPU
in the summer of 1937 and his wife and two children were then turned
out of the Lux.'

She said nothing to that, and I continued: 'Perhaps you're also
interested in the fate of Comrade Piatnitzki, and Comrade Valetzki,
and Krayevski and Lenski, and all the others from the Comintern?
They all went the same way as Tchernin.'

At that she turned on her heel and marched off. I learnt afterwards
that her name was Paleckova. She was the leader of the Czech Communist
women in the camp. Clearly, as far as prisoners with red triangles were
concerned, I was an outcast. I went back to Block 2 to supervise the distribution of the afternoon tea. There they all sat, fifteen to a table, singing
in concert. Most of the songs they sang were dreadfully sentimental ditties.
One they liked in particular was about a lover who climbed the mountain
to pick an edelweiss, a white alpine flower, for his sweetheart, fell and was
found by his maiden still clutching the edelweiss he had picked for her,
but now it was red – red with his blood.

At my table sat Else Krug, and her speciality was sadism. 'What about
a little Nature study?' she would ask, and then she would delve into her
great fund of reminiscences. Up to then I had considered myself a fairly
enlightened person and I had read a certain amount of scientific literature on the subject, but Else's stories of the requests she met with in
the course of her profession and how she complied with them made my
hair stand on end. And she was quite a likeable personality, cheerful and
helpful. She never whined like the others, and she never made hypocrit-

ical repentance or expressed any intention to reform. She told her stories in a dry, matter-of-fact way, and there was a certain professional pride in her attitude. She knew what she was, and she insisted that she was a good one. You never heard her say: 'When I get out of here I'll lead a different life.' Instead, she would say reflectively: 'A few more years' camp and I'll find it difficult to earn 300 marks in a night. Ah well, I'll have to invent something special to make up for it, the only Asocial in such a position.'

Else was in charge of the kitchen gang, which consisted entirely of Asocials, and there was great competition to get into it. There were potatoes, carrots, turnips and cabbage in the cellar, and not far away such delicacies as canned food and jam. What an opportunity for stealing! And what terrible dangers to be run! Yet Else had succeeded in managing her gang for over a year without a 'report'. The stealing was organised and kept within reasonable bounds, and its booty was always fairly divided amongst them all. Else's achievement was particularly striking because the Asocials were naturally treacherous; they had no sense of loyalty whatever and they were perfectly ready to betray their nearest and dearest for any immediate advantage, particularly for food. And yet Else kept that gang of fifteen or twenty women in strict order by sheer force of personality.

However, it couldn't go on indefinitely, and after about eighteen months of it someone did betray her, and off she went to the Bunkers. After that she had to spend a year in the Punishment Block. I was no longer in Block 2 by that time, but I saw her occasionally. Now and then we even found an opportunity for a whispered chat – it was forbidden to talk to prisoners from the Punishment Block.

'Grete,' she said on one occasion, 'they think they can get me down with work, but they're wrong; I'm tough. I can get through it better than any of them.'

It was in 1940 that Himmler first introduced corporal punishment into Ravensbrück for offences against camp discipline. The women to be flogged were tied to a special whipping block and at first the Camp Commandant Kögel himself administered the punishment. It was his little pleasure, but before long such punishments became so frequent that it was hard work, and then the task was delegated to the SS Overseer Drechsel and to one or other of the SS women. In the end they must have got tired of it too, for then volunteers were asked for from amongst the criminals, with extra rations as the incentive. It was easy enough to find volunteers, and after that two criminals and a Polish woman carried out the floggings.

In the winter of 1941–2 the extermination of prisoners by gas began in Ravensbrück. Else Krug was taken from the Punishment Block and brought before the Camp Commandant Kögel.

'Krug, you are to be released from the Punishment Block to carry out floggings.'

Else refused. Kögel, who was not used to having even his slightest whim frustrated, was furious, but Else was firm.

'No, Herr Camp Commandant; I never beat a fellow prisoner.'

'What, you dirty whore! You think you can pick and choose. That's a refusal to obey an order.'

Else shrugged her shoulders, but she was grimly determined.

'Take the whore away,' snorted Kögel. 'You'll have cause to remember me, I can tell you.'

A few weeks after that incident Else was sent off with a Sick Transport to the gas chambers. Else knew where she was sent and that this was Kögel's revenge.

Ravensbrück Camp lay in a hollow. To the north beyond the camp wall was rising sandy land on which grew a few stunted pines. Towards the south the ground sank gradually and ended at a morass. Later this was incorporated into the camp, filled in and built over with further huts. The first block which was built in this way gradually sank into the soft ground, and in order to lessen the weight the second block was left without a proper roof and covered instead by tarpaulin sheets. Towards the end the overcrowding was very bad in Ravensbrück, and to add to the miseries of the prisoners the drainage system was constantly over-flowing. In the summer months the huts in this low-lying part of the camp were permanently surrounded by a *cloaca*, which froze hard in winter. A small concentration camp for male prisoners holding about 1,000 men abutted on to our ground. In the west, behind the build-ings of the Kommandantur, which was outside the camp wall, lay the Fürstenberg Lake. Prisoners who were sent outside the camp to work declared that it was surrounded on all sides by water and marshland.

The Hunters and the Hunted

One morning the camp siren sounded earlier than usual and it was not the ordinary long-drawn-out howl to which we were accustomed, but a more urgent sound which had something frightening in it. The Block Seniors hurried their charges out of the huts. They were tremendously excited and urged them on to even greater haste. 'Hurry. Hurry. Line up. Someone's escaped.'

Within a very short space of time, we were all lined up in our usual places. The camp personnel was aroused like a disturbed colony of ants. Wardresses with dogs ran here and there. The Camp Commandant stood surrounded by his underlings, giving furious orders. The sound of motors starting up made the air throb. The SS was preparing for a manhunt. In the meantime, the roll-call proceeded hurriedly. One prisoner was missing from the Punishment Block. It was a gipsy woman named Weitz. In the night she had left her hut by climbing out of a window. She must have crossed the camp street, made her way up to the iron gates of the camp – although the police dogs roamed around off the leash during the night – climbed over the roof of the SS canteen, hardly ten yards from the SS guardroom, made her way up to the wall, which was topped with live wire, put a blanket and pillow she had brought with her over it for insulation and then got over it and sprung down to freedom. The first intimation of her flight was when the blanket and the pillow were spotted still on the wire in the morning.

We stood there silently and watched the preparations for the hunt. With all my heart, I longed that she should succeed; that she should make her way safely through the trees and the marshland to some safe hiding place. But the dogs! They were already straining at the leash, and the whole male and female SS was mobilising to be after her.

The prisoners in the Punishment Block from which Weitz had escaped were women who had offended in some way or other against the camp rules. They were serving various terms there, ranging from three months to the whole period of their stay in the camp, according to the severity of their offences. Amongst the thousands of women in the camp were naturally some who were hardened criminals, and sooner or later they were caught breaking the strict rules of the camp and ended in the Punishment Block. Naturally there was a much higher percentage of these hopeless cases there, and their presence made it a hell for the others. Violence, theft and treachery were everyday occurrences. And at that time the Block Senior was an Asocial who ruled by brutality and violence. The prisoners there received the same rations as we did, but they performed the heaviest work and in consequence they were always hungry. On account of the escape, all the prisoners in the Punishment Block were deprived of three days' rations. As a result, a wave of hatred arose against the unfortunate woman.

It was already midday and we were still standing and waiting. I felt cold, hungry and miserable. Behind us those who had lost consciousness lay in rows on the ground. They were not allowed to crawl back into the comparative warmth of the huts.

And then at last they came. A group of wardresses with dogs, SS men and the Camp Commandant Kögel. And driven along in front of them, stumbling, pushed and kicked, was a miserable bundle of rags, the gipsy

Weitz. The dogs snapped at her legs and tore at her clothing as she staggered forward. Like this the whole group moved right through the lines
of waiting prisoners. Then it disappeared into the Punishment Block.
What happened there I learnt later. The Camp Commandant himself
kicked and pushed the exhausted woman forward. She was bitten all over
her body by the dogs and covered with blood and dirt. The prisoners
in the Punishment Block had been waiting all the morning lined up just
as we had, and, in addition, they knew that her attempt at escape was
to cost them three days' food.

'There she is,' he said. 'It's her fault that you'll get no food for three
days. Do what you like with her.'

And the majority of the prisoners rushed at her, kicking her, striking
her with their fists and belabouring her with stools until she dropped
unconscious to the floor. After that, the bundle of bloody rags was
dragged out again and pulled along the ground before our horrified
eyes. Kögel followed behind and to each line of prisoners he declared:

'Take a good look at her. That's what will happen to any of you who
attempt to escape.'

The gipsy Weitz died a little later without recovering consciousness.
The SS had made an example of her for the benefit of all of us.

During the whole year 1940 only forty-seven prisoners died in
Ravensbrück. In later years the mortality rate of 'natural deaths' was about
eighty a day, not counting those who were sent to the gas chambers,
and more than half had been beaten, starved or frozen to death in the
punishment cells. The prisoners who worked in the sickbay had to fetch
the corpses from the cells. They often found them frozen to the floor
or mummified from starvation.

Whilst I was still in Block 2 I saw a woman who had been flogged.
Her buttocks and thighs were black and blue in ugly weals. In many
places the skin had burst under the blows, and crusted blood made a
tracery of stripes. The woman had been caught stealing a piece of bread.
Our stupid Block Senior delivered a speech on stealing and its consequences. 'I'm not a thief,' the woman replied; 'but I was so hungry
I hardly knew what I was doing.'

In our hut there was a prisoner who regularly stole the aluminium
cups. Afterwards they would be found neatly arranged in her own locker.
Every time she did it there was a tremendous hubbub and the prisoners
who had lost their cups fell on her and beat her. She had been reported
again and again, but neither reports nor punishment nor blows made
any difference. Even her fellow Asocials realised that she 'had a screw
loose'. There was a high proportion of such women amongst the Asocials
and their lot was unenviable, for they were beaten and ill-treated by their

fellow prisoners as well as by the guards. There were also the bed-wetters whose failings were regarded as malicious. They were terribly beaten and often forced to spend the night in the damp washroom, but, of course, it did no good; quite the contrary, for they lived in constant anxiety and their condition grew worse. It was the same with the epileptics. Under the camp conditions their fits grew more and more frequent and more and more violent. They, too, were regarded with disgust and loathing by the other prisoners. And then there was the great number of venereal patients whose health was undermined by the experiments of the SS doctor, Sonntag.

There was an eighteen-year-old girl named Erna in our block. Her head was rather too big for her body and she, too, 'had a screw loose'. She hardly spoke except to utter impotent threats. She was much teased and persecuted by the other Asocials. If an aeroplane came anywhere near the camp, she would rush to the window or out on to the camp street looking up at it, her lips moving rapidly in an excited monologue.

'Erna, your airman's coming for you. He'll jump down on his parachute for certain today. Keep your eyes open.'

Erna continued to look for her airman until the day they took her away to the gas chamber.

We had a Block Register, which was kept in the Block Office. All particulars of the prisoners were written down in it. One day I saw an entry: 'Poremski, Eugenia; Asocial; born in Moscow.' She was on the 'B' side of the Block, and that evening I went over to 'B' and asked the Hut Senior which prisoner was Eugenia Poremski. She called out the name and a woman in her late twenties with dark eyes and an aquiline nose came out to me in the corridor with an anxious look on her face. I told her I had come to see her because she had been born in Moscow. Her face lighted up. 'Moscow!' she exclaimed. 'Do you know Moscow? Do you speak Russian?' And when I spoke to her in Russian she embraced me and began to sob. She was the daughter of White Russian emigrants and a niece of the Czarist Minister, Stolypin. She was in camp for having led an allegedly asocial life. After that we often chatted with each other. She was not very well educated, but she was intelligent and she suffered greatly from her life amongst prostitutes. Our acquaintance went on for some years and then she was sent away to work in a munitions factory.

One of the worst features of German concentration camps was that no term was fixed for release. That 'not knowing how long' was one of our worst tortures. As far as I was concerned, I had given up all hope, but amongst the Asocials there were many women who never ceased to reckon with their release. Those who could 'read the cards' were in great demand. For a piece of bread, there was always a happy future: quick freedom.

Human beings in concentration camps are different, and they are not inmates for long before they change. During my years of incarceration I had ample opportunity for seeing my fellow human beings without their normal civilised mask. It is not so easy to watch oneself. When people ask me how I managed to survive seven years of concentration camp in Russia and Germany I can only say that, apart from the fact that my physical condition was always good and my nerves well-balanced, I never let myself slide into a state where I lost my self-respect, and, above all, because I always found people who needed me. Again and again I was given the good fortune of friendships of human relations.

Apart from the real criminal and asocial elements, most of the women were ordinary human beings – housewives, mothers and young girls who differed very little, in fact not at all, from the housewives, mothers and young girls outside the camps. In the first years there were very few conscious enemies of the regime in the camps – just the 'old' Politicals and the Bible Students. Later on their number was increased by women from the resistance movements in the occupied countries. These latter women found it easier to stand the camp life. They had fought for a cause and the fact that they were now in a concentration camp was proof of their danger to National Socialism. It strengthened their self-respect and helped them to hold their heads high. But the majority of the prisoners were 'innocent'; they were unable to understand why this terrible fate had befallen them at all. Each of these prisoners hung with all her being on to the memory of what she had left behind: her husband, her children, her home. And here she was now, despairing and helpless, in a concentration camp, with no knowledge of how long she would have to stay there. She was drilled like a soldier and made to react like an automaton. At no time of the day or night was she ever alone. Everything she did was done in the company of others. At every step, at every word, she came up against strangers – strangers who were suffering as she was. Amongst the hundreds in her hut there would be perhaps one or two to whom she felt attracted, but the majority she would find odious and intolerable in all their ways and habits.

She was made to work excessively hard; she was half-starved; she was made to stand still and freeze; and it even happened that she, an adult human being, a woman, a mother, a young girl, would be shouted at, bullied and even beaten. Every newcomer in a concentration camp goes through a terrible period in which she is shaken to the core, no matter how strong her physique, how calm her nerves. And the sufferings of the newcomers became worse and worse each year in Ravensbrück, and in consequence the death rate was highest amongst them. According to character, it would take weeks, months, or even years, before a prisoner resigned herself to her fate and adapted her being to existence in a camp. It is in this period that the character of the individual changes. Gradually the interest for the outside world and for the other prisoners declines. The reaction to horrifying events grows less intense and does not last so long. It is a process of hardening, until soon the news of death sentences, executions, floggings and even atrocious tortures causes no more than a faint reaction of horror which is over in a few minutes, and then there is again laughter and talk, and the camp life goes on as though nothing had happened.

I observed the same change in myself. I remember that when I was a newcomer in the camp I was shocked and horrified when the women fainted at the roll-call, and in particular when a gipsy woman suffered the same heart attack each time because she was unable to stand immobile so long. And yet in 1944 when I had to go to the sickbay for some reason or other I calmly picked my way through the dying as they lay in the corridor choking out their lives.

Christian morality declares that suffering ennobles the sufferer. That can be only a very qualified truth. Life in a concentration camp showed the contrary to be true more often than not. I think that nothing is more demoralising than suffering, excessive suffering coupled with humiliation such as comes to men and women in concentration camps. That is true of individuals and probably of whole peoples. Concentration camp is not like an ordinary prison. The one great blow, the loss of freedom, is only the first, and after that you are made to suffer, deliberately made to suffer, constantly. Blows are bad, but there are worse things – constant provocations and constant humiliations. When the SS struck, you dared not strike back. When the SS bullied and insulted, you had to keep your mouth shut and never answer back. You had lost all human rights – all, all without exception. You were just a living being with a number to distinguish you from the other unfortunates around you.

And unconsciously you were tempted to revenge yourself on your fellow prisoners for the injuries you suffered. I am not thinking here of those prisoners who occupied some post and were able to maltreat those in their charge. That is a chapter on its own. No; I mean the ordinary women prisoners. This was at its worst amongst the Asocials, most of whom had not the faintest vestige of human solidarity. There it was a fight of all against all. But the same thing in a milder form could be seen amongst the other prisoners, even amongst the conscious Politicals. They were envious and jealous of each other. If one seemed to get a trifle more food, a slightly larger piece of bread, a slightly bigger portion of margarine or sausage, there were immediately hateful scenes of anger and resentment.

In the first years the Politicals, Asocials and criminals were kept

separate in German concentration camps, but later on, particularly when
the camps became overcrowded, this practice ceased. Like the GPU in
Russia, the SS discovered that non-segregation made it easier for them
to manage the prisoners, for it tended to increase the existing rivalries,
jealousies and differences. To facilitate their own task, the SS also introduced what was called 'self-administration'. This system placed a part of
the responsibility on the prisoners themselves, and unless prisoners of
upright character occupied the various camp posts, which was the exception, it merely added new oppression and misery to the lives of the ordinary prisoners, for when Asocial or criminal elements managed to get
such posts they exploited them to the advantage of themselves and their
favourites and to the suffering of their fellow prisoners.

In the best case, the job of the Block or Hut Senior or Gang Leader
was not an easy one to carry out justly. The prisoner in such a post had
the difficult task of guarding the interests of her fellow prisoners and at
the same time to see that as far as possible the orders of the administration were obeyed and conflicts and irregularities avoided. More than
once have I seen a sudden change come over a woman chosen for such
a post. From an ordinary cowed and docile creature, I have seen her
change overnight into a domineering, ruthless fury who would brook
no contradiction, make the others treat her with respect she most certainly
did not deserve, scatter punishments and threats of punishments far and
wide, and unscrupulously take things for herself which properly belonged
to all. A woman like that – and there were many of them – could make
the lives of several hundred of her fellow prisoners become a never-
ending torture instead of merely a dull misery.

I have already spoken of 'bed-building' and locker-tidying, but such
a woman was also in charge of the distribution of food, clothing and
so on. What an opportunity for favouring her toadies! And in later
years, when we were allowed to receive parcels from outside, what an
opportunity for bribery and corruption! Some of the Block Seniors, in
particular, zealously copied the manners of the SS Block Leader and
established a reign of terror around them until they were indistinguishable from the SS apart from the uniform. Such women were mere executive organs of the SS in the ranks of the prisoners, 'SS
might-have-beens'. One word from a Block Senior to the SS Block
Leader and there was punishment for the unfortunate prisoner who
had incurred her displeasure.

On the other hand, a good Block Senior could soon manage her SS
Block Leader, usually a woman of low intelligence, divert her from too
frequent controls, prevent reports and punishments, and quite generally
improve the conditions of her fellow prisoners and assure them peace

and quiet in their free time at least. From 1942 onwards, when the so-called 'Sick Transports' began to be organised, the Block Senior held practically the power of life and death over her fellow prisoners. It was she who was instructed to draw up the list of those who had 'physical or mental defects' or who were incapable of work. Women who went off with such transports ended in the gas chambers. There were, however, some Block Seniors who managed to protect the old and unfit prisoners from these transports for years.

As Block Leader of the Jehovah's Witnesses

From the time we first tumbled out of our bunks to the time we had to line up outside for the roll-call there was three-quarters of an hour in which to wash, dress, build beds, tidy lockers and eat our 'breakfast'. That would not be too easy in the best of circumstances, but think what it meant in a hut with 100 other women all rushing around intent on doing the same! We pushed and shoved each other in a race to get through the narrow corridors between the bunks and get into the wash-room first. Queues immediately formed in front of each tap. One combed herself, the other cleaned her teeth, the third splashed everyone in the neighbourhood as she washed, and the air was blue with bad language and abuse. There were more queues in front of each WC and then queues for 'coffee'. Everyone was tearing around at top speed, buffeting everyone else. And then the siren would start up to call us outside for the roll-call and the Block Senior would begin to bellow 'Fall in!'

One morning the SS Block Leader Drechsler paid us a visit. She was obviously in a bad temper and she began to shout furiously to speed up our efforts. She abused and bullied us left and right, and all who got in her way were clouted viciously.

'Get out of here,' she shouted; 'and sharp about it. Do you think you've got all day to hang about in? Get a move on or I'll report the lot of you.'

She was in a mood, and when the prisoners were all outside she marched into the dormitory of 'A' Hut, which was mine. She gave one look at the beds: 'Where's the Hut Senior?' she shrieked. I went forward and received a flood of abuse.

'Do you call that bed-building? Those beds are more like hammocks. I've had just about enough of this piggery on "A" Side. Report in the office after roll-call.'

When the roll-call was over and the members of the Labour Pool and the knitters had returned to the huts, one of the women from my group began to complain bitterly to the Block Senior that her bread had been stolen in the night. At that moment the door to the office opened and the angry face of Drechsler appeared.

'What's all this noise?' she asked.

The Block Senior explained.

'Who stole your bread?' Drechsler demanded, turning towards the woman who had complained.

'Lina from Table 6,' she replied at once.

'Get the woman and bring her in to me,' she ordered, 'and the rest of you come as well. We'll get to the bottom of this, or I'll know the reason why.'

With a sinking heart, I went to find poor Lina, an old woman with the wrinkled face of a worried baby and a high-pitched, childish voice. She was hopeless; even before I had told her what it was about she began to deny having stolen any bread. She was mentally defective, and we all knew it. Before the door of the office I whispered hurriedly: 'Don't forget to announce yourself properly or Drechsler will beat hell out of you this morning. She's feeling like it.'

Inside Lina stammered out her name and number, and the examination began. The verdict was a foregone conclusion once the Block Senior had reported that Lina had already been caught stealing bread. When I saw that Drechsler was about to write out a report, I intervened.

'Frau SS Leader, you're dealing with a mentally defective. Lina's not responsible for her actions. Everybody knows she's not all there.'

Drechsler stopped her writing and looked up at me with her mouth open in astonishment at my temerity. For a moment she seemed unable to grasp the enormity of my offence, but then she recovered tongue:

'Your mouth's too big; that's what's the matter with you. Of all the insolence! And an idiot like you is Hut Senior. Small wonder "A" Side's like a pigsty.'

She got up from her chair and came round towards me, still talking. 'You've been Hut Senior too long, and this is it. I'll report you to the Senior Supervisor. Understand? Dismiss. All of you.'

As we closed the door behind us, she was talking to herself indignantly: 'What a nerve! I've never known such a thing in my life.'

I didn't mind losing my position as Hut Senior; in fact, I was glad of it – but a 'report'? I felt miserable and apprehensive.

The next morning I was 'called out' to go to the office of SS Senior Supervisor Langefeld. I waited in front of the door and after a while Marianne Korn, Langefeld's secretary, came out. She was young, blonde and pretty, but the conviction of being one of the élite – she was a Bible Student – gave her an arrogant and condescending look.

'Go in, Buber,' she said. 'Frau Supervisor is ready to see you.'

I went in and announced myself in the routine fashion. Frau Langefeld was sitting at her desk. At first she did not look at me at all, but glanced out of the window. She seemed nervous and shook her head as though she were shaking her hair out of her eyes.

'You are Hut Senior with the Asocials?' she asked.

I was about to say 'I was', but I altered it to a simple confirmation. Her next question found me quite unprepared.

'Do you think yourself capable of being Block Senior?'

'No; I don't think so,' I stammered. 'I don't think I'm suitable at all. I'm already in trouble as Hut Senior.'

She took no notice of what I said. 'Very well, then,' she continued: 'You are to be Block Senior with the Bible Students in Block 3. You must remember that Block 3 is the Inspection Block, and you must pay particular attention to constant neatness and orderliness, because you never know when there might be an inspection, and everything must be in perfect order at any time of the day or night. Go and get your things and take them straight to Block 3 now.'

That was the end of the interview, and I left in a state of great astonishment to carry out my orders. I had expected punishment – perhaps even the Bunkers – and instead I was promoted. It was not until later that I gradually learnt the background of this extraordinary happening. The Block Senior of Block 3 was a certain Käthe Knoll. She was known as a Political, but she had not been a member of any political party and she never made any reference to the reason for her arrest. Later on I happened to see her file card, and on it was the note: 'Twice convicted for theft.' She was probably one of those 'Politicals' who had made an incautious remark about the Nazis and been overheard by a zealous informer; there were many like that.

By 1940 her name was notorious in the camp. She considered herself to be the best and most efficient Block Senior in the camp, and this opinion was shared by the Camp Commandant, Kögel, who had therefore entrusted her with the most important Block Senior's post. With the backing of Kögel, her position seemed impregnable. Not only did she comply with all the camp rules and regulations most strictly as far as those under her were concerned, but she led them a dog's life, even outdoing the SS in chicanery. She already had the death of one prisoner on her conscience, the Political Sabo, whom she had reported and who had then been sent to the Bunkers, where she died. This did not disturb her in the least, and she went on bullying and tormenting the inmates of Block 3, keeping them in a constant state of anxiety and suspense. She even succeeded in making 'reports', although the prisoners in Block 3 were all Bible Students and model prisoners.

Now, SS Senior Supervisor Langefeld sympathised with them. She admired their constancy and respected their religious convictions. Through her secretary, Marianne Korn, who was herself a Bible Student, she learnt of the hell they were suffering in Block 3 thanks to the zeal and malice of Käthe Knoll. For the moment she could do nothing for them, because it was impossible to get rid of a woman who enjoyed the confidence and favour of the Camp Commandant himself, but she watched Käthe Knoll like a lynx until finally she caught her red-handed in a self-seeking offence against the camp regulations. She then put the worst possible interpretation on it and formally made a 'report'. Even the Commandant could not shield the culprit against his own Senior Supervisor, and so Käthe Knoll went off to the Bunkers to which she had condemned so many others.

But now the problem arose of finding a suitable Block Senior, someone Langefeld and Marianne Korn could rely on to satisfy the formal requirements of camp discipline and yet treat the Bible Students decently. Whilst they were still discussing the difficult question, SS Leader Drechsler arrived, indignantly demanding the removal and punishment of the Hut Senior of 'A' Wing for insolence, describing her (me) as 'a hopeless idiot who had had the nerve to declare that another idiot couldn't be made responsible for an offence because she wasn't right in the head'. Here was the God-sent solution of Langefeld's difficulty: such 'a hopeless idiot' was exactly what she wanted to look after her Bible Students. And so I was promoted Block Senior.

With mixed feelings, I took up my duties that afternoon at Block 3. It was situated on the right-hand side of the camp street opposite Block 1, which contained 'old' Politicals. There was a very different atmosphere here. The place was silent and smelt of cleaning powder, disinfectant and cabbage soup. Two hundred and seventy women sat at the tables and ate their meal in silence, and hardly a word was spoken. It was not what I had been used to, and I found it a little overpowering. As soon as I went into the room, a tall, blonde woman rose, led me to a seat and served me with a bowl of cabbage soup. I hardly knew what to do. Should I tell them who I was and why I had come? Ought I to deliver a speech in this expectant silence? Should I tell them they could talk, so that I could have some noise around me?

Wherever I looked along the tables there were the same modest smiling faces. All of them had their hair tied at the back in a tight bun, and they sat there in perfect order and ate their food as though they were all on the same string. Most of them seemed to be peasant women, and their lean faces were brown and wrinkled from the sun and the wind. Under each bowl there was a little cardboard mat – 'because otherwise there might be rings on the table,' as I learnt subsequently. The floor in the corridor and between the tables was laid out with big sheets of brown paper in order that prisoners coming in from work outside should not dirty it. At the door were brushes and scrapers, and no prisoner ever entered without first removing the mud and dirt from her clogs. After the meal one of the prisoners came up to me:

'Block Senior, may I go into the dormitory, please? I've forgotten something there.'

I gave her permission, and before she entered the dormitory I saw her take off her clogs and go in with stockinged feet. In the meantime, several women collected the bowls and spoons of all of them and carried them off to be washed. I sat where I was, still feeling a little strange and miserable in these new surroundings, and very uncertain of myself. The siren had not yet sounded for the afternoon 'labour parade', but without any special instructions or encouragement one after the other left the hut to line up. Many of them wore solid leather boots and lined, striped jackets – at this point I must mention that in the previous September the whole camp had received field-grey stockings, wooden clogs and jackets. The clothing of most of these Bible Students had been issued in the early days of concentration camps and it was made of better and warmer material. Many of these women had been in prison and concentration camp for years. Like the 'old' Politicals, their camp numbers were all low, and in this respect the Devil won a minor victory over them, for they were guilty of a certain modest pride in the fact.

As soon as the others had gone out, the duty squad got to work. It consisted of the tall blonde, Geesche, who was a Friesian, a Berliner named Friedel Schwann and a Saxon named Ella Hempel. They rapidly collected the paper on the floor and put it away neatly for use next time, dusted all ledges and carefully examined the tables for possible stains.

The Hut Senior of 'A' Wing came in. Her name was Bertel Schindler and she was a political Czech from Pardubitce. She was a different and altogether more human and approachable type than these humble and yet somehow self-sufficient sectarians. I liked her friendly face and lively manner from the beginning, and it was clear that we should get on together. The talk opened with an outburst of indignation against my predecessor, in which, somewhat to my surprise, the duty squad of Bible Students joined zealously.

Then they instructed me in my duties as Block Senior and told me exactly what I had to do on inspections when the much-feared Camp Commandant Kögel arrived with his visitors. I practised springing smartly to attention and rattling off my report on the state of the block. Thanks to them, too, I was told at once of all the little ways and tricks of Kögel.

My Hut Senior of 'B' Wing was Grete Bötzel, a German Pole, a thoroughly hateful person and a worthy subordinate of Käthe Knoll. It took me some time before I could assert my authority as Block Senior sufficiently to make her treat the Bible Students with some degree of consideration, and all the time she was there we lived on a footing of unspoken hostility. Later on she left us to become Block Senior elsewhere, to our great relief and to the misfortune of those who came under her control.

A Realm of Orderliness

I was taken round on a tour of inspection of this 'model block' of which I was now in charge. There were 275 prisoners – all Bible Students. All of them were model prisoners and all of them knew the camp rules and regulations inside out and obeyed them to the letter. One locker looked exactly like the other, and all of them were models of cleanliness and neatness. All the towels hung on the locker doors in exactly the same regulation fashion; every bowl, plate, cup, etc., was clean and highly polished. All combs were cleaned daily and each toothbrush was carefully searched for any stain or clogging. Not a fingerprint was visible on any door. The stools were scrubbed spotlessly clean and always neatly stacked when not in use. Not one of the prisoners ever broke the regulation that feet must not be put round the legs of stools for fear of marks. Dust was removed everywhere, even from the beams across the hut, for our hut had no ceiling and we looked up straight into the roof. I was told that some of the SS overseers went round with white gloves, passing their fingers over ledges and locker tops and even climbing on to the tables to find out whether the beams were dustless. The table tops seemed to be polished, and I discovered that this effect was obtained by pressing down the wood inch for inch with the back of a shoe-brush. The windows shone and you could quite literally have eaten off the floor, which was thoroughly scrubbed daily.

The office of the SS Block Leader was a picture of cleanliness, and the locker where the cleaning materials and utensils were kept was dazzling; every pail and bowl shone like a mirror. Lavatories and washroom were equally clean. Two women of the duty squad spent hours on them. But the culminating point of all this neatness and cleanliness was the dormitories, each containing 140 beds. The bed-building here was an astonishing achievement. Straw sacks and pillows were like boxes, each with its clearly defined edges, one exactly the same shape and size as the next, the whole forming absolutely impeccable rows. The blankets were all carefully folded in exactly the same way and exactly the same size, and all laid out on the beds in exactly the same pattern, showing exactly the same number of squares on the mattress coverings. At the end, neatly piled under the last bunk, lay the sticks and boards with which this marvel was achieved. On every bunk was a card bearing the name and number of the prisoner who slept in it, and on the door was a carefully drawn plan of the dormitory showing each bunk and exactly who slept in it, so that anyone inspecting could tell at once where everyone was.

In the day room there was a record showing just which table had to be first with the distribution of 'sweet soup' or the Sunday 'extra ladle' of *goulash*, and so on. Inside the door of each locker was a card on which the name and number of the prisoner responsible for it was neatly inscribed, and in the office were plans showing the exact position of everything in the block and just where each prisoner sat and slept and stood at the roll-call. There was also an exact record of every letter despatched and received – and so on and so on; lists, plans and graphs without end. And now I was in charge of all this complicated purgatory of cleanliness and order. The thought depressed me and I almost began to think that the lousy mud huts of Birma were preferable to this pedantic nightmare.

It was a strange life I now began to lead in Block 3. Whilst I was Hut Senior amongst the Asocials, the whole day had been occupied with some duty or other and disturbed with some new fear. With the Bible Students my life ran very smoothly. Everything went like clockwork. In the mornings, when everyone was intent on getting her jobs done before the roll-call, no one spoke a loud word. In other blocks the Block Seniors and Hut Seniors had to shout themselves hoarse before they could get their charges out into the open and into line, but here the whole procedure went off silently and without a word from me, and the same was true of everything else – the distribution of food, lights out, and all the rest of the prisoners' day.

My chief task with the Bible Students was to make their lives as tolerable as possible, to ward off the chicanery of the SS Block Leader, and to further the interests of each individual to the best of my ability. I had an opportunity of helping them in particular on the daily journey with sick prisoners to the medical post. What the Block Senior said to the SS matron or the SS doctor was usually decisive, and in this way I could usually obtain a 'bed card' or a permit for 'inside work'. In addition, occasionally there was a possibility of getting hold of aspirin tablets and similar medicaments, and securing more frequent changes of linen, and things of that nature.

Nothing was ever stolen in Block 3. There was no lying and no tale-bearing. Each of the women was not only highly conscientious personally, but held herself responsible for the well-being of the group as a whole. I had not been there very long before they realised that I was their friend and then they took me unreservedly into their community. During the two years I was with them as their Block Senior nothing ever happened to mar the relation of absolute confidence which existed between us.

Once this relationship had been established and I was quite confident that none of them would ever betray me, there were many things I could do for them – for instance, I saved the older and physically weaker prisoners from standing for hours at the roll-call with all sorts of excuses and tricks. I could not have done that with the Asocials, for those who were better able to stand the strain would have betrayed me to the SS in their resentment at the idea that anyone was being favoured.

The Bible Students formed the only homogeneous block amongst the prisoners at Ravensbrück. Apart from one or two Dutchwomen, they were all Germans, and they all belonged to the International Association of Bible Students. When I first went to Block 3 I had only the vaguest idea about their religious convictions and why Hitler disliked them. Dislike is a mild word to describe his attitude towards them; he denounced them as enemies of the State and persecuted them ruthlessly. Before 1933 an earnest, bespectacled woman had rung my bell and tried to persuade me to read a pamphlet about the imminent destruction of the world. I had refused politely, regarding her fears, or hopes, as premature. And now I lived my life amongst hundreds of equally earnest and sincere believers, and as they did not regard me as 'a vessel of wrath', they naturally tried to win me over to their beliefs – 'bearing witness' as it was called in their sectarian jargon.

Even as a child I had not been much interested in religion, and during the scripture lessons I had usually read some other and more interesting book under the desk. It was not easy for me to grasp just what their religion was all about, or to pin them down to anything concrete which was capable of logical discussion, particularly as I soon found that without exception they were simple-minded women of little or no education. They came from small towns or country villages, from peasant and lower middle-class families, and occasionally from working-class families, but then of the unskilled labourer type. It was useless to talk about natural science to them; they merely answered with a self-satisfied quotation from the Bible, which, to them, was a complete refutation of anything I might have said. And once when I innocently mentioned Darwin and natural selection a horrified hush descended as though I had conjured up the Devil himself.

It was not long before they realised that I was a very unlikely convert so they gave up their efforts, but they continued to show me their sympathy and never ceased to hope that one day I might 'see the light' and thus avoid the fate of the damned. As far as I could make out they believed that the whole of humanity, with the exception of Jehovah's Witnesses, was soon to be cast into everlasting darkness when the world came to an end. After that Jehovah's Witnesses would live on in the 'Golden Age' after 'Armageddon', at which Good was to triumph finally over Evil. The poor little crippled ugly duckling Erna would sit there and rave in her high-pitched, squeaky voice about all the wonders that awaited them. She was to rise again in the body, which was to be perfectly beautiful, and enjoy all the peace, happiness and good things she had missed on earth. Nation would no longer lift up sword against nation, the leopard would lie down with the kid; and the calf and the young lion and the fatling together, and no one would hurt or destroy in all His holy mountain. And there would be no more dying and everyone – the survivors – would live happily ever after and there would be no end to their felicity.

This simple and satisfactory belief lent them strength and made them able to stand the long years of concentration-camp life and all the indignities and humiliations and still retain their human dignity. They were given cause to prove, and they proved, that death had no terrors for them. They could die for their beliefs without shrinking. How much easier it is for a religious martyr to die for his faith, for he believes that everlasting happiness and glory await him on the other side. The political martyr must be content with sacrificing himself that others, future generations, may one day enjoy the fruits of his sacrifice.

It was not their belief in the imminent destruction of the world 'so as by fire' which made these people enemies of Hitler's State, but their opposition to all established organisations, both political and religious, to Hitler's State and to the Catholic Church, both of which they regarded as 'instruments of the Devil'. They regarded the Nazi regime as the work of the Antichrist, the crowning of the diabolical which was, as the Bible prophesied, to stand at the end of days and be followed shortly afterwards by the casting of all unbelievers into Hell. At the same time they took the Sixth Commandment seriously and in consequence they were determined opponents of all wars and all military service. Their constancy in this respect cost many of the male Witnesses their lives. The women of the sect also refused to perform any work which in their opinion was calculated to further the war effort. As usual in such complicated questions, they were guilty of many inconsistencies, and in the concentration camps they were the most highly prized and most sought-after workers. They cleaned the houses of the SS officials and the quarters of the overseers; they looked after the children of the SS in their children's homes; they served as maids to the Camp Commandant and other SS officers; they tended the SS kitchen garden; and they fed the SS bloodhounds, police dogs, pigs, chickens and rabbits. Their sense of duty and their feeling of responsibility were unshakeable; they were industrious, honest and obedient – in short, they were ideal slaves for the SS. They were even given special passes permitting them to leave and enter the camp for their work, for, as the SS finally realised, no Bible Student would ever dream of trying to escape from a concentration camp; that would have been tantamount to rejecting the crown of martyrdom. The Witnesses were, so to speak, 'voluntary prisoners', for all they had to do in order to secure their immediate release was to sign the special Bible Students' form which read: 'I declare herewith that from this day on I no longer consider myself a Bible Student and that I will do nothing to further the interests of the International Association of Bible Students.'

There were piles of these forms in the SS office, but up to 1942 very, very few were ever signed. However, later on, when the persecution against them grew more brutal and ruthless, the weaker sisters began to sign, though even then they were the exception.

'I don't understand why you don't sign this ridiculous form,' I said one day to an elderly 'Witness'. 'After all, promises made under duress have no moral significance and no binding value. And outside you could carry on with your work.'

'No,' she replied firmly. 'We could not reconcile that with our consciences. To sign the SS form would be to pact with the Devil.'

They gladly suffered for their beliefs, particularly as they were convinced that the more they suffered the greater their reward would be after the forces of Good had triumphed at 'Armageddon'. It struck me as an accountant's form of morality, but they were obviously not conscious of it. If one of their 'sisters', as they called each other, won the crown of martyrdom, they showed no trace of sadness or horror. 'She has passed over. She is happier than we are,' they would say at the news that another of their friends had suffered death as the culmination of their often horrible sufferings in the camp.

Before I became their Block Senior, they suffered much from the fact that Käthe Knoll did her utmost to prevent them from engaging in religious discussion with each other. At the slightest suspicion she would threaten them with 'reports'. This was a dreadful deprivation for them because they lived in the Bible and all their thoughts revolved around it. Everything that happened had to be corroborated by some text or other in the Scriptures; and everything that happened from the beginning of the world and would still happen to its end was all prophesied in the Bible, if you could only find the right place. They even found their own personal fates prefigured in the Word. To stop them from talking about it all and comparing notes – 'studying the Bible', in short – was a kind of Chinese torture, and Käthe Knoll had applied it with malicious zeal.

I had been their Block Senior for some time before I discovered that my 'Bible Worms', as they were known in the camp, possessed Bibles and Bible Students literature. Under Käthe Knoll's regime they had never dared to smuggle them into the block, and they had probably read them in spare moments at their outside work and left them hidden in safe places. But under my benevolent regime – which, incidentally, was also prophesied in the Bible – they began to bring them in, hidden in pails and floorcloths and so on, when they came in from work. When I discovered it I suggested that it would be less dangerous if they hid them somewhere in the block, and this suggestion was enthusiastically adopted. After that Bible studying went on quite openly in the block in the evenings and on Sundays. And in bed at night, before the SS women came round with their dogs, they would sing their hymns softly. My job was to see that they had ample warning of danger and an opportunity to hide away their forbidden literature. When we left Block 3 and moved to Block 17, which was situated in the newly built second camp street, we had a ceiling to our hut and then we carefully made a cache between ceiling and roof for all this forbidden material.

'Grete,' they said, 'every day we thank Jehovah that He sent you to us. Our sufferings were terrible and we never ceased to pray that He might have mercy on us. And, you see, He did.'

I got this in varying forms from all of them at one time or another, and it was usually followed up by another attempt at proselytism, from which I would fly out into the fresh air with a hurriedly murmured: 'Yes, yes. Good. That's all right.'

Inspection

But in the meantime I was running no small risk. I was Block Senior and responsible for everything that went on. It was the 'Golden Age' of my life in concentration camp – post-Armageddon so to speak – but how I managed to survive inspection after inspection headed by that brute Kögel without landing in Punishment Block or Bunkers I don't know to this day. The risk was increased by the fact that even conscientious Bible Students are human, and under my mild regime they began to fall away from their former exemplary state and be guilty of various minor infringements of the camp rules. For instance, gradually they became every bit as adept at 'organising' coffee-making and potato-cooking as the inmates of any other block. And because it happened, no matter what care was taken, there was the danger of discovery. And I was responsible. If Kögel had found out even once, my fate would have been the Bunkers.

But there was a still more dangerous game I played. When a prisoner felt ill she had to report through me to the medical post. The acid test was the thermometer. According to its reading, the sick woman would be sent into the sickbay, be permitted to do 'inside work', or be sent out mercilessly to her ordinary labours. Now, amongst the 'Witnesses' there were quite a number of older women who, although they had no fever, were just so weak that work was really beyond them. The only way to spare them and let them have a day off from time to time was for me to give false reports of the numbers in the gangs, and this I did. What would have happened to me if this had been discovered I hesitate to think. It was made more difficult by the fact that we were the Inspection Block, but somehow or other all dangers were circumvented and I was never found out.

To reduce all risks to a minimum, we organised a constant watch. One of the four members of the 'Duty Squad' was always stationed at the window which overlooked the camp street, from which side danger was most likely to come. In addition, around eleven in the morning and three in the afternoon, which were the most dangerous times, I would invent some pretext or other for leaving the block and going outside to look around, or I would send my Hut Senior out for the same purpose. And then a stout shield was Marianne Korn, Langefeld's secretary. She knew what I risked, and at the least sign of danger she would find some means of sending us warning.

As soon as the warning sounded, 'They're coming!' all the prisoners who were in the block without 'inside work' permits would rush off and lock themselves in the lavatories. Those who were in bed right at the end of the dormitory were told to keep as quiet as mice; all the pots with potatoes, soup or coffee were whisked away; the window was opened to let out any possible smell of food; those who were properly present hastily sat down at the tables and began to work on socks; and I hastily adjusted my headdress in the regulation fashion and buttoned up the top button of my dress. Then I would march smartly towards Commandant Kögel and his herd of visitors to welcome them at the door. On such occasions my legs invariably felt as though they were made of india-rubber.

According to the rank and significance of his visitors, Kögel would be dressed in ordinary or gala uniform complete with all his clinking load of medals. Coming smartly to attention, clicking my heels, and keeping my arms to my side, I would report in the appropriate subaltern voice:

'Block Senior Margarete Buber, No. 4,208. Report obediently Block No. 3 occupied by 275 Bible Students and three Politicals, of whom 260 are at work, eight have hut duties and seven permits for inside work.'

Kögel would stare at me with his watery blue eyes, his clean-shaven jowls twitching, and grunt something. Then I would go ahead on the routine inspection, opening one door after the other, and the first three lockers. And as we approached the prisoners properly and legitimately present, I would snarl 'Achtung!' whereupon they would all spring up like jacks-in-the-box. All the visitors, whether male or female, SA, SS, or what-not, would invariably be impressed by the shining tin and aluminium. Kögel was usually the only one to put questions to the prisoners. If anyone else attempted to do so, he would immediately intervene. Each time he would ask one of the women present, 'Why were you arrested?' and invariably the answer would come: 'Because I am a Witness of Jehovah.' That would be all the questioning, for Kögel knew from experience that these incorrigible Bible Students never missed an opportunity for a demonstration. 'Carry on,' he would order, and the prisoners would then go on with their knitting or whatever other work had been specially prepared for such a contingency.

After that the visitors would look into the dormitory, and invariably there would be loud exclamations at the spotless order they found there. At which Kögel would shout:

'Block Senior! How much time have the prisoners between reveille and roll-call?'

'Three-quarters of an hour, Herr Camp Commandant.'

And then Kögel would point to the beds. 'Three-quarters of an hour, ladies and gentlemen,' he would declare with pride. 'And in that time look what my prisoners do: bed-building, dressing, washing, locker-cleaning, coffee-drinking and then roll-call. And look at these exemplary beds. Or perhaps you think there are boards under the blankets?' And then he would go over to one of the beds and turn back the covers and smack the mattress with his whip. 'Look at that straw sack. See how it's packed. That's merely one of the results of the work we do here to educate the prisoners back to a life of order and cleanliness.'

Then he would regularly stride to the window, which was immediately opposite the window of the next hut, whose far window was immediately opposite the window of the one beyond, and so on right down the line, so that visitors could gaze right through all the huts on that side and see neverending lines of bunks. With a proud movement of his arm, Kögel would embrace the lot, saying in an impressive voice: 'And all those huts are just as clean and orderly as this one; you can take my word for that.'

And his visitors would crowd round the window and look through with admiration at the evidence of the great work being done in concentration camp Ravensbrück to educate the enemies of the State and other inferior elements to be good and useful citizens of the National Socialist People's Community.

After 'A' Wing, exactly the same ritual was performed in 'B' Wing. And once the cigarette-smoking, stamping, clinking mob had trooped off, the prisoners locked in the toilets would tumble out again in great relief, the work would be shoved to one side and the pots with food would reappear on the tables or on the stove. Once again we had survived an inspection.

But on one such inspection it was almost all up with me and my heart sank into my boots. When the inspection was almost over and the crowd was about to move off, one of the visitors asked Kögel whether he might inspect the lavatories.

'Why, of course,' answered Kögel jovially. 'Of course. And you'll find the same cleanliness and order there as everywhere else. Block Senior, lead the way.'

I led the way in despair. I went to open the first WC door, quite expecting to find it locked because it contained three or four prisoners hiding themselves from Kögel's sight, but to my surprise it opened and proved to be empty. The inquisitive visitor went in and pulled the plug. The water closet flushed according to plan and with a fatuous smile on his face he expressed himself as satisfied, adding: 'During the war I was interned in England. The water closets never functioned properly there. It just shows you the difference in culture.'

And then they did go. I had to sit down and recover. My heart threatened to choke me and my legs refused to support me any longer. But really I needn't have worried at all – it was all in the Bible.

Modern Martyrs

Although the SS Senior Supervisor Frau Langefeld favoured and protected the 'Witnesses', one of the leading overseers, a woman named Zimmer, regarded them as her *bête noire*. She was between fifty and sixty years of age, a typical old prison wardress, and she had the reputation of dearly loving the bottle. The 'Witnesses' whose job it was to clean her quarters reported that she was about as dirty and untidy as a woman could possibly be. When she came to our block, it was usually the prelude to an inspection by outsiders. Frau Zimmer was satisfied with nothing; not even the most exemplary bed met with approval in her eyes, and she never missed an opportunity to abuse and bully the Witnesses.

'You old hags,' she would say; 'sitting around here and squawking about Jehovah. Why don't you go home and look after your children and your husbands? Get back to your households, you stupid old women.'

The Bible Students and Frau Zimmer were old enemies from the days of Lichtenberg, the first concentration camp for women.

But my 'Witnesses' were not always talking about Jehovah and the coming Golden Age, particularly on Saturdays, when the post was distributed. Then they had letters from their husbands. Many of these men were also Bible Students, and they were in Buchenwald, Dachau, Sachsenhausen and other concentration camps for their beliefs. But some of the women received letters from home, and they all contained the same urgent pleadings. I remember one of them:

MY DEAR ELLA, – When will you make up your mind to come home at last? The children are asking for you every day. The household is going more and more to rack and ruin, and the children aren't getting the proper attention. The garden is overgrown with weeds. How can you be so hard-hearted and leave your nearest and dearest like this? I'm sure God can't want you to do that.

And when she read it Ella dissolved into tears. Her distress and agony of mind were so obvious that I intervened.

'What your husband says is right, Ella. How can you make them suffer on your account? Why don't you go home to them?'

But Ella dried her tears and looked defiant.

'You're a child of this world,' she declared. 'You can't understand. Jehovah demands that His followers should leave wife and child – and that means husband as well – and follow Him.'

And with that she seized cloth and bucket and began cleaning the floor with great determination.

These 500 women had become Bible Students for various reasons. Some of them were 'Witnesses' because their husbands were. These were, so to speak, the 'moderates'. A few of them came from Bible Student families, and some of these were very young, hardly in their twenties. However, the great majority had 'seen the light' at some time or other and been 'saved'. In the majority of such cases the women came from very poor circumstances. They had always had to struggle hard in order to live. They had been deeply disappointed in life and most of them were unhappily married. One might fairly say that the great majority of these women had lived unhappy lives and therefore they were not in love with this life and hoped for something better in a future world.

They fled from the burden of responsibility this life placed on them and sought refuge in the role of martyrs, and in the name of Jehovah they condemned all the 'worldly-wise'. Once they were Bible Students, their lives changed; from being wretched and miserable, oppressed and hard done by, they suddenly became members of 'the Elect'. Their former resentment at their own personal fates changed into an arrogant contempt for everyone and everything which did not belong to their own little sect. Each of them felt herself the chosen instrument of God's wrath and wallowed with joy in the thought that the whole of humanity was soon to be plunged for ever into fire and brimstone. Only the few thousand 'Witnesses' were to survive this cosmic holocaust. Apart from their religious fanaticism, most of them were good-natured, helpful souls and I got on well with them.

But on one occasion – it was in the spring of 1942 – an incident took place which was more than I could stand. I have already mentioned that by this time the 'Sick Transports' were being organised – that is to say, the unfit were being sent to the gas chamber. It was the duty of the Block Seniors to report the names of sick and unfit prisoners in their charge. Naturally, I always insisted that I had no one who was not capable of work. Any indisposition was always purely temporary. But amongst my lame ducks was a woman of about fifty named Anna Lück. She was suffering from tubercular glands which suppurated and so from time to time she had to be bandaged. For the most part we managed to keep her in bed, but one day, when she had to go to the medical post for treatment, the SS doctor saw her and put her name on the 'Sick Transport List'. I heard of this only a few days later from a friend who worked at the medical post. By that time it was too late to do anything; the list was already completed and signed. Only one way of escape remained open and that was to persuade her to sign the 'Bible Student Declaration'.

With a heavy heart, I went to her bunk to tell her the news. My face must have betrayed me, and she knew at once that something serious was wrong; probably guessed that she was to go with the 'Sick Transport'. Her eyes seemed unnaturally large in her sunken features as she stared at me in horror. I told her without beating about the bush exactly what had happened, and that the only way to save her life was to sign the Bible Student undertaking without delay. And then I used all the force of argument and persuasion I could muster to get her to agree to sign. The fear of death is a potent factor even in a sick, middle-aged woman for whom on the face of it life can offer very little, and in the end she agreed.

But less than half an hour later Ella Hempel accosted me with an expression of mingled indignation and reproach.

'How could you!' she exclaimed. 'Grete, I didn't think it of you. That you could join the Devil and make common cause with the SS.'

'What are you talking about, Ella?' I asked in astonishment, completely at a loss to understand the reason for her outburst. 'What do you mean, I've made common casue with the SS?'

'You've advised Anna Lück to sign the undertaking and lose her immortal soul. How could you do such a thing? It's wicked.'

My patience was at an end this time. 'Wicked!' I repeated furiously. My voice rose and for the first time in my life I shouted at a Jehovah's witness: 'You talk to me about being wicked and you want to send her to the gas chamber. Fine Christians you are. Her soul, or whatever you call it, isn't in your keeping. Tell me any Christian commandment that justifies letting her go to her death like a mangy cat? Is that sisterly love? She's supposed to be your sister, isn't she? A fine religion you've got. Not only do you let your children go to Nazi children's homes and be maltreated, but you even want to help the Nazis slaughter your own sister. And all in the name of God. Get out of my sight. You make me sick.'

Ella turned and fled, leaving me snorting with rage. I assumed that from now on we should be enemies, but no, after that her attitude was servility itself, and it was then I began to dislike her.

One day one of the Bible students came to me and declared that henceforth she and her sisters would no longer eat blood sausage. Let me explain the background. Up to 1943 we received, in addition to our bread ration of about 500 grams (just over one pound), a plate of vegetables and five or six potatoes cooked in their jackets, and, in the evening, soup. On Saturdays and Sundays the evening meal was cold. It consisted of about twenty grams of margarine and some cheese on Saturday, and about two ounces of sausage, sometimes blood sausage, on Sunday. But then things gradually got worse. Pod vegetables disappeared entirely, the fat in the food became less and less, the weekly portion of fat stopped altogether, and jam was reduced to about a spoonful a week. The sugar was stolen by the SS and we got none. And in the end all we could get in the prisoners' canteen was a very inferior sort of fish paste and something quite horrible described as 'vegetable salad'.

In that situation any refusal to eat what was, after all, a superior item of food was serious, but a young witness, Ilse Unterdörter, discovered in the Bible a line about letting the blood flow into the ground, and this she interpreted as meaning that Jehovah's Witnesses must henceforth eat no blood sausage. However, she did not succeed in carrying all her sisters with her. Within the community there were three 'fractions': the extremists, the wavering middle and the moderates. These fractions fought each other fiercely, every bit as fiercely as political fractions struggling for control do. They accused each other of treachery and abused their rivals with rude names culled from the Bible.

About twenty-five of the extremists firmly refused to eat any blood sausage. Always on the lookout for a workable compromise, I tried to minimise the dispute and declared that those who didn't want to eat blood sausage need not do so; they could have liver sausage instead; the two sorts usually came up together. But no, that wouldn't do at all; it had gone far beyond the blood sausage and developed into a demonstration in honour of Jehovah. The extremists wanted to provoke the SS. They hungered and thirsted after martyrdom, so they drew up a list of the names of all those who refused to eat blood sausage and presented it in the office. At first the SS only laughed: very well, if they didn't want blood sausage, they needn't have it; and if they didn't have blood sausage they didn't need margarine, so that was stopped as well. But when as the result of fierce disputes between the fractions another section was won over to the extremists and a second list went in, the SS adopted draconic measures: our peaceful Bible Student Block was presented with a hundred Asocials, all of them specially chosen blossoms – the 'morons', the bedwetters, the epileptics, the women with tics of all kinds. That was our punishment.

Denunciation, theft and brawling became part and parcel of our daily lives. The Asocials immediately began to denounce the 'Witnesses' for Bible studies and religious discussions; they stole everything they could lay hands on; and, feeling themselves the representatives of authority, conducted themselves generally in a thoroughly aggressive and provocative fashion. And how sad it was for me! But to the credit of my 'Witnesses' be it said that they rallied to me in my difficulties and supported me in every possible way. Thanks to them, we managed to struggle through for six months – as long as the scourge lasted – without serious trouble.

The affair was finally resolved in a simply grotesque fashion, and by this time I was quite prepared to see the hand of Jehovah in it all. When the invasion came, I did my best to isolate the trouble-makers. I kept the 'Witnesses' at separate tables so that they could discuss their affairs during meals without the danger of denunciation, and at night I put the Asocials in the top bunks and the 'Witnesses' below. However, as it transpired, the authorities – the prime mover in the scheme was Frau Zimmer, who was only too glad to have an opportunity of making life difficult for the Bible Students – must have picked us out all the notorious bed-wetters in the camp, and night after night it rained down on the innocents in the bunks beneath.

One day our old enemy, Frau Zimmer, came in to survey her handiwork. She immediately spotted my separation of the sheep from the goats and turned on me indignantly.

'You needn't think I'm blind,' she declared. 'I know perfectly well you shield and protect the Bible-punchers here. You're responsible for the whole farce. Don't you dare separate the Bible Worms and the Asocials, do you hear? The whole idea is that they should be together. I don't want any more of this jawing about Jehovah. Do you understand?'

'Certainly. Very good, Frau Leading Overseer.'

And off she waddled in high dudgeon. Well, that was it; I had to mix them all up and hope for the best. It was at this point that Jehovah intervened. The Bible Students accepted the Asocials like long-lost sisters: Were they hungry? Were they! Would they like an extra piece of bread? Would they! And so it went on. I watched this Christian charity in operation with mixed feelings, but it worked. The Asocials were softened up with kindness and friendliness, and then a campaign began to show them the light. In quite a short space of time there were quite a number of Asocials – a gipsy, a Pole, a Jewess and a Political – who presented themselves at the SS office, declaring that henceforth they wished to be regarded as Jehovah's Witnesses and demanding the lilac traingle for their sleeves. When it got too bad, the SS just stormed and raved at the converts and threw then out. In the end the SS got so fed up that they removed the Asocials from our block and peace descended again. I breathed a sigh of relief, and the 'Witnesses' held a prayer meeting to render thanks to Jehovah.

Milena

In October 1940 – I had been Block Senior only for a short time then – the Hut Senior of the new Reception Block 7 came to me with a message of greetings from Lotte Henschel, who was amongst the newcomers. Thanks to the authority of my green Block Senior armlet, I was able to invent some excuse for visiting the Reception Block. Our meeting was a great joy to me, for we were old friends, and I had been so long without a real friend. We met again during the exercise hour of the newcomers as they walked up and down along the camp wall. At intervals along the grass were the warning boards with their yellow skull and crossbones. It was then that she introduced me to Milena Jesenska.

Milena was a Czech journalist who spoke German with a soft Slav accent. She shook hands with me almost without bending her fingers and immediately asked me not to press too hard. She was almost crippled with rheumatism contracted during her imprisonment. Her joints were swollen and she was almost always in pain. During the long standing at roll-calls she shivered with cold and at night she could not get warm under the thin blankets. Her face had the typical greyness of the long-term prisoner and in her eyes was the evidence of much suffering. But when I first met her in 1940 her spirit was unbroken and she was cheerful and courageous. With her dark eyes and her jaunty curls, she was a good-looking woman, but in her long camp dress with boots too large for her she looked like a scarecrow with a lovely face.

She had heard of my fate from Lotte, and as a journalist she was anxious to question me about my experiences. Questioning to extract as much information as possible in the shortest space of time is a journalistic art, and it was one she had thoroughly mastered. Walking up and down along 'The Wailing Wall' as she called it, I told her all she wanted to know. From the beginning we were friends and we remained so throughout four bitter camp years until her death. I became much attached to her and her state of health caused me constant anxiety. I was so afraid I should lose a new-found friend.

In 1930 she had joined the Czech Communist Party, but she was too independent a spirit to make a good Party member in the circumstances which already existed in the Communist Parties by that time. The trouble came to a head in 1936, and in 1937 she was expelled from the Party. She worked for Czech newspapers up to the time of the German invasion, and then she took part in the Czech resistance movement and assisted Czech airmen and other officers to escape abroad. In 1939 she was arrested by the Gestapo in Prague, and she had been in prison or concentration camp ever since.

The Czech Communists in Ravensbrück knew her political attitude, but they tried to win her over, and through their influence she obtained light work in the sickbay. We had not known each other more than a few days when Palečkova, the leader of the Czech Communists in the camp, asked whether she knew that I was a Trotskyite who spread slanders about the Soviet Union. She replied that she was quite able to judge for herself about what I told her. A few days later they delivered an ultimatum: she must choose between them and me. She chose at once, and from that time on she had to cope with the enmity of the Czech and German Stalinists in the camp. For four years she was subjected to their hatred and chicanery. It was not so bad as long as she ws still fairly well in health, but as she became more and more ill she suffered terribly from their persecution. Day after day she had to share the same room and breathe the same air as her enemies. In such circumstances there are a dozen and one opportunities for petty cruelties every day.

And what they found most difficult to forgive was her refusal to share their facile optimism. From the very beginning the war ended every three months; every few weeks a new revolution broke out somewhere or other; and Hitler was assassinated a dozen and one times. Optimistic rumours swept through our camp constantly, and as the next one arose the old one was forgotten. When they were repeated to Milena, she plucked them to pieces mercilessly – and got herself still more hated for her pains. When Hitler attacked Russia in 1941 the camp was swept with pro-Russian enthusiasm, in which not only the Stalinists, but almost all the other Politicals joined. But Milena answered the enthusiasts with a picture of what Europe would be like if it ever came under Russian domination. Even I argued with her, but when I look back on her words now they seem like Sibylline prophecy.

'If ever I get out of here alive, I don't suppose for one moment I shall be able to return to Prague,' she would say. 'But where should I go?' For my part, I did not believe that the Western Powers would be so blind as to allow the Russians to drive forward into Europe, but, together with her, I forged many a plan for us in the future. The Stalinists told us that when the Russians came we should both be put against the wall or sent to Siberia. When that threat began to look real as the Russians came nearer and nearer to our camp, I was glad that Milena was dead. At least she had died in bed without having to suffer that.

Thanks to her work in the Medical Post, Milena was able to save the lives of many of the prisoners. She deliberately falsified returns, and each time she risked her life. In 1941 she tried to secure the release of Lotte on medical grounds. Lotte had served four years' hard labour before she came to us and her state of health was very bad. At that time prisoners with tuberculosis were often released from Ravensbrück and so Milena faked a sputum test which showed Lotte to be suffering from tuberculosis. Lotte was admitted into the TB station and and application for her release was filed. It was at this time that the so-called Sick Transports were introduced. The first of these transports left Ravensbrück whilst Lotte officially was suffering from tuberculosis. The terrible suspicion was first aroused I don't know how, and it was quickly confirmed. A lorry returned with the clothing and personal effects of all the women who had gone off in the first transport, and then we knew. They had been sent to their deaths. And Lotte was in the TB station! Her fate was certain. Milena was in a terrible state, but somehow or other she managed to arrange for new sputum tests and, of course, they were all negative. Lotte had made a miraculous recovery and she was discharged. Milena and I breathed again.

Whilst I was still Block Senior with the Bible Students, Milena often came to me and we would sit together in the Block Office talking whilst she warmed herself at the fire. 'Just to sit somewhere in a field again under a tree with the sun shining!' It was the picture which was always in her mind. Deep down in her heart she knew it would never be realised – and so did I. What I had told her about my experiences in Birma inspired her to write a book – if ever she recovered her freedom – a book on concentration camps under two dictatorships, with roll-calls, marching columns, and millions of humiliated slaves, in one dictatorship in the name of Socialism and the other for the benefit of the Master Race.

The summer of 1941 was hot. Night work had been introduced in the garment shops and the undernourishment and exhaustion of the prisoners became more and more obvious. The legs of many of the women began to swell, and often they were covered with boils and eczema. Then one or two cases of paralysis occurred. It is possible that these cases were the first fruits of SS Dr Sonntag's experimental venereal cures. By the time the number of cases had risen to twelve, the camp authorities began to get worried. Rumours spread through the camp that infantile paralysis was rife in Mecklenburg, and then the camp was declared in quarantine. The prisoners were confined to their own barracks and no columns went out to work. The women who worked in the kitchens were not allowed to return to their barracks at nights and had to sleep in the washrooms. Barbed wire was erected to prevent contact between the various blocks. The SS authorities no longer came into the camp proper – except Frau Zimmer, who considered herself immune. From time to time she would waddle from block to block to ensure that camp discipline was still being upheld.

The prisoners were delighted; it was like a holiday. Only the fact that case after case was carried out from the huts on stretchers to a special isolation barracks spread fear and alarm. All the cases showed the same symptoms; they were suddenly unable to move their limbs. One thing should have been obvious to the SS medical experts: neither the 'old' Politicals nor the Bible Students were affected; all the cases occurred amongst the Asocials, the gipsies and the 'Polish love-birds', as the girls and women were called who had had Polish boyfriends and been caught. After about a week the number of paralysis cases had risen to 100. A veritable flood of disinfectants poured over the camp. Everything was disinfected – the lavatories, the washrooms, the day rooms, the dormitories, even the kitchen utensils – and our food tasted of it. Each block delivered up its food containers separately, and each time the receptacles were carefully washed out with disinfectant. During exercise the prisoners of each block were kept strictly segregated from the others.

After two weeks of this strict quarantine regime a commission of medical specialists arrived. They were well versed in all the symptoms of infantile paralysis, and it did not take them long to discover that there was nothing of the sort in our camp. The whole affair turned out to be an epidemic of mass hysteria. Dr Sonntag revenged himself on his patients for his discomfiture. Violent electric shocks were administered to them, causing them to spring up in horror and demonstrating that they had the full use of their limbs. That method was a little hard on one or two cases of rheumatic fever and on the women Dr Sonntag had crippled with his experimental venereal cure, but it put a swift end to the epidemic of infantile paralysis in Camp Ravensbrück.

A Neighbour's Death

As the years passed more and more women were sent to concentration camp until even with overcrowding our camp could not hold them all and had to be extended. Behind 'The Wailing Wall' a new line of wooden huts was erected and then an entrance was knocked through the wall and prisoners put into these new huts. My Bible Students and I were all transferred to Blocks 17 and 19, and a strange battle began, fought out with persistence and obstinacy, for permission to take along the old mattresses – they had been given such a wonderful shape by years of hard work. Our new block, No. 17, was painted inside with real white oil paint and had a whitewashed ceiling. For concentration camp conditions, it ranked as 'lovely'.

During 1940 and 1941 many transports of Polish women were brought into Ravensbrück. It seemed almost as though Hitler had determined to wipe out the Polish people altogether. All sections of the population and all ages were represented. A rumour arose from somewhere that many of these women were under sentence of death, and that a whole transport had been sent from Warsaw to Ravensbrück for the sole purpose of execution. In the spring of 1942 ten of these Polish women were called out and taken to the Punishment Block. Shortly before the evening roll-call the camp street was cleared and all prisoners ordered back to their huts. Prisoners working in the kitchen and the medical post saw these ten women led across the camp square barefooted and in long frocks without belts, looking like medieval penitents. As they went out of the camp gates, they turned and waved cheerfully, perhaps in the hope that some of their friends who had been left behind could see them.

Shortly afterwards the evening siren howled for the roll-call. It was about six o'clock. We stood there in our thousands and waited as usual. Everything was silent, and then suddenly from the other side of the camp wall sounded a rattle of shots, followed a second or two later by several single shots. We did not need to be told what had happened. The first executions had taken place in Ravensbrück. Opposite us stood the women of the Polish Block, and I could see their lips moving in silent prayer. Behind the wall the pines caught the evening sun as usual and gradually the host of crows settled down again on the roof of the Kommandantur.

The faces of the women around me had changed. We knew that a new and terrible period had opened up for Camp Ravensbrück and our hearts were heavy with dread.

That was only the beginning. From then on executions frequently took place on the other side of the camp wall whilst we were drawn up and waiting in silence, our nerves charged, our ears strained for the volley. Sometimes there would be screams, and in our minds we pictured the scenes taking place just out of our sight.

Wicklein, the Adjutant of Camp Commandant Kögel, supervised the executions. They were carried out by a special squad of SS, who were brought in for the purpose. From my Bible Students who worked in the SS Canteen, I learnt that these men were first given a big meal and plenty of spirits in the canteen before going off to do their work.

In the winter of 1941–2 a 'Medical Commission' arrived in Ravensbrück. Before their arrival all the sick and incapable had been listed through the Block Seniors, and we were given to believe that they were to be transferred to another camp, where they would have only light work to do, or, if necessary, to sanatoria. All these prisoners, in so far as they were not already confined to their beds, had to file before this Commission, which sat in the washrooms. Then the Commission departed, only to return a little later. This time all the women in the Jewish Block had to parade before them.

The first Sick Transport left Ravensbrück at the beginning of 1942. The women were put into lorries, the lying cases being bedded on the floors of the lorries on straw. Milena and I already suspected the truth, but the next day our suspicions were confirmed. A lorry arrived bringing all the personal effects of the sick prisoners, including their triangles with numbers, their toothbrushes and so on. Amongst the debris were even crutches, an artificial leg and several sets of false teeth. The sick prisoners had gone to their deaths. The terrible news swept through the camp at once, and hundreds knew they must expect the same fate, and yet they still hoped. They invented all sorts of explanations to deceive themselves: the prisoners had been given new clothes for the sanatoria, etc. They preferred to ignore the artificial leg and the sets of teeth. After that these Sick Transports went off frequently, and with gruesome regularity one

lorry returned the next day bringing back all the effects of the slaughtered prisoners. After the sick, hundreds of Jewish prisoners went the
same way. One of them arranged to hide a secret message in the seam
of her dress. It was found: 'We have been brought to Dessau. Now we
have been ordered to strip. Goodbye.'

Both Sick Transport and executions went on regularly and our days
became terrible. More and more women were brought into the camp.
They came from all the occupied countries of Europe. And then the
children arrived . . .

The first one was Angela, a little nine-year-old gipsy girl; dirty and
ragged, but as pretty as a picture. She would trot around during the
exercise hour amongst her numerous relatives, and the eyes of the women
would follow her sadly. The women embraced her, gave her bread, and
petted her. She and a second arrival were then handed over to the SS
Supervisor Massar to be taught a little Nazi discipline.

At the sight of the first children, all the women found their eyes
strangely wet, but it was not long before children were such a common
sight that they attracted no further attention. Jewish mothers came with
their children from Holland, Belgium and France. A curly-haired cherub
sat on a stool in the waiting room of the Medical Post and played with
a teddy bear. It was a little child from Turkey and it played around innocently amidst the turmoil of worried mothers who had been ordered to
come for a 'medical'.

Children were now part and parcel of the camp life. They turned out
at five o'clock in the morning with their mothers and stood around for
hours in cold, heat, rain and wind. As they did not work, they were not
even given a ration of potatoes, but just a wretched mess of dried vegetables and a small ration of bread. They were always hungry and they
trooped daily from hut to hut begging for food. At first the motherly
feelings of the women were deeply moved at the sight of these poor
mites begging for a crust of bread, and so they got plenty, but before
long the little beggars were just a nuisance.

One Sunday in 1943, Lotte Henschel, Maria Gropp and I were
strolling through the camp when we found a little girl of about three,
clutching a miserable rag doll to her heaving chest and weeping bitterly.
She was lost and didn't know what hut she belonged to. It was very
easy for young children to get lost, because one hut looked just like the
rest, and if the children were not old enough to know their numbers
there was no way of telling one from the other. Lotte picked up the
child and we went from block to block trying to find where it belonged.
In every block nervous and irritable women were engaged in various
tasks, and we could find no one who knew the child or was even suffi-

ciently interested to help us. None of the Block or Hut Seniors recognised the child, which in the meantime had fallen asleep in Lotte's arms. She woke up when we were in the Office of the Jewish Block, and at the sight of all the Jewesses around declared indignantly: 'I'm not a Jewish child. I'm a Romany.' There was racial pride even in the voice of this three-year-old. From there we went straight to the gipsy block and found her mother.

In 1944 a gipsy camp where men and women had been interned together was disbanded and the women came to us. Husbands and wives were separated. The men and all the male children of twelve and over were sent to other camps, whilst the women and girls and the boys below twelve came to us. Many of the children were babes in arms. One evening the camp street was alive with children and I learnt that they had been ordered to line up to go to the kitchen and get a spoonful of synthetic honey each. Ragged and with broken boots, but all holding aluminium mugs in their hands, they formed into line. One or two twelve-year-old boys were in command and in the end they got some sort of order into the crowd, and then the march began, all the children singing, 'We're marching on to England,' the popular Nazi song which had got a bit out of date by that time.

The war against Russia brought the SS new masses of slaves for its concentration camps. When we expected our first big transport of Russian women prisoners, the Czech Communist Palečkova volunteered for work in the wash- and delousing rooms in order to be amongst the first to welcome the Russians. What actually happened when the great moment arrived I can only guess. She probably greeted the Russian women with great enthusiasm and told them that the Communist prisoners in Ravensbrück were in full sisterly solidarity with them. Whereupon many of them cursed her. And then no doubt she appealed to them to conduct themselves in a German concentration camp in a fashion worthy of their great Socialist Fatherland – only to hear further curses and abuse. Like all the Communists in the camp, Palečkova nourished great illusions about these Russian women and expected to find them all prodigies of Socialist education, for, of course, they would all be enthusiastic supporters of the Soviet regime and great admirers of the Russian Bolshevist Party. Instead of that, her heroines turned out to be an undisciplined horde of primitive, illiterate thieves and hooligans who hated Stalin and all his works and were not backward in saying so.

Palečkova suffered a terrible shock. She was obviously very depressed, and she never ceased to assure the other Politicals that they mustn't think all Russian women were like those who had come to Ravensbrück. Soon afterwards she began to display unmistakable signs that her brain had become unhinged. Her friends did their utmost to prevent the camp authorities from noticing anything, but it was impossible, and in the end she was taken away to the sickbay. When an attempt was made to give her a sedative injection she was seized with a frenzy and the SS doctor ordered her removal to the punishment cells. Bible Students who worked there reported that her condition was hopeless; she refused to eat and spent her days raving and shouting, 'Stalin, I love you.' Two weeks later she died and her body had wasted away almost to a skeleton.

At the beginning of 1942, the first big transport of approximately 1,000 women was sent off to Auschwitz. This was the first time we had heard of the concentration camp there, and no one yet knew the dread significance of the name. Many of the 'old' Politicals even volunteered to go there. With the transport went SS Senior Supervisor Langefeld and the two most popular camp messengers, Bertel Teege and Liesl Maurer. Frau Langefeld's place was taken by a fury named Mandl. You're never so badly off in a concentration camp that it can't get worse, and this Mandl was a sadistic beast. Under her ægis, the hated roll-call took on a new terror. Her special amusement was the hunt for curls. Whilst the prisoners stood silently to attention, she would stride slowly along the ranks inspecting all the women's heads. If she discovered a curl or a lock of hair peeping out from under a headdress she would bellow at the offender to step forward. Then she would tear off the unfortunate woman's headdress and box her ears savagely left and right, often kicking her in addition. The offender's number was noted; a 'report' went in and her hair was shaved off. Once ten women who had had their hair shaved off in this fashion had to parade in single file past us all as we stood at the roll-call. Round the neck of the first offender was a placard with the words: 'I broke camp discipline and curled my hair.'

Mandl also lengthened the agony of the roll-call by insisting that at the 'dismiss' the prisoners should march off in column to the huts and not just break up.

At about the same time my Bible Students were bitten by a new bug. This time it was the refusal of all work connected in any way with the prosecution of the war. I have already mentioned that they were often inconsistent in this difficult and almost insoluble problem, and there were always debatable points. The extremists, in particular, were constantly agitating for an extension of passive resistance. The first group to take action were those who up to then had been looking after the Angora rabbits. They declared that the combings of these animals were being used for war purposes and therefore their religious convictions would no longer permit them to continue the work. After that the garden gang refused work on the ground that the vegetables were being sent to a military hospital.

In all about ninety of the 'Witnesses' joined the new resistance movement. They were assembled and taken to the courtyard of the Punishment
Block, where they were left standing for three days without food as a
punishment. Then they were put into the Bunkers. However, there were
not enough dark cells to hold them all, so one wing of Block 25 was
cleared, everything taken out and the windows painted over, and they
were put in there. The already exhausted women had no blankets, no
mattresses and nowhere to sit except on the floor. Here they received
their bread ration every day and normal rations once every four days.
Whilst the struggle was still proceeding a new order came from Berlin
that refusal to work was to be punished with seventy-five lashes, and all
these women, many of whom were between fifty and sixty, received three
floggings of twenty-five lashes each. I saw them in the washroom about
a month afterwards. They were like walking skeletons, and their thighs
and buttocks were covered with ugly weals. Many of them looked as
though they had gone off their heads. In the end they were released,
but then they refused to stand at roll-calls, declaring they would stand
up for Jehovah, but not for the SS. They were distributed amongst all
the blocks and the Block Seniors received orders to have them present
at the roll-call under all circumstances. The more humane Block Seniors
had their recalcitrants carried out, but many of these poor old women
were dragged along the ground. They all refused to stand; many of them
could not have stood if they had wanted to. And there they sat hunched
up like bundles of rags.

The SS Camp Leader Redwitz seemed to take a delight in bullying
and mocking these wretched women. He ordered them to stand up, and
when they paid no attention, he began to bellow. It still had no effect,
so then he ordered the 'camp police' to fetch buckets of water and pour
them over the squatting women. One of the moderates in my block
whispered to me in confidence: 'Grete, you know, the evil spirit has
entered into our extremists.'

Redwitz was a newcomer to our camp and it was to him we owed
the introduction of 'camp police'. A few days after he arrived he was
striding down the ranks when he stopped in front of one of the prisoners,
looked her up and down, and ordered: 'Report to me in the Office.'
The woman was known as 'Leo'. The two had met before. Redwitz had
been a policeman, and at a Communist demonstration which had become
disorderly 'Leo' had boxed his ears. He had a good memory and he
recognised her again years afterwards in Ravensbrück. When she reported
to him in the Office, he said curtly: 'From today you're a camp policeman
and responsible for the maintenance of discipline and good order in the
camp.' As it turned out, he had made a good choice, for 'Leo' shouted,

bullied, beat up the prisoners and threatened them with the dreaded 'report' as though she had been in the SS all her life.

Late one afternoon on a burning hot summer's day the labour gangs were returning from work. Tired, sweating and covered with dust, they dragged their feet along in their wooden clogs. One gang of about thirty women was particularly noticeable. They were all Jewesses and they had obviously not been in the camp long, for they were terribly burnt by the sun. Their faces, and their bare arms and legs were an angry red and their hands which hung down at their sides were raw and bleeding. They had obviously been engaged on 'brick-throwing'. It was the worst possible work and a gross piece of brutality to put women on it whose hands had not yet become hardened by manual labour. The bricks came up in barges and they were then unloaded by long lines of women who had to throw half a dozen bricks at a time to each other until they were finally piled up where they were wanted. The hard, rough bricks quickly tore soft hands to pieces.

After the roll-call I had to go to the Medical Post with several of my Bible Students who needed attention, and there I saw the Block Senior with her thirty Jewesses, most of them middle-aged women, housewives and mothers. She had brought them along to get something for their terrible sunburn and for their hands. We had always thought SS Dr Sonntag was about as bad as a man could be, but his successor, SS Dr Schiedlausky, was even worse. As soon as he caught sight of the Jewesses, he began to bellow: 'Jewish cows outside. Right outside. Take them away altogether.' The Block Senior made an attempt to pacify him and persuade him to give her medicaments, but it was no use and she had to take her charges away.

The women spent a night of torture, and the next day their faces, arms and legs were covered with blisters. Their Block Senior tried again, and this time she was lucky enough to arrive when Schiedlausky was not there and so her charges were bandaged. But two days later she brought them along again to have the paper bandages renewed and this time Schiedlausky was there and drove them off again. The women all had high fever; the blisters were suppurating and the stench was awful. Two days later the Block Senior brought them along again, and this time the bandages were taken off and replaced. The state of these women was dreadful and the neglected bandages proved to be full of maggots. Many of them could hardly stand and had to be given bed cards for the sickbay, where several of them subsequently died.

Schiedlausky was assisted by another SS doctor named Rosenthal and a woman doctor, and they were almost as bad as he was. An SS Matron supervised the carrying out of their orders. Between them, these four established a reign of terror at the Medical Post. Sick prisoners reported first to their Block Senior and she wrote down their names, and then, after the first labour roll-call in the morning, she would take them – in column of five, of course – to the Medical Post. As there were already about 10,000 women in Ravensbrück by 1942, there were 100 or so going sick every day. They had to stand outside in all weathers until they were let in in batches. In the ante-room they had to take off their clogs. The SS Matron stood at a table and took them one by one according to the lists given to her by the Block Seniors. She was a tall, angular creature with a cadaverous and embittered face and big red ears that stood out almost at right angles from her head. She was almost grotesquely ugly, but it was not that that mattered; she had not a drop of the milk of human kindness in her whole make-up. It was she who sifted the applicants for medical attention and decided whether they should be allowed to see the doctor or not.

The would-be patients approached her desk singly and explained what was the matter with them. If anyone mumbled or whined, out she went, irrespective of what was wrong with her. If the others who were waiting their turn dared to whisper amongst themselves, the whole lot were ejected. If a patient leaned against the wall in exhaustion, out she went too. In this way the SS Matron saved the doctors a lot of work. If a woman was brought in on a stretcher and happened to be a Jewess or a gipsy, she would shout, 'Corridor case.' Before long all the prisoners knew what that meant. The hopeless cases were laid out in the corridor of the sickbay. For two days they were given narcotics, and on the third day they came into the 'death chamber', where either the SS Matron or one of the doctors despatched them with an injection of Evipan in the heart muscles. Every seriously sick prisoner was threatened with this fate, and the result was that no matter how sick a prisoner was she would not go to the Medical Post as long as she could stand.

The actual bandaging, dressing, taking of temperatures and so on, was all done by prisoners who worked in the Medical Post, and what these prisoners did for their unfortunate fellows is beyond words. Cramped into a small place behind the SS Matron, they had a table with instruments, ointments, medicaments and bandaging material. They took all temperatures, and many of the women owed their 'fever' – and, in consequence, a day or two off from labour – to them. Surrounded by a jostling crowd of prisoners, they treated boils, eczema, cuts, sunburn and all other minor complaints, and handed out aspirin and other medicaments.

One day a transport of pregnant women was brought into the camp. They had all been arrested for 'intercourse with foreigners'. In the first

years at Ravensbrück pregnant women were released if their offence was
considered a minor one, or sent out of the camp to have their babies
and brought back again afterwards; their children were taken away from
them. A different course was adopted with these women. The SS had
ordered that 'the fruit of their shame' should be aborted, and SS Dr
Rosenthal was entrusted with the operations. Many of these women were
in the seventh and even eighth month, and, of course, an operation in
such circumstances meant great danger for the life of the mother. No
doctor outside the camp would have operated when pregnancy was so
far advanced. But Rosenthal operated with the assistance of one of the
prisoners named Gerda Quernheim, who was a nurse by profession.
Milena told me that quite often at these operations the cry of new-born
children could be heard, but only for a moment or so.

But it was not only pregnant women who had had affairs with foreigners
who came into the hands of Rosenthal and Quernheim. Any pregnant
woman who came into the camp was handed over to them. The camp
had no arrangements for newborn babies, and these two between them
got rid of them all. Rosenthal and Quernheim had an affair with each
other, and the most dreadful rumours circulated about their professional
activities in the camp.

In January 1945, I was in the sickbay for a while, and in the bed
below mine was a peasant girl from Schleswig-Holstein, who had been
sent into the camp with a transport of pregnant women. She had
been a strong, healthy girl, but an operation in the eighth month of
pregnancy performed by Rosenthal had torn the urethra, and the girl
was now a physical wreck. Before long she was destined to be despatched
by Rosenthal and Quernheim. Another of their victims was a young
Ukrainian girl. When they approached her bed, the sick girl sprang out
in terror and fled, Rosenthal and Quernheim dashing after her. She ran
down the corridor and jumped out of a window. Of course, she was
caught and brought back. After a while there was silence. A Polish woman
who had been in the sickbay at the time and witnessed the gruesome
hunt told Milena, who sought an opportunity to slip in to where the
dead girl lay. Her face had been badly bruised and beaten and there were
injection marks in her chest.

In the summer of 1942 twenty young Polish girls who had been
brought into the camp with a transport of women sentenced to death
were picked out to see the doctor. SS Dr Oberhauser examined them.
About six of them were picked out and kept in the sickbay. The news
caused a panic amongst the women in the Warsaw and Lublin transports, particularly when it became known that these six perfectly healthy
girls were being kept isolated and closely guarded in a special ward to

which none of the normal prisoner assistants had access. At the same
time an operation room with the very latest medical equipment was set
up. Then the well-known German medical luminary Professor Gebhardt
arrived with a staff of assistants. We often saw them crossing over to the
operation room in their white overalls.

The camp was a prey to rumours. Some thought the women were
being sterilised; others that some terrible experiment was being
conducted on them. At first it was impossible to discover the truth, for
only SS nurses were allowed into the ward, but after a while these nurses
got tired of their precautions and the ordinary prisoner assistants were
allowed in for cleaning and so on. They reported that the six girls were
obviously in pain and that all of them had their legs in plaster casts. It
turned out that Professor Gebhardt was using these young Polish girls
for experimental transfers of bone and muscle.

After a while these girls were released. They hobbled around the camp
with great difficulty. Some of them no longer had calves and their legs
were like matchsticks. Others could walk only on their toes. But that
was not the end of it. Gebhardt's experimental urge was insatiable, and
further victims were chosen. Soon all secrecy was abandoned and the
work proceeded quite openly. Rumour had it that tetanus experiments
were being performed. Many of the women died. Those who survived
were sent back into the camp on crutches, and soon the 'guinea-pigs',
as they were called, became part and parcel of our camp life. These
women had one faint ray of hope – perhaps now that they had been
used for experimental purposes they would not be shot after all.

The Camp is Growing

That same summer big building operations went on. The workers were
prisoners from the neighbouring men's concentration camp. Large, solidly
built, modern factory buildings were erected by the German firm Siemens-
Halske, together with new barracks for another 1,000 prisoners. With
these new additions Concentration Camp Ravensbrück consisted of thirty-
two living blocks arranged in three streets.

The size of the camp increased, but the number of inmates increased
still more rapidly, and before long three prisoners were sleeping on two
mattresses and sharing lockers. Up to 1942 Camp Ravensbrück had
been free from lice, but owing to the overcrowding the laundry could
no longer cope, and we received clean things at more and more lengthy
intervals. There were no longer regular supplies of straw for the
mattresses. There was not enough footwear and other articles of clothing

to replace worn-out items, and the quality of the replacements grew worse and worse.

The SS still tried to maintain the old discipline, but in the rapidly deteriorating conditions it proved impossible. In 1940 and 1941 no prisoner would have dared to tread on the grass plots, but now when the roll-call was over the women would rush over them, even treading down the flowers, in order to get to their labour gangs more quickly. Prisoners climbed in and out of the windows of the huts because there was always a jam at the narrow doors. The more and more numerous columns of Russian prisoners also did much to change the outward face of Ravensbrück. Raids on the kitchen gangs took place. Prisoners bringing bread from the kitchen over to the huts were often attacked on the way by sudden descents of marauding bands and robbed of the bread, and it was the same with other food. The SS answered this degeneration of camp morals by strengthening the 'camp police', who were entitled to use violence towards other prisoners and make 'reports'. In this way a body of professional spies and informers grew up. The new Camp Commandant, Suhren, and his Gestapo assistant, Ramdohr, organised a spy system in the camp. Previously there had been, as far as we knew, only one Gestapo agent amongst the prisoners, a Swiss woman named Carmen Mori, but now Ramdohr recruited many more and rewarded them for their activities with food stolen from Red Cross parcels.

Up to the autumn of 1942 all prisoners in Ravensbrück received the same rations, and no one got any more, except such prisoners who were employed in the kitchens and the stores and were able to steal. But after that prisoners were allowed to receive food parcels from friends and relatives, and for many of them this was salvation. The granting of permission to receive food from outside was not introduced in order to ameliorate our lot, but in order to increase our labour capacity without cost to the State, for from about this time the SS began to be keenly interested in us as labour power in the war effort. Before long we were working eleven hours a day, and some of the workshops had day and night shifts.

However, with the introduction of food parcels from outside the prisoners were abruptly divided into two social groups: the haves, who managed to get enough to eat, and the have-nots, who were always hungry. The French and Russian prisoners never received food parcels. The gipsies, Asocials, and a great number of the minor Political offenders received very few. Although many of those who did receive them shared their good fortune with others, the great majority of the prisoners were dependent on camp food, which was rapidly deteriorating. It was inevitable that in the circumstances there was a great wave of demoralisation. Anything could be bought with food; the Block Seniors, the Hut Seniors and all other prisoners enjoying some sort of authority could be bribed with food. Before long the regular receivers of parcels were better dressed than the others and even had 'servants' to wait on them, 'build' their beds, wash out their dishes, and so on.

The situation grew even worse when prisoners were allowed to receive parcels of clothing, and the articles thus introduced into the camp created a lively market, with bread, margarine and other foodstuffs as currency. However, those who benefited most from the food and clothing parcels were the SS, who first stole out of them whatever they pleased. One or two of the Bible Students were appointed to new confidential jobs: the sorting and storing of the things the SS stole. Although the parcels sent in to the prisoners from outside were regularly pilfered, the main source of ill-gotten goods was the parcels sent to the camp *en bloc* by the International Red Cross. Prisoners, of course, were still being sent to the Bunkers and flogged for theft.

One summer a column of male prisoners under SS supervision came into the camp to lay new drains immediately behind our block. The windows of the huts looking out on to their place of work were screwed down and there were severe penalties for any woman prisoner who tried to get into touch with the men. Under Camp Commandant Kögel, no male prisoner had ever entered the women's camp, and if a column of women had accidentally met a column of men outside the camp, then one of the columns had to halt and face about whilst the other column went past. But with the enlargement of the camp and the degeneration under Suhren, such precautionary measures fell into disuse.

All day long we could hear the bullying and bawling of the camp *kapos* and the women were deeply touched. What no longer moved them when it happened to their own sex seemed dreadful when it happened to men, and the women would hang on to the window ledges in order to catch a glimpse of the men through the cracks. What a dreadful state they were in! Their camp clothing hung on their skinny limbs like sacks. The only well-fed men amongst them were the *kapos*, invariably criminals. These petty tyrants were armed with sticks, and when they thought that a prisoner was not working hard enough they would belabour him savagely. On the second day we managed to establish contact with the men. They were working directly under our window right against the hut wall and we could talk to them through the window cracks. Our Bible Students wanted to know whether any of their men were in the male section of Ravensbrück, and our Czech Hut Senior wanted to know about her countrymen.

After a while we even succeeded in finding a way to smuggle food to them: bread, carrots (which could be bought at that time in the canteen) and margarine, which we stole from the kitchen stores. A day or so later one of the men denounced us. As Block Senior, I was called to the office to give an account of my stewardship. I was questioned by SS Senior Supervisor Frau Mandl. Of course, I knew nothing whatever about it and had never seen the slightest sign of anything of the sort. Fortunately, the women in other blocks along the line the men were working had done the same thing, so the responsibility was not entirely ours and it was impossible to find out just who had done it. Mandl was furious with me, but she had nothing to go on and so I escaped with nothing worse than a dressing down.

However, a day or so later I was called to the office again.

'Get your things and go to Block 9,' Mandl ordered. 'You are to be Block Senior there from now on.'

Block 9 was the Jewish block, and transports of women were sent off regularly to be killed. I was horrified.

'SS Supervisor, please send me for outside work. I'd do anything rather than be Block Senior there.'

'Are you refusing to obey orders?' she snapped.

'No,' I replied. 'Of course I'll go if you order it, but please put me on outside work. I've been Block Senior long enough.'

She looked at me doubtfully and hesitated; but it was not often a prisoner asked to be put on outside work, so finally she agreed: 'I think you're right. Very well; outside work, then.'

I had been with the Bible Students for almost two years and the parting was not easy. As an 'old' Political, I was transferred to Block 1 and came into the same hut as Milena, which was a great delight to both of us. I was treated with suspicion by the others, but before long we began to engage in political discussions. Almost all the German Communists not only hoped for a Russian victory, but even believed that the Hitler dictatorship would be overthrown by a proletarian revolution. They had lost none of their illusions, and they still exaggerated the least signs of revolutionary activity in a fantastic fashion. According to them, Communist influence in Germany was rapidly on the increase, and when I pointed out that very few new political prisoners were coming into the concentration camps, they replied that that was because they were all being put in prison.

'And what about the inevitable suspects?' I asked. 'At least they are always sent to concentration camps.'

But the explanation, it appeared, was that the illegal Communist Party was functioning so effectively that the Gestapo was unable to make wide-scale arrests. They still lived in the Communist cloud cuckoo land of 1933 and they were incapable of drawing the slightest practical conclusion from the ten terrible years which had passed since then.

And the Russian Communists we had were an odd lot of internationalists. There was a young Russian who had been in the medical corps of the Crimean Army. One day one of the 'old' Politicals, a woman who had done ten years' hard labour for her political activity before she came to Ravensbrück, turned enthusiastically to this young Russian, and declared:

'After the war we'll build up Socialism in Germany just like you're doing in the Soviet Union, Shenya.' And Shenya's eyes lighted up ecstatically: 'Yes,' she replied. 'After the war everything will be Russian, everything Russian.'

Politicals from Block 1 who worked in the Kommandantur smuggled newspapers into the camp and we were able to read the bulletins of the Army Command from the front. These naturally gave no nourishment to the hopes of the Communists, but in addition there was an endless stream of 'confidential reports' concerning mutinies at the front, the collapse of German positions, revolutions, and what not, which were very heartening for them. Through newcomers to the camp we learnt, with some delay, the reports of foreign wireless stations. These proved more reliable, and often we would find them confirmed, perhaps weeks later, in small print somewhere in the *Völkischer Beobachter*.

From the late summer of 1942 we began to have air-raid warnings in Ravensbrück, and far away on the horizon at night, in the direction of Berlin, we could see the glow of searchlights. More and more often squadrons of Allied bombers droned overhead when we lay on our straw mattresses. It was a heartening sound for the foreign prisoners, and every time there was a heavy raid on some German town they were more cheerful the next day. It was different for us. I, too, longed for a German defeat in the field, because I was convinced that that was the only way to get rid of the Nazis, and until they were defeated there could be no hope for Germany; but the bombing of German towns was different. Men, women and children lived in them, and many of them were enemies of National Socialism just as I was. The bombs and incendiaries rained down on the just and the unjust alike, but chiefly on the just, because most of the Nazi high-ups would be safe in their deep shelters or well away from the bombing. That side of it was depressing for me.

Work for the 'Reich'

The next morning after my transfer to Block 1 I lined up after the roll-call with the kitchen-garden gang. There were fifteen of us, and after we had been carefully listed we marched off singing, 'Roses are blooming in my homeland.' It was the first time for two years I had seen the outside world. We marched along the Fürstenberg Lake. The banks were thick with rushes and plants, and in the distance behind the trees we could see the spire of Fürstenberg Church. Marching along the sandy paths, we finally arrived at the chicken runs and pigsties of the SS and came to a halt in front of the greenhouse.

Our gang was in the charge of an SS wardress who was new to the job and none too sure of herself. By profession she was a waitress in a restaurant. The SS head gardener, Löbel, gave us our work. The lucky ones, amongst whom was my friend, the singer Eva Busch, came into the hothouse. Others went into the kitchen garden, and the rest were put to carting mould. I was put on the mould-shifting. The kitchen garden backed on to the male prisoners' camp, and through a hole in the wall men shovelled mould taken from the lower-lying marshland at the other side of the camp and we shovelled it away. It was very hard work and we were kept at it, because the men on the other side worked faster than we did and if we let the heap get too large there was trouble. From time to time I looked with delight over to where the garden was blooming. The sight of the flowers filled me with a feeling of exhilaration, but after a while I lost interest. I was not used to the work and it was not long before my hands began to blister. After that it was torture, particularly as the mould was wet and heavy. 'Garden work outside' sounded very attractive, but after you have slaved for nine hours shifting mould, or pushing heavy wheelbarrows full of manure, even beautiful flowers cease to interest you. We got no extra rations for this heavy work, so we 'organised' a supplement to our food supply. Some of the Bible Students looked after the sties, and we arranged with them to leave us a pailful of cooked potatoes intended for the pigs in a certain hiding place, and we filled ourselves up with them.

The camp garden grew flowers and plants to decorate the quarters of the SS and to fill the beds in front of the Kommandantur and elsewhere. Great attention was paid to this, and the beds and lawns looked a picture. From the outside Ravensbrück was neat and clean to look at – a whited sepulchre, to talk in the language of the Bible Students. Prisoners did all the work. We dug, carted earth and manure, hoed, weeded, sowed and planted. It was hard work and we were kept going, but nevertheless membership of the garden gang was much sought after, particularly as the SS head gardener had none of the usual SS manners. He was a decent, humane man. He never bullied or cursed us, and he never threatened us with 'reports'. He was a reserved and silent man and he rarely said a word more than was absolutely necessary. He knew perfectly well that when the tomatoes, cucumbers and so on were ready for picking, we ate our fill and even stole some of them to smuggle back with us into the camp, but he never made any attempt to stop us.

Eva Busch reigned in the hothouse. She was a well-known actress and singer in Germany, the wife of the composer, Ernst Busch, and it was easy enough for her to influence Löbel. When she told him what an expert gardener I was and suggested that I should work in the greenhouses with her, he agreed and I was emancipated from the heavy work outside. The next one we managed to get into this relative paradise was Lotte Henschel. The most important service anyone could render a prisoner in Ravensbrück – and, I suppose, in any other camp – was to get her a job where she had an opportunity to supplement her rations. The garden gang was fortunate in this respect.

Whilst I was Block Senior I lived in a constant state of suspense. Danger threatened from all sides; not only for me, but for the hundreds of women in my charge. But in the garden gang, as soon as I got into the greenhouse, I led an almost idyllic life. Years of imprisonment in a concentration camp in constant fear of punishment and in constant, unwilling obedience make grown-up women act like children as soon as the pressure is relaxed a little, and so it was with us. We laughed at anything and demanded no very high standard of humour. Eva, Lotte and I decided to make ourselves an aquarium in a place which had been cemented out to hold water. Whilst kneeling at the compost heaps and supposed to be potting plants, we were really intent on collecting frogs of all shapes, sizes and colours, and anything that came to hand for our collection. Then we would solemnly carry them off in empty flower pots to add them to our aquarium. We put a board or two in the water to give the poor things a rest from swimming, and when we were unobserved we would stand and watch our handiwork with childlike delight. But as soon as the door opened we would all three engage enthusiastically in some routine work or other, watering plants that had already been watered, dashing around with potted plants, and generally creating an appearance of ceaseless activity.

It was easy enough to eat tomatoes or cucumbers in the greenhouse, but it was much more difficult to smuggle them back into the camp for the others, but we succeeded in all sorts of ways. Tomatoes and cucumbers were taken in under our armpits, and in pails of mould which allegedly this or that supervisor had ordered. And one day Lotte, who was tall and thin, even smuggled out a bundle of gladioli under her dress for Milena.

Few, if any, of the other prisoners were as fortunate as we were. Many of them worked for Siemens-Halske winding spools for wireless and other electrical equipment. Before any prisoner was chosen for this work, she had to undergo an intelligence test, which consisted in twisting a piece of wire in a certain fashion or folding a piece of paper according to directions. An engineer named Grade, who had been fifteen years with Siemens-Halske, carefully chose the most suitable women, and he was always asking the SS for the women with the highest 'intelligence quota'.

The work was carried out in exactly the same fashion as in ordinary Siemens-Halske workshops. Civilian foremen led each gang and the departmental overseers were old Siemens-Halske employees. In each workshop was an SS supervisor entrusted with the maintenance of camp discipline. The production of each prisoner was carefully controlled, and payment was by result. Wage sheets were made out each week and normal rates were paid, but not to the prisoners. The wages were handed over to the SS and the prisoners got nothing. If a prisoner failed to perform her quota, she was tackled by her foreman. If that did not help, then along came the SS Supervisor and boxed her ears. When even that did not cure her of her 'laziness', she got a 'report' and landed in the Bunkers. On the other hand, prisoners who exceeded their quota received coupons valued at fifty pfennige or one mark, to be expended in the camp canteen – though all they could buy in later years was salt and cheap fish paste.

Grade, who was in charge of this camp branch of Siemens-Halske, was a slave-driver who would have been an ornament to the SS. For him a prisoner was a source of labour power and nothing else. She had no rights; she was just a work-beast. If any woman proved unsuitable, he would denounce her to the SS authorities as a good-for-nothing. The chief reason for his slave-driving was his fear that he would be sent to the front. If he proved himself an efficient manager by keeping production high, Siemens-Halske claimed him and he remained exempt.

The 'extremist' Bible Students had been making themselves a nuisance again, and so they were all packed off with the next transport to Auschwitz. That was in the autumn of 1942, and at that time we were still not quite certain about what happened to the transports which went to Auschwitz. A little while later I had business in the neighbourhood of the Punishment Compound, and there I recognised about a dozen of the 'extremist' Bible Students who had been sent to Auschwitz and had now returned. I managed to speak to one of them, Rosa Hahn of Ischl.

'They've sent us back,' she said. 'I'm certain we're going to be executed, but before we die I must tell you that terrible things happen in Auschwitz. You won't believe it I know, but living human beings are thrown into the fire, including little children. Jews chiefly. All day long the smell of burning flesh hangs over the camp. You can't believe me; I know it. But I'm speaking the truth as sure as I stand here in front of you.'

Once she had been a very good-looking woman, but now her face was sunken and her skin like parchment. Her eyes burnt feverishly. I didn't believe her; I merely thought that now she had gone completely off her head. I wanted to get away. It was dangerous for me to be found anywhere near them.

'You'll be put in Block 17,' I said. 'I'll come over and see you this evening. So long.'

'Oh, no we shan't,' she insisted. 'We've been brought here for execution, I tell you.'

The next day all the extremist Bible Students were taken away in a prison wagon, and the day after that all their things came back, complete with triangle and number.

THE ABYSS

As Secretary to the Senior Supervisor

The hated Frau Mandl went off to Auschwitz with a transport and who should return in her place but Frau Langefeld. When she discovered that I was no longer Block Senior with the Bible Students, she wanted to know the reason. I told her and she listened carefully. 'Hm,' she said finally. 'How would you like to work with me in my office?'

'Why, yes,' I said. 'I would, of course, but it hardly depends on what I like.'

She made no comment, but shortly after that I was installed. Frau Langefeld, as Senior Supervisor, was practically in charge of the camp, and it was her duty to see that the instructions received from the Camp Commandant and his Adjutant were carried out. All the female supervisors in the camp were under her orders, and it was she who appointed the Block Seniors and Gang Leaders. All the administrative figures of the camp went through her hands, including roll-call labour gang tallies. And a very important part of her work was to sift the 'reports' made by the overseers against the prisoners. It was she who decided whether a 'report' was justified and should go through to the Camp Commandant; and the comments she added were usually decisive for the punishment the Camp Commandant meted out. His decision came back to her subsequently for execution.

Another important task she had was to reply to enquiries concerning a prisoner's conduct. For instance, the 'Political Department' would ask for information about a prisoner from time to time: how long she had been in camp, how she had conducted herself, how many times she had been punished and whether she could be considered to have 'improved'. Such an enquiry usually meant that the release of the prisoner in question was under discussion. She would then be called to the office for an interview, and in that five minutes or so Frau Langefeld had to decide whether the woman was 'suitable' for release or not. On her answer, favourable or unfavourable, the prisoner's fate usually depended, though, of course, in the last resort the Gestapo was responsible for releases. The Commandant naturally added his recommendations, but as he rarely knew much about the prisoners he usually went by what Frau Langefeld said. There was another SS Senior Supervisor in addition to Frau Langefeld, a woman named Gallinat, but she was in charge of outside camp affairs.

A Woman with her Doubts

Frau Langefeld was about forty-two years old. She came from the Rhineland, and had been strictly brought up against a patriotic and nationalistic background. During the First World War her one regret had been that she had not been born a man so that she could bear arms for her country. The loss of the war and the subsequent occupation of the Rhineland by the French had been a terrible humiliation for her patriotic pride. It was in this mood that she had first fallen in with the Nazis, and Hitler had become her ideal and hero. During the inflation period, her family was ruined. She got married, but her husband soon died, and left her with a child to look after. She got work in a public welfare organisation and later became a prison wardress. In 1936 she became a Supervisor in Lichtenberg Concentration Camp for Women, and later Senior SS Supervisor.

I was now in the place of Marianne Korn as her secretary, and I sat with her day after day in her office. Amongst the prisoners, she had the reputation of being 'decent', for she never used violence towards them as so many others did. Even before I had any chance of private conversation with her, she struck me as troubled with inner conflicts and governed by inhibitions and inferiority feelings. Her nerves were always in a bad state, and she had all sorts of nervous habits. Before she spoke she would always have to clear her throat once or twice, and she was endlessly stroking her dress straight, or shaking a non-existent lock of hair out of her eyes. Sometimes she would stop in the middle of a sentence and stare out of the window for minutes at a time.

She treated most of the SS Supervisors with a certain arrogance, but it was a defensive measure to ward off all familiarities. With one or two whom she liked she was just the opposite, and in their presence she made no secret of her hatred for the SS. In such moments my presence did not embarrass her and she would speak quite openly. Once during a battle with SS Storm Leader Seitz to obtain winter clothing for the prisoners,

she hung up the receiver after a bitter telephone discussion and declared:
'That man Seitz ought to be made to stand naked on the camp street
for a few hours so that he could learn what it is to feel cold.'

It was not long before I found myself in a position to exercise considerable influence on her in favour of the prisoners, particularly when the
'reports' came in. The prisoners concerned would wait outside until they
were called in for examination. On one occasion a hungry Asocial was
brought in from the Punishment Block charged with having stolen a turnip.

'Did you steal the turnip?' asked Frau Langefeld.

'Frau Senior Supervisor, I was so hungry; really I was,' came the
answer, broken with sobs.

'But if everyone stole turnips there would soon be none left for anyone
else,' said Frau Langefeld.

'But Frau Senior Supervisor, I was so hungry . . .'

The woman was sent out of the room. The case was clear. She had
stolen the turnip and the 'report' was justified. But if it went forward,
as it ought to, it meant solitary confinement and perhaps a flogging. I
intervened.

'Frau Senior Supervisor, I know the woman from when I was Hut
Senior at the Asocials Block. She would never survive the Bunkers. Her
only hope is to get out of the Punishment Block. A "report" would rob
her of all hope of ever doing so.'

Frau Langefeld said nothing, considered the case for a moment or
two whilst her mouth twitched nervously, then with a sudden gesture
she tore up the 'report' and flung it into the waste-paper basket.

It was easier still for me when Russian and Polish prisoners were
brought in, for then I acted as interpreter and could give what replies
I liked to her questions. And it was not long before I noticed that she
had a shocking memory, and I took advantage of this very often to 'lose'
'reports' altogether. I always took the 'reports' where serious punishment was to be expected and hid them behind a sheaf of other papers,
and then waited to see whether any enquiry came from the Supervisor
who had lodged them. If nothing happened after a while, then the
'reports' disappeared for good. And when I heard that a Supervisor was
conducting herself with exceptional brutality towards prisoners, I took
the first opportunity to bring the matter to the notice of Frau Langefeld,
with the result that the woman was usually removed.

Every Friday she went together with the Camp Commandant and the
SS doctor to witness the floggings, and every time she came back she
was in a state of great nervous tension and obviously controlling herself
with an effort of will. She was a strange woman. I remember on one
occasion a gipsy woman named Judith Horvath, who had ten children

and whom she knew from Lichtenberg, came before her. She spoke to the woman so consolingly and with such great kindness that I was quite moved. But if it happened to be a Jewess, or if she was making up the list for a transport to Auschwitz, her face was distorted and her voice hateful.

She had been Senior Suprvisor in Auschwitz for six months, and she knew all about the gas chambers and about the fate of Jews there. She had succeeded in securing her transfer back to Ravensbrück thanks to influence in higher circles.

'Auschwitz is the most horrible place the mind of man could conceive of,' she said to me once. 'I can never get over it that the Bible Students I took there came to their end. But at least Teege and Maurer were saved.'

These two owed their lives to her. With great difficulty and after a personal intervention with Himmler, she had succeeded in saving the lives of these two Communist prisoners and securing their release. But the people she admired most of all were the nationalist Poles. They were heroes to her, and those who were sentenced to death were martyrs who died for their country. On the other hand, she supported the master race ideas of Hitler and approved of Nazi Germany's claim to overlordship. She firmly believed that Hitler and Himmler were humane and idealistic men who had no idea of the things done in their names by the corrupt and morally degenerate SS who ran their camps. And just as she worshipped National Socialism, so she had no doubt whatever in the final victory of the German arms, though she condemned the deportation of millions of foreign workers from their own countries to work in Germany as inhumane and a political error.

We began to discuss political affairs more and more frequently, and it was not difficult for me to refute her arguments. Before long I had not only shaken her conviction in a German victory, but I had also made her see the concentration-camp system through the eyes of its victims. In consequence, her inner conflict grew more and more painful. I made her see that all these terrible things were not the isolated acts of one or two wicked and corrupt SS officials, but the natural and logical consequence of the whole dictatorial regime instituted by her hero, Hitler. How far I succeeded in convincing her it is difficult to say, but at least she, the Senior SS Supervisor, listened attentively to all I had to say, and I know she thought about it a great deal. One day I dared to ask her point blank how she could reconcile her co-operation in the running of a hell-hole like Ravensbrück or Auschwitz with her conscience as a woman and a mother. For a moment she did not reply; then she said hesitantly: 'Don't you think I do some good here in my work? Don't you think the prisoners would be much worse off if they had someone else over them instead of me?'

That was true enough.

How tense the relationship was between Frau Langefeld and the SS I realised only gradually, and it was only after my job as her secretary had come to an end that I learnt that from the moment she came back from Auschwitz the Camp Commandant Suhren, and the Camp Leader, Bräuning, had systematically set to work to bring about her downfall. They not only carefully collected material against her, but they also made her work as Senior Supervisor as difficult as possible.

In the winter of 1942 we awaited a big transport of Russian women from the Medical Corps of the Red Army. These women were all nurses or doctors who had been captured in Sebastopol. The German author-ities apparently considered that a concentration camp was the right place for them. A special block was prepared for them and surrounded with barbed wire to isolate them from the other prisoners. When they got out of the goods train in which they had been transported, some of the SS women immediately began to kick and beat them. They were all in uniform and they arrived at the camp in strict military order. They obeyed their own leaders implicitly, and the whole reception procedure went off smoothly in complete silence. When these women were naked in the washroom Commandant Suhren and Camp Leader Bräuning deliber-ately went in amongst them. Frau Langefeld came back to her office in great excitement, loudly condemning the provocative shamelessness of the SS leaders and praising the dignified attitude of the Russian prisoners of war.

The appearance of these women of the Red Army made a deep impres-sion on the many Russian and Ukrainian prisoners who were already in the camp, and the 'camp police' intercepted a number of messages they tried to smuggle through. They were brought to Frau Langefeld, who passed them on to me for translation. It was quite clear from their contents that the Russians and Ukrainians were frightened at the appear-ance of these, so to speak, official Russians, and were anxious to put themselves in a favourable light, so that together with hymns of praise in favour of the Soviet regime and the Red Army were the full names and camp numbers of many of the prisoners. It would have cost them dear had I translated accurately, but instead I turned them into senti-mental messages of greetings and they were thrown into the waste-paper basket. But what I didn't know was that the SS were watching Frau Langefeld carefully, and when no 'reports' came through as a result of the finding of the messages they had the next one that was intercepted translated themselves, and its contents were very different from my translations. That was one of the things which was later brought up against Frau Langefeld.

Ravensbrück now held many thousands of women prisoners and more and more wardresses were necessary to control them. Ordinary recruitment was not sufficient to supply the demand, and so Camp Leader Bräuning used to go out on recruiting drives to factories and other places where there were many women. He would have the women workers called together and then address them in glowing terms on the wonderful career that awaited them in the rehabilitation centres – he never mentioned the words 'concentration camp'. As the pay was good and the food ample, recruits soon began to come in, for the work in war factories was hard and conditions difficult. After every such campaign Ravensbrück would receive a score or so of young working women as wardresses.

Before they were put into uniform they all came in a body to be seen by Frau Langefeld. Most of them were poorly dressed, rather nervous and hesitant in their unaccustomed surroundings, and more than a little intimidated. Frau Langefeld would give them a lecture on their duties and then send them off to their quarters. I often noticed them nudge each other in astonishment when they saw prisoners passing. At first these women would be sent out in company with an experienced wardress to show them the ropes, and during the first week almost half of them would come weeping to Frau Langefeld and ask to be allowed to go home. She would explain to them that only the Camp Commandant could release them once they were enrolled, and that they must therefore go to him. Very few of them had sufficient courage to do so. They were afraid of being dressed down by an SS officer, and so the great majority of them stayed on and got used to their new profession. After all, it was, as they had been promised, light work, and well paid, and their food and quarters were good. And many of them changed out of all recognition once they got into uniform. Top boots and a forage cap stuck at an angle on their heads gave them a feeling of confidence and superiority.

The Commandant and the SS Camp Leader instructed them in the practical side of their work. From the beginning they were taught to stifle any sympathy with the prisoners, who were always presented as morally degenerate and worthless, and in addition they were threatened with dire punishments if they violated the service regulations and had any other than strictly official contacts with their charges. Day after day these new recruits had strictness and severity drilled into them, and they were always accompanied by the worst of the old wardresses, all brutal, bullying, reporting, ear-boxing types. And during their free hours their only male companions were SS men. Again and again one could observe the same transformation: these young working women were soon every bit as bad as the old hands, ordering the prisoners around, bullying them and shouting as though they had been born in a barracks. There were, of course, exceptions, but not many.

The relations between Frau Langefeld and the SS authorities became more and more explosive. The SS had quite a lot of material against her, but as they well knew, she also had material: she knew of many instances of corruption and embezzlement in which the Camp Commandant and his officers were involved. Their aim was to prove her inefficient and secure her dismissal. The most active intriguer in this respect was the hated and feared Gestapo man, Ramdohr. He would put prisoners in the Bunkers even without a 'report', beat them up himself, douse them with cold water, and leave them without food in order to extort 'confessions' from them. The name Ramdohr was sufficient to make many women in the camp tremble. He would search about all over the camp, turning out the lockers and even emptying the straw out of the mattresses in his hunt for illegal material.

In the winter of 1942–3 two Polish women, who worked in the kitchen, managed to escape from the camp. They hid behind the camp refuse bins after they had been loaded into a lorry to be taken away as usual. When their absence was noticed, they were already far away; they had managed to reach a railway station and get to Berlin. One of them was recaptured a year later and brought back to the camp. The other one was reported to have been shot dead whilst attempting to cross the frontier. As more and more gangs worked outside the camp, particularly on the local farms, it was easier for prisoners to escape, and about a dozen more escaped without the SS being able to recapture them. I always experienced a feeling of delight when I had to take their cards out of the general index and put them in a special box-file marked 'Escapes'. Of course, a scapegoat had to be found for this, and it was Senior SS Supervisor Langefeld, who had failed to put a sufficiently alert wardress in charge of the gangs . . . and so on.

Frau Langefeld took advantage of every opportunity to talk to the 'old' Politicals, and in particular with the Austrian Rosl Jochmann, the German Maria Fischer and the Pole, Helena Korova. When new Block or Hut Seniors had to be appointed, she always took the candidates proposed by the Politicals, and this naturally did not remain unknown to Ramdohr and his spies. On one occasion two Politicals, Anni Rudroff and Emmi Ambrusova, were reported by Storm Leader Dittmann, Anni because she had not got new numbers ready in time for a transport of prisoners for a munitions factory, and Emmi because she had made some tea for herself in the canteen where she worked. A 'report' from a Storm

Leader meant six months in the Punishment Block at least, and I did my best to persuade Frau Langefeld not to forward them, but it was a serious matter, and after some hesitation, at last she sent them on to the Commandant. A few weeks later his verdict came through: six months Punishment Block for each. Again I did my best to influence her, pointing out that Anni was innocent, whilst Emmi's offence had been a bagatelle. This time I tried to persuade her to intervene with the Commandant; again she hesitated, but in the end she sent the two of them back to their huts instead of sending them to the Punishment Block, and promised to get into touch with the Commandant. Every few days I reminded her of it, but it was obviously an unpleasant matter for her and she kept putting it off.

That was in the spring of 1943. Then a chit came through from the 'Political Department' asking for ten Poles with numbers between 7,000 and 10,000. I knew that they were death sentences. The women were fetched from their block by a Camp Messenger. I sat at my typewriter and looked through the window. As they came across the square I noticed that two of them were on crutches.

'Frau Langefeld,' I exclaimed. 'They're going to shoot the guinea-pigs. They're coming now.'

She sprang up, gave one glance out of the window and then picked up the telephone receiver and demanded to speak to the Camp Commandant. I sat there listening anxiously to one side of the conversation.

'Storm Leader, is there any confirmation from Berlin that the guinea-pigs are to be executed?'

I don't know what answer came through, but she hung up the receiver and turned to me:

'Go out and send the two prisoners on crutches back to their block.'

In April Ramdohr put three 'old' Politicals, Rosl Jochmann, Maria Fischer and Maria Schwarz, in the Punishment Block. At the same time he had the Camp Messenger Marianne Scharinger brought to the Kommandantur and cross-examined for hours. Marianne Scharinger was formally registered as a criminal. She had been assistant to a doctor who had been arrested for abortion operations, an offence which was regarded as criminal. Apparently she was unable to withstand the bullying and the threats, for she gave way and made incriminating statements against Frau Langefeld and me.

One morning in April Frau Langefeld had left the office after a telephone conversation with the Kommandantur, and I was alone in the room waiting for her to return when Ramdohr marched in with his secretary, Löffler.

'Come with me,' he ordered, and I walked out between the two of them. I was taken to the Punishment Block, where Ramdohr searched my pockets.

'Why have I been brought here and searched?' I asked.

'You've got a nerve to ask,' he replied. 'It's only because you've systematically suppressed "reports" and destroyed messages intercepted from prisoners; that's all. What's happened to the punishment orders for Rudroff and Ambrusova? Don't you deceive yourself: we've had our eye on you for some time, and we're up to all your tricks. You've interfered with official documents and conducted Communist agitation.'

I started to defend myself, but Ramdohr cut me short.

'You'd better not say anything now,' he declared. 'That's not all by any means. I'll leave you in this cell for a while and you can think about whether it's worthwhile to lie or not.'

Löffler handed me over to Binz, who was the SS Supervisor of the Punishment Block, and she called a Bible Student who acted amongst other things as searcher. I had to strip and then I was given a thin shift and knickers, a summer dress with short sleeves, stockings and a towel. My shoes were not returned to me. Then Binz led me away until we came to one of the cells on the ground floor which was empty. The cell door slammed behind me and I was in the dark. Feeling my way around, I knocked into a stool which was fixed to the floor. I sat down on it and tried to get my eyes used to the darkness. There was a faint glimmer under the door. Then I began to accustom myself to the cell layout. There was a small leaf table attached to the wall which could be raised and lowered, and a wooden bed-rack also attached to the wall which could also be raised and lowered, though it was now locked. In one corner near the door was a water closet, and on the other side were cold central-heating pipes. Opposite the door was a small window, but it was so closely covered that neither light nor air came through. The cell was about four and a half paces by two and a half. After a while I got sufficiently used to the arrangements to be able to walk up and down without fear of knocking against the stool.

Naturally I was upset by the unexpected turn of fortune, but if Ramdohr thought he was going to intimidate me he was mistaken. You get used to darkness. Would he cut off my food? I felt sorry I had not finished up all my bread that morning. Would I be beaten? I remembered all the horrors of the punishment cells: the prisoners who had been beaten to death; those who had starved to death; those who had gone mad. I grew frightened. And outside there was Milena. She needed me. Who would look after her when her fever recurred? At night she would sob on her mattress: 'If only I could be dead without dying! But to die in this place like a dog!' When I was with her I could console her; even make her believe that one day we should be free again. But now I realised clearly that she was lost, irretrievably lost. And me?

Suddenly the light was turned on from outside and I stood blinking. Someone was at the peephole. It was Ramdohr looking with satisfaction at his latest victim.

The Bunkers consisted of a rectangular cement building with about 100 cells along both walls at ground level and on the first floor. In the middle was a large space with iron stairways and landings leading to the upper cells. At one end of the building was the reception room, an office for the Supervisor, a room in which examinations took place and another one with the whipping block, where every Friday the floggings took place. There was also a washroom with showers.

Dark Arrest

After striding up and down in the cell for a while, I began to distinguish the noises which I could hear on the other side of the door. There was the loud and raucous voice of Binz; the sobbing and crying of prisoners; the barking of dogs; men's voices; and loud laughter. Everything sounded hollow and echoed as though in a swimming pool. After a very long time I smelt the well-known aroma of camp soup. That meant it was already evening. Then I heard the clatter of utensils. Steps approached and I heard cell doors being opened, and once a woman's voice began to whine: 'But, Frau Supervisor . . .' The steps passed on and then there was silence. So I was to have no soup.

It grew cold as the evening wore on. From outside the building I heard the sound of singing as a column came in from outside work. There were still some hours to go before night fell, and then the long hours of the night until morning. My bare arms were already covered with goose flesh. I heard the muffled sound of the camp siren, then a little while afterwards the light was switched on in my cell and an eye appeared at the spy-hole. No doubt it was Binz making her rounds. She put the key in the cell door, but to double-lock it, not to open it. The light went out. After a while the faint shimmer under the door went out too, and I was in complete darkness. They had not even unlocked and let down the bed for me to lie on, or given me a blanket.

And then the fight against cold, hunger and tiredness began. I would sit down on the stool, draw up my knees and press my bare arms between my thighs to get a little warmth into them. As soon as I nodded off for a moment, I would overbalance and wake up with a jerk, and then walk up and down the cell again: five steps there, five steps back, carefully skirting the stool each time. I tried sitting on the floor with my back against the wall, but it was so cold and damp that I was soon chilled to the bone. With the towel rolled up for a pillow, I curled up on the floor – if only my arms were not bare! And then I remembered that there was newspaper stuck behind the closet pipe. I got it out and spread it carefully on the floor. It kept one shoulder and an arm from direct contact with the stone. Yes, it was warmer – or not quite so cold. Such a night seems endless, but it did end, and at last I heard the siren sound for the morning roll-call, and noises began to come from the other side of the door.

But the day was no different from the night, except that the light was switched on for five minutes for the cell to be swept out. For the rest the only light was the faint glimmer under the door, and it seemed even colder. My stomach was empty and I began to experience pains. Strange lights danced before my eyes like balls of coloured fire, and when I closed my eyes tightly it was lighter than ever. A whole universe of celestial suns passed rapidly before my eyes. Once I heard men's footsteps and then I sprang up and turned my back to the door. If Ramdor looked in, he should not see my face. The light went on and the cell door was opened. It was Ramdohr.

'Well,' he said, 'how are we feeling today? Are you ready to make a statement now?'

I made no reply.

'Very well,' he said with a mocking grin. 'I can wait.'

And with that he went out and the cell door closed behind him. The electric light went out. I wonder when he'll fetch me for questioning, I thought. At night probably. He can't prove anything against me. Would Frau Langefeld use her influence for me? I was certain she would. But had she any influence left? Everything they accused me of incriminated her too, for it had all happened in her office.

For a time I forgot hunger and cold, but then I smelt food again and my mouth watered. I crouched down in the corner between the closet and the wall and pulled my dress over my shoulders. It seemed not so cold there. Every time when steps sounded in the corridor I sprang up and began to walk up and down the cell.

In the second night I had dreams – dreams of bread. There they were, mountains of crisp, golden brown loaves piled up in front of me, but when I went to take one I always woke up. I crouched down over a dish full of macaroni and was about to wolf it up like a dog when I knocked my head on the closet. At least I could get water from the tap next to the closet, and drinking helped for a while. On the third day the pangs of hunger had gone, but the desire for a little warmth was overwhelming.

Punctually at the same time every morning the light was switched on and the cell door opened and then one of the Bible Students handed in a brush and pan for me to sweep out the cell. She never said a word and her face wore a set look of suffering and sympathy. It was always the same expression; as though she wore a mask.

'Give me some more paper, please,' I said.

She nodded and went out hurriedly as though she were afraid I might ask her for something forbidden, perhaps a piece of bread. The Bible Students carried out their work with more conscientiousness than a Nazi would have done. What might the SS not have thought of them if one of them had been discovered breaking the rules!

I covered the floor with paper in the corner between the closet and the wall, and there I sat hunched up with my hands over my face so that no one could see me through the spy-hole. I ceased to distinguish night from day and vegetated in a dull stupor. A pulse beat quietly in my neck. What a pity that the eiderdowns which covered the floor in front of me were not there when I put my hand forward to draw them over me! And then strange people began to come into my cell. They shone like phosphorus and seemed not to touch the ground. They were friendly and smiled at me, and I felt peaceful and happy. I was not hungry, and even the cold was no longer so bad. But they teased me with the broom, and I covered my face and longed for the darkness.

It was the morning of the eighth day (so I learnt later) when the light went on and the hatch of the cell door was opened. The rough voice of Binz sounded sharply:

'Get a move on, Buber. Don't you want any bread?'

I got up and staggered to the door. There on the lowered hatch was a bread ration and a mug of hot coffee substitute. I took the bread and the mug incredulously and went over to the table. The light went out at once but I had the bread in my hands and the smell of it in my nostrils. No bread ever smelt as good as that.

After my seven days' fast I received normal camp rations every fourth day, and on the days in between I was given bread only. It is difficult to say which is worse: to have no food at all, or to have only enough food to keep you hungry all the time. At the end of my fast, Binz also let down the wall bed and I was given two blankets, a sheet and a cover for a mattress, but no mattress. In the phraseology of the Gestapo, that is called 'Strict dark arrest with hard sleeping'.

After I had drunk the hot coffee substitute and chewed some of the bread, I felt better, and my will to live returned. I washed myself down with cold water and when I went to spread out the towel on the central-heating pipes I found they were warm. I pressed myself as close to them as I could, enjoying the warmth that came through them to my body. After that the heating was turned on every day for half an hour.

In the afternoon Supervisor Binz took me out of the cell and ordered me to take a blanket with me. For a wild breathless moment I thought I was to be released, but no. I was taken up the iron stairs and along the gallery until we reached the last cell in the row, and there I was locked in. The crack under the door was a little wider, and it was not quite so dark as in the other cell. In addition, the place did not smell so damp and mouldy, and in consequence it did not strike so cold. During my short journey from one cell to the other the sun had been shining through the glass roof down into the basement – real May sunlight, heartening and thrilling after the darkness. Outside it was spring, and animals and plants enjoyed the sun, but in the Bunkers behind a hundred steel doors prisoners sat cold and hungry in the darkness.

A young Russian was brought in whilst I was there. She had been caught stealing. She kept screaming in Russian, 'Oh, God! Oh, my God!' and kicking against the door of her cell. From time to time Binz would descend on her in wrath, boxing her ears, kicking her and setting the dog on her. She even poured cold water over her, but still the Russian kept on screaming and moaning. It was horrible, and I put my fingers in my ears to keep out the sound. It was hours before she finally fell silent, probably from sheer exhaustion. Binz gave women who caused trouble short shrift. If someone hadn't folded her blanket just right (in the dark) she would get her ears boxed or be kicked, have her food stopped for three days, her blankets taken away and the bed locked up against the wall. There were women who were constantly incurring her rage, and punishments showered down on them. That meant certain death in the end.

When I had been in the Bunkers for some weeks, dependent almost the whole time on my sense of hearing alone for any contact with the outside world, I learnt to distinguish the voices of many of the inmates. I recognised the steps of all the wardresses, and Ramdohr's steps in particular, and I knew exactly which cell they had halted in front of. The worst day of the week in the Bunkers was Friday, when the floggings took place. Women were dragged out of their cells or brought in from the camp to suffer this punishment.

One night Ramdohr had me brought out of my cell for an examination. Unexpectedly, nothing further was said about suppressed 'reports',

destroyed messages or interference with official documents, and all the
questions he asked concerned private conversations that I was alleged to
have had with Frau Langefeld about the building up of a spy organisation against Camp Commandant Suhren and SS Camp Leader Bräuning,
and alleged Communist propaganda.

'I have asked for five death sentences,' Ramdohr told me, 'and as an
example to the camp they won't be carried out by shooting, but by
public hanging in full view of the whole camp.'

I gathered the impression that Frau Langefeld must be under arrest,
and I tried to get confirmation or denial from the Bible Student who
brought in the brush and pan every morning. At first she refused to say
anything at all, but finally she whispered that Senior SS Supervisor Frau
Langefeld was no longer in office.

After a while I managed to communicate with my neighbour in the
next cell. The walls of the Bunkers were well suited to this. We waited
until everything was quiet and then we crouched down at the dividing
wall and knocked to attract the other's attention. If we then spoke close
up to the wall the words could be heard on the other side. The prisoner
in the next cell was Betty Schneider, an Asocial, and in consequence our
conversational possibilities were limited. She was also being held by
Ramdohr. She had worked in the furriers' workshop, where furs and fur-
lined coats which had belonged to Jews who had ended in the gas chambers were unpicked to be used for military jackets. Very often the former
owners had sewn valuables into their coats, and for a time there were
rings, jewels and other valuables going the rounds in the camp. Some
of the male prisoners, who also worked in the shop, had tried to bribe
the guards in order to smuggle the valuables out. Someone had given
the game away and Betty was involved as an accomplice.

By accident, I discovered that Eva Busch was also in the Bunkers, and
I was caught calling out to her. The Bible Student had just brought in
my coffee substitute when along stormed Binz, rushed into my cell,
seized my coffee and poured it away, shouting, 'Three days starvation
for you, my lady, and no bed and blankets.' And, unfortunately, Eva was
caught as well.

For another three days I took up my position in the corner between
the closet and the wall, and this time my senses seemed to go much
more quickly than the first time I had been left without food. I became
exhausted much more rapidly. On the third day the hatch was opened
before the usual time for distributing the rations. It was the Bible Student.
'Grete,' she called. 'Come here quickly. I've got something for you. It's
from Milena.' I dragged myself to my feet and staggered to the door
with difficulty, and from her blouse the Bible Student pulled a little

parcel. 'Quick! Quick! Take it. Milena sends you her warmest greetings. Hide it, for heaven's sake.'

The tears rolled down my cheeks. Milena had not forgotten me. The parcel contained sugar and bread. Instead of my looking after her, she was looking after me.

Ramdohr had me out again for questioning, and when I still refused to say what he wanted me to say he declared that he was sick and tired of my constant denials and that he would arrange for my transport to Auschwitz with the comment, 'Return undesirable'. His first attempt at intimidation – the story of the public hangings in the camp – I had taken with a pinch of salt as one of the usual blood-curdling threats made to extort statements, but the threat of transfer to Auschwitz was a different matter; that sounded only too probable. Back in my dark cell I had plenty of time to recall and think over what Rosl Hahn had told me about Auschwitz. And it seemed to me that I could already smell charred and burnt flesh. At first I thought it was an illusion, the power of suggestion to an overwrought mind, but it was so persistent and penetrating that I got into touch with Betty and asked her whether she could smell anything. The answer came back:

'Yes, of course. Didn't you know the crematorium they've built behind the Bunkers has started up?'

I had been in dark arrest for over two months and in that time I had missed the latest addition to the amenities of Ravensbrück.

Every fourth day I was given half a litre of turnip soup or dried vegetables and six potatoes cooked in their jackets, and I summoned up all my energy and will-power to put aside three of the potatoes so that I could have one every day with my bread. I put them between the central heating pipes where it was coolest and where they were likely to stay fresh longest. Of course, it was dirty there, and it was impossible to find a clean spot in the dark, but in my position cleanliness was not a prime necessity of life. The thought of food occupied a great deal of my attention in the Bunkers, though I tried to keep my mind on the past and to think of poetry and songs. On my interminable march up and down the cell I would sing or recite poetry. Some days the songs were cheerful; on others they were sad. I did my best to keep my spirits up by thinking of all the wonderful things I would do when I got out, and by refusing to think of the much more probable future of gradual starvation, sickness and death.

As soon as the light was switched on in the morning, and the dustpan and brush handed in, I would sweep up like mad in order to spend the rest of the precious time the light was on by reading the scraps of newspaper provided for lavatory purposes. The paper consisted of squares cut up from the SS paper, *Das Schwarze Korps*. Hurriedly, I would try to fit the pieces together so that they made a whole. In this way I managed to piece an article together which cheered me up for days. It was entitled 'And then a Miracle happened!' It described the desperate situation in which Frederick the Great found himself after his defeat at Leuthen. All seemed lost – and then Elizabeth of Russia suddenly died and the whole political situation was transformed in his favour. Obviously, the article was a parallel to the present situation of Hitler. If all they could hope for was a miracle, then for me and my like there was hope.

One morning before the Bunkers were officially awake the hatch of my cell was cautiously opened and the Bible Student produced another package from Milena. My pleasure was spoiled by the horrible state of fright the woman was in. 'Grete,' she pleaded, 'please let me tell Milena you don't want her to send you any more; it's so dangerous. Please let me tell her that. Please, Grete.' She was in such a state of nerves and almost hysterical fear that I had no alternative but to agree: 'Very well,' I said coldly. 'Tell her I forbid her to send me anything else.'

At the beginning of July – I had not been taken out for questioning for a long time – the light was switched on and SS Supervisor Binz and a prisoner came into my cell. I thought it was a search, but the prisoner brought in a pair of steps and proceeded to uncover the window of my cell and let the light in. The pleasurable shock was so overwhelming that I quite lost my head. I can't remember whether I prayed, wept or sang – I probably did all three in turn. When they were gone, I pulled myself up to the window. It took all my remaining strength, but with one foot on the table I could lean over precariously and hang on. The summer air was delicious; heady, almost like wine, and I breathed it in deeply until I was giddy with it. The sun was shining and I could see beyond the camp wall. There was a tall chimney I had never seen before. The brickwork was yellow and new. That was no doubt the crematorium. I could see the pines and in the distance the church spire. And the sky was blue. How can I make anyone realise what a simple everyday scene like that meant to me? I remained there drinking it all in greedily until my strength was exhausted and I had to let myself down again.

There was another great pleasure in store for me that same day. The cell door opened and two other women were sent in. It was Maria Graf and Presserova. They stood there with pale, colourless faces, just like mine must have been, and were at a loss, like shy children in an unaccustomed situation. My heart was full to bursting point and I just looked at them with delight, and when they spoke their voices seemed lovely. All the misery and pain I had suffered disappeared in their company, and the gruesome, ghostly life I had been leading receded into the past almost as though it had never been true. The days no longer consisted of dark, endless waiting. There were fellow human beings to talk to, and even though there was still anxiety, at least it could be shared, and the mere presence of the others gave me courage.

Their situation was not enviable. Both of them were expecting severe punishment. When the Bible Students refused to attend to the Angora rabbits any longer, a new group had been given the work. It consisted of German and Czech Politicals, including Maria Graf and Presserova. A civilian was in charge of the work. He was so small in stature that they nicknamed him 'The Little Coachman'. From all accounts, he must have been a splendid fellow and a courageous one too. He did everything he possibly could to make their lives easier, and he even began to smuggle out letters for them. And after a while he arranged to receive the replies in his own home in Fürstenberg. He also obtained special medicine from Prague for one of the Czech prisoners who was suffering from pernicious anæmia.

Unfortunately, he was denounced by someone, with the result that all the members of the group found themselves in the Bunkers, and the sick Czech girl as well. The Little Coachman and his wife and daughter were arrested and sent to concentration camps, and Ramdohr even travelled to Prague to question the relatives of the sick girl. The members of the group were all told that their relatives had been arrested in connection with the affair, and one of them broke down and confessed everything. In the end, Maria Graf received twenty-five lashes, but Presserova was unexpectedly released, together with the sick Czech, whose condition had grown so much worse in the Punishment Block that she was sent to the sickbay, where she died. All the others, including Maria Graf, were sentenced to a term in the Punishment Block.

Compared with what went before, the time I spent with Maria Graf and Presserova seemed almost serene and happy. We chatted and sang together, and I learnt a number of Czech songs by heart. We shared our food and our joys and sorrows, and every evening Maria, who was a practising Catholic, would kneel down and pray fervently.

Mental Derangement and Recovery

After I had spent ten weeks in the Bunkers, I was suddenly released and sent back to the camp without further questioning and without any explanation. I greeted the relative freedom of the camp square and the huts with more enthusiasm than I did my final freedom years later. The very next day I fell ill. My body could not stand the regular meals. I was given 'inside work' and for the greater part of the day I lay peacefully on my straw mattress whilst Milena looked after me. From her I learnt that Frau Langefeld had been arrested and brought before an SS court charged with a variety of offences, including that of having shown sympathy towards the Poles. She was discharged for lack of evidence, but removed from the service.

I recovered slowly and after a week I could get about again fairly normally. My first journey was to the Polish Block, where, I was told, Helena Korewa wanted to see me. When I arrived, she cautiously showed me a leaflet dropped by the Royal Air Force about the flight of Hess to England. Polish workers had found it in the wood and brought it in with the greatest possible precautions. The penalty for possessing such a thing would have been terrible, but for us that piece of paper was like a magic talisman.

The very next day – I was still in bed – along came SS Supervisor Schrörs and roughly ordered me to get up. She then thoroughly searched my mattress. She seemed to be looking for something in particular, but, of course, there was nothing there. 'Come along with me,' she said when she had finished, and I followed her to the office with new despair and anxiety in my heart. What could it be this time? So soon after the other. Before I had had a chance to recover. I suspected that it was something to do with the RAF leaflet.

In the corridor of the office, waiting to see the new Senior SS Supervisor, a woman named Klein-Träubel, stood Helena Korova, her daughter and another Pole named Bella Hallina. It seemed clear that the leaflet had been discovered and that my visit to Helena had been reported. We were unable to exchange a word whilst we were waiting. The Camp Leader Bräuning passed us and went into the office. After a while an SS Supervisor came out and took us all to the Bunkers. Supervisor Binz greeted me mockingly: 'What! You here again! It didn't last long, did it?'

I made no attempt to discover the cause of my new misfortune; it seemed only too clear. This time I was put in Betty Schneider's cell. In the meantime, she had gone back to the Punishment Block. And then it began all over again. For a week I was kept in absolute darkness without food. After that I received my daily ration of bread and normal rations once every fourth day. The same misery and suffering, the same hunger and sleeplessness, the same noises outside the door. My mind began to wander and I was no longer sure whether I had really been let out of the Bunkers or not. Perhaps it had all been a hallucination. By the second week everything had become unreal. I no longer knew where I was, whether it was day or night or when the longed-for fourth day was due. I lived in feverish dreams peopled by the characters of song and poetry. Maria Graf and Bella Hallina were in the next cell, and from time to time they called me back to reality by knocking, but as soon as the conversation ceased I slid back again into my fantasies.

I spent five weeks in the Bunkers this time, and not once was I taken out for questioning. At the end of that time – it was on a Sunday – the cell door was opened and I was released, together with Helena Korewa, her daughter and Halina Bella. I never discovered why we had been sent to the Bunkers.

This time I hated the light and the reality of the camp. My release was no pleasure to me. I closed my eyes and longed for the darkness, and tried to live again in my fantasies. Milena needed a very great deal of patience to bring me back to reality.

A quite striking change had taken place in my absence. The prisoners who strolled up and down the camp streets were dressed in coloured summer clothes of all kinds, though on the back and front there were patches in the shape of a cross to mark them as prisoners. The gipsies, in particular, were as bright as tropical birds with all sorts of coloured scraps. And the regulation step the SS had taken so much trouble to teach us had disappeared – another sign of how the camp discipline was loosening. It appeared that camp clothing was so scarce that the SS had distributed the clothing of women who had been sent to the gas chambers amongst the prisoners. Those who received parcels from outside were even allowed to wear their own clothes. Only the gangs who went outside the camp to work still had to wear the old regulation camp uniform.

Before the clothing stores there were heaps of this clothing, and hundreds of pairs of shoes neatly tied together as the women had been instructed to tie them when they had to strip for the gas chambers, though many of the shoes had obviously been tried on and tossed back separately on to the heap by prisoners. At first the garment workshop had cut out patches back and front and sewn in material of a different colour, but later on this proved too tiresome and so the clothing was just daubed back and front with white paint.

The disappearance of the uniform clothing was another factor which increased the dirt and disorder in the camp. The old warning placards, 'A louse may mean your death!' were still around, but in the meantime the louse population had increased enormously and some of the blocks were hopelessly infested. From time to time the camp authorities took measures against the pest. Huts were fumigated and the women were called out in batches to have their clothing disinfected, and kept waiting around naked for hours in cold rooms, and when their clothing came back there were often living lice still in it.

During my second stay in the Bunkers a welcome change had come over the Medical Post. The SS Dr Rosenthal and his favourite, Gerda Quernheim, had been arrested – not for the murders they had committed

– the SS had no objection to that – but for systematically stealing gold
teeth from the mouths of their victims. In that respect they had poached
on the preserves of more powerful people. Rosenthal was sentenced to
seven years' imprisonment, and Gerda Quernheim was sent to Auschwitz.
SS Dr Schidlausky was also transferred, and the SS now began to use
the services of German, Czech, Russian and Polish doctors amongst their
prisoners, with the result that a visit to the Medical Post lost its terrors,
though, to tell the truth, some of these doctors treated the sick prisoners not much better than the SS doctors before them, and some of
them shamelessly favoured the sick of their own nationality. However,
most of them did their best with great devotion in extraordinarily difficult circumstances – circumstances which became worse and worse towards
the final years of the camp's existence, when prisoners died like flies of
typhoid, tuberculosis, dysentery, pneumonia and other causes. The situation was greatly aggravated by the terrible overcrowding. Sometimes
there were as many as four women to one mattress. Sheets were changed
only for those who worked in the kitchens and the SS offices, and a bath
became a great rarity. At the same time, prisoners were working eleven
hours a day and their food was barely enough to keep body and soul
together.

More and more prisoners were being sent out of the camp as mobile
labour gangs for munition factories, airfields, and other war undertak-
ings. Conditions were bad and the food was even worse than in the
camp; in addition, there was the danger from bombing. When I was
strong enough to work again, I did my utmost to evade being put into
one of these gangs, and through the good offices of Polish prisoners
with whom I was friendly I managed to get myself attached to their
'Forestry Gang'. The leader of this gang was Mother Liberak, a good-
hearted and motherly soul to whom quite a number of the Polish
'guinea-pigs' owed their lives. The SS Overseer was a nineteen-year-old,
good-natured and harmless girl from Ulm named Eugenia. Excellent
relations existed between her and her Polish charges, who called her
'Sherija'. Letter-smuggling was an understood thing, and although it was
strictly forbidden Mother Liberak would take 'guinea-pigs' out with us
into the woods every day, provided they could walk there and back
without attracting attention. When we arrived at our place of work, they
could sit or lie down all day.

We had to pass the SS quarters and go down the road in the direction of Fürstenberg until we came to the woods, and Mother Liberak
had to slow down our pace again and again in order that the 'guinea-
pigs' could keep up. The first time I accompanied the gang it was a
misty morning, and the trees, the moss underfoot and the brown leaves

of the undergrowth were covered with hoar frost. I had quite forgotten how invigorating it is to walk through woods with the soft, mossy ground underneath and twigs cracking underfoot. And the autumnal smells! They were indescribably lovely. When we came to the hut the gang had built of branches and leaves, a jay flew up suddenly in front of us, chattering indignantly. The axes and other tools were kept in this hut to save the trouble of carrying them backwards and forwards. Eugenie was on such good terms with her Poles that she confidently accepted their word that no one would try to escape, and she would often retire into this hut with her dog and go to sleep, leaving us to our own devices.

The forester would come along with his dog, exchange friendly greetings with the prisoners, most of whom he knew by this time, and show Mother Liberak the trees which were to be felled. Then the two-handled saws would get to work – but not too zealously. The work was hard, of course, but there was no one to drive us and we didn't overexert ourselves. Towards midday the forester would suggest that the time had come to burn the brushwood. We all knew what that meant. Some of the prisoners would go off to fetch potatoes and the others would prepare the fire. The branches hissed and smoked and soon there was a glowing heap of ashes into which we inserted whole potatoes. When they were done we all sat down and ate them. The life with the Forestry Gang was a real joy, and whilst I was with it my health improved tremendously. The whole thing was possible only because of the good relations which existed between the SS Overseer Eugenia and her Poles, and because of the humanity of our forester.

Unfortunately for me – or so it seemed at the time – I was transferred after a while to the garment workshop. I had not been expelled from my woodland paradise for long when it suffered the final fate of all good things in concentration camp. Ramdohr and his spies found out about the idyllic conditions which existed in the Forestry Gang, and all its members were arrested, together with the SS Supervisor Eugenia, and put into the Bunkers. The prisoners were later let out of the Bunkers and kept in the Punishment Block, but Eugenia stayed behind and in April 1945 she was still there.

My transfer to the garment workshop came about by an unexpected accident. In Mother Liberak's gang, you could take the day off occasionally, and when my turn came round I stayed in the camp with Milena. We were strolling along talking about towns and trees and such things when Milena suddenly began to talk about her little daughter, Honza – that is to say, she had been small four years before when she had been brought to see Milena in prison in Prague. But life went on outside and the children grew up while their mothers stayed in prison and concentration camp.

'They grow up into girls and young women,' said Milena, 'and naturally they almost forget their mothers. And their letters get so formal.
You hear that they're learning to play the piano and getting on very
nicely, and that they're doing very well at school, and things like that.
But I wish she would sometimes tell me what sort of a dress she has
and whether she's started wearing silk stockings yet.' And she sighed.

When we came to the end of the camp street and were just going to
turn round and go back who should come round the corner face to face
with us but the SS Labour Organiser Dittmann. He spotted me at once.

'What are you doing in camp during working hours?' he bellowed.
Unfortunately, he knew me only too well. He had a permanent lump
on one side of his face, which was now red with fury.

'I'm sick and on "inside work", Herr Labour Organiser,' was the only
lie I could think up on the spur of the moment. Fortunately, Milena
wore her yellow armlet which showed that she was entitled to be in the
camp and he made no attempt to browbeat her.

'You weren't long enough in the Bunkers,' he said. 'Perhaps you'd
like another dose? Report to me tomorrow, otherwise there'll be trouble.'
And with that he stamped on his way. There was nothing for it, so the
next morning I reported to his office. He had me in to see him personally, threatened me with a 'report' and told me that I was being transferred as a punishment to Workshop I. 'Report to Oberscharführer Graf,'
he said. 'I'll telephone him and let him know you're coming.'

THE DEAD AND THE SURVIVORS

Slaves of the Assembly Line

Workshop I was a large well-built factory with big windows and modern lighting. Over 400 women worked there on electric sewing machines making SS uniforms. There were three such workshops, a cutting room, a weaving room, a furrier's workshop, a repair shop for damaged uniforms and a repair workshop for machinery. No less than 3,000 prisoners worked in this factory. There were also buildings where stocks and other requirements were kept. The whole complex was separated from the camp by a wall. Up to the end of 1943 the prisoners who worked there still lived in the camp, but afterwards the SS began to have buildings erected for them next to their work, thus saving quite an amount of time otherwise wasted in roll-calls and so on.

There was such a noise of machinery in the great hall that you could hardly hear yourself speak at first. Hundreds of machines were going at once and the place shook. Moving bands carried the work along from prisoner to prisoner, and the women had to work ceaselessly to keep up. The cutting room delivered the parts, which were then assembled on special tables and laid out on the moving bands. One prisoner sewed a back seam, the next a front seam, the next sewed in one arm, the next the other, the next the collar, and so on down the line until the finished jacket was handed over to the controller, an SS man, to be examined for faults.

Each line of workers had their fixed quota, and if this was not achieved there were blows, punishments and 'reports'. The prisoner forewoman scolded, the SS Overseer bullied and the SS Inspector hit out whenever he felt inclined. When I sat down at my machine and heard the dreaded word 'quota', I was reminded of Birma, where the prisoners also lived in fear of not being able to perform the amount of work fixed for them. In Siberia the camp authorities forced the prisoners to do their utmost to fulfil the labour quotas by cutting down their rations if they didn't;

here in Ravensbrück the same effect was achieved by blows, punishments and 'reports', followed by still more severe punishments.

I had never used a machine before and although my first job was comparatively simple, the machine 'ran away with me', and I could not fulfil my quota. The thread was constantly breaking and the needles too. What I should have had to suffer if I had been an unknown newcomer! Beaten by the SS man, had my ears boxed by the Overseer, been bullied by the forewoman. But an old 'Ravensbrücker' finds friends everywhere. A Czech forewoman named Nelly observed my difficulties and she covertly sewed a pile of the bands I was supposed to be doing and put them on my pile, and I was saved. And little brown-eyed Anička from the repair workshop, whose job it was to go from machine to machine doing running repairs and making any necessary adjustments, quickly replaced my broken needles so that I did not have to ask the Overseer every time and probably get my ears boxed for asking too often.

We worked in two shifts of ten hours each, which were later extended to eleven hours. At nights the windows were tightly closed and curtained for fear of bombing attacks. After a few hours the air was so thick with fluff that it was almost impossible to breathe. Bent over their machines, the women worked desperately to fulfil their quotas. They dared not look up or stop for a moment. Next to me was a young Ukrainian girl. I noticed that her lips moved all the time she was working and I realised that she was singing. I smiled at her and she smiled back, and I had another friend in Ravensbrück.

The terror of our workshop was the SS Unterscharführer Binder. The night shift was usually the time when he went on the rampage. Suddenly even above the noise of the machinery his brutal bellowing would sound, causing all the women to stop their work for a moment in fright and look up. Binder had found another victim: some poor wretch who was not working fast enough, or who had sewn a crooked seam, or perhaps just someone he hated. His cheeks would puff out and his face go purple from the shrieking, and then, with a maniacal look on his face, he would seize his victim, bang her head against the machine, drag her off her seat and punch her until blood poured from her nose. The man was a sadist; he had to see blood every night. Then he would let his victim fall in a heap to the floor and stand over her gloating. There was a wiry little Frenchwoman who was his particular enemy. No matter how he maltreated her, she never ceased to pour out a stream of vituperation in French. It made her the pride and admiration of the whole workshop, and it stung Binder into frenzies of impotent fury.

At midnight there was half an hour's pause during which each prisoner received a mug of coffee substitute and ate the bread she had brought with her – unless, as often happened, the whole shift was made to work through the pause as a punishment. Many of the women had to work through without a bite, for they had already eaten up their bread ration during the day. The Ukrainian girl next to me never had anything to eat and I shared my bread with her. When we did not spend the rest of the pause sleeping with our heads on our machines we would talk. Her name was Nina, and her father had been a teacher in a small town in the Ukraine. It was easy to see that she had loved him dearly. Obviously he had been a man of some education and culture, and he had taught his daughter very much of Russian literature, particularly the poems of Pushkin, which she could recite by heart. She was delighted to find that I could speak Russian and she taught me many Russian folk songs. When I had mastered a new one and sang it to her, it gave her a childlike pleasure, and then we would sing it together in the rattle of the machinery. Her father had been taken away by the GPU in 1937, leaving her mother to bring her up, together with two younger sisters. When the war came and the Germans broke into the Ukraine, hunger had driven Nina to take work in an Army canteen. In ignorance of what she was doing, she let herself be recruited, together with many other Ukrainians, for work in the Reich. She was put in a munitions factory in Germany, where she was so unhappy that she tried to make her escape and return to the Ukraine. She was caught and sent to Ravensbrück.

Nowhere did the many air-raid warnings cause such pleasure as in the workshops at Ravensbrück. When the warning came through and the lights were extinguished, every prisoner looked for somewhere to go to sleep. Usually Anička, her toolbox under her arm, would seize me by the hand and drag me in the dark into the storeroom, where the SS uniforms were piled up. They served us as beds. Whilst the Allied bombers roared overhead and made the windows of the factory rattle, we were usually fast asleep, and there we stayed until the 'All Clear' brought us back to the hated machines again. The more often there were raids, and the longer they lasted, the more brutal became the regime in the workshop. Binder's example was followed by others. There was hardly a moving band at which the Overseer and the forewomen did not beat the prisoners, and SS Overseer Lange, a tall, raw-boned woman with unnaturally large hands and feet, followed the example of her male colleagues with particular brutality. But even here there was one exception, an SS man named Seipel who came from Hungary. He was a big, angular man with dark, sad-looking eyes. The women under him were never struck. He did not even shout at them, and he could be seen going from machine to machine, bending over, giving advice, and sometimes taking the woman's place to show her how it had to be done.

Naturally, the women loved him, but the longer he was there the more clearly he demonstrated how unsuited he was to be an overseer in an SS slave shop, and no doubt his superiors – and in particular Binder – did not fail to notice it. In the end he was sent to the front. It was a sad day for the women and they went around with downcast looks. About a fortnight later he came into the workshop for some reason or other. Immediately, the women spotted him; the machines stopped and there was a sudden demonstration of joy. But their hope that he had come back to work was without foundation. He smiled and shook his head. Probably he had just come in to fetch some paper or other, before going off. It was a demonstration to his humanity which must have consoled him and made him proud.

The man responsible for Workshops I, II and III was SS Ober-scharführer Graf, the man with whom Dittmann had threatened me. He was more intelligent than men like Binder and the others, but no less of a brute. He never beat a prisoner in public, but in his office he was like a savage, beating up women with the buckle of his belt and hurling them against the wall. In order to forestall 'sabotage', the women in the workshops were chosen from all nationalities and all categories, and Germans, Czechs, Poles, Politicals, criminals and Asocials all worked together. In addition, the control was so strict that not a badly sewn seam could get by, and for stealing a small piece of stuff there was a beating followed by a 'report' and still further punishment. One of Lange's chief pleasures was searching the women when work was over.

Many of the slaves worked willingly. I am not referring only to the criminal types, whose servile attitude to the SS was notorious. There were Communists who put their hearts and souls into the work – for instance, Maria Wiedmeier. She had occupied a prominent position in the Communist Party and had been almost ten years in prison and concentration camp, and yet she worked for the SS with such zeal and conscientiousness that one might have thought she was 'building up Socialism'. In fact, Graf was once heard to remark: 'Wiedmeier – now, that's one for you! I don't know what I'd do without her.' She had a responsible position in the workshop, being in charge of distributing the material to the tailoring workshops. Another one who worked with zeal and devotion as though for a noble cause was Olga Körner, a handsome, middle-aged woman with white hair, who had been a member of the Communist Party for many years before her arrest. She lived for her work and talked about nothing else.

One of the best workers in the shop was a young Ukrainian named Rema. In the summer of 1944 the SS introduced 'food bonuses' for good work in order to give the prisoners an incentive. By that time I was already working in the office. This Rema was extraordinarily adept at her work and she could do almost twice as much as the other machinists with ease. One day Graf ordered me to take her a package of food as a reward for her work. Incidentally, this food was stolen from the International Red Cross parcels sent into the camp. When I handed over the package to Rema, I spoke to her in Russian.

'You ought to be ashamed of yourself working so hard for the SS. And what's more, you'll make things worse for the others. They'll be expected to do it as well.'

But she smiled up at me shamelessly: 'I'm a very good worker,' she said proudly. 'It's only right that I should get something extra, isn't it?'

Milena's End

My work at the machine was ended by Maria Wiedmeier, who suggested to Graf that I should be placed in charge of the distribution of thread and buttons. Why she favoured me in this fashion I never understood, but there it was. Graf was very favourably disposed towards her on account of her industry and efficiency, and he usually followed her suggestions. He did so on this occasion and I was emancipated from the slavery at the machine. Maria Wiedmeier was firmly convinced that after the war the Communist Party would seize power in Germany, and she always told the Russians and Ukrainians of her group to write to her after the war 'c/o Central Committee of The Communist Party of Germany.' But as an old and experienced Communist she was well aware that Communist policy could change, and did change, from one moment to the next, with direful results for those who had just previously been on top. Perhaps she thought it not impossible that in the event of a Communist seizure of power Heinz Neumann's star might rise again. Stranger things than that have happened. She knew my relation to him, and therefore perhaps her consideration to me was a sort of long-term insurance policy.

After the terrors of the electric sewing machine and the constant fear of lagging behind the quota, the work of handing out materials was child's play. Women came from all the moving bands to ask for thread, etc. Amongst the hundreds of women I already knew quite a number. One day a young girl came. She was dressed in a camp outfit which was too big for her and was held together in the middle with a piece of string instead of a belt. Her face was grey and her dark hair was covered with fluff from the camouflage stuff on which she was working. She had the brown, friendly eyes of a child, and I liked her at once. When I had an opportunity, I spoke to her. It was the beginning of my friendship

with the Norwegian prisoner, Lille Graah. Shortly after our first talk, all
Norwegian prisoners received coloured aprons from the Norwegian Red
Cross and Lille appeared with one of these aprons. It was the envy of
the workshop. However, it violated the first principle of all prison life:
never, never attract attention. She was caught in some harmless offence
against the rules, lost her job of material-fetcher for her moving band
and was set to a machine as punishment. She had to sew in sleeves and
was in constant danger of lagging behind her quota.

The winter of 1943–4 was probably the worst period of all in
Ravensbrück. We got news of the situation at the front from time to
time, and we knew that Hitler's star was on the wane. That cheered us
up and gave us hope, but the fact was that many prisoners were rapidly
coming to the very end of their strength. If they were to be saved it
was a matter of weeks, not months, or perhaps a year. But there was
nothing we could do. We had to wait helplessly, hoping against hope,
and seeing every new day claim hundreds of victims. Merely standing
for hours at the roll-calls was an agony in the cold, and scores of women
suffered from frostbite. The doctors were unable to keep pace with the
innumerable amputation cases, and many women died of gangrene.

In the beginning a carter named Wendland used to come from
Fürstenberg and take the dead away, each in a separate coffin and wrapped
in a paper shroud with frills at the end, something like a frill round a
ham-bone. As time went on, more and more prisoners died, and
Wendland's business prospered greatly and he bought himself a lorry.
But when the crematorium was built the SS took charge of the disposal
of the dead. By this time prisoners were so thin that two corpses could
be got into one coffin easily; they were only flat boxes of rough, unplaned
wood. At first four prisoners would carry the coffin to the crematorium,
but later they were provided with a cart, and dealt with up to fifty corpses
a day. They would load perhaps half a dozen boxes into the cart and
then trundle it off to the crematorium. That was a prisoner's 'funeral'.

It was in this terrible winter that Milena's health took a very serious
turn. Her powers of resistance were broken and her will to live exhausted.
She began to speak more and more of death. 'I shan't survive this camp,'
she would say. 'I know it. I shall never see Prague again. If only Herr
Wendland had come for me! He always looked so friendly in his duffle
coat.'

It was with a great effort that she dragged herself to work every day
as usual, and the fear of injections and the Sick Transports kept her going.
She always had a temperature, and the new SS doctor examined her and
declared that one kidney was diseased. At his urgent advice, she agreed
on an operation. She still wanted to live, as all human beings want to

live, and particularly as a prisoner wants to live to get back one day to freedom and her loved ones. For Milena it was primarily her daughter and her far-off home in Prague. She survived the actual operation, and for a while she even seemed to get better. She was firmly convinced that she would recover, and even I began to do more than just hope, but the recovery was very slow – too slow – and then it stopped altogether. For three months my camp life consisted chiefly of the quarter of an hour I spent at her bedside in the morning before the roll-call.

She was in a room with five others, all hopeless cases. Naturally, it was strictly prohibited for me to go there, but my luck held and it was only on the day Milena died that the SS Matron caught me, and then it didn't matter any longer. She died on 17 May 1944, and she believed up to the last that she was going to recover. Something precious had gone out of my life with Milena and I felt very near despair. Life seemed to have no further point. When they came to take her body away, I asked permission to go with it to the crematorium. That last little piety was some small consolation. It was a typical spring morning and a warm rain was falling when two prisoners lifted the coffin on to the cart. Somewhere in the rushes of Fürstenberg Lake a bird was singing a melancholy little song. Perhaps the guard at the gate thought it was the rain that trickled down my cheeks.

The World Outside

In June we heard the news of the successful invasion of the Continent by British and American troops. We were overjoyed, but my joy was tempered by the fact that I had no one near with whom to share it. If Milena had been alive to experience it! It was the first real harbinger of freedom. But freedom for me had been bound up with Milena for so long that now I regarded it almost disconsolately. My days were sad and I wept into my pillow at night. For so many years all our desires had been in common and all our plans for the future made together. Lotte Henschel, Maria Graf, the little Norwegian Lille and the Czech Anička shared my sadness, and it brought us closer together.

During the time I was ill I had managed to send my first illegal and uncensored letter to my mother. A Polish girl smuggled it out for me and it arrived safely. Although I did not directly express my despair, the greater freedom of expression must have permitted my mother to realise it. She discussed the situation with my brother-in-law, Bernhard, and he suggested that from then on he should write the monthly letter and send off my parcel. Bernhard was a doctor and he had been both in prison and concentration camp after 1933, so that he knew how to write to prisoners. His letters to me were a deep source of consolation. They gave me back my courage and my determination to survive, and I read them to many of my companions. We had not seen each other for over ten years, but he wrote as though it had been only yesterday. In his first letter announcing the despatch of a parcel there was a sentence: 'Be careful with the box; they're difficult to get.' That obviously had a meaning.

A big parcel arrived with food and sweets. It was beautifully packed like a Christmas parcel, the various items wrapped up separately and tied with ribbon. On a slab of chocolate he had scratched: 'All the best. Bernhard.' We were like children on Christmas morning when we opened it. Little things – childish things, perhaps – but very important to anyone in our position. And when we had taken everything out we turned our attention to the cardboard box itself. Sure enough, it contained another surprise. Carefully concealed in the sides were three coloured reproductions: two of Van Gogh, the famous *Three Ships on the Strand* and *Sunflowers*, and one of Renoir, *The Country House*. The first works of art in our concentration camp. Those three pictures gave us a tremendous amount of pleasure. They spoke of another world and another life, and they fortified our belief that one day we should be free to enjoy all the things they symbolised.

Bernhard was an absolute master in the art of illegal communication. Despite the strict censorship, he played never-ending variations on the theme, 'When will the war be over?' and our hopes for a speedy ending were greatly encouraged by what he said. One day he sent me a box with twelve eggs. On each egg there was an artistically executed miniature: flowers, birds, rabbits, kids and so on. The supervisor at the parcel office was nonplussed, and because such a thing was beyond her ken she was suspicious, though she didn't quite know why. At first she refused to hand over the precious eggs, and it took me all my powers of persuasion to make her change her mind. In the end she submitted with very bad grace. I rushed off with the eggs and we squatted together on the ground studying them all very carefully. Most of them seemed quite innocent, but there was one which we finally decided was the message. It represented the legend of Perseus and Andromeda. There was the monster writhing round the egg. On its tail was a minute, hardly visible *Hakenkreuz*. Andromeda stood hopefully chained to a rock, whilst Perseus, in German Army uniform, complete with steel helmet, thrust his sword deep into the neck of the dragon. Finally, we discovered worked into Andromeda the word 'You' and into Perseus the word 'Us', and we were convinced that before long the Army was to strike a blow against the Nazi power.

In a further parcel, which also contained a number of these miniature sketches, all of them apparently quite innocent, we at last found
the more detailed message we had been hoping for. It was hidden in a
package of 'V for Victory Drops'. Even that message was guarded, but
its purport was clear. It informed us that a concert was going to be held
in Bernhard's unit at which, not a solo or a quartet, but a full orchestral
work was to be performed. We discussed this message from every possible
angle and came to the conclusion that the Army was preparing to over-
throw Hitler and bring the war to an end, particularly as in his ordinary
letter Bernhard informed me that my sister was soon going to have a
baby – a piece of information which was possible, but very unlikely. We
were tremendously excited and we lived from day to day with our hopes
and expectations excruciatingly strained.

The world knows what happened. The venture failed. The next monthly
letter which arrived after the unsuccessful attempt on Hitler's life was
written on black-edged notepaper and informed me that unfortunately
the child had died at birth. It was a great disappointment, but my brother-
in-law still managed to find consoling words for us, and his letters did
much to help us get through the difficult months up to January 1945,
when all postal communication with the outside world ceased.

The misery and overcrowding in the camp reached its worst pitch
with the arrival of hundreds of women who had been evacuated from
Warsaw. At the invitation of the German occupation authorities, these
women had placed themselves 'in German care'. They were promised
safe accommodation and care in the Reich, and, relying on this, they
had packed everything of value they possessed which was portable and
left their homes. They found the safe accommodation and care in
Ravensbrück Concentration Camp. They arrived with cases and boxes
containing all their worldly possessions, and they stood around in the
camp in hundreds, well dressed and warmly clothed, many of them in
fur coats, looking at us in horror and dismay. Some of them had even
brought their pet dogs with them, and one woman had a canary in a
cage.

We were strictly forbidden to go anywhere near them, but as soon as
the first of them had passed through the Political Department, they
realised what was happening. They were all registered in the same way
as ordinary prisoners and called on to hand over their valuables 'for safe
keeping'. In the washrooms they had to strip and the SS took away all
their clothes and gave them the pitiful rig-out of ordinary prisoners.
Then they were taken off to the Reception Block. When the hundreds
who were still waiting saw what had happened, they hastily took off rings
and ornaments and tried to bury them in the ground, and tore up their

papers and private letters in order that the SS should not get hold of them.

These evacuated women, and, in general, all those who fell unexpectedly into the hands of the SS in Ravensbrück, had the highest death rate of all. Their fate had been so unexpected and had come so suddenly that they were psychologically unprepared for it. Many of them did not survive the first few months. In addition, the conditions they were suddenly pitchforked into were worse than any we had previously had to cope with. The camp was in a sorry state. The windows of the huts were mostly broken. Instead of the straw sacks which we had had to 'build' so carefully, there were now dirty and lousy paper sacks with a few shavings inside for them to lie on, no mattress covers, no sheets and only a thin blanket for each woman. In order to get more women into a hut, all the bunks were pushed together so that a three-tiered mass sleeping stage was formed, something like we had been used to in Birma.

The social differences in the camp were never so glaring as during the last year of its existence. Crowds of children hung around the blocks of the better-off prisoners begging for food, whilst ragged, half-starving figures rummaged in the waste-bins for scraps of food. Other prisoners were well dressed and well fed, according to their influence in the camp. There was one woman who might have been strolling along the streets of the West End as she took the greyhound of the SS Camp Leader out for exercise. The huts in the low-lying part of the camp were permanently surrounded by sewage overflow, but elsewhere the SS was still laying out new flower beds and lawns, and planting decorative trees.

The 'industrial complex' outside the camp proper had built its own accommodation for its workers, and Lotte Henschel, Maria Graf and I had to leave the camp and take up our quarters there. In comparison with the old huts, these new ones were gloomy and cramped. For the sake of economy, they had no day rooms, no washing accommodation and no proper 'beds'. The prisoners were packed into four huts, and for the 4,000 of them there was one common washroom, with lavatories around it. Before long, owing to overcrowding and a general administrative breakdown, the water supply failed in the lavatories and the thousands of women had to attend to their needs in the open. The primitive latrine trenches which were dug quickly became intolerable. Things were declining to a Siberian level, and by the end of 1944 there was not a great deal of difference left between Ravensbrück and Karaganda.

Lille, Anička and I were quartered in the second tier of the mass bunks. At least we were quite near the window. We could not sit upright, and we had to crouch down all the time, and there we sat, ate, chatted and slept. We three formed a little family, sharing everything we had, and in the evenings and on Sundays we received our visitors. There were Margrete and Birgit, the Norwegians, Lotte and Maria, the Germans, Inka, the Czech, and Kouri and Danielle, the French girls.

Sick to Death in the 'Revier'

One day I was again promoted; why, I don't know; and I don't think Maria Wiedmeier had anything to do with it this time. From handing out thread, buttons and so on, I came into the office. Together with a Dutch prisoner named Ilse Heckster, I had to look after a card file of all the prisoners working in the tailoring shops. Those who were sick and had 'inside work' or 'bed cards' were reported to us and we had to place their cards in a special file. It was an easy job, but, as it soon turned out, it had its dangers, and I nearly ended up in the Bunkers again. I knew from experience the agonies of working at the machine, and the constant fear of lagging behind. We were now all working an eleven-hour day, and in consequence the number of prisoners who were 'legally' sick steadily increased. But to go sick 'legally' you had to have a temperature, so when women came to me and begged and prayed to be put in amongst the sick I did so, until after a while I had about a score or so of such 'illegal' sick cases registered in the file.

This swindle went smoothly until one day SS Oberscharführer Graf told me that the SS Dr. Treite wanted a full list of all the sick cases in the workshops for control purposes. I broke out in a cold sweat. There was only one hope for me and the 'illegal' sick cases, and that was Emmi Görlich, Treite's secretary. She was a Political, and I hoped to be able to persuade her to cover us. I took the list to her, explained the situation and urged her to help us. She was obviously not keen, and all I could get out of her was a vague semi-promise: 'I'll see what I can do.' However, I went away fairly confident that she would help us. She knew the conditions in the workshops and she knew the trouble we should all get into if she let us down. But two days later she rang me up and declared with assumed indignation that there were twenty-five prisoners sick without 'inside work' or 'bed cards', and what had I got to say about it. I slammed the receiver down and rushed off to Graf in desperation. He already had the list, but had not yet grasped its significance.

'Herr SS Oberscharführer,' I burst out. 'They've made a mistake in the office. I expect their files have got into disorder. There have been so many cases lately. Let me take the list and put the matter right.'

He hesitated a moment: 'But here's Dr Treite's signature,' he said doubtfully. 'It must be in order.' But in that moment he was lost, for I picked up the list and fled. I came face to face with Emmi Görlich and overwhelmed her with reproaches. She shrugged her shoulders: 'I didn't say I would cover you,' she said, 'and I don't see why I should. I have to work. Let them work if they're not sick.'

I gave her a piece of my mind and then rushed off to the Block Seniors of the women concerned. I managed to save fifteen of the women whose Block Seniors were decent enough to come forward and declare that the women had been sick, but were now well again. The other ten were mercilessly drubbed by Graf and given a 'report'. But strangely, and to my great relief, it didn't occur to him that I had had any hand in the swindle and so I got off scot free.

In the autumn of 1944 I suffered an attack of typical camp boils. This affliction was very painful and in the conditions of camp life it quite often proved fatal. A young Czech medical student was in charge of the outside medical post. I knew she was a staunch Communist, and I put off having my boils attended to until I was simply driven to go by pain and discomfort, because I knew that for her I was a 'Trotskyite' and more or less the scum of the earth. However, in the end I just had to go, and I stood in a long queue hoping for the best. The conditions under which she had to work were even worse than in the camp, for she had no proper room, and her medicaments, bandages and so on were just piled on to a table in one corner, whilst queues of patients formed up between the mass bunks. When my turn came she was friend-liness itself, and I was sorry that I had not gone to her before. She attended to me carefully and efficiently, and I was very favourably impressed. My attack proved obstinate, and no sooner had I got rid of one boil than another came to take its place, which meant that I became a regular patient of Inka's – such was her name.

On one occasion she attacked me politically, half in fun. I don't know what I replied, but she said she would like to have a chat with me and ask one or two questions. That evening we walked round and round together, and in reply to her many questions the history of the 'Trotskyite' was disclosed. Despite her youth and her Communist faith, Inka was quite intelligent enough to be objective and to draw her own conclusions. In particular, she seemed to resent the dictatorship of the Czech Communist group in Ravensbrück. The upshot was that she got into trouble with the other Czech Communists, but became firm friends with me. At first they were content to warn her, but when that had no effect they began to threaten her with disciplinary measures unless she broke off relations with me. This she refused to do. The great 'Communist authority' in the camp was a Russian professor named Ewgenia. Inka knew her well, of course, and quite early on in our acquaintance she had asked Ewgenia what she knew about Heinz Neumann. It appeared that Ewgenia had never even heard of him. Later on, when threats proved of no avail, Inka was called before Ewgenia as the decisive Party authority and informed, to her great surprise, that Heinz Neumann was a criminal who had blown up Russian factories in the Volga district, thereby killing many hundreds of Russian workers. This was laying it on a bit too thick, and Inka reminded Ewgenia that only a month before she had not even known who Heinz Neumann was.

In the meantime, my boils did not get better, and in January 1945, I developed blood poisoning. But for Inka's care and assistance, I should have died. She managed to secure my transfer to hospital, and there she succeeded in treating me with stolen Prontosil. I was on the danger list and not expected to recover, but thanks to Inka I did. Our friendship continued, despite all the efforts of the Czech Communists to prevent it, and in the end they decided to expel her from the Party for maintaining friendly relations with 'the Trotskyite Grete Buber', and to forbid the other Czechs from having any further communications with her.

At the end of January 1945, we learnt that the SS had arrested our enemy, Ramdohr. Perhaps the Camp Commander Suhren thought that Ramdohr was getting to know too much about all the corruption in which he was involved. Whatever the reason, the news was received in camp with a sigh of relief.

The Killing Continues

Every morning before the SS appeared for duty, I used to slip into their office. On the wall was a large-scale map of Europe, and on it carefully marked with little flags was the situation at the fronts – no longer according to the official reports of the German Army Command, but according to the enemy broadcasts, to which they secretly listened during their duty hours. During the day we could read on their faces what the news was, and as it grew worse and worse they were correspondingly depressed. Binder took it out on the prisoners by maltreating them more than ever, and Lange followed his example. Graf, as I have already said, was more intelligent, and his attitude towards us gradually changed. He even began to talk to us amiably. During one conversation with Ilse Heckster and me, he even admitted the possibility that Germany would lose the war. That was in the winter of 1944–5.

'And what would happen to you then, Herr Graf?' asked Ilse with assumed sympathy.

'Hm. I suppose I'd be arrested and sent to Siberia. But perhaps that wouldn't be so bad. Wiedmeier would have my job, and I'd have hers. She'd put in a good word for me. Well, let's wait and see.' And he laughed in a rather hollow fashion. Herr Oberscharführer Graf was beginning to feel distinctly worried. It filled us with glee.

As the Russian advance drove deeper and deeper into Europe, the concentration camp at Auschwitz was evacuated and the women brought back further into Germany. Several thousand of them arrived at Ravensbrück, half-starved and exhausted by the terrible journey. They were crying desperately for water and none was given to them. The kitchen prisoners asked permission to give them coffee substitute, and this was allowed, but when the great tub of hot liquid was wheeled out to them hundreds of women fought madly to get at it first. They kicked, punched and clawed each other, and in the scrimmage much of the coffee was upset on the ground. It was only after 'camp police' and SS overseers had clubbed right and left that some sort of order was restored and it became possible to distribute what remained of the coffee.

The Auschwitz prisoners were a very different type – or perhaps it is more correct to say that they had been made into a very different type by conditions in the extermination camp. Only the toughest had any chance of survival there, and the one aim of all the prisoners was to remain alive. They were brutal both in appearance and manners. In the first period of their invasion, it was possible to recognise a prisoner from Auschwitz at a glance.

They had not been in the camp long when a rumour went round that, in order to lessen the pressure, all old and unfit prisoners were to be sent to another camp in Mittweida for light work. The prisoners of one block after the other were paraded and an alleged doctor named Winkelmann, who was said by the Auschwitz prisoners to have chosen those to go to the gas chambers, walked up and down the ranks indicating by a jerk of the thumb who was to go to Mittweida. The old and unfit were taken away in lorries. A little while later new Block Seniors were chosen from amongst the 'old' Politicals to go to the Youth Camp Uckermark, which lay a little distance away beyond the workshops, and where youthful offenders had once been held. When they arrived, they found the old and unfit prisoners who had been taken from Ravensbrück. We thought Ravensbrück was just about as bad as a camp could be, but from what they said the conditions under which these poor, old and sick creatures now vegetated were even worse: roll-calls which lasted even longer than at Ravensbrück, less food and even worse food, no warm clothing and no medical attention. Naturally, they were dying like flies.

In 1944 a second crematorium was built on the other side of the Bunkers, and the black, stinking smoke which belched out of the two chimneys became one of the ordinary features of the Ravensbrück scene. The prisoners were on familiar terms with the idea of death, and it played a big role in their witticisms. 'There goes poor So-and-so' was a constant joke when there was a sudden big belch of smoke, and the overseers and SS men were fond of telling us that the only way we should ever leave Ravensbrück would be 'up the chimney'.

A few days after the departure of the old and unfit prisoners, Anička came to me excitedly and called me out to look at something. Behind the Bunkers the sky was aglow. The crematoria must have been working at full blast.

'We haven't had so many extra dead during the past few days, have we?' I asked. She shook her head. 'Perhaps there's a new epidemic of typhus.' We had a terrible suspicion, but it was not until we managed to speak with one of the new Block Seniors that it was confirmed. About forty women had been picked out by Winkelmann, and SS overseers had written their camp numbers on their bare arms with indelible pencil. When lorries came to take them away, the women already suspected what was to happen to them and they screamed and struggled and refused to go. A company of SS men had been necessary to force them in by violence. Then the lorries had driven off to the crematoria.

During one of these transports a forty-year-old Polish woman managed to escape unnoticed in the dusk. She hid herself, but she was found the next day by an SS man and brought into Ravensbrück. Under pressure, she admitted that she had come from Uckermark, and she was then taken off to the Bunkers to be held there until the next transport was ready. On the way she shrieked: 'We're not being taken to Mittweida. We're being sent to the gas chamber.' In the first 14 days of February 1945, 4,000 women were gassed in Ravensbrück.

In the winter of 1944–5 the glow at nights was almost always there. Every woman of fifty, every woman with grey hair, every woman who had been ill – particularly those who had survived typhus, but were now such skeletons that they were not fit for work – trembled when Dr Winkelmann came round. It was said that he just took a glance at face and hair and passed his verdict of life or death on that. Women with grey or white hair began to dye it as well as they could. They made a paste with water and soot from the ovens and darkened their hair with it. But the next rumour was that Winkelmann judged solely by the legs. A woman with thin, bony legs or with thick ankles and swollen legs was lost. There was nothing anyone could do about that. The only salvation open was to get into one of the workshops or one of the labour gangs, because he chose his victims from those who were left behind as unfit for work.

One morning the 'camp police' cleared the grounds. Everyone left behind had to disappear into the huts. I knew nothing of this, because I was working in the office of the garment factory. For some reason or other, I had to go into the camp. When I came out into the open the place was bare as though the air-raid warning had sounded. I looked round in surprise, and then I saw a column of women coming up the main street of the camp towards the gates. Innocently, I stood there and watched the strange procession. The women were in column of five and they were holding each other's arms. Two SS overseers lashed at them with leather thongs from time to time to urge them on, but they still advanced at their own pace. Their faces were expressionless. It was almost as though they were sleepwalking. I gazed in fascination at this procession of the dead. One of the SS overseers spotted me and began to bellow at me.

'Get out of it!' she shrieked. 'Get out of it! It'll be your turn soon enough. Get out of it now unless you want to join them.'

I needed no second telling, and I bolted into a nearby hut. When I returned to the office, Oberscharführer Graf was there.

'Did you see that column they were taking to be gassed?' I asked. 'I saw it by accident when I went out, and one of the overseers threatened to send me with the next column.'

At first he pretended not to understand. Then he burst out angrily: 'Oh, she did, did she? Well, I'll have a word to say about it before they send any of my prisoners to be gassed. What I say goes here.' And he went out and slammed the door.

In the last year at Ravensbrück many children were born. There was an efficient midwife in the sickbay, and when the maternity cases became more and more numerous the SS even set up a special maternity ward. The idea that the babies were to be allowed to live delighted us all, but the SS made no provision for milk, and as the mothers were too under-nourished to be able to feed their infants, the babies were fed on pap made from dried vegetables. Hardly one of them lived more than a month or so. There they lay in rows, crying with hunger and colic, their tiny, wizened faces all wrinkled up. A Czech girl named Eliska, who was very fond of children, had volunteered to help, but after a few weeks she declared that she would have to get out of it if she were to rescue her sanity, because all she had to do was to stand impotently and watch them starve to death and then carry out their little corpses, sometimes five or six a day.

On Sundays we would often go back into the 'old' camp visiting, particularly to our two French friends, Kouri and Danielle. The French

Block was terribly overcrowded, and it was difficult to force a way through the door. Anicka and I used therefore to climb through the back window straight up on to the top layer of the bunks, where the two had their straw sack. There we would crouch and talk. Kouri, whose Christian name was Germaine, would often tell us about the time when she had been on an expedition to the nomad tribes of North Africa. She was an ethnologist. Both Kouri and Danielle were so-called 'NN' prisoners. No one in the camp knew what it meant, but it was obviously something disagreeable, for they were not allowed to write letters or to receive parcels or letters. Later we learnt that it was a special Gestapo category. Kouri had her old mother in Ravensbrück. The mother was tougher and healthier than the daughter, but on account of her age she was in constant danger.

One day at the beginning of 1945 it was rumoured that all 'NN' prisoners and Jewesses and gipsies with children were to be sent to Mauthausen. There was no doubt in our minds as to what that meant – the gas chambers. Kouri and Danielle had to be rescued. The transport went off, and both the girls succeeded in evading it by hiding themselves. However, so many others did the same that there was a great danger that the SS would organise a systematic round-up of the missing prisoners.

One Sunday towards the end of January, I was already in the sickbay in bed in the 'Death Chamber', when the window was opened from outside by Anička and Lille, who told me excitedly that a 'General Appell' was to take place and that some hiding place must be found for Kouri and Danielle, for, obviously, the SS was out to round up the missing prisoners. We considered every possible plan, and then I proposed that Kouri, who was small and thin, should smuggle herself in to me and hide under my covers. This was done and she crawled down under the blankets and made herself as thin as possible. There was only one double-tiered bunk in the room, and below me was a dying woman who had lost all interest in life. Kouri told me that Danielle had found a hiding place in the roof of one of the huts, where she hoped not to be caught.

We heard the siren sound for the prisoners to assemble, and we heard the usual bellowing of the SS Overseers and Block Seniors. Everyone had to be present at a 'General Appell', and whilst the prisoners stood waiting, search parties went throughout the whole camp and into every room. However, they were not likely to look under my bedclothes, and if they did – well, that would be just too bad for both of us. We heard the noise of lorries starting up and driving off, and various other sounds, but nothing out of the way. Then after about an hour steps sounded in the corridor. Kouri popped her head under the clothes and squeezed up as closely to me as she could on the far side of the bunk. I was half lying on her. The door opened and three uniformed men came in: SS Drs. Treite, Trommel and Winkelmann.

'How many sick in this room?' asked Treite. His head was just about on a level with my bunk.

'Two, Herr SS Doctor,' I answered in a weak voice.

'What's the matter with you?' he asked.

I told him and he gave one look at the dying woman below me, and turned round and went out with the two others. The door closed behind them. We were saved, and Curie came up for breath. After a while the siren sounded the end of the 'General Appell'. We were just wondering how best to smuggle her out again when suddenly the window was opened from the outside and Danielle's horrified face appeared.

'Germaine,' she stammered, 'they've taken your mother away to the gas chamber.'

Kouri sprang down from the bed, her face contorted with sudden emotion. 'My God!' she sobbed. 'My God! How could I have thought only of myself! My mother. My mother.'

She needed all her strength to clamber out of the window. A little while after the two had gone, Anička came along in tears to tell me that her friend, Milena Fischerova, who had been in the TB Station, had been dragged out of bed, together with many other TB cases, and loaded into the lorries just as they were, without even being given time to dress. They had been driven off to the gas chambers lying one on top of the other as though they were already corpses. Anička was on the verge of breakdown.

The Last Days of Ravensbrück

During the last six months in the camp there was a great increase in political discussion, particularly, of course, amongst the Communist prisoners. The unpolitical foreign prisoners made no distinctions in their hatred of everything German. All Germans for them were the same as the SS, and as they hated the SS, so they hated all Germans. It was interesting to note that the foreign Communists in the camp more or less shared this view, and regarded their German comrades as almost outside the pale. They invented a political explanation to cloak their patent nationalism: the German Communist Party could not be regarded as their equal because it had not succeeded in preventing Hitler's accession to power by a revolution and because during the twelve years of National Socialist rule it had not succeeded in overthrowing the Nazi regime. They enthusiastically accepted the idea of the guilt of the whole

German people; and the German Communists made no attempt to defend themselves.

When I asked, 'Who first took up the cudgels against Hitler? Who were his first victims? How many thousands of German political prisoners were being murdered in Hitler's concentration camps when Comrade Stalin was shaking hands and concluding a pact of friendship with him? And who handed over German political refugees to Hitler?' there was no reply. Nor was there when I pointed out that Marxists usually spoke in terms of classes and not of whole peoples.

When it retreated, the German Army took a tremendous amount of booty with it. In our 'Industrial Complex' alone there were three sheds packed full with a great variety of looted property. However, the lack of spare parts, and even needles and cotton, became more and more hampering, but that did not prevent the SS from trying to get the same labour quota out of its slaves. In the spring of 1945 they were still making SS uniforms for use in the following winter! The Russians had reached the Oder, but work on a new factory extension still went on in Ravensbrück.

Towards the end of January the electric power began to fail. Suddenly, during a busy shift, the motors would stop and everything come to a standstill. This began to happen more and more often and for longer and longer periods. And night after night Allied bombing squadrons roared overhead towards Berlin. It was no longer the camp siren which determined the rhythm of our lives. Higher powers had taken a hand in the game. But although the end seemed to be very near, the glow still lit up the sky over the crematoria, and Winkelmann still walked through the lines picking out his victims.

The closer and closer the Russians came, and the more and more obvious the collapse of Germany's resistance, the more talk there was amongst the prisoners about their probable fate. How would the camp break up? Would the SS carry out their threat to shoot all Politicals when the end came? There was a rumour that in one of the more easterly camps the SS had just fled head over heels as the Russians approached, and we hoped that our SS would do the same. Many of the prisoners began to make their preparations for freedom. They collected clothes and cloth stolen from the SS stores, and rucksacks became the most sought-after objects in the camp.

I no longer had the same strong desire for liberty. When Milena was still alive, it had meant that we should see our first town together, walk through our first fields together, hear the song of the birds in freedom together, and then settle down to writing our book about concentration camps under the two dictatorships. Now that Milena was dead, the thought of release no longer moved me so much, but still I was not

altogether indifferent, and the thought that the Russians would reach
Ravensbrück before the Americans or the British made me anxious and
afraid. I knew what my fate would be if the Russians got there first: the
Stalinists would denounce me to the GPU at once. If the Russians came
first, my only chance was to get away on my own. A number of Polish
prisoners knew what would happen to me if I fell into Russian hands
again, and they told me that when the time came I could rely on their
help; they had already made their plans. It was a consolation.

One day Inka came rushing into the office of the garment factory to
me, her face beaming.

'Come out,' she exclaimed. 'Come out and have a look.'

She dragged me by the hand and we ran outside. Wonder of wonders!
Three large white busses bearing the insignia of the Swedish Red Cross
drove into the camp, and the men with them began to unload great
piles of parcels. It was quite clear to us: The war was over. Hitler had
been defeated. The International Red Cross had taken over the camp.

We danced for joy, but it was too soon. The Red Cross vans went
off, and soon afterwards an SS lorry came along and stole a great number
of the parcels. However, there were still so many left that each prisoner
got one. The SS declared that a committee of prisoners should distribute
the parcels, everything except the cigarettes – which the SS stole. We
could hardly believe our ears, but it was true, and the prisoners filed up
in long lines to get them. Some of them were unable to wait until they
got back to the huts. They just sat down there and then and began to
gobble what they found inside. The whole camp was in festive mood.
All rules and regulations went by the board and none of the SS or the
overseers made any attempt to interfere. Many women made fires in the
open and began to warm up the food. In the sickbay there was a parcel
on the bed of each patient, and they lay there with beaming, happy faces.
Unfortunately, for many it was too late, and in other cases the unusually
rich food merely hastened the end.

The next extraordinary event was the departure of 300 Frenchwomen
under the ægis of the International Red Cross. At first their representatives in the camp refused to go until the French prisoners being held
for gassing in Uckermark were also sent. After some discussion, the SS
gave way, and in this fashion many Frenchwomen whose doom had
seemed certain were saved and sent into freedom with the first transport of the International Red Cross from Ravensbrück.

There were still many French prisoners left in the camp; there had
been far more than 300; and amongst them were Kouri and Danielle.
A second French transport was being prepared, and I sat down and wrote
for hours, setting down in detail all the crimes I had witnessed during

my long stay; then I gave the document to Kouri. If I didn't escape alive, at least my evidence should be heard.

When the electric power failed in the workshops the women usually had to sit around doing nothing until it came on again. But one day Graf came out of his office.

'You can all go back to your blocks,' he said.

At once there was a tremendous uproar. The women sprang to their feet and, shrieking with delight like children let out of school, they rushed for the doors. They all felt that their term of slavery in Ravensbrück was over. Then the prisoners who had been working and living outside returned to the camp, and Lotte, Maria and I were able to renew many old friendships. No one did any work any longer, except in the kitchens, and we all lived as though on holiday. We had stolen back the cigarettes which the SS had stolen from us and now almost all the women in the camp walked around puffing away cheerfully.

One Saturday in March all the Norwegian prisoners were told to assemble, 'With things'. Hundreds of shouting, happy women accompanied them. A great crowd of prisoners surrounded them as they lined up. Our Lille was pale with excitement and hardly knew whether to laugh or cry. She was happy to be going home, but she was anxious about us. We were not yet saved by any means. Anička and I put a bold front on it, but we were not happy except for Lille. What was going to happen to us? Should we ever see our friends again? Or ever be so close to human beings again as we had been in Ravensbrück?

Since January we had received no letters from outside, and what we knew about the military situation was chiefly rumour. At the beginning of April the West Front was said to be along the Elbe and the East Front along the Oder. The rumour went round that the SS was preparing for flight. Like us, they were providing themselves with rucksacks, and Graf, Binder and the rest were making good use of their last opportunity to feather their nests. The valuable stocks of cloth disappeared overnight. There was another rumour that charges were being laid to blow up the workshops when the enemy approached. And those of us who were left wondered anxiously whether the SS would carry out a massacre before they went.

On 18 April SS Oberscharführer Graf sent for Ilse Heckster and me to come to his office. We went unwillingly, resentful at the disturbance of our relative freedom in the camp. When we got there, Graf gave orders in his usual tone, as though nothing had happened.

'Inform all the prisoners attached to the garment workshops that from Monday, 23 April all the workshops will carry on again as usual and all prisoners must be in their normal places.'

We were so astonished that for a moment we remained silent. We wondered whether he had gone off his head. Then Ilse Heckster spoke in a tone she would never have dared to use towards him formerly:

'And I suppose we'll all be supplied with treadle machines by that time, Herr Oberscharführer?'

He frowned, but made no comment on her tone.

'No,' he said; 'by that time Ravensbrück will have electric power again.'

'Really,' she went on. 'How interesting! And what grid will it come from?'

'From the north,' he replied tamely.

Ilse was clever. She had got Graf off his perch, and she was determined to find out as much as she could, so she led him on with a show of sympathy. We could see that he was eagerly drinking it in, and then in a changed voice and an air of communicating confidential information he said:

'Of course, I ought not to speak to you about it, but I'm sure I can rely on your discretion. You were both always very reliable [I remembered my experiences in the Bunkers]. You see, on 20 April – that's the birthday of the Führer – our new secret weapon comes into operation. With one blow, it will change the situation on all fronts in our favour. Within a very short space of time we shall have cleared German soil of the enemy.'

'Oh, how wonderful, Herr Graf!' we both exclaimed, and then we went off. When we got outside we burst out laughing, and Ilse tapped her forehead. 'Poor lunatic!'

On 21 April, Cilly, our Block Senior, came in from the office with a list of names of prisoners – they were all Germans and Czechs – who were to assemble, 'With things'. And my name was amongst them. There was immediately a babel of voices. 'You're going to be released.' 'You're going off.' 'Lucky devils.'

I could hardly believe it. I had already thought out what I was going to do if the Russians came: go with the Poles, if that worked, and slip away in the confusion on my own if it didn't. The one possibility I had never even considered was that I should be released before the Russians arrived. Anička, Inka and I embraced each other and did 'Ring a ring of roses' for joy. They had been more worried about my fate than I had suspected. Then I collected my things. We went through lines of cheering, waving prisoners to the office where about sixty German and Czech prisoners were lined up. They were all 'old Ravensbrücker' who had been in the camp for five years and more.

They had already begun to read out our names when an old acquaintance staggered up with difficulty. It was a prisoner we all knew as Melody because she could whistle so melodiously. Of course, it was forbidden, and she had been punished on a dozen occasions for entertaining us with her art. She had been ill in bed when the news came that her name was on the list of those to be released, and with her last strength she had got up and dressed and made her way forward.

'Stand on either side of me and support me,' she said. 'If they notice how knocked up I am, they may keep me back. Once I'm out of this hole, I'll get well again in no time. Just think of it – to see Berlin again!'

Her eyes shone. Sheer will-power was keeping her on her feet. Even when her name was called and she had to go into the office she managed to keep upright. We were afraid they would notice her state and keep her back, but she managed it, and when she came out again she sat down on the ground to rest, her face happy and smiling, whilst we stood around her to guard her from prying eyes.

After that we all had to go to the Political Department, almost carrying Melody along in our midst. It was 21 April 1945, but they had the effrontery to give us a chit stating that we were released from concentration camp Ravensbrück and had to report to our local Gestapo office within three days under pain of arrest and punishment. We didn't know whether to laugh or be angry.

Then, in our camp clothes, with different coloured patches fore and aft, with a few slices of bread to keep us going on the way, and the chit that served us as a transport warrant, we set off through the camp gates 'in column of five' – for the last time. SS Overseer Binz accompanied us until we were outside the camp precincts and on the way to Fürstenberg.

'Halt!' she bellowed. It was the last order she gave us and we obeyed it meekly.

'Frau SS Overseer Binz,' someone piped up. 'I live in Cologne. Can you give me the address of the local Gestapo there? I shouldn't like to be late in reporting.'

Everybody laughed and Binz made an angry face.

'You can do what you like,' she snorted, 'and go where you like. From now on regard yourselves as fugitives.'

And with that she turned round and went back to the camp. We started off on our own towards Fürstenberg. So this is freedom, I thought. For the first time for seven years there's no one just behind me to tell me what to do and where to go. I could sit down by the roadside if I wanted to. Or go across the fields. Or go back.

Strange, we were still in column of five. Old habits die hard. One or two of the weaker ones dropped back. Gradually the idea seemed to spread that we were free. There was no need to march in rank. We could walk at our own pace. As though by common consent, the ranks broke. Then someone with a voice which sounded as though it had been used to command shouted:

'We can't go into Fürstenberg like a straggling lot of sheep. Keep in column of five.'

But the deadly potion of freedom was beginning to have its effect. Those who had been slaves were now beginning to be free, and there was a chorus of indignation and one or two threats to the would-be commandant.

'You get yourself out of the habit of bellowing at us like that or you'll end up badly.'

The bent spines were beginning to straighten.

THE GIFT OF LIBERTY

The World Without Barbed Wire

We found the railway station at Fürstenberg crowded with refugees and soldiers who had lost or deserted their units. Railway communication to the south had been cut, we were told, and the Russians were driving forward towards Berlin from the north. We stood around helplessly, not knowing where to turn. There was no siren here to govern our lives and no one to tell us what to do. After years of slavery in which all our actions had been laid down for us, and in which we had never been able to take an independent decision, we were now faced with the necessity of fending for ourselves and deciding for ourselves. None of us was used to it. None of us felt confident. I learnt later that in confusion and desperation some of the women even went back to Ravensbrück. The chaos of freedom, with its demand for personal initiative, proved too much for them and they fled back to slavery.

I went up to a group of soldiers and asked them if they had a map and a piece of paper and pencil they could give me, and whether they knew where the fronts ran. They produced a map and showed me where they thought the fronts were. In the east the Russians were still on the Oder, but in the north they must already be near Berlin, and at any time they were expected to renew their offensive in the east and drive forward over the Oder. The Americans and the English were still on the Elbe and seemed unwilling to advance any further. I asked them whether they thought I could get through to Potsdam between the two fronts. I hoped to be able to find my mother and go with her from there into the American or British lines.

According to them, it was still possible, but how long it would remain so it was impossible to say. They sketched out the route on a piece of paper for me and then advised me to wait for the train which would leave tomorrow. With that I should be able to get as far as Neu-Strelitz, and after that I could try my luck along the south-west road. I took their advice and spent the night in the station. There were air-raid warnings several times, but we took no notice of them; we weren't used to taking cover in shelters.

The next morning Emmi Görlich spotted me and came up. I had very good reason to harbour bitter feelings on account of her attitude in the camp. Through her refusal to help me when I was in trouble, I might have landed in the Bunkers again and finished up there, and now she wanted me to help her. Could she and Helene Kretschmar come with me? They were at their wits' end and didn't know what to do. Helene had survived two attacks of typhus and twice she had been saved at the last moment from the gas list. She was still very weak and I couldn't see her walking far. However, I told them what I proposed to do and said they could come with me if they wanted to.

The information about the train was right, and it duly arrived. We had to fight to get into it, but with the help of my soldiers we succeeded. At last it started up. There were a number of soldiers who sat together and were strangely silent and uninterested in what went on around them. It was some time before I realised that they were blind. They had been evacuated from an eye hospital further east. A Home Guard asked us what the different coloured patches on our clothes meant, and when we told him we were overwhelmed with sympathy. They made a collection for us and gave us money and food, and much good advice.

It was then I learnt that Potsdam had been heavily raided and that the suburb in which my mother lived had been razed to the ground. It was at that news that all my courage seemed to ooze out of me. The determination to get to Potsdam and my mother had given me a hold in all the confusion and chaos, and now it was gone. What was the use of going on when my mother probably lay under the ruins? What did it matter where I went or what happened to me? The train arrived in Neu-Strelitz and passed through without stopping, and I didn't care any more. It passed through all stations in the same way and stopped only in Güstrow in North Mecklenburg. Apparently someone had ordered that all refugees should be dumped as far north as possible.

We got out and stood around on the platform, jostled by hundreds of soldiers and refugees. None of us had the faintest idea what to do next or where to go. What was the use of freedom like this? Finally, we made our way out of the station. The town was crowded, and everyone seemed to be afraid of air raids. We tried to find somewhere to rest, and we were directed to a camp for fugitives. Another camp? We looked at each other. But what else was there to do? We made our way there and found it terribly overcrowded with men, women and children. The bugs, the lice, the straw sacks and the thin soup reminded us of Ravensbrück.

There were no more newspapers and no source of reliable information. All we had to go on was rumour. Güstrow was already being hurriedly evacuated. We got into conversation with a group of soldiers who had 'withdrawn' from the Oder. From what they said it was clear that the Russian offensive had already begun. After that all the news concerned the Russian advance. That at least stung me into action. If I didn't know quite what I wanted, I knew perfectly well what I wanted to avoid at all costs. I borrowed a map from the soldiers and worked out a route for myself towards the west. Party Communist though she was, Emmi Görlich didn't fancy staying behind to meet the Russians. There were already the ugliest of rumours about the way they treated civilians, and in particular women, and she decided to go with me. Helene didn't want to go, but she didn't want to be left alone either, so she came too.

We made our way out of the town towards the west. My plan was to get through to the American lines just as quickly as I could, and with the information the soldiers had given me I had mapped out the shortest way. By the side of the road were abandoned tanks, burnt-out motor-buses and other transport debris, and the road itself was crowded with fugitives. Most of them were on foot, but some were in farm carts with what goods and chattels they had been able to rescue, and from time to time cars drove past with household goods strapped or tied on to the roofs. Everyone seemed to have the same idea – get westwards away from the Russians.

Every half an hour or so we had to stop to let Helene rest, but we managed to press on with some difficulty until the late afternoon, when she declared she could go no further. So we went to the nearest farm-house and asked for shelter. The place was full of fugitives, but we found room in the barn. We slept that night in the hay looking up through the damaged roof to the stars. The next morning we prepared ourselves to continue our journey. The peasant woman was a friendly soul, and she asked us what the strange patches on our clothes meant. When we told her that we had just been released from a concentration camp, she was all sympathy at once and took us in to her 'best room'. Excitedly, she asked us which camp and whether there had been any Bible Students there. We told her there had been many, and then I remembered that there had been a woman named Klärchen Mau from Güstrow there. She knew Klara Mau quite well, and then she told us that she and her husband were themselves members of the International Bible Students' Association.

After that the place was ours for the asking. She gave us a wonderful meal of potatoes and bacon with rich sauce; prepared us a room with real beds and real sheets and blankets; and urged us to stay with her until we had recovered our strength sufficiently to go on. It was a very tempting invitation, and both Emmi and Helene urged me to accept it, which I did for the time being. At the bottom of the garden at the back there was a clear little stream in which we washed our clothes. It was a warm spring day and the hot sun quickly dried them. Behind the stream was a lush meadow and I crossed a little bridge into it. It was a proper country meadow with long, thick grass and many buttercups and other wild flowers. Just what I had always dreamt of both in Birma and Ravensbrück. The stream flowed and rippled over a stony bed into a lake. I walked along its course to the bank where there were thick rushes and a row of willows. Freedom was sweet after all, and life was sweet to enjoy it. Above me in the blue sky there were aeroplanes. I could hear their motors whine and drum as they weaved around. It was mere background noise as far as I was concerned, and I paid very little attention to it. The sun shone, the water glistened and the grass was incredibly green and beautifully soft under foot. I was happier than I had been for a very long time.

And then suddenly there was a nerve-shattering crescendo roar. I looked up in horror and saw the planes diving down straight at me, and through the roar as they plunged down came the savage rattle of their guns. I flung myself down into the sand and pebbles by the lake in a panic of fear and tried to claw myself into the ground, pressing myself desperately up against the bank. O God, O God, I thought, let me live. Just a little while longer. Not now.

Three or four planes screamed down in a steep dive, firing as they came, and then swept up into the sky again. I lay there sweating. It was my first experience of low-flying attack. Peace came back to the countryside and I got to my feet feeling very shaky. Needless to say, I had not been their objective. There was military transport on the road some distance behind me and out of my sight. A cloud of smoke began to rise. Probably they had set fire to tanks or lorries. For the moment I had had enough of my country walk, and I hurried back to the farmhouse. When I arrived it was to find another reminder that I was not yet in a position to think of country idylls. The never-ending stream of fugitives which rolled on towards Schwerin brought news that the Russians had crossed the Oder and were only a few miles away from Güstrow. And then from the distance I heard the sound of gunfire. It was high time we got under way.

In the meantime, the peasant and his wife had decided to go too, and his cart with horse and ox stood before the house. They loaded one or two of their best pieces and we piled our rucksacks on top, and then we all set off, the peasant leading his ox through the crowd on the road, the horse walking behind, and their little son sitting against our rucksacks. The man's face was as calm and unmoved as though he were just going to town on some farm errand. From time to time we were forced to the side of the road when cars and lorries full of soldiers, many of them officers, and groups of motorcyclists overtook the civilians on the road.

Halfway to Schwerin a Military Police post stopped all civilians and turned them into a side road. The main road was to be kept free for military traffic. Our wheels were now crunching through sand and the ox had to pull heavily to get along. Towards evening we came to a little wood and decided to halt. The signs and sounds of war had come much closer. Again and again we could hear the howling roar of planes as they dived in to attack, and the rumble of gunfire was almost uninterrupted. In several places on the horizon there were clouds of black smoke and we could whiff burning even through the smell of the pines. We made ourselves as comfortable as possible and went to sleep. The two peasants slept under the huge feather pillows they had brought with them, their little boy between them.

When we woke up in the morning we were wet with the dew. The peasant and his wife were already awake and had been talking over their situation. He had decided that they would never make the American lines before the Russians arrived, and so they intended to stay where they were until the fighting passed them and then make their way back to the farm, to see what they could save. Helene declared that she could not go on, and decided to stay with them. For me there was no decision to be taken: I was not going to wait for the Russians, whatever happened. If they caught up with me . . . But in the meantime I would press on. Emmi decided to go with me, so we parted from the others and made our way across the fields in the direction the peasant had indicated.

We decided to avoid the roads as far as possible on account of the low-flying planes. I had had one experience and I didn't want any more, though I had not even been on the road during the attack. After a few hours' march through the forest we came to a road overhung with trees. Underneath them, stretching away on both sides as far as we could see, were military stores and piles of arms and equipment. We were just about to cross and get away from such a dangerous spot as quickly as possible when the low-flying attack we had feared began. There was the rushing scream of diving planes, the rattle of guns and the constant explosion of anti-aircraft artillery. We turned and fled back into the wood for our lives, rushing through the undergrowth and tearing our skirts and stockings on briars.

We stopped only when we came to a clearing, and then we decided that we had lost our way. We sat down and calmed ourselves. It was a typical forest clearing, and war and sudden death seemed far away. Emmi still had a tin of Nescafé she had saved from her Red Cross parcel. I got water from a nearby pool. It looked rather brown, but we were in no position to be particular, and I made the most wonderful coffee in an aluminium saucepan we had with us. When we had drunk it we felt much better and started on our way again greatly strengthened. We had no watch, but we judged that it was late afternoon, so, as we both knew just about as much as townsmen usually do know about the habits of the universe, i.e. that the sun sinks in the west, we went towards it. We came across a path and followed it. At a crossing we met two soldiers and I asked them the way.

'Who do you want to get to,' one asked, 'the Russians or the Americans?'

'The Americans,' I replied.

'So do we,' he said. 'So you'd better come with us.'

'But you're going east,' I objected. 'That's where the Russians must be. That's where we've come from.'

And then one of those silly arguments about matters of fact started, and after a while I wasn't sure any longer whether the sun sank in the west or not. Fortunately, however, a motorcyclist came along, and the soldiers stopped him to see what he had to say about it. He supported us and the two soldiers gracefully gave way. The motorcyclist also told us that the Russians were only a few miles away by this time and that the Americans were in Bad Kleinen, which was a day's march further on. We should press on until we came to the railway line which led to Bad Kleinen. We couldn't miss it. The news that the Russians were so near lent us – well, not exactly wings, but it did spur us on.

Even when the sun went down we still pushed on and we reached the railway line soon after dark. From this point, according to the motorcyclist, it was only just over ten miles to Bad Kleinen. On the road by the side of the line groups of soldiers were making their way towards the town. None of them was armed and most of them had no pack of any sort. We joined them. Although it was night, it was quite light enough to see what was happening. They were all going forward at a good pace and even wounded men were hobbling along as quickly as they could. Suddenly one or two soldiers began to run and then almost everybody followed their example. Emmi and I trotted after them for a few paces, but then we had to give up. It was as much as we could do to keep walking and we were both terribly thirsty.

'What's the matter?' we asked the men who ran past us. 'Why are you running?' But no one answered. Sitting by the side of the road was a wounded man and we asked him.

'Oh,' he said wearily, 'every now and again there's a rumour that the Russian tanks are just round the corner, coming up. Somebody starts running and then they all run.'

We pressed on again. We were making for freedom, but all these soldiers were hurrying to imprisonment – but at least they preferred to choose their prison. Along both sides of the road the debris of war was lying in disorder – rifles, anti-tank guns, machine-guns, ammunition boxes and all sorts of kit which had been abandoned. We came to a level crossing and there was a light in the keeper's hut, so we went in to ask for a glass of water. To our surprise, a table in the room was piled up with tinned food, chocolate, cigarettes, packets of raisins and other good things. The stuff obviously came from Red Cross parcels. The man's wife explained that her children had collected it. Soldiers who had plundered a train had flung what was left of their booty away as they approached the American lines. They were not going to risk being treated as looters.

We drank our water greedily and went on our way. What the woman had said was true; the tins and packages were scattered all over the place. Eagerly we filled our rucksacks with them. We also noticed torn photos of men in smart SS uniforms, and the ridiculous Nazi 'Ancestor Pass', which guaranteed that its holder had no Jewish blood in his veins. Apparently the ex-Nazis were not anxious to be found with such things in their possession either. But as we tramped on our rucksacks seemed to get heavier and heavier, and we got more and more exhausted.

And then from behind us we heard a train approaching. If only we could get on it! It was not going very fast, but too fast for us to attempt to board it. And then, as though by a miracle, it clanked to a halt on the line quite near us. It was an odd sort of train, made up of mixed carriages and goods trucks, and it was crowded with men, women and children. With a last access of energy, we ran towards it. If only we could get on it! When we got there, our strength was no longer sufficient to climb up, but one or two men who were in a goods truck were kind enough to haul us in, and there we lay completely exhausted.

After a while the train started up again and moved slowly forward. It appeared that this was the last train to leave Neu-Strelitz before the Russians arrived. Railwaymen had coupled it up and taken an engine to get their wives and families away. After a while it came to a halt again and it seemed this time as though it could go no further. One of the men got out and went forward to discover what was the matter and why we were standing there so long. He came back with the information that there were five Red Cross coaches on the line in front of us full of wounded, and that no trains were being allowed to pass through the American lines.

Gradually it began to get lighter. It was cold and my legs were stiff. The thought of walking was a torture and my feet were sore and blistered, but I was not going to give up now. We must be quite near Bad Kleinen.

'I'm going to get out and walk on,' I said to Emmi.

She was doubtful about the wisdom of that, but I was quite determined, and so she came with me. The men in the wagon tried to dissuade us.

'They'll shoot you if you attempt to go into their lines,' they said, but I was determined. We hobbled along the side of the track, and as we passed the other carriages we were warned again and again that we would be shot. The idea had literally no terrors for me. For one thing, I didn't believe it. I didn't believe the Americans would shoot down two women who approached their lines in daylight, and it was nearly daylight. And for another I was cheerfully prepared to risk being shot by Americans rather than be taken prisoner by Russians.

We came up with the hospital train. There were five coaches, all with white flags up. As we passed the leading coach, we could see the railway station of Bad Kleinen. It was quite empty. Not a living soul was to be seen anywhere. We climbed up a flight of steep steps which led up the western side of the cutting and when we got to the top we saw the Americans. They stood there silently spread out in open order. Without hesitation we made our way towards them. I confess I felt a twinge at the sight of their tommy-guns, but the Russians were behind us, and then, as former concentration camp prisoners, our consciences were clear.

We came up to the nearest man. He had a round, red, friendly face and he looked at us curiously. In my broken English, I explained that we were prisoners who had been five years in Ravensbrück Concentration Camp, and that I had previously been in concentration camp in Siberia. If the Russians caught me, I should be sent back there again. Would he please let us pass through to safety?

He looked at our miserable clothes with the coloured patches, whose significance I had explained to him, then he casually moved what was probably a wad of chewing gum from one side of his mouth to the other and drawled: 'OK, sister. Go through.' And he made a gesture of invitation with his hand. I never heard such a beautiful arrangement of words before in my life. I could have flung my arms round his neck and kissed him, only the thought that I couldn't have looked very appetising restrained me. Joyfully, we hurried past.

We had not gone more than a few paces when he called after us: 'Hey, girls. Wait a minute.' God, I thought, he's changed his mind. He's going to send us back. He strolled slowly after us and then beckoned us to follow him. We came to a house with a sentry at the door. 'Wait here,' he said, and he disappeared inside. We waited in a fever of impatience. He's going to ask his superiors, I thought. We seemed to have got hold of a non-commissioned officer. He had rank stripes upside down on his arm.

After a while he came out again with a tall, smiling officer, who looked at us, but said nothing. Our soldier went round behind the house. A few minutes later there was a sound of horses' hooves and he drove out with a farm cart and pair.

'Get in,' he said. 'You've walked enough by the look of you. You're going to ride now.'

Horse and Wagon

Hardly had I taken hold of the reins when the horses started to pull and to drag us over the bumpy field. The small cart wobbled as if it were going to fall over any minute and we frantically clutched the narrow board – our coachman's seat. Not we, but the horses chose the direction and at the end of the field they turned, as if this were a matter of course, on to a narrow path that led westwards. When our cart came to the soft wagon tracks, I jokingly said 'brr!' Immediately the horses stood still. I breathed easy and my cramped hands loosened up. 'Well, Emmi, what do you say now? Could you have imagined that we two would be given a real cart and real horses as a present? And that an American soldier should have such an idea? Too bad my English isn't any better. We didn't even thank him properly and he certainly doesn't realise how glad we are . . . But why are you so quiet?' I turned my head and noticed Emmi's tortured face. Her hand clutched my upper arm.

'I'm so afraid of the horses. Just imagine them running away with us!'

'Ah, what nonsense!' I said unthinkingly. 'Why ever haven't you any guts?' Crossly I tried to remove her hand. But my anger disappeared as fast as it had come; I encouraged the two brown ones with a 'hüh!' clicked my tongue and wiggled the reins – exactly as I had learnt as a child from my father's drivers. And to my considerable surprise the horses started moving again.

Although I was still rather confused by the sudden turn in our fortunes, I already started to think about our journey's end. As I couldn't go to Potsdam, I remembered Thierstein, the small village in Lower Bavaria from where my father had come, where my grandparents' farmhouse stood. Without considering for a second the enormous distance between Mecklenburg and Bavaria, I decided there and then to make this the goal I was striving for.

'Emmi, we are going to Bavaria, to Prague, to wherever we want. Now the world is ours.'

A feeling of great happiness overcame me – suddenly the world had changed. The aimless flight had come to an end; with this free choice of an objective, the road to freedom had opened. Seven years of dependence dropped off me and the joy of living was like a high. Everything around me happened as if for the first time: the pink-tinted anemones at the forest's edge, the silver of the birches' trunks, the new grass that appeared through last year's mouldering leaves, and the smell of the earth. Beyond the rocking heads of the horses the wagon tracks of the forest path led uphill and met the blue of the spring sky.

We reached the top of the hill, and now the path led steeply downwards to the shore of a small lake. But the skills of a coachman have to be learnt. Our cart had no brakes and I did not know how – by pulling tight the reins – to make the animals themselves slow down the cart with the help of the shaft chains. Thus the cart again and again hit their hind legs and forced the poor creatures into a gallop. When fortunately at last they stood still down by the lake, we trembled just like the tortured horses, and for the first time I understood Emmi's fear and the deep sigh of relief with which she jumped off the coachman's seat.

The cart was a German 'Trainwagen', and to our delight we found under old military blankets a dented bucket and half a sack of oats. I ran down to the lake with the bucket. At the foot of the hill the sandy shore dropped steeply to the calm surface of the water. At some time in the past, masses of sand slid into the lake. I squatted down at the water's edge, and let the bucket sink and drift in the gentle current.

As if this were understood we already spoke about 'our' horses. We had loosened their snaffles, so they could feed and drink, and we stroked their soft warm mouths. But they scorned the oats and barely drank. Whatever could be wrong with them? They hung their heads so sadly and wearily. And Emmi was right, one of them, the dark-brown one, limped – maybe he had a sore hoof. Who knew what exertions they had undergone? Perhaps an entire war with advances and retreats. I would have loved to untie them and led them into the meadow, but thought it might be better to find a good stable for them – possibly in the next village.

Soon we entered a highway. Here all hell was let loose and we could advance only very slowly. The road was clogged by innumerable wagons with fleeing people. Two streams passed each other, one miserable, often unmoving, that persistently made its way westwards; the other loud, warlike, in the opposite direction. Whenever a motorised column raced by us, whenever a tank drowned all other noises with its deafening din, our light-brown reared up and pushed the cart to the edge of the ditch. If only I had known better how to handle the animals. In front of us the wagons on the trek moved in regular rhythm, their horses perhaps already used to flight. Whenever we were forced to stop and I looked longingly at the dark forest, whenever my attention waned, a sudden jump of the light-brown pulled me back to reality. The small jeeps raced by with an annoying clatter. Slowly my optimism began to vanish. And when I discovered that the snaffle had rubbed sore the light-brown's mouth, I nearly forgot the happiness of freedom and was desperate. But we were tied willy-nilly to the animals and the cart. Like a warning, the sides of the road were littered with cadavers of horses, their bellies horrifyingly extended and their tongues hanging out. On its left and on its right side the highway was edged by deserted guns, burnt-out wagons, bed linen and broken furniture, and among them were crosses, again and again, sometimes crowned by steel helmets. Slowly we pushed through this no man's land. Here and there water had collected in the bomb craters, their torn edges reflected in calm ponds.

The wagons banked up. Very slowly we advanced to an American barrier. The nearer we approached, the more numerous were the trekkers who were not being let through. They assembled in the meadow by the road. The people stood around next to their miserable belongings, stretched their legs and swore.

'We come from the Ravensbrück Concentration Camp. An American soldier gave us this cart and these horses.'

'OK. You can pass.'

Already the sun had turned orange and sunk amongst the trees of the endless highway. We drove in its direction. When darkness fell we reached a village, completely worn-out. My arms ached from the unusual effort of holding the reins; even getting off was painful. For the horses we found room in a stable. I was very grateful. Then we also found a place for the night for ourselves. In the barn we spread our military blankets on the straw. It was pitch dark and from some corner the crying of a child could be heard. A woman hissed impatiently. The straw rustled incessantly. The barn had to be full of people. Dust settled on our lips. Emmi couldn't fall asleep, nor could I. I could still feel the swinging of the cart and behind my closed eyes passed – like a film strip – trees, meadows and fields, then again there were swaying wagons. Our nerves fluttered in excitement. Both of us must have lived for too long behind camp walls and barbed wire, and now, on our way to freedom, we couldn't absorb the mass of unaccustomed impressions as, with our newly awoken joy of living, our senses had to deal with too much.

Next morning a farmer – himself a refugee – helped us to harness the horses, as he had noticed my clumsiness. 'Nah, missies, you won't get far with those,' he said as farewell. We rolled silently through the sunless morning. In a small hamlet we were stopped again and this time not allowed to pass. Each time we repeated our explanation about coming from a concentration camp and wanting to go home – but this American reacted by shaking his head stubbornly. At last another American – apparently an officer – asked us if we were ready to transport German wounded to Schwerin to the military hospital. We thought about it for a moment. To drive to Schwerin meant making a big detour, almost going back. Nevertheless we agreed. The American disappeared into a house. Soon he reappeared, behind him six German soldiers in dirty, untidy uniforms, their faces exhausted, with bandaged arms, legs or heads. Next to the youthful round face of the American these figures looked old and used-up. With difficulty they climbed on to the cart, sat down on its sides and carelessly put their loam-smeared boots on our rucksacks and the military blankets. As we started, one of them groaned. He looked like an officer – his uniform had a more elegant cut. He had no badges – perhaps they had been pulled off. He clutched his bandaged head and stared ahead, looking drunk and muttering something over and over. I understood a few words like 'can't survive the disgrace. I should have finished it before they took away my pistol!'

'Shut your trap!' snarled the one sitting opposite him. 'You'll have time enough to hang yourself!' Then all of them were quiet and in me arose a painful feeling of helplessness towards these unknown German soldiers.

When we reached the first barrier, the prisoners had to get off. They were led into a house and the Americans told us to wait. After some time had passed, only three of our wounded returned. The others were kept there. I wanted to know what had happened to them and was told that they were not wounded at all, but had only pretended to be in order to avoid becoming prisoners of war. We continued our drive and suggested after a while that we stop for a rest. The soldiers were much in favour and soon a meadow on the water's edge was found. When we opened our rucksacks and showed our treasures, the soldiers offered to share their food with us. We decided to cook soup together. Emmi and one who talked like a Berliner lit a fire. I ran for wood while the two others with their bandaged legs unharnessed the horses. But our horses were curious animals: instead of enjoying the tender spring grass, they shook their heads angrily, as if they wanted to get rid of flies, and touched the ground noisily in mistrust with their swollen lips. They seemed not to know what to do in a meadow.

We sat on the grass, above which the smoke of the wood fire spread, and the first conversation started. The Berliner wanted to know from where we had come. 'KZ, yes, we have heard about those already. Looking at you, it follows. You look so different. And these funny clothes . . . Yes, but tell us, why were you arrested?'

We told them about Ravensbrück.

'Is something like that at all possible? These swine have arrested thousands of women! We really did not know anything about this.'

'And you also never have heard anything about the gas chambers of Auschwitz? Never anything about millions of murdered Jews?' we asked.

'You know, there were always whispers about terrible things happening in KZs but we had no idea as to what really went on there . . . Nevertheless I must admit that once, years ago, I saw a column of women in striped dresses at a building site. I suppose they were Jewesses. Women wearing a "*Hosenrock*", with a sheepdog on a leash, were guarding them. But who would think immediately about gassing?'

'Yes, whoever!' we agreed.

In the meantime the food was ready and we all sat together around the fire and spooned up the soup, courtesy of the Red Cross.

In front of the military hospital in Schwerin we took leave of the soldiers, wishing them a speedy recovery and a short imprisonment.

At a street corner we stopped and began to consider what to do next. 'However can we get rid of the horses and the wagon?' We argued that it was necessary to return the present of an American soldier to the Americans. In front of a public building we found a US soldier. I tried to explain the problem to him. He listened reluctantly and with incredulity, moved the chewing gum from one cheek to the other and finally rejected our offering with a grunt: 'Whatever should I do with your damned horses? I don't want them.' What now? We could not simply leave these poor animals to their fate.

While still thinking about it, I noticed at the opposite street corner a man with a sack on his back, leaning against a garden fence. He looked like a farmer. 'Emmi, should I ask this man if he wants the horses and wagon?' I climbed down from the driver's seat and approached him. As I described our situation and offered him the cart and horses he grinned knowingly. After a short examination he agreed. I was somewhat surprised. What a peculiar farmer this was who could make such a quick decision.

When he told us that he knew how to work with horses, I handed him the reins and we asked him to drive us a little way in the direction of Ratzeburg. 'Can do – but not today. Tomorrow, if that's all right with you.' He called us '*du*' and told us that in a village near Schwerin he had relatives in whose house he hoped to find his wife. 'If you want to come with me I will drive you tomorrow morning to Ratzeburg. Agreed?' We agreed. As soon as the farmer got hold of the reins our horses looked like new. They started trotting and even the lame dark-brown one suddenly knew how to pull.

Emmi and I sat happily in the back of the cart and I was glad to have nothing to do with the horses any more. Darkness descended. The new owner of our cart turned round and examined us thoroughly. Then he pointed at the paint crosses on our dresses. 'Anyway, where are you from?'

'From KZ Ravensbrück.'

'That's what I thought,' called our farmer as if he had been reunited with dear old acquaintances. 'So we are colleagues. I come from Güstrow.'

'Güstrow?'

'From the penitentiary, of course,' he answered without any hesitation. Emmi and I looked at each other, suppressing laughter. A nice 'colleague'. Whatever did he do?

But he readily explained to us: 'Three years for illegal slaughtering.'

Then he started telling stories about the penitentiary. He was funny and lively, and we had a wonderful time. Something mysterious did link us to him, our 'colleague' who also had sat behind bars. Then he pointed at a thick, blunt church tower on the horizon: 'That's where we're going. My relatives live there. I hope my wife is with them. And the children. I have been away for nearly three years. We were living in Stettin. From there they were evacuated some time ago.'

As darkness slowly descended, we bumped towards the village. Shortly before the entrance to the place we turned. In front of us lay a small farm. We stopped, descended and walked together with the 'Güstrower'. Nobody appeared. In these wild days we had learnt to distrust rules.

Our friend signalled us to stop. He went to a door and knocked. At first, everything remained quiet. He knocked again and a voice said, 'Who is there?'

'It's me, Heinrich! Is Berta here?'

Pause.

'Do you understand, Anna? It's me, Heinrich. I'm back from Güstrow. I'm free again.'

'You are back from Güstrow? Have you finished doing your time?' Anna's voice was ice-cold with rejection. 'Whatever do you want here? We want nothing to do with you. Berta is not with us. We don't know anything about her, we don't know anything at all. Look for her some-where else.'

In the darkening twilight I saw Heinrich shrugging his shoulders.

'Could I at least stay with you for the night? I have two horses and a wagon. The animals should be fed. There are also two women from the KZ with me. Couldn't we stay overnight in the barn?'

'No!' declared Anna categorically. 'Nobody can stay with us. Get going! Perhaps somebody in the village will take you in.' As she shuffled away I heard her scolding: 'Jailbirds and KZ-lers! That's just what we need!'

Slowly we returned to the cart. Heinrich spat disdainfully. 'That was the sister of my wife. For this damned bunch of farmers we are nothing but subhumans. Never mind. We'll find some place to stay.'

Next morning, when we started out at dawn in the direction of Ratzeburg, the rain came pouring down. Water sprayed from above, from below, from everywhere. We sat wrapped in the army blankets and were in high spirits. On a truck parked in the middle of a field, I noticed a new complete set of kitchen furniture, gleaming with varnish. 'I'll pick that up later on my way back,' confided our 'colleague'. 'Decent of you to give me the cart. This is going to be a good business; one only has to stick to it. Everyone is still busy fleeing and there are no policemen. The former one has fled and who knows how soon a new one will arrive.'

We passed villages hidden behind the veil of rain. Then there was a forest and I noticed with pleasure how the water ran down the tree trunks covered by grey moss. This was followed by an open field and at a distance from the road in the depressing grey stood large manor houses with their extended farm buildings.

Then a peculiar cavalcade passed us. In an elegant dog cart two old people sat wrapped in colourful plaids, he with a white beard, she wearing a very old-fashioned hat. Beside the cart a young girl rode astride. She wore tight pants, her head was bare, and she let the rain run over her head and face without paying any attention to it. Her attitude showed that she took note neither of the bad weather nor of this flight. If you had to leave, desperate as you were, seemed to be her attitude, on no account should you let anybody notice it.

Shortly afterwards I read on a signpost the name 'Lützow'. I pointed it out to Emmi and we started to sing with all our might, 'This is Lützow's wild daring hunt! This is Lützow's wild daring hunt! . . .' Our Güstrower joined in enthusiastically. When Ratzeburg came into sight, another road sign caused me to have a further outburst of gallows humour: 'Ziethen' . . . Thus, in flight in the streaming rain, passes Prussia's glorious tradition.

Meetings with the Past

We had said goodbye to our 'colleague' and waved at the cart as it hurried away. How sad that we had to part. A curious solidarity connected us to this jailbird. We had understood each other without wasting many words. Although his idiom was not exactly the same as ours, we knew what he was talking about and vice versa. He had been quite right: we were indeed colleagues in the best sense of the word.

Now we were pedestrians again, and in the rain, too. The tough Mecklenburg loam stuck in clumps to our feet as we approached an estate. At the gate we stopped as if rooted to the spot. In the large yard, ringed by stables and farm buildings, something extraordinary was going on. Open fires burnt in the middle of the yard and there was cooking in kettles of all sizes. In one corner a pig had just been butchered. Almost hidden by old oak trees, the façade of the manor-house gleamed in the background. Outside in the rain stood tables, chairs, cupboards, armchairs. Out of the windows more furniture and household equipment was being thrown, caught by men and women, and quickly carried off. Out of the attic flew bundles of straw and pressed hay. People with sacks on their backs hurriedly left the yard. In this chaos a group of women stood quietly by the door, possibly the housekeeper and her maids. Silently and passively they watched the goings on. At a fire young girls were singing a Russian song, their faces lit by the flames, reflecting the joy of liberation. We watched a while, then walked slowly away across the yard. Why we didn't stay I can't say. Perhaps because we were Germans – ex-KZ prisoners but nevertheless Germans – and therefore didn't belong to this celebration of the freed slaves?

Immediately behind the manor in the ditch by the road sat an abandoned Volkswagen. The rain pelted down on its shiny wet top. As a joke I tried the door handle. It opened and, without further ado, we got in laughing, happy to have found shelter from the pouring rain. We removed our dirty boots and lay down on the soft seats.

'How wonderful it is to be in the dry. Now we only need a few litres of petrol and in no time we would reach Bavaria and Prague.'

This thought was so tempting that I forgot all the roadblocks and blown-up bridges, and thought for the first time of the towns, the plains and mountains we would pass on this imaginary journey to Bavaria. Like children at play we started to push the levers and to handle the controls. Then, out of curiosity, we opened the various compartments and found there the remains of an unknown private life: skin lotion, comb, notepad and shoe-cleaning utensils. I felt as if I had entered a strange home without permission and we had to make a bit of an effort to decide to take the shoe brushes with us.

Through the dim windows of the car we saw more and more farmers arriving to join in the plundering of the manor. After looking around furtively, they carried away sacks and even dragged bundles of straw over the wet paths. In contrast to the matter-of-fact attitude of the freed '*Ostarbeiter*' standing near the fire, these plundering farmers looked to me like mean thieves.

Then, in the unaccustomed warmth of the closed car, we fell asleep, and only gnawing hunger woke us.

The rain had stopped. We got out and stretched our stiff limbs. How good it would be to eat something warm, we thought. A few hundred metres further along stood a tenant's cottage. Perhaps they'd give us a few potatoes. The cottage was stuffed full of people. In the entrance, in the kitchen, everywhere men, women and children pushed each other. On the stove stood at least ten different cooking pots full of potatoes or some kind of soup. In spite of the crowd the housewife greeted us as we voiced our request: 'Just wait a minute – the potatoes will be done in a moment.' We squatted on the steps outside the front door and ate ravenously. Around us the children made a racket. Then the housewife stepped outside. She was thin and her face was careworn.

'Do all these many refugees live with you? Do they have to stay, because they can't get on?'

The woman shrugged her shoulders. 'I don't know,' she answered indifferently. 'They can't all stay with me. But after the "*Ostarbeiters*" have done looting they surely will leave. Then the refugees can perhaps live at the manor. But what do I know? Everything will turn out as it's meant to do. The likes of us can't change anything. But where do you want to go?'

'My friend to Prague and I to Bavaria.'

She opened her eyes wide. 'On foot perhaps?'

'Sure!' Bavaria and Prague were, for this woman who may never have been further away than Schwerin, unimaginably distant. For her everything was incomprehensible anyway. Some people walked on foot to faraway countries, others abandoned house and farm with a cart full of bed linen and kitchen utensils. What could one say to all that? I asked her if we could stay overnight anywhere in the neighbourhood. She described in detail the way to the next manor, that might well still be occupied and not plundered. I asked her if her '*Gutsherr*' had by any chance been a Nazi. She looked at me suspiciously and said, 'Sometimes the big Party bosses came to him for the hunt. Where else could they have gone?' Emmi asked her about the peculiar people who were dragging along sacks and bundles of straw. The '*Häuslersfrau*' looked around fearfully, then said very quietly, 'Those are the farmers from the next village.' Her voice sank to a mere whisper as she assured us that the 'master' – she meant the owner of the manor – would return soon and then something terrible would happen to them. And that would be quite in order: 'Where would we be if this accursed "*Polenpack*" were to get the upper hand here? I have always said that it is a bad thing to have them in the country. They are dirty and lazy and capable of any crime.'

I felt sickened by this outburst of hate, and tried to make clear to this indoctrinated woman that the Poles and the Russians, like all the other foreign workers, had been dragged by force to Germany and treated like slaves. But with this woman my defence reached the wrong address. She scolded me and shouted, 'Aha, then you also come from this dirty country back there?'

'No, we come from a KZ.'

She took a step in our direction and clasped her heart. 'From a KZ? My God, this must have been terrible! Just imagine, a few weeks ago I saw an entire train of men in striped uniforms. They were from a KZ. It was terrible, how these poor people looked. And in the village they said the SS had shot some of them over there in the forest. Those who couldn't continue walking. Think how awful! I could not keep from crying. Poor starved people who could not continue walking, this "SS-Pack" just mowed them down. Oh, what an awful world!' And she wiped the tears from her face with the back of her hand. After a pause of shocked silence she picked up the thread of the conversation and, as if to justify her outburst of anger of before, the hard words came from her lips: 'But concerning the Polish rabble you definitely are mistaken. If nobody stands behind them with a whip, they don't work at all.'

I gave up and stayed silent, as here any additional word would have been spoken in vain. Then we thanked the tenant woman for the potatoes and departed. From behind us through the dusk we still heard the singing of the Poles and the Russians.

Emmi and I walked along the soggy paths lost in thought. Soon it would be night and we would have to find a roof over our heads. Somewhere afar glimmered the first lights. The mud of the path was furrowed by uncounted wagons and we made our way slowly. When it was dark, we suddenly saw in front of us a refugee wagon covered with a tarpaulin, the last in a long line. No people were to be seen, perhaps they were at the manor to fetch water or feed for the horses. Some dogs, which had been tied between the wheels of the wagons, were barking. From time to time the crying of a baby could be heard through the tarpaulin. We walked along the row of wagons, which seemed to have

.no end. The road was absolutely blocked; even the paths that led into the road from both sides were full of stationary wagons. It was like a huge military camp. At last we fought our way through the confusion and dirt up to the manor. From somewhere appeared a man in riding breeches and high boots, who looked like the inspector of the estate. In reply to our question he pointed his finger towards one of the barns. 'You can sleep there. But only in this one, not in the others. Understood?' Abruptly he turned round and disappeared into one of the stables.

We groped our way into the barn that was already pitch dark inside. Yet the darkness was full of voices, noise and movement. It stank of turned-up dust and wet clothes. After uncounted numbers of people had spent a night on them, the hay and straw had turned into a kind of chaff and, due to the damp, had stuck together in the form of small, hard, flat cakes. Somewhere we found a space for our blankets. Around us we heard many voices, young and old, male and female, voices in broad East Prussian, in comical Saxon and in flippant Berlin dialects. Only after we had lain down quietly could we distinguish between the different conversations.

A young male voice cried loudly, inconsiderately and impudently, 'Whatever do you want? We have lain in much worse dirt. Nothing can shock us any more. Now the theatre is over, thank God, and we can over-come this as well. It would need something very different to rattle us. Renate, pass me another sip of the schnapps ['Negerschweiss'], this bloody dust settles all over one's brain. Just like in a mass grave.'

'Nah, hold your horses!' This was another voice, just as young, just as flippant, this time a girl's. 'Now it's Johnny's turn to get a lid full.'

'Johnny, naturally it's always him! Do you want first to soften him up a bit?'

'Shut your trap! Renate knows who has had his turn and who hasn't!' This was another girl's voice, nearly interchangeable with the first.

'And after all it was me who pinched the stuff,' Johnny could be heard to say in the background. 'And what's more, my dear, don't you forget that I am your topkick!'

'Aye, aye, Mr Sergeant Major,' screamed the first one, sneering. 'If you by any chance assume . . .'

'Don't make such a racket here. You aren't in front of Welikije Luki!'

My flesh began to creep. Don't I know this tune? Our guards in Ravensbrück talked just like that. But then I had to listen to another voice, a very quiet, monotonous voice that appeared to be directed at nobody but that, nevertheless, one could not escape. 'Our grandmother had been sitting for hours back on the wagon without moving. One couldn't see her face, it was covered because of the cold; then my husband went there to look and she had already been dead for hours. Simply frozen to death. We could only lay her at the side of the road, not bury her. The Russians were just behind us. And Pachulke's two little ones also froze. They had to throw them out of the wagon.'

I groped for Emmi to make sure she was near. It was difficult to breathe. But the voice returned like a prayer wheel: 'All the time we had to keep moving, otherwise we would have turned stiff. Then there came a village. They said the Russians would be there at any moment. We wanted to get indoors somewhere to warm ourselves. But we couldn't any more. My little girl cried and cried . . .'

Then somebody barked, making the entire barn start, 'Man, move your feet from my rucksack. Damn mess! Here one can't see one's hand in front of one's eyes. Four years we spent at the front, in order then to have to sleep on filthy straw in our own home country. Couldn't this lot at least have hung up a stable lantern?'

'Don't make such a fuss. If it doesn't suit you, you can always join the werewolves.'

'Shut your trap!'

But still it wasn't quiet. Emmi had moved close to me.

Again there came a voice from another corner: 'I'm curious if our Herr Führer still talks as highfalutin as before. Now when he himself is in for it?'

'But boys, how can you talk like that about our Führer!' This was an old voice, a farmer's East Prussian broad voice. 'Wasn't he like a real father to us? It isn't his fault that he has so many spoilt children. It's the officers' fault . . .'

'Nah, Granpa, you surely are one of those who got a farm from the dear Führer, aren't you. When Adolf divided up the "Polish corridor"? I can just imagine it. Before, you had no bed under your bum and after it you were "Village farmers' leader". Wasn't that great? Wasn't it? Nah, you too will have to learn.'

'Hang it all, do finally stop talking politics. The old pig-head doesn't understand a word of it anyway. We must have quiet at last.'

'. . . and then my little girl was dead. We couldn't even stop. The Russians were just behind us . . .'

'That's enough, do turn in and get a few hours' sleep.'

'Shut up, silly ass!'

Next morning the cackling of the chickens and the lowing of the cows awakened us. Gleaming bands of dust shone through the gaps in the walls and through the open door of the barn. Outside the sun was shining. I looked at the unknowns whose conversations we had listened to last night. The two girls had just woken up and were sitting on their blankets, their faces puffed with sleep. Their dishevelled hair, with its wild permanent waves, was full of dust. Although still quite sleepy, they started the morning with a noisy conversation in the same tone that we already knew from the previous evening. In comical contrast to this language and to their ravaged looks were the highfalutin names that they called each other by: Irene and Renate. They devilishly resembled our guards in Ravensbrück. As yet I didn't know to which category of German girls these two belonged. Then I noticed their field-grey skirts and grey shirt blouses. So these two were 'army helpers' in Hitler's army. Now I could explain to myself their curious language: it was the soldiers' jargon of the Second World War. Later, when fetching water at the pump, by chance I stood next to Irene. If one ignored the horrible hair she was quite nice-looking and she was friendly too. She immediately offered to push the handle of the pump for me, while I rinsed out my mug.

'Where do you want to go?' she asked in a trusting way.

'To Bavaria.'

'Actually I should go to Berlin, but there are the Russians and I don't fancy being raped by them. I prefer to go to western Germany together with a few comrades. Somewhere we'll find a place. Are you also walking in the direction of Boizenburg? Then we could stay together for a while. But when the American roadblocks start again we have to disappear sideways into the bushes. Our comrades naturally don't want to become prisoners of war.'

So we passed through the gate of the farmyard and spent a radiant morning walking with these boys and girls. The three ex-soldiers wore a curious get-up: army pants and they'd picked up civilian jackets somewhere. They continued to be loud and to speak their miserable German, but towards us – it must be the KZ – they behaved with a nearly formal politeness that was touching.

For a second and a third time we circumvented a roadblock, leaving the highway, walking in single file over narrow paths that crossed the still sparse undergrowth of the May forest.

Suddenly one of the boys ran towards a few pieces of paper that were spread over the forest floor. 'Do come here,' he screamed. 'Newspapers! They must have thrown them down from a plane.'

We crowded round him and read the boldly printed headline: 'Hitler commits suicide! The corpse drenched in petrol and lit in front of the "Bunker" . . . Goebbels and his family swallowed poison . . .' The lines blurred in front of my eyes. I didn't notice that the news was already several days old. Around me there was an uncanny silence. So now the moment that we had awaited so long had arrived. And all the dead, my dead, were not granted to live to see it . . .

A volley of rude words of abuse pulled me out of my numbness.

'You can't go on.' The soldier had now declared this three times already and had ordered us back with a gesture that could not be misunderstood. Just as stubbornly I pushed in front of his nose my most valuable document, my document of discharge, and translated hesitatingly, searching for words, its idiotic text: that I was 'detained' in the Ravensbrück Concentration Camp for political reasons and that I was obliged to present myself within three days at the 'Stapo' post of my native village. The whole thing was ridiculous if one looked at the world into which we had been released. No wonder weapon, no hope of final victory and not even a Führer. And particularly, never again a 'report' at a 'Stapo' post, or whatever those places of horror were called.

But this document did not interest the small American with his crooked steel helmet at all. He didn't know any German and wanted to be left in peace. Stubbornly he repeated, 'You can't go through.' This was his last word.

'Come, Emmi!' We turned round cursing and went back the way we had come. So we would have to wander back half a kilometre, find the side roads and circumvent the roadblock. In order to move more quickly we had separated not long before from our travelling companions, the soldiers and the army assistants, who had taught us this method. But the nearer we came to the south of Mecklenburg the denser were the roadblocks. Mostly, our documents of discharge, or even the word 'KZ', worked like an 'open, sesame'. But sometimes we could just as well have shown the document to a wall. Whenever the word 'KZ' didn't have its effect immediately and a conversation developed, I searched my memory in despair for English words, and again and again I heaved a sigh of distress and: 'Oh, if only we had a dictionary . . . !'

On a village road we met two boys, still children of about fourteen or fifteen. They had large dark eyes in dark-brown faces and, as they sat so nonchalantly on a wall dangling their legs, we asked them the way. I listened to their language and knew they were gipsies. Then I noticed on the lower arm of one of them the tattooed prisoner number. So then, Auschwitz! The boy had noticed my look and nodded, grinning. 'You too?'

'From Ravensbrück.'

'And where to?' was his next question.

We told them.

Then we wanted to know what their plans were and one, the more outgoing of the two, explained to us calmly that they didn't know as yet, but that they were quite enjoying themselves.

'We'll get somewhere anyway.' And then he asked suddenly, 'Have
you already eaten eggs?'

'Eggs? No. Where should we get them from? We are glad if we are
given potatoes and bread.'

'Given!' He shook with laughter. 'One "organises" them. Something
like that you don't get as a present. But my friend and I, we eat eggs
every day. We have already eaten at least fifty. And chickens, too!' He
slid down from the wall and let himself fall into the grass of the ditch.
He rolled around like a young animal and suddenly it was obvious that
he enjoyed life. We sat down next to them.

'When did they let you go?' I asked.

'Not at all.'

'Bolted?'

'Not that either.'

'Was your camp freed?'

'No. They evacuated us.'

I thought of the death march of the Auschwitz prisoners. 'But not
from Auschwitz, surely?'

'That too. But that was already in winter, wasn't it. Then we came
to Parchim and from there started the new march.'

'Was it very bad?'

'For this one it was.' He pointed to his comrade. I turned towards
the other boy and noticed that he seemed weak and ailing. The brown
colour of his skin looked like make-up.

'Are you friends?'

'Yes, since Auschwitz. We were always together.' He dug his friend
in the ribs tenderly.

'How many were you in your camp when they evacuated you?'

'A hundred thousand at least. It was a line that never ended. The
worst thing was that the SS shot all those who couldn't walk on. All the
time we heard the banging.'

'Did you run away during the march?'

'What do you think? We couldn't do that any more. No, that was
entirely different. But first something happened with him.' He pointed
again to his silent comrade. 'This one collapsed.'

'And they didn't shoot him?'

'They would have if they had noticed,' said the boy and the other
one turned away, quite embarrassed. 'He never wants me to talk about
it, he is ashamed. But we can tell you, you also are from the "KZ". He
gave in by the second day. Naturally that was because of hunger. For
weeks they had given us nothing but a cup of soup and a slice of bread.
I also was finished, but I am stronger than he is. More and more often

he sat down in the ditch. It was awful. Each time I was waiting for one of those dogs to come and finish him. I was begging and threatening him. But he was just stubborn. Then I always pulled him up again and we went on a bit arm in arm. But soon I couldn't walk myself any more and dragged him on with the greatest effort. Then he started to talk nonsense and was no longer right in his head, and on the third day I gave up. Our legs wouldn't work by then and we sat down next to each other in the ditch.' The boy was silent, pressed his hand to his mouth and bit his finger. All the joy of life had suddenly disappeared from his eyes, leaving him with the face of an old man. Then, sighing deeply, he started talking again: 'God, it was awful. To expect that any moment the high boots would appear next to one and that suddenly there would be a bang; that everything would be finished all at once. And next to me sat this one and whispered all the time, "Do let me die, do let me die . . ." and I couldn't say anything to him but "shit, stop it at once!".' Then he stopped, all embarrassed, and looked at us. And the former happy grin was back, and with it the previous lively boy's face. He made a disparaging gesture with his hand. 'It's good that you too know all about it!'

'Yes, and how did things go on?'

'I started talking to him like to a sick horse: "Don't talk nonsense about dying. Now we nearly have made it. It cannot last much longer. Now you are not permitted to die!" But at last he didn't understand me any more. When I looked up, I always saw only the legs of our men, who dragged themselves onwards along the road. I called. I begged that they should take us with them. But nobody cared about us. They had enough to do to cope themselves. After all, we were only gipsy boys. Each time I heard boots approaching, I bent down over him and pretended we were talking. They mustn't notice how down he was. I didn't dare to look up and when the steps stopped, I always had only one thought: now it is finished. His lot was better. He didn't understand anything any more. But me . . .' He stopped and quietly became absorbed in thought. 'Lorries and tanks went by. Sometimes I shouted they should give us a slice of bread. But they must have been afraid of the SS. They didn't stop. Then I must have fallen asleep. I woke up scared when the brakes of a car screeched next to us. Now, I thought, now it has happened. First I closed my eyes in fear, but then I couldn't stand it any longer and raised my head. There in the road directly in front of us stood a white bus with a red cross. A man got out and came towards us. He had a strange uniform. I started trembling with fear and shook Franz violently. Then I threw up my arms. When I think of it now I could burst out laughing. The man looked friendly. He said something, but I didn't understand him, no doubt because I was so confused. He had a cup in his hand and a parcel. In the cup there was coffee. Real proper coffee. He held the cup' – he pointed to his friend – 'to this one's mouth, but by this time Franz couldn't swallow. The coffee spilt down on both sides, but a few drops must have got in anyway. Because after a few seconds he opened his eyes. Then the man took a packet of biscuits from the parcel and I could see all that was in it. Wonderful! Colourful tins, paper bags and tiny packages all made of transparent stuff. The man was just offering Franz a biscuit and I couldn't stand it any more. I simply said, "Please, dear sir, do give me something too, just one biscuit." And he immediately threw an entire packet into my lap. I would have loved to swallow them all at once. I never had eaten anything so delicious.'

'And how did it go with your friend?' asked Emmi.

'It's hard to believe how fast he recovered. By the time I had finished all my biscuits he was already drinking his coffee properly and then came the turn of the biscuits. Masses of prisoners were crowding round the white bus. Everyone got a parcel, we too. What a bother I had then with Franz. He didn't want to stop eating. And that, you know, is dangerous. We lit a fire at the side of the road and cooked in the new tins, as did the others. Everybody was laughing and enjoying themselves. Long after the white bus had left I learnt from the men that it had been the Swedish Red Cross.'

'And you were free?'

'Yes, the SS had run away in the meantime. We stayed for a few days in a barn until Franz could walk again and then we started to wander. Do you also like Mecklenburg that much?'

Before we took leave of the two boys we passed a short course in stealing chickens and eggs. We had great fun and I promised to use our new knowledge soon. The four eggs that we got as a present from the gipsy boys we boiled shortly afterwards on the shore of a small lake.

In front of a tiny house surrounded by a tidily tended small garden sat an elderly woman. Her face was friendly and calm, as if she had no notion of what was happening around her. We asked her for some fresh water. She got up immediately, smiled and asked us in.

We went with her into a kitchen and, as the door shut quietly behind us, we were suddenly removed to another world. The shelves along the walls were decorated with colourful cut-out paper trimmings. On them stood in a straight line and perfect order stone jugs with their blue onion pattern: sugar, salt, flour and semolina, and smaller ones for cinnamon, nutmeg and pepper. I was moved and thought of my childhood, of our kitchen in Potsdam. But could something like that still exist? Did the earth never shake here even a single time to get these jugs out of line? The old woman with her tidy apron stood at the stove and warmed coffee and milk for us two vagabonds. We sat at the kitchen table, a large comforting cup in front of each of us, sipping the precious drink. Then the old one led us with motherly words through her carefully tended front garden and when parting I got an uncanny feeling. I did not dare turn round to look again at this untouched remnant of a lost era.

The End of the Splendour

All tired out, we reached the first houses of the small town of Zarrentin. On the right in the dusk lay a calm lake, on the left stretched a high wall. On this day our way had been awfully long. Our strength was fading. Already from afar I saw that we hadn't reached the end of our troubles. At the town entrance there was an American roadblock. The soldier didn't let us pass. All my arts of persuasion were in vain. I started to despair, as here no walking around was possible: on one side the lake, on the other the wall. So eventually I lost my composure and began to weep. 'We are sick and exhausted, and could not walk the many kilometres back to the last village.' When the soldier saw my tears he instantly started fidgeting with embarrassment, lifted his hand and shouted almost commandingly, 'OK!' We hastily ran by him as if somebody were chasing us.

Quickly we went to the town hall to find a place to sleep.

But at the town hall there were crowds of people, who all, just like us, were without any shelter. There was no more room – the town was inundated with refugees. We pushed forward to the clerk and showed him our documents of discharge. He pondered for a quite a while.

'You come from a "KZ", therefore you actually could try the monastery. Former prisoners of war are there, perhaps you can find a place.'

'What kind of prisoners of war are they?'

'Mainly Frenchmen, but also Russians, Poles and other previous "*Ostarbeiter*". Surely you can go there; as "KZ" people you have the right to a place.'

The monastery had until recently been a hostel of the Hitlerjugend. Even before we arrived there, noise and laughter reached us. Male voices competed in shouting. We didn't feel comfortable at all. We should have loved to turn round. How would these strangers receive us? 'KZ' all right, but after all, we are Germans. From the open windows of the building next to the monastery I heard loud Russian words. Then we passed the main gate and entered a large room with many two-tiered wooden beds along the walls. As the men noticed us, the noise stopped abruptly. Nobody said anything.

Then I addressed one who was sitting nearest to me: 'We come from a "KZ" and are looking for a place to sleep. We are very tired.'

The Frenchman didn't ask a single question. Without hesitation he called into the hall, 'Marcel! André! Out of the beds. They are for the women. You can lie on the floor.'

Without any resistance the two removed their possessions from the straw mattresses. These beds were the most beautiful ones in the hall, just next to the window. Confused, we sat down. Then, immediately, the merry noise started. A few asked us where we came from. When they heard 'Ravensbrück', more of them came over. They wanted to know if and when the French were freed, whether Ravensbrück also had a men's camp and how many Frenchmen had been there. We provided information as well as we could and it turned out that amongst the Frenchmen in the hall, quite a number had themselves been in a concentration camp. The conversation developed quickly and animatedly. Our tiredness disappeared.

Naturally, some also wanted to know why we actually had been imprisoned in the KZ. So I started, for the first time in freedom, to tell roughly about my experiences in the Soviet Union, the time in Siberia and the extradition to the Gestapo.

The Frenchmen listened silently, but soon I noticed how some of them became disapproving in a peculiar way – even almost hostile. Their looks appeared to say: Can you actually believe her? And at that point one of them put it into words: 'If I have understood you right, you want to claim that although innocent you were arrested in the Soviet Union?'

'Yes, it was just like that.'

'Do you really believe that the Germans – and you, you surely are a German? – that they never conspired against the Soviet Union?'

With this sound my mouth dried up and my heart started to flutter. The memory of the interrogation at the arrival block of Ravensbrück came back, the declaration of war of the Communist fellow prisoners. Could it be possible that now, even after liberation, something similar might happen? Should I not be believed even here? Did these Frenchmen too walk through the last decade blind and deaf? For the Communist prisoners there were mitigating circumstances, perhaps they had to cling to their political belief in order not to recognise the awful senselessness of their fate. But here in liberty, no, here I would not let myself be called a liar, here one must fight for truth. Let the Communists hear it, even if it breaks their hearts.

'Did you not realise from my report that I lived as a Communist emigrant in Moscow, that I fled as an anti-Fascist in 1933 from Hitler's Germany? Try to realise once that back then, for my husband and me, who had been members of the KPD for one and a half decades, our land of emigration, the Soviet Union, represented the only real force against Fascism. And we should have conspired against this country? Should have made common cause with our deadliest enemies, the Nazis?'

'But maybe you had, without knowing it, come into contact with some undercover Nazis? There certainly existed in the Soviet Union, just as in all other countries, a "Fifth Column". And you can't really take it amiss that the Soviet Government defended itself against Nazi spies. Shouldn't Hitler's attack have convinced you that the Soviet Union was constantly in danger? If you, as Germans, were arrested, this certainly had its reasons.'

'Haven't I already told you that during the "big cleansing" from 1936 to 1938 Stalin arrested and brought to trial not only nearly all the old Bolshevists and fighting companions of Lenin, but also deprived millions of Soviet citizens, simple workers and farmers, of their freedom? Amongst these masses of imprisoned people the foreigners were a tiny percentage. Do you honestly believe that all these people worked for the "Fifth Column" of the Nazis?'

'I don't know which crimes these people committed, but do you really want to make us believe that in the Soviet Union innocent people were arrested?'

The man was pale and tense, and regarded me as if I were his bitterest enemy. He was a Communist and therefore couldn't and wouldn't give in. How could he deal so fast with such a bitter truth?

'All you are saying here nearly sounds as if Stalin wasn't a bit better than Hitler. Could that actually be your opinion?' He asked this in an imploring voice.

'Yes, that is it. Between the misdeeds of Hitler and those of Stalin, in my opinion, there exists only a quantitative difference. To be sure, Communism as an idea was originally positive, and National Socialism never was positive; it was, since its origin and from its beginning, criminal in its aims and its programme. I don't know if the Communist idea, if its theory, already contained a basic fault or if only the Soviet practice under Stalin betrayed the original good idea and established in the Soviet Union a kind of Fascism.'

This reply made the listeners, who until then had been sympathising, turn cool and reserved, and it looked to me as if they all moved away from us. I started to feel almost guilty as these people had received us in the beginning with open arms and without any suspicion. Now the atmosphere was poisoned. For the first time a dull fear about the future overcame me. Could that really mean that in the days ahead too there would be believing Communists, people who, in the free world, would go on to do Stalin's criminal business?

Luckily, at this tense moment Auguste, who was both a person who commanded respect and kitchen chef, called both of us to the table and I was more than glad to be relieved for the time being of the continuation of discussions with our friendly hosts. Auguste had prepared a meal for us, so it happened that we received from this former French prisoner of war the first festive meal at liberty. There were roast pork and potatoes. These tempting long-forgotten fragrances made our strength of character disappear. We simply couldn't say 'no', although we should have known that these delicacies were poison for our sick stomachs. We dined, laughed and told each other comical stories from the camp. The recent hostile debate was forgotten. We were good comrades and felt linked by the same suffering, now overcome.

During the night Emmi and I became seriously ill. The rich meal had finished us. For the next three days our hosts tended us with tea and Zwieback, and not a single word concerning politics was spoken. Even my Communist opponent knew how to behave towards the sick and the weak.

We were still lying miserably on the beds when one of our Frenchmen came running, laughing and screaming, into the hall, jumped on a chair and shouted, 'The Germans have capitulated without conditions! The war is over!'

Together we sang the 'Marseillaise' . . .

Two days later the news arrived that the former French prisoners of war were being taken back to their homeland by truck. A wild mood of departure took hold of everybody. We asked Auguste whether they couldn't take us with them for a bit. He thought it over but, as we were women, he didn't find a way to smuggle us into the transport.

The trucks stood in the yard of the monastery and our friends, laughing, threw their luggage on to them. Then they climbed up. We shook many hands and wished each other good luck. Together with us in the yard stood a few German girls, the girlfriends of the few young Frenchmen, who had arrived in the monastery two days ago. The other men treated the girls haughtily. Quite lost, they stood taking leave and the tears ran down their faces. I felt particularly sorry for them.

Quiet came to the monastery of Zarrentin. Everyone had gone. Emmi and I decided to rest for a few more days. The Frenchmen left us all their provisions. We could live on them for weeks. As for now we were only allowed to gobble them up with our eyes, because we were still ill.

I recall these last peaceful days in Zarrentin with particular joy. The weather had turned warm, nearly summery. On a hill above the lake sat the Gothic monastery and next to it a beautiful old church. Behind the monastery lay a yard covered by lush grass with ancient linden and chestnut trees, framed in a wide curve by country houses. On the hill down to the lake the lilac blooms smelt sweetly. Slowly Emmi and I walked along the garden paths.

The leaves of the chestnut trees were still so tender that they couldn't stand the strong sun. They hung down limply as if in exhaustion. At a fence leant a curious couple: on the street side a young American soldier, in the garden a brown-eyed girl in a light dress, a German. They smiled at each other and everything was as it should be. Only later did I come to understand that here spring was stronger than the strict orders of the occupying forces. As yet the American soldiers were forbidden to fraternise with the Germans.

Actually I had not realised that life in the lonely house with broken doors could be not without danger for us two women. It was so peaceful all around. Yet on this night, which was to be our last in Zarrentin, we would have had great need of a locked door. It may have been near midnight when I sat up, scared, in my bed. From somewhere an unusual noise could be heard. I held my breath and listened; steps were approaching the entrance of the hall. Then the beam of a flashlight jerked over the wall and somebody groped forward, searching. Suddenly the light was turned on. He had seen us. We lay in the remotest corner of the hall in two beds, one above the other: Emmi in the top bunk, I underneath. The American staggered through the room directly towards us, stopped, took off his helmet and tossed it on the table. Then I saw his face. He was completely drunk. With a few uncertain steps he reached my bed and slumped down at its end.

Still quite sleepy, I sat up abruptly. My first reaction to this night visit was less fear than rage. I hissed, 'Get out! What the hell do you want here?' To be sure, that was a silly question as I knew only too well what his merry intentions were. My next thought was how to keep him off me. But there was no time to think long thoughts. Already he had grabbed my feet and tried to grope along my legs. I gave him a kick. 'Get out, you should be ashamed of yourself!' That he was not, but retreated to the end of the bed. I knew from my bad experiences in Siberia that now, if at all, there was only one salvation: talk, talk and talk.

'Which town do you come from, from the north or from the south,' I asked abruptly as well as illogically.

And already it had worked: 'New Orleans,' he grunted.

Quickly on: 'Are you married?'

'Oh yes!' To my astonishment, he removed his hand from my feet, put it into his uniform pocket and fumbled awkwardly for his wallet. 'This is my wife.' And he laid the photo of a smiling blonde on my blanket.

'How pretty,' I continued. 'Do you also have children?'

Immediately the next photo lay on my knees. 'My son!' Even through his drunk voice still trembled a father's pride.

I assumed I had won. But my triumph was premature. He quickly returned his photos and grabbed with his free hand my legs that – as a precaution – I had pulled up. Now I hissed as loudly as I could, 'To hell with you, you're married! Can't you wait even for the short time until you are back in New Orleans with your wife?'

Despite my less than sparse English vocabulary, he understood immediately and retorted with emphasis, 'I don't wait a single day longer!' He had come so close to me that his alcohol-laden breath hit my face.

In despair I called Emmi, who until then had remained absolutely silent: 'Emmi, for heaven's sake help me! What can I do against this drunk? Run out and fetch somebody!'

From above came her voice: 'Grete, do ask him is he has a dictionary.'

For a moment I lost my voice, dumbfounded, but then I gave free vent to my anger and shouted, 'Idiot, for what this one wants he doesn't need a dictionary.' Now I was at my wit's end and started hitting him and screaming angrily, 'What, you pretend to be an American, an American, who are said to be gentlemen? You are anything but a gentleman!'

He loosened his grip, stared speechlessly at me for a moment with bloodshot eyes, got up uncertainly, grabbed his helmet and staggered out of the hall. He left the light on.

The next day we were back again on the road. With grey faces we sat down in the ditch more and more frequently. The illness had returned. For the first time my courage left me entirely. I quarrelled with Emmi because of her mention of the dictionary and told her nastily that she was a coward. This was certainly a result of her weakness and actually I was sorry about it. Whatever else was left to us but to comfort each other?

'I am finished. What shall become of us? Will we ever reach home alive?' I groaned and held my tummy.

'We cannot remain sitting here,' pleaded Emmi. 'If only my damn rucksack weren't so heavy . . .'

The rucksack was another touchy topic and again a new quarrel with

Emmi threatened. She tended to take with her anything she found. Before she left Ravensbrück, she 'organised' for herself a few sets of underwear from the looted goods ('*Beutegut*') of the SS. In the ditch she found further valuable items. Despite the abundance, strict order prevailed in this rucksack. One could envy her this: each item neatly packed in its special bag. Emmi's rucksack was a reflection of herself, who marched through the chaos as spotless as possible, with hair tightly combed back and arranged flatly in the shape of a pretzel at her neck. Emmi's fantasy never disturbed her balance and I could understand that she basically considered me an adventuress.

'Why don't you at least throw out some of that stuff that you drag around with you in your rucksack?' I asked her with annoyance.

'Throw away? Whatever are you thinking of? I don't own anything any more. My husband has divorced me while I sat in Ravensbrück . . . I have no relatives and have to start all over again. Can't you understand at all how hard this is?'

She began to weep and I considered myself heartless and brutal. 'Emmi, don't be afraid. First of all you'll come with me to Thierstein, where we are already near the Bohemian border. And there you can stay as long as you like.'

'How nice that would be! But no, I can't, I have to get to Prague as quickly as possible.'

'You'd better not do that, as you are a Sudetendeutsche. Better wait and see what happens. You have to take into account that in Czechoslovakia – after all that has happened – they have a bad opinion about the Germans. As you know, there were masses of Nazis amongst the Sudetendeutsche.'

'True enough. But what has that to do with me? Why should the Czechs do anything to me of all people? Haven't I worked for years with the Czech Social-Democrats and, just because of that, sat in a KZ!'

'Yes, that's all true. But can one know if the Czechs after this war still differentiate between Germans and Germans? I, anyway, would advise you at first not to go to Czechoslovakia.'

'I have to go home. Naturally, you cannot understand that. I belong in Prague . . .'

We stood in front of the shop window of a small suburban bakery. Next to us stood a thin, dark man, who wore a handkerchief knotted at its four corners. There was a smell of freshly baked bread. The man asked us shyly, 'Do you have coupons?' I noticed the red triangle with the printed 'F' on his jacket: a Frenchman from a KZ. Therefore one of us.

'Do you have money?' we asked in return.

He nodded with resignation. 'Money, yes, but they don't give you anything without coupons . . .'

'Have you already been inside?'

'Yes.'

'And you left without anything?'

Could such a thing happen? The monstrosity of this situation only became clear to me at that point. Here stood one of the liberated, one of those who survived hell, was hungry, craving a slice of bread, he even wanted to pay for it, and a German baker dared to refuse him by answering: 'We don't give anything without coupons!'

Now Emmi and I stood in front of the counter, the Frenchman's money in our hands.

'We would like to have three loaves of bread!' My voice trembled with excitement. Here it was no longer only the matter of the bread, of hunger. This was about something much worse . . . 'Here is the money, we don't have any coupons.'

'No coupons?' said the baker woman haughtily. 'I am sorry, we don't sell anything without . . .'

I interrupted her: 'I know. But we come from a KZ, have no coupons and are hungry.'

'Nevertheless, I cannot give you anything, I treat all customers equally. Go to the municipality and get coupons.'

This was too much. 'If three loaves of bread are not on the counter immediately . . .' My voice gave out.

Then a hand touched my arm and a young woman said soothingly, 'May I help you with my coupons? Please, I'd like to do it . . . I am so sorry about it . . .'

Embarrassed, I said nothing but 'thank you'. With the loaves under our arms we stepped outside to our comrade. In Boizenburg, the small town in Mecklenburg on the Elbe river, entire rows of houses lay in ruins. On our way we had seen already many ruined houses. Most of them had been single farms that had been burnt down in the last days of the war, often still smoking or full of the smell of burning. Now we stood, shaken, in front of the first cold ruins and I caught myself again and again in the attempt to reconstruct in my imagination the house from the remnants of the walls, to imagine the old look of the street. I still could not grasp that one could ever get used to this horrible picture.

In the streets of the suburb we met groups of former prisoners on their way to the centre of Boizenburg. In their striped rags with triangles and prisoner numbers on the jacket and on the legs of their pants, they looked like scarecrows. What perverse imagination could have invented this prisoner garb? If only one could soon relieve these poor people of their disgusting uniforms, I thought. Emmi and I were forever sitting down and scratching with knives at our paint crosses in order to look at last like normal human beings. It remained completely incomprehensible to me that some of the former people of the KZ – and I already experienced this in Boizenburg – continued also after the liberation to wear this insulting costume with a kind of pride, or even demonstrated with it their special position. There exist curious forms of exhibitionism.

In front of the municipal building of Boizenburg swarmed the usual crowd of refugees. Here there was the first provisional welfare centre for former KZ people. It operated night and day to cope with the stream of newcomers. Everybody was examined. I soon understood how necessary this was, because we heard that some criminal and asocial prisoners had exchanged their green or black triangles with the red one of the 'Politicals', looted the villages and 'confiscated' the former possessions of the Nazis. We were told that near Boizenburg an asocial KZ couple had joined up and claimed to be male and female physicians. Consequently they received from an American occupation centre all available benefits, even a car. Thus they drove around with the Red Cross flag flying from their radiator and lorded it, until at long last they were exposed by a political prisoner who had recognised them.

In Boizenburg each prisoner received money, food coupons and vouchers for soup once a day. At the inn 'Mecklenburger Hof', a mass lodging, Emmi and I were put up. As in a huge sanatorium, bed stood next to bed, but ceiling and walls still revealed the former purpose of this room. They were hung with faded paper garlands, the decoration of a party with dancing that would apparently be the last for a long time.

The first days we spent dazed by the crowd of people and lay in bed almost all day long. Only with great effort did we succeed in walking through the city at noon in order to receive soup at the provisionally arranged food supply for the masses. All the 'KZ'-lers were granted a positive benefit; they didn't have to queue up for the distribution of food.

Wherever we listened we were assured that the crossing of the Elbe was prohibited for German civilians. All bridges had been blown up by the Nazis, but the emergency bridge was to be used only by the Allied military.

'Why hasn't anyone started a ferry?' I asked, astonished. They informed me that it was strictly forbidden to cross the river. Everybody who tried was arrested immediately. One of them even claimed that the Allied soldiers shot at people who tried to cross by swimming. Others related that the floating bridge would be opened for traffic in three weeks at the latest. So we obviously had to expect a longer stay in Boizenburg.

Emmi suggested that we should look for a job where perhaps we would get something to eat. This sounded like a wonderful idea – by the way, one very typical for our 'KZ'ler mentality – and we immediately walked together to the employment office. It was quite astonishing that in Boizenburg this institution was working again already, with a new head appointed by the occupying forces. We presented ourselves there and learnt that people looking for work had first to register with the military government and obtain a recommendation. We received this peculiar document and returned to the employment office.

'We would like to work somewhere.'

'To work?' repeated the clerk as if he had misunderstood us. 'You were in the KZ for years and still you haven't had enough of it? Are you now not more in need of rest a while?'

'Yes, that is so. If the Elbe were not blocked, we would go on tomorrow to get home as quickly as possible. Only there can we recuperate. But here in Boizenburg . . . You know, we actually would like to have a workplace where one gets something to eat.'

He wrote down our names and enquired where we had been put up. 'The Mecklenburger Hof is actually not a good place for resting,' said the understanding head of the employment office in farewell.

Shopping for our food with coupons turned each occasion into an enjoyable event, no matter how little there was available. What a grand feeling it was to have money and food coupons in one's hand, and to be able to decide whether one bought only one hundred grams of butter instead of one hundred and fifty, instead of a whole only half a loaf of bread and to know that the time of begging for a few potatoes or a little bread had passed, and that the KZ ration finally lay behind one. We stood in line in front of a shop. I enjoyed the mixture of people on the streets and was glad that I again could be one out of many in a town. Suddenly the blood rushed to my heart. Somebody was walking over there in high boots, a shopping net in his hand; I could only see the neck, the back of the head.

'Emmi, quickly, hold my bread! I'll be back in a moment!' And with that I began to follow this man. I had no choice, I had to. He turned into the main road. I followed him. The distance became shorter and shorter. I couldn't fit my speed to the measured step of those high boots. Nowhere was an American soldier to be seen. What should I do? Grab him by the arm and say: 'You are arrested!' No, he would knock me to the ground with a blow of his fist and escape. Then he even stood still and I was forced to overtake him. If only he didn't recognise me! Thank God I was not wearing the coat with the give-away remnants of the paint cross. On the wall there was a notification of the occupying forces. I stopped and pretended to read it with interest, and noticed in the remotest corner of my vision that the man continued walking. The boots overtook me and I followed. There was no end to the road. Nowhere was there an American or an auxiliary policeman. Then the man turned right into a side street. Soon it would be too late. On the left lay the port offices of Boizenburg and in its yard an American guard walked up and down. I ran across the road, jumped over the barbed-wired fence, rushed towards him and pointed with my hand in the direction the man had taken: 'There is a Gestapo man from the KZ Ravensbrück. Arrest him!' The soldier put his rifle on the ground and ran after him. At the same time I saw four other soldiers running. Now Ramdohr also tried to flee. I can't remember how long it took until he was brought in. I didn't even notice what was happening around me. Only when they came near me with him and I saw his face was I horrified. It wasn't him at all. I had been mistaken. 'Are you Ramdohr?' I asked uncertainly. 'Yes.' Fear had so distorted his face that it was barely recognisable. 'Frau Buber, you are doing me wrong. I also once was a Social Democrat . . .'

'Shut up!' interrupted the American soldier.

The Commandant of the harbour office wrote a protocol. Then we were being loaded into a covered car and driven to the commander of Boizenburg. Next to us sat two Americans with machine pistols on their knees. When we arrived at the major's office, in front of the door stood, as usual, waiting 'KZ'ler. They must have recognised Ramdohr, as he had raged for years also in the men's camp of Ravensbrück. Afterwards, when he was taken away to prison, the men fell on him and beat him up despite the protecting Americans. At the Commandant's I was asked for my address. Then I was allowed to go.

During the week after this two Americans arrived in order to inter-rogate me. They recorded everything I had to say about Ramdohr: that for years in Ravensbrück he tortured, beat and killed women, that he was the horror of the camp. I related my own experiences with Ramdohr during my fifteen weeks of dark arrest. After these statements the Americans asked me some peculiar questions:

'How do you know that Ramdohr was an SS man?'

'All the members of the guard units of Ravensbrück belonged to the Waffen SS.'

'You would have to prove that first.'

'I can't.'

The next question was just as astonishing: 'You claim that Ramdohr was a Gestapo man? Do you have any proof for this claim?'

'Proof? I was a prisoner and could not enter the Kommandantur of the camp. But I observed Ramdohr in his activity as Gestapo man and he himself has interrogated me in prison.'

'That is not enough, as Ramdohr claims to have been a detective sergeant and not a Gestapo man. He also claims not to have been a member of the SS. Did you ever see him in SS uniform?'

I was no longer sure. In fact, he always wore civilian clothing. But suddenly I remembered a Sunday in prison . . . 'Yes, once. At that time I was being held in the camp prison. Then Ramdohr opened the flap of the cell door and in its frame I saw him in SS uniform.'

When the Americans moved out of Mecklenburg and the British took over the occupation, they brought Ramdohr to Lüneburg. Later he was sentenced to death in the Hamburg trial of the guard units of Ravensbrück.

Among Former Comrades

After just a few days Emmi got a job at the hospital of Boizenburg. Again, I had to stay in bed. The recuperation didn't work out. Each evening, Emmi faithfully brought half her hospital meal to my bed.

'As soon as I am all right again, we definitely have to find a way over the Elbe, even if we have to swim across.'

Emmi soothed me: 'Wouldn't it be better to write to the American Commandant, or even better just go and see him? If the prisoners of war and the foreign "KZ"-ler are permitted to cross the floating bridge, why ever shouldn't we?'

'You're quite right. Here, too, they don't differentiate between Germans who were Nazis and Germans who fought against the Nazis. Actually, it's incomprehensible!'

The next day, while Emmi was at work, I went alone to the Kommandantur. But there they didn't even consider letting me in. Some snot-nose of an interpreter, a German, snubbed me, took the letter I had prepared as a precaution and advised me to be patient.

One evening two well-mannered men appeared in the dance hall of the 'Mecklenburger Hof', looking for the two of us. They addressed us as 'Comrade Emmi' and 'Comrade Grete', and with '*du*'. And one of them invited us quite formally to move to his house. So we arrived at the fisherman's house of the K family: a small, crooked, red-brick cottage with a hunchbacked roof made of reeds. At the door, Mother K welcomed us like old friends. The daughter and the little son came, and we were led into the living room as if we were long-expected relatives. There was not even a minute of awkward silence. They talked without restraint in the '*plattdeutsch*' dialect, laughed with us and were extremely human and natural.

As yet I had no idea who our friendly hosts actually were. 'Comrade Emmi?' 'Comrade Grete?' Communists by any chance? Then I noticed the long bookshelves that occupied nearly half of the wall and tried quickly to decipher titles on a few of the books. Exactly: Marx, Engels, Feuerbach . . . Now there remained no doubt. I wished myself back at the mass camp at the 'Mecklenburger Hof'. I really did not fancy discussions, disputes without solutions. I simply was tired. How beautiful and cosy was this little house, but not destined to grant me some peace, even for a short time. And these warm-hearted, good people? Would they continue to be friendly and to treat us as one of them as soon as they knew that I was no longer their 'comrade' and did not share their faith any more? Wouldn't they, as soon as I told them the truth, instantly become my bitterest enemies? I leant back in the armchair with a sigh and enjoyed the cosy room where one could feel at home. It reminded one a little of a boat cabin with its furnishings so carefully arranged. This impression was strengthened by two miniature sailing ships that stood covered by glass on cupboard and bookshelf. I got up in order to look at these works of art more closely.

Martha, the daughter, came over to me and said that their father had made these himself and had rearranged the entire little house. The little ships had been built during the long period of unemployment. Then he earned quite good money by it. 'Father actually is a rigger,' she said, full of pride. And I asked what kind of profession that was. 'Once they were the experts for the rigging of the sailing ships,' she explained to me. 'Father started as a sailor and later on he worked in Hamburg in a shipyard.' Now I could understand his sailor's face and the curious slightly rolling walk. 'Then, with the long unemployment started the hard times, but it became really bad only under Hitler.' Martha was silent. Mother K called from the kitchen that we should take a look at her realm and with a happy face she confided to me that she had just got some meat and fat 'under the hand' so that in the evening, when they also had invited friends, there would be a good meal. Then she led Emmi and me to 'our room', an attic that was shining white with freshly made beds and dainty mull curtains. With our worn-out shoes and faded clothes we felt quite out of place amongst this delicate splendour.

When we were sitting again at the round table in the living room, Father K returned from work. Naturally, the topic 'concentration camp' was started immediately, but the faces of this family did not show any signs of guilty conscience or, as we had noticed so often in these weeks of freedom, an embarrassing kind of exaggerated compassion. These people discussed the entire problem quite objectively; it even sounded as if they all were experts.

'Now I want to show you my treasures,' said Father K and walked to the bookshelf. First of all he took down a thin volume and put it in front of us on the table with a solemn expression on his face: *The Communist Manifesto*. The next book: *Rosa Luxemburg: Russian Revolution* . . . Why exactly this book? Rosa Luxemburg? Could this K actually be a member of the opposition? He pointed to the entire remarkable row of volumes of Marx and Lenin, and told us that in 1933 he had buried these books carefully in the garden, and that they had survived there twelve long years.

'They did become a little mildewed, just like ourselves. But that doesn't matter. Now we are free and now they can stand again on the bookshelf. You two certainly can understand what this means.'

I felt goose pimples forming on my body in little separate spots. Now it would have to come out. Until that moment I had had a faint hope that the Ks perhaps were Social Democrats. But *Rosa Luxemburg* twelve years buried in the garden? No, here hope was lost.

'Do tell me, Comrade Grete, one of the "KZ"-ers in the Mecklenburger Hof said that you were the wife of Heinz Neumann and that Heinz had been arrested in Soviet Russia. Is that really true?' I nodded. Until then at the Ks' place I actually had not mentioned Siberia and everything before, had wanted to postpone it as long as possible for the sake of peace.

'Do you also know', continued Father K, 'that I have known Heinz? He spoke here in red Boizenburg. What a good speaker he was! And how right he was with his slogan "hit the Fascists wherever you meet them"! If only everybody had done this, we wouldn't be sitting today in this mess. You really have to know that I and a small group broke with the Communist Party as early as the end of 1931. Then they called us Trotskyites, but we never were that and today we aren't either. Even at that time we saw through the fraud, we noticed what kind of wind blew from Moscow and that those in Berlin in the Central Committee had just to obey. It wasn't about the fight against the Nazis any more. The Comintern was used only for what was useful to the Russians. And when we had left the Party, I sat down and tried to find in my books an explanation for this treachery. If you look closely, Rosa Luxemburg had seen it all coming . . . When the time had come in 1933, we soon had other cares. One after the other was taken away . . .'

After a pause, during which I experienced a long, long forgotten feeling of happiness, K hesitatingly, and with uncertain words, directed

the following question at me: 'Comrade Grete, what do you actually
think of Soviet Russia? You have been there, haven't you? To us, you
surely can tell the truth . . .'

And I told it to them . . . In the meantime several friends had arrived
at the fisherman's cottage. All of them former members of the KPD,
members of the opposition who, like K, had left the Communist Party,
yet had remained anti-Fascists imprisoned by the Nazis for many years
in penitentiary or KZ. For them the imprisonment had been doubly
difficult. Their Communist fellow prisoners had declared them to be
Trotskyite traitors; they suffered from this, but even more from the
continuous political doubts that didn't leave them any peace. They still
considered themselves to be Communists; they believed that they were
the fighters for the true teaching, despite the fact that their ideological
foundation was already damaged at all its corners. They didn't dare yet
to doubt Lenin, let alone the October Revolution or even Marxist theory.
The great traitor was called Stalin . . .

'Don't you too believe that in the Soviet Union everything would
be different if Lenin hadn't died so early?' This was one of the usual
questions.

When I described the 'Big Cleansing' and the show trials, I noticed
how little my listeners knew of this terrible truth and what a great impact
it had on them. They didn't even dare ask questions. Only Mother K
said naïvely, 'When one listens to you, one almost has to believe that
what is said about the Russian soldiers is also true, that they really follow
orders from above and loot, rob and rape? I always had thought that
what the Nazi press printed about Soviet Russia was pure atrocity propaganda? But there seems to be some truth in it. When you tell about
your arrest and that of thousands of old good comrades, and about the
methods by which the NKVD forced them to confess, and about these
terrible trials, one could go mad.'

When in my story I got to the extradition to the Gestapo, Comrade
M couldn't control himself any longer and cursed: 'These filthy killers!
Will we ever be able to pay them back? And the Stalin–Hitler pact?'

F related that one of his acquaintances, an old comrade, committed
suicide when this shameful pact became known.

Emmi had long gone to sleep and the faces of my new and yet so
old friends were now, after they had heard something of the truth,
confounded and confused. For whatever did we live, for what did we
fight, for what did we suffer?

'The worst is that we cannot even be really glad about the liberation,
because are we not also guilty of the present chaos? Did we not, as
former Communists – even without knowing it – ruin the Weimar

Republic at the order of the Russians?' It was Father K who posed this question.

But here comrade T protested energetically: 'Do you actually want to state by this that the Social Democrats with their policy of the "smaller evil" did not assist in bringing the Nazis to power? Would not Europe look entirely different if they had not already failed in 1918?'

'If, if . . . By the way, the SPD did not fail only in 1918 – that had already happened in 1914, but the failure of the SPD doesn't free us of guilt. We should not have believed and maintained party discipline, we should have hit the table with our fists. Whenever I remember the "red people's decision" ['*roter Volksentscheid*'] even now my stomach is flipping!'

'Quiet!' cried Mother K suddenly. She turned up the radio to its highest volume and we heard the signal of the BBC: '. . . –, . . . –, . . . –'. 'Off this we lived in the years of the war. Here we sat together, often ten of us, with locked doors and tightly covered windows. It is a miracle that they did not catch us all.'

We stayed until dawn. I had met the first like-minded persons since my liberation, people who turned away from the Communist Party of Germany after long, painful doubts and broke with their Communist worldview. The path of suffering hadn't ended yet for them, but already they had known the pain that a Communist feels when he loses his political faith and has to reorientate himself in this life – lonely and banished. Tired out by the effort of talking, I nevertheless was filled with courage and optimism. Just like K and his friends, there must be thousands of other 'formers' in Germany, I thought. Together with them, we would manage to expose the Soviet lie.

During the following days we rested in earnest; during the day we lay in the sun in the little stone garden next to the house where each patch of earth sprouted flowers and leaves, or went to the Elbe meadows down at the bank of the mighty river. There, some American soldiers were swimming and others played an improvised game of baseball.

A few days later Father K related a rumour that the Russians would occupy Mecklenburg and Thüringen, and that the Americans were already in the process of pulling back.

'This would be complete madness, the Allied forces cannot do such a thing!' was my first reaction. 'They are not suicidal.'

'But they don't seem to me to be very far-sighted politicians either,' said Father K bitterly. 'Why, actually, did they have to let the Russians advance to Berlin? Even now they could chase them back across the River Oder. They would only have to knit their brows angrily. It is simply ridiculous what the refugees tell about the Russian Army and its equipment. I don't want to think what would have become of them without American help.'

'But what will become of you, if the Russians are allowed to come as far as the Elbe?' As soon as I had said it I was bitterly sorry about the question, as I saw the fearful looks of Mother K and Martha. 'But no, they couldn't possibly do something like that.'

Months later – meanwhile I had already reached the end of my journey – I received a devastating letter from Father K. What we did not want to believe had occurred. The Russians had pushed forward to the Elbe. Bitterness and fury spoke from each line of this letter. 'The situation here is like that which may have prevailed before the Flood. The so-called Communists call it Socialism and are defending murder, looting, stealing, fraud and dictatorship as something better than Hitler-Fascism . . . What do the Communists in the Reich actually say about this barbarism . . . ?'

I could have answered this question of old K, but the reply certainly would not have satisfied him.

Crossing the Elbe

Two French 'KZ'-lers who were given permission by the Americans to cross the Elbe, in the abundance of their joy about their forthcoming homecoming presented us with their bikes. In this period without trains and petrol, bicycles were probably among the most valuable items of property.

Bad news became more frequent, and now day and night American trucks, tanks and canon clanked over the main street of Boizenburg in a westward direction. Emmi and I decided to practise bicycle riding for a few days and to find a way across the Elbe – whatever might come. In Boizenburg it was being said that near Lauenburg there existed a secret ferry that in the early morning hours brought the refugees in a fishing boat across the river. One day after another went by, but Emmi didn't have the courage to leave. She was afraid of the open road, she was frightened by any risk. To my proposal first to ride at least to Lauenburg to check if there did indeed exist a crossing, there always came the same fearful objection: 'But haven't you heard that they arrest all those whom they catch near the boats? Let's go once more to the Commandant of Boizenburg, perhaps he will yet let us cross the floating bridge.' We tried it, but in vain.

In the meantime the Americans had moved and Mecklenburg was under British occupation. I stood in the market place and was astonished by the curious exercising regulations of the British when 'changing the guard'; old memories of Potsdam arose in me and it seemed as if this army had much more in common with the old Prussian one than with its Allies the Americans. With those one couldn't notice any drill at all, they actually were all civilians in uniform.

Together with a fresh wave of refugees arrived new and threatening rumours of the entry of the Russians into Mecklenburg. Now it was Father K who urged me to leave and, as Emmi was still hesitating, I finally decided to go alone. It was difficult for me simply to leave her to her fate. How would she manage at all with her lack of initiative? How in this chaos would she find her way home on her own? But there was no choice; I had to leave her.

Martha accompanied me. She wanted to take me to relatives in Lauenburg, where I was supposed to stay the night.

But shortly before reaching the goal, our journey came to an abrupt end. The bridge over the Elbe–Trave Canal had been blocked for any civilian traffic by the British. They wanted to prevent the refugees from streaming into town. In a meadow along the canal hundreds of refugees camped with their wagons, patiently waiting in the hope of advancing at some time. I started to negotiate with the guard, but he didn't even consider it necessary to answer me.

'Would it not be better', proposed Martha, 'to come back to Boizenburg?' I was quite tempted to say yes. There, in Boizenburg, was the peaceful family, there were the people whom I had learnt to love, a house, a bed, whereas here were the dividing river and hundreds of kilometres of uncertainty in front of me. But to turn back upon meeting with the first obstacle? No, that was out of the question. There still was the goal that had to be reached. But why did I aim so resolutely in the direction of Thierstein anyway? Was it mother, whom I was longing for and whom I had to reach by any available means? Yes, because there was my home. 'Martha, I have to stay here and wait like the others. I'm sure they'll let me sleep under one of the wagons. Anyway, I have a blanket for the night.' But then, when I saw Martha's red skirt disappearing along the highway, I felt quite sad.

Beyond the meadow, at the bank of the canal, there was a pine plantation. Maybe a protected place for the night could be found there. I rode along a path by the canal bank. In the distance rose the remnants of a blown-up bridge. Here the entire canal was certainly no broader than twenty metres and I was unable to understand why this narrow stream of water should prevent my advance. Unawares, I had arrived at the ruins of the bridge and discovered with astonishment that one of its arches had survived the destruction. And along this arch led an untouched wooden footpath. Without considering how dangerous a risk this was, I removed the rucksack from the bicycle and groped my way carefully along the path. This done, it was back to the bicycle – my most valuable possession. This life-threatening enterprise also succeeded and, covered with sweat, I sat down on the forbidden canal bank, full of joy and not without pride at having fooled the British.

In Lauenburg I could not find the Ks' relatives and wandered around for a long time before finding at long last a place for the night in a stable crowded with refugees. There they agreed that there was a secret crossing over the Elbe and explained to me the place where the boat crossed. However, one had to arrive at the bank at the crack of dawn, because only thus did one have a chance of being taken. In the town there was a state of emergency and Germans were permitted to be on the streets only between five o'clock in the morning and ten o'clock at night. Whoever was caught in the hours between was arrested. They described the way to the bank of the Elbe and next morning at four o'clock I left the stable, a lonely bicycle rider with beating heart. There was no sign, far and wide, of an Englishman. Nowhere was there a human being of any kind. I arrived at the bank and, to my great disappointment, saw more than a hundred people standing in an orderly line. A single fishing boat went back and forth to ferry five people at most on each journey. At this place the Elbe was broader than a kilometre and there was a strong spring current. My hope faded with each half-hour. 'If we are lucky, the English commander sleeps late today. He notices us only at breakfast,' said my well-informed neighbour.

'Can he see us?' I asked, astonished, as we stood behind the undergrowth of willows at the bank.

'Yes, distinctly.' And he pointed in the direction of Lauenburg. 'His villa lies up there on the hill. When he is drinking his coffee, he takes his binoculars and sees our boat going back and forth. That annoys him, of course, as it is forbidden and he himself has given the command. Then he immediately orders a unit of soldiers to come here.'

'And what happens then?'

'That changes. Sometimes they arrest the people, sometimes they only chase them away and confiscate the boat.'

'Have you ever experienced that? How come there is a boat today nevertheless?'

'Well, there always are clever heads who find a new one each time.'

At nearly eight o'clock – in front of me there were still thirty to forty people – somebody called out, 'The English are coming!' People ran in all directions. I grabbed my bike and dashed through the bushes along the river bank. Let's get away as fast as possible, so they don't catch me,

I thought. In dense bushes covered with nettles I first hid my bike, then crept in myself. From afar one heard shouts and curses. That lasted for quite a while, then the noise seemed to move away. I was already starting to creep out of my hiding place, when quite nearby the bushes were crackling. I bent down and stopped breathing. With a genuine Prussian 'Nah, do get out of there!' a man bent the greenery apart: a German auxiliary policeman. 'Come on, come with me!' He gave the order in the tones of yesterday.

'What do you want of me?'

'Don't talk so stupidly; you know full well that the English have forbidden the secret crossing of the Elbe. Now you have to take the consequences and wait in a refugee camp until orderly conditions have returned!' That's just what I need, I thought. Out of the camp and back in again!

My voice started shaking with fury. 'Did you suggest to the English to look for the people here in the bushes?' Dear God, if he had had a rubber truncheon I would have caught it.

A second one joined him. 'Why do you get so excited? We are acting according to the orders of the occupying forces. If it were our decision, we wouldn't prevent anybody from crossing the Elbe. Don't make our work more difficult.'

As my last attempt failed to convince the two that I, as a former 'KZ'-ler, should at least be left in peace, I gave up. Burnt by the nettles on calves and hands, and with a red face, I arrived as one of the last between the two policemen at the edge of the meadow. There they were already loading the people on to two trucks. I was astonished that nobody defended himself. At a distance stood British soldiers and an officer. They wanted to put me in a camp? Barbed wire, barracks, guards, commands? I threw the bike on to the grass and ran to the officer. 'Sir, after seven years of concentration camp you can get me to a refugee camp only by force. Here is my document of release. Do let me go back to town.'

He glanced at the paper. 'You can go.' A little further on in the ditch my nerves gave out. I had to throw up.

'Miss, do you perhaps know where here in Lauenburg one could find a place to stay?' I asked the first human being I met as – leaning on the bike – I walked back into town. Her lips were painted red like fire, her eyebrows pencilled and she wore a bright spring dress.

'That will be difficult,' she said in broad East Prussian. 'We also are refugees and live down there in the wooden shack near the canal.' She pointed to a run-down shed. I had already said 'thank you' and wanted to walk on, when she stepped closer to me and looked searchingly into my face. 'Do you realise that I know you?'

'That can hardly be true, I look like many other people.'

'No, I can't be wrong, I know exactly who you are.' But then she hesitated. I thought I had met one of the peculiar people who, from a need to talk, meet 'old acquaintances' everywhere.

'But from where do you know me? When did you see me?'

'1940 and 1941.'

'That's impossible, then I wasn't . . .' I almost said 'in Germany'. 'I wasn't here at all!' What silly talk. I was annoyed.

'But you were our Room Elder [*Stubenälteste*] in Ravensbrück in Block 2 with the Asocials!' Was she ashamed or did she pretend to be? She appeared to be blushing under her make-up.

'Yes, that's true, I was Room Elder there for two months. How long were you in Ravensbrück?'

'Until 1941. Then I was released and immediately conscripted for service. Later, we had to flee here from East Prussia from the Russians.' She rummaged eagerly in her bag for cigarettes. They were English.

'Now we can smoke as many cigarettes as we want, can't we? No longer do we get twenty-five lashes. Dear God, when I think of it! And the SS bitches!' She laughed and offered me a cigarette. Her fingernails were carefully manicured and painted a glaring red. 'Where do you want to go now?'

'First across the Elbe and then to Bavaria to find my mother. If only I were already on the other side of the river.' I told her about my experience with the auxiliary policeman and she demonstrated her disdain for this kind of man with a few juicy curses.

'Do you know, the English are so decent, they certainly wouldn't do such a thing. The Americans also were not bad, but the English are more refined. Really noble people, I tell you.' So she was content with her new customers. I threw the cigarette stub into the canal and wanted to say goodbye. 'That is out of the question! Now you naturally have to stay with me. How ever could I leave my former "*Stubenälteste*" standing in the street? Naturally, our emergency flat isn't as nice as we used to have it at home, but a place for sleeping can be found. My mother will be surprised when I arrive with an old acquaintance from Ravensbrück.' Without waiting for my consent she grabbed the bike, turned round and led me down a small hill to the bank of the canal, through a devastated industrial area, past bombed-out warehouses, idle cranes and inactive tugboats. The shed had two rooms that were separated by a small corridor. In each room lived a family. My East Prussians were six persons, the others were five. It stank of floor rags and boiled potatoes.

When the mother heard of our old acquaintance, she became quite

effusive. 'Do sit down, miss, food will be ready in a moment. Only potatoes with sauce. If I had known . . .' She had wrapped an old faded
dressing gown round her abundance. She resembled her daughter: the
same broad farmer's face that, however, was much changed by age. The
cheeks had dropped, the nose was swollen and shapeless. But on to her
forehead fell carefully curled and, as it seemed to me, even dyed strands.
Then there was a father, who claimed to have been a carpenter. In addition, there were also two younger brothers and an older sister. The
brothers collected cigarette stubs for their father's pipe and in addition
brought home free potatoes, wood and coal. The two sisters provided
the family with English tins, cigarettes and many other good things that
could be found in the British Army. Even coffee was available. I soon
noticed that in this family there was no refugee atmosphere. They
possessed the admirable adaptability of the asocials. I observed with
amusement that they had beautified even their temporary housing. On
the wooden walls they had stuck with pins colourful postcards and pictures
cut out of journals, the mirror in the corner was framed by paper flowers
and beneath it, on an upended wooden box, rested powder boxes and
curlers.

'You have made yourself quite comfortable here,' I said approvingly.

'Yes, one does what one can. But I can't think back to our beautiful
flat in Königsberg or I'd start crying.' She sniffled and wiped her eyes.
Wide awake and interested, she then asked me if I had already received
ration cards for Lauenburg. I said no. 'Lieselotte, do go with the lady
immediately to the municipality so that they give her some. That would
be laughable. You have the right to a double ration!' I was silently
amazed. 'Lieselotte, of course, has already demanded the addition. All
who were in a KZ have that right. It was announced on the radio.'

Lieselotte obtained ration cards for me with ease. 'This is my comrade
from the concentration camp,' she introduced me. With the help of my
document of discharge she visibly rose in the esteem of the officials.

After we returned to the shed, the entire family deliberated how I
might cross the Elbe in the safest way. 'If you go out into the street
during curfew, it makes no difference if they catch you at two or at four
o'clock. We will wake you up tomorrow at half-past one, and then get
you down to the shore so that you are the first.'

That naturally made sense to me. 'But if the British arrest me for a
second time, what then?'

The father joined in: 'Yes, miss, you have to risk it. Nothing dared
nothing won . . .' Then they started telling stories about arrests by the
English, about confiscated boats and shootings. Obviously they were not
especially good psychologists.

In the evening six straw sacks were laid on the floor. Lieselotte let me have hers and slept with her sister. It was still quite dark when the mother woke me. She had made coffee and smeared many slices of bread. 'You have to take something for the road. You never know how things might turn out.' Then she even put a small bag of tobacco and cigarette papers into my hand. Dawn broke just as I – after saying friendly goodbyes – left the shed and rode over the cobblestone pavement. If only the damn bike didn't make such a racket, I thought. Then I crossed the dyke and arrived down at the meadows covered by a light fog. As soon as I reached the bushes at the bank, nothing more could happen. I found yesterday's place: not a single human being, but also no boat. On the opposite bank something dark appeared to lie. Was it perhaps a boat? But what help would that be? I looked around me at a loss. It was absolutely quiet. Even the water streamed noiselessly. Should I swim across? Yes, that would be possible. But it would mean leaving my bike and everything else.

Then there was a rustle in the bushes. I was afraid. Oh God, it was certainly the police. A young man, his bike next to him, came out of the bushes with a friendly 'Good morning. So I am the second. But where is the boat? The British have pushed it to the other side. A bad business.' We smoked a cigarette, thinking hard. By that time a third person turned up. He, like the other, had spent the night in the bushes. Both men were soldiers, who wanted to escape in order to avoid becoming prisoners of war. 'Well, there is only one solution. We two swim over to the other side and you in the meantime watch our belongings – agreed?'

Slowly the heads of the swimmers moved away. The current was very strong. I saw how they were being pulled further away all the time. I hoped nothing would happen to them. The water was still very cold. They reached the opposite bank a few hundred metres downriver. Then I saw them do something to the boat. Nearly an hour had passed and they hadn't returned. What could have happened? Then I noticed a third man. They were running back and forth. At long last the boat started to move away from the bank. As they came nearer I noticed that all three were holding wooden slats in their hands and paddling strenuously in order to move forward. The British had thrown the oars into the water and the current had carried them away. Therefore the swimmers had first to ask in the nearest farm for a few bits of wood. The third man was an 'Ostarbeiter', a Pole, and he offered to help us. Three bikes and four persons was not an easy load for the boat. 'So, miss, here is your piece of wood. Now you really have to help us, otherwise things with go wrong!' One could handle the 'oars' only while standing. The water moved along the boat just a few centimetres beneath the edge of the boat. The current made me dizzy, I was afraid I'd lose my balance at any moment. We had reached the middle of the river when the boat started spinning round and round. 'Harder, miss, harder, don't give up!' A blow missed and a spray of water drenched everybody. Thank God they laughed. And then we overcame the current and were approaching the safe shore. Arrived there, I pulled out my little bag of tobacco, thanked the '*Ostarbeiter*' for his help and wanted to give it to him as a present. Full of indignation he refused: 'I didn't help expecting payment. You need that yourself.' On landing I cycled speedily down the dyke and on to the high road in the direction of Celle. I had done it! No obstacle remained and, overflowing with joy, I tried to ride with no hands. Now at last I was free altogether, entirely my own master.

COMING HOME

A Dramatic Report

The highway led through the Lüneburger Heath. Birch trees, crooked pines and boggy ditches lined the road. A hundred metres from the road the wilderness with rushes and rustling swamp grass began. On the sandy hills the broom flowered golden and the wood larks sang as though their throats would burst. On this road to Celle I didn't meet anyone for kilometres on end. The stream of refugees had been blocked on the other side of the Elbe. All alone, obsessed with going on, this first day away from the crowds was sheer joy.

Towards midday I started to feel hungry and turned into a side road where a signpost promised a village nearby. In front of me were spread out beautiful wide houses with their huge thatch-covered roofs, and as I tried to decide which would be the friendliest, I noticed a large sign made of cardboard fastened to the gate of a yard. Reading it set me trembling: 'Here looting is forbidden. This farmer has saved the life of a Jew!' Without thinking twice I opened the door and found myself in the large cool entrance hall. A short young man approached me from the back and asked in peculiar German, 'What do you want?' I requested, as so many times before, something warm to eat or drink. The man confused me completely. This must be the Jew whose life had been saved. Surely he was a 'KZ'ler, with his short hair and peculiar looks? 'Do wait here, I go to the farmer's wife.' I heard voices and the clatter of dishes. Then the door opened and he cried, 'Do come in, we are just eating!'

In the kitchen sat the farmer, his wife and a girl. The dark-eyed young man offered me a chair as if he were the master of the house. In silence, they spooned sour milk from a large bowl. Then the farmer's wife looked up in a friendly way and encouraged me, nodding. A spoon lay in front of me, as well as a heap of steaming boiled potatoes, which I started to peel with the handle of the spoon as the others were doing. I had one single wish: that they should start a conversation in order to put an end

to my embarrassment. I totally forgot that farmers do not speak while
they eat. To my great relief the young man at last broke the silence:
'Where are you coming from?' I told them about my successful crossing
of the Elbe. Then he wanted to know where I was from. I had hardly
uttered 'KZ' before he almost embraced me. 'Farmer, here you see a
colleague of mine. From Ravensbrück! Oh, how nice! How do you
happen to come to our village?' I replied with another question: 'And
what are you doing here? I read the notice on the gate. How was all
this possible?'

The farmer's wife led me into another room, treating me like a distin-
guished guest. She put coffee cups with golden rims on the oval table
and ran excitedly back and forth. My KZ colleague didn't stopped talking
even for a minute. He wanted to know everything about Ravensbrück.
Again and again he turned to the master of the house: 'Do you see,
farmer, that's how the "KZ"-lers are. Innocent people! Are you hearing
it? Women, thousands of young women did they treat worse than animals.'
The farmer only nodded and looked away.

At long last I got B to tell his own story. When I heard that his time
of suffering started in Poland, my first question was, 'How was it possible
for you to survive?' 'I lived from one watch to the other.' 'What has
that to do with watches?' 'It was like that. After the first "*Aktion*" at
our place in Poland, when the Germans started to drag away the Jews
– that was in the winter of 1941–2 – we consulted with our father and
mother how one could save one's life. They thought that we big ones,
my sister and I, should enter a labour camp of the SS voluntarily, as we
had learnt a decent trade – I am actually a watchmaker and my sister is
a dressmaker. We travelled to Kraków. Everywhere we heard that the
lives of Jews were in danger. So we didn't hesitate any longer. When
saying goodbye my sister said, "When the war is over and if we survive,
I will wait for you in the flat of our aunt here in Kraków. Don't forget!"
Soon I noticed that even in the labour camp one wasn't safe from being
killed. One "selection" followed the other. I had registered immediately
as a watchmaker and already during the first few days an SS man gave
me his watch with the order to repair it as quickly as possible. Then it
became clear to me that as long as I hadn't finished repairing his watch,
my life was safe; there was no chance that I'd be sent on transport. And
I managed to arrange things so I always got a new watch for repair
before the last one was finished. The SS men always had watches that
didn't work. So I lived for more than two years from one watch to the
other. I was sent into a work commando, then into a proper concentration camp and my life all the time depended on a watch. But once – it
was at the end of 1944 – things after all went wrong. A *capo* ordered

me to repair his watch. He wanted to pay me with a slice of bread. I
didn't dare to say no and tried to repair it secretly in the workshop, but
a fellow prisoner had listened to the conversation and he threatened to
tell the SS about me if I didn't give him the watch. I begged and pleaded
with him not to inform about me. I couldn't give him the watch, the
capo simply would have killed me. All was in vain. He reported me and
I was put in the punishment unit. There things deteriorated with great
speed. Soon I was a "Muselmann" and went on transport to Bergen-
Belsen. With this, my fate should have been sealed, but despite all, it
turned out differently.'

As B talked he groaned and gesticulated as though he were living
through all the horror once more. His forehead was covered with sweat
and his eyes were bloodshot. 'In Bergen-Belsen they put together a transport for clearing work in Hamburg. They needed one thousand men.
About five thousand applied. All wanted out of this hell, each of them
wanted to be among the one thousand chosen. The prisoners hit each
other on the head with sticks to get to the front. Using all my might
and skill I crept between the legs of the fighting men and succeeded: I
belonged to the thousand and once more I was safe.

'In Hamburg it was very good. We got bread, worked in a shipyard
and the people treated us in a friendly way. After a few weeks the rumour
went around that we should be returned to Bergen-Belsen. It was clear
to all that this would be the end. Without quite understanding why I
did it, I stole at my place of work a pair of civilian pants, a jacket and
a cap. For any emergency that might come up I also took a pair of
tongs. I can't even say if I had planned the escape. I simply took the
chance. When we were put in the freight car and the others were sitting
on the floor, entirely dull and desperate, I tested first the two doors of
the wagon to see if perhaps something could be done there. The SS
guards couldn't see us, as they were posted outside the wagon in the
brake man's hut. Unfortunately the doors proved to be locked too well.
Above, just under the roof, there was a small window, which interested
me. The screws that held the grille were all rusted. I had to deal with
six of them. I pulled myself up with the left hand at the crossbeam of
the side wall and worked at the screws with the tongs. At first it looked
hopeless, and I was ready to give up. Then one started to move. With
redoubled strength I turned and rattled on. Again and again my arm
gave out and I had to take a break. None of the others appeared even
to notice my dangerous activity. After I had removed four screws a
Russian prisoner asked me, whispering, if I intended to flee. "You take
me and my comrade too?" I nodded. From then on things progressed
with lightning speed. One of the Russians supported me from below.

The grille came off. I pushed out my head. It was pitch dark. As agreed, I first threw out both wooden shoes and listened. Everything remained silent. Then followed my bundle with the civilian clothes, I jumped out of the slow train and rolled down the embankment. Immediately after me came the Russians. Nothing moved. As soon as the tail-lights of the train had disappeared I stood up and took a deep breath. The Russians came and we looked in the dark for quite a while for our precious wooden shoes and the clothes bundles until we had found everything. I quickly put on the civilian clothes over my camp rags and suggested to the Russians to turn their jackets inside out so they wouldn't be recognised at once as 'KZ'-lers. We were done and I asked my two comrades to disappear quickly into the safe forest. Then one of them turned to me and said, "You Jew, we not go with you!" That hurt! But we are used to it.'

B stopped and wiped the sweat off his forehead. The farmer's wife, who had listened all the time as if turned to stone, quickly left the room. Only now did I notice that the tears were running down my face.

'So I walked alone for many kilometres on paths, over meadows and fields. When dawn was breaking I saw from the edge of the forest – and I didn't want to believe my eyes – the outlines of the so familiar one-storey barracks which, however, were not surrounded by barbed wire but by a simple fence. It was a camp for free "*Ostarbeiters*". I had an idea. Work and food I could get from a farmer if I could pretend to be an "*Ostarbeiter*", but a place for sleeping nobody would give me. So I decided in the evening in the dark to try to climb over the fence into the camp and to sleep there. On the other side of the forest there was a village. I knocked at a door, said that I was an "*Ostarbeiter*" and if perhaps they had wood that needed chopping. They did. But a place for sleeping, even only in the barn, to this they didn't agree. It was early in the morning when I started with the wood chopping. Due to hunger I could hardly stand any more on my feet. I thought all the time, if only they had pity on me and gave me something to eat. I couldn't think about anything else and when the housewife called "come in for break-fast," I forgot all caution.

'I ran more than walked and was just about to politely remove the cap from my head entering the kitchen. At the last moment I remembered. Then – woe is me – the shaved line running down the middle of the head would immediately have given me away as an escaped "KZ-ler". In order to correct this mistake, I then ate the dark bread in small pieces and very slowly, as if this breakfast was the most natural thing in the world and not the first bite for somebody half starved. Very gratefully – it really can be said – I worked until midday, but then it nearly happened.

The farmer's wife put a big bowl full of vegetables and potatoes in the middle of the table. As I had never eaten from a plate in Germany, as we do in Poland, but only always out of tin bowls, I assumed that the farmers in Germany have the same customs. This bowl was twice as big as those I was used to, but anyway I was among free Germans. Without thinking much, I took it, pulled it to me and wanted to start to eating. With the spoon moving towards my mouth I stopped, seeing the astonished eyes of the farmers, and pushed the bowl back into the middle of the table with an embarrassed smile. Nobody said anything and then all dipped their spoons into the common bowl.

'Evening came and I left behind me a mountain of chopped wood. The farmer hummed contentedly, I could return tomorrow morning. I hesitatingly walked through the forest towards the camp. It was already completely dark and I climbed over the fence and sat down in the first barracks behind an open window. Pulling up my knees under my chin, I spent the first night sleeping. Quite early in the morning I crept out again, crossed the fence without any obstacle and walked through the forest to the farmer. For two nights everything went well, but in the third there was an air-raid warning. "Lights out!" shouted the guards and one of them went checking with his flashlight through the barracks. He arrived at the door behind which I sat trembling and shone light on my toes that were visible under the door. Then it had happened. They grabbed me, pulled the cap off my head and saw the treacherous shaved line. "Where have you come from, Jewish pig? Aha, run away!" They hit me in the face. I noticed nothing more, knew only that finally I had lost. When the air-raid warning came to an end, one of them brought me to the police. Now, this is the last night, I thought.

'In the morning they had phoned Bergen-Belsen and the order came to bring me there, because from the Hamburg transport several had escaped, for whom they were still searching. In the afternoon I was driven away by two policemen in a car. In a small place they had to stop because again there was an air-raid warning. They brought me to the mayor's office. As the "All Clear" came only hours later, we spent the night in a room there. I was ordered to sit in the back of the room on the floor. One policeman sat at the table with his back to the wall, the other on a bench opposite him. It was absolutely quiet in the room. I must have fallen asleep as I suddenly sat up, scared. The policemen snored; they had laid their heads on the table. Just by accident I looked at the door.

'Slowly I rose and stared. The key was in the lock, they had forgotten to pull it out. What happened then was no longer done by myself, it was somebody who used his last chance to stay alive. Between the back of one of the policemen and the wall, there was a space perhaps not even twenty centimetres wide. Silently I squeezed myself through, with the shoes under the arm. The policemen snored. Two steps away I stopped and said tonelessly, "I have to go." The policemen snored. Then I was at the door. Noiselessly the key was turned. I pulled it out, pushed down the handle. My heart stopped beating and my breathing didn't work either. Nothing made a noise. I succeeded in closing the door, groped the key into the lock and turned it. While pulling it out my courage suddenly disappeared. I left it there. There was a long corridor. I found the front door and ran through dark streets, over open ground, a forest and only then did I suddenly collapse. My body trembled as if with St Vitus's dance. Foam covered my mouth and I lost consciousness. How long that lasted I don't know. When I awoke in the morning, I was lying in the forest hidden deep in the bushes . . .

'I believe they didn't find me because I remained quite close to the village. Something like that they probably couldn't imagine. In the very next village I knocked on a door and it was the door of this house here, in which we are sitting now. My salvation was that the farmer let me sleep in his barn. I hid the prisoner's stuff, which I was wearing under my civilian clothes, in the hay carefully. Now it was the beginning of April and one wasn't cold any longer. I chopped wood and waited for the friendly invitation to the meals. I never left the farm even by one step. After several days somebody entered the gate, coming straight towards me: an SS man. I put the axe down and expected to be hit in the face. "How long are you working here already?" he asked me. "Nearly a week," I answered. "Where is your farmer?" I pointed with my hand towards the house. "When you have finished today, come to me for chopping, understood?" he said when leaving. Luckily this didn't work out as the farmer refused to let me go.

'In the village there also were prisoners of war. On 12 April a Frenchman came jumping into the yard and shouted excitedly, "Come quickly! The English are here!" I followed him slowly. Tanks were driving along the village street. But what did this actually mean? I didn't understand, what this should have to do with me. But two days later, on the 14th, again there were tanks on the square in front of the house. There also stood a little boy, who had a swastika made of metal on his cap. A French prisoner of war pulled it off, broke it and threw it to the ground. Then the blood shot to my head and I knew: now the time has come! That is the end of the horrors. Now you are allowed to live. On this 14 April 1945 I was born a second time. I danced and sang our songs. Then I ran to the farmer, took off my cap and showed him the shaved line. "Farmer," I called, "do you know that I am a Jew and fled from Bergen-Belsen?" Then our old one said simply, "So, I thought so immediately, that something with you was not in order. Now we do not have to be afraid any more." But I thought differently. I assumed that now the Germans would be dealt with, now those from Bergen-Belsen would come, would loot and set fire to everything. Therefore I wrote the note that you have read outside. In the meantime I know that this had not been necessary at all. Of the Bergen-Belseners nobody has taken revenge, they must have been too near the end, they simply lacked the strength . . .'

Five years later I happened to meet B once more. I was waiting at Tempelhof Airport to fly from Berlin to Frankfurt. Among my fellow travellers was a face that reminded me of somebody. I was sure that I knew this man. Our plane was already one hour late starting because of fog. Whereas the rest of the passengers sat bored in the big hall, that young man was walking back and forth restlessly, going again and again to the information desk as if any lost minute were important to him. An official entered the hall and immediately he ran up to him and I recognised B's voice.

Then, in June 1945, he felt strong enough to travel home. But for him it wasn't as straightforward as for us Germans. His route led through the now opened concentration camps, where he enquired after his relatives. He asked the freed prisoners and searched in the leftover card indexes to see if their names appeared anywhere. Finally in Gross-Rosen he succeeded. He found the name of his sister and heard that she was supposed to have survived the horrors. Full of new hope, he set off towards his Polish home town. Nobody was there and nobody knew anything about the fate of his family. Almost in despair, he remembered Kraków and the words of his sister back then at the last goodbye in the spring of 1942. She was indeed there and she was waiting for him. 'Only the two of us are left of the entire family, all our relatives were gassed.' So ended the description of his homecoming.

Then I wanted to know where he was living and heard to my great astonishment that B had settled in West Berlin. He showed me photos of his wife with his one-year-old son and, with special pride, pictures of his shop. Above the shop window was displayed a much too large sign, 'WATCHES', and beneath it his name. I couldn't understand why he had chosen Germany, the country that had inflicted such horrors on him. I asked why he hadn't gone to Palestine. He answered, shortly and dismissively, that he didn't belong there, that he was no farmer, he had other tasks. As I went on suggesting that he choose another country as homeland, should not remain in Germany since one couldn't know whether some day there wouldn't be another war, he offered me the following shocking explanation: 'Don't you know that for us Jews it doesn't matter where we live? They can catch us anywhere. If the Russians should occupy all of Berlin, if there were war again, we should certainly be sent to a KZ, this time perhaps to Siberia. One can't escape one's fate. But one thing I have to tell you. Despite everything, my life has been worthwhile.' With this sentence his eyes lit up and I, quite moved, thought how good it was that he was so happy with his wife and his little boy. Then his voice became solemn: 'You have to know that I have made an invention. And what an invention! It has already been patented in four countries. Nobody can take this from me any more. This will remain even if I should be liquidated . . .'

We sat next to each other on the aeroplane and he tried to explain to me, with the help of his watch, this amazing invention. He was quite in love with his work. Then he talked of the future: 'But that is not everything, I have four more inventions in my head. I wish only one thing with all my heart: to have a few years of freedom and life to be able to work out also these inventions and to realise them.'

. . . As If Nothing Had Happened

The sun was sinking when on the highway to Celle I arrived at a sign-post. I turned. After a few minutes the path became a straight avenue lined with chestnut trees that led to an estate. There I planned to spend the night. From the stables the clutter of pails and the friendly mooing of cattle could be heard. A door to a kind of kitchen stood open facing the yard. I leant the bike on a tree and approached. Several women were busy pouring milk through cloths into the pails. In the back of the room a centrifuge hummed. Suddenly I had a craving for milk still warm from the cow. 'May I have a place to sleep for the night – here on the estate?' Nobody answered. I repeated my question in a friendly way – perhaps they hadn't heard. 'Please wait until madam comes. She decides things,' said one woman with a half-turned-away face, as if she wanted to prove that the importance of her activity didn't even allow her to lift her head. I swallowed my anger and turned briskly towards the yard, walking past the large stables that testified to the wealth of this place and noticing the carefully layered dung heaps that revealed the exemplary order that reigned here. I opened a garden door that led to a park and stepped hesitantly on to a path covered with reddish gravel. Between the trunks of old trees I caught glimpses of the wide façade of the manor house. From there voices could be heard. The path led to a square full of flower beds. Round a laid garden table a group of people sat in the friendly evening sun. I remained standing in the shadow of the trees in order to enjoy this beautiful colourful picture of prosperity and peace: bright summer dresses, well-dressed young men, a well-preserved old man and at his feet a shining black-and-white mastiff. They laughed loudly and carelessly. With my next steps the gravel crunched, the mastiff raised its head and started to growl. Someone examined me, slightly amazed and a bit bored. The old man held back the dog. To my question concerning the possibility of spending the night I again was referred to the 'Gnädiges Fräulein'. As I turned away to wait somewhere in the park, the old man asked me, 'Where have you come from? What's that peculiar badge you have on your blouse?' (B had advised me to sew the red cloth triangle of the political 'KZ'-lers to the blouse for safety's sake.) I explained this to the old one. His face revealed shock, but before he could say anything, one of the young men asked, 'Do tell me, was it really as bad in the camps as now is being claimed everywhere? The millions of gassed people certainly are an invention of the Americans! You, anyway, seem to have got through quite well.'

And there I stood emaciated, in rags, covered by dust, and I wished for nothing so much as the strength to punch this presumptuous impudent creature's face. A previously unknown hatred took control of me and gave me words that I hadn't been capable of until then. I wanted to know from those sitting round the table whether they knew of Bergen-Belsen, the extermination camp that was situated less than ten kilometres away from their idyllically untouched home. Whether, perhaps, they had heard this name? I regretted that the opportunity had been missed to sit for a day and a night in front of the heaps of dead bodies rotting in Bergen-Belsen unburied when the Allied troops freed the camps, all those who wanted to turn the crimes of the KZs, the millions killed, into a horror story.

In a white shirt, riding breeches and boots the 'Gnädiges Fräulein' came into the garden. The company turned to her vivaciously, visibly relieved at this interruption. The old one asked his daughter, as it were in my name, for a lodging for the night. She addressed her answer to me: 'In the house we have nothing available, but you can sleep in the barn.' The old one wanted to object, but his daughter shut him up brusquely: 'Who is responsible for the management, you or I? I am fed up with being disturbed all the time.' Silence. I let them show me the barn and when we arrived in the farmyard I asked the manageress if she would sell me half a litre of milk.

'No,' was the answer, 'we are not allowed to, the milk is rationed.'

Immediately behind the servants' quarters a small river flowed through willows and dense alder bushes. There the air was cool and

filled with a strong bog smell. Through the shallow clear water I could
see the rust-coloured pebbles on the bottom. I sat on the wooden
step made for the laundresses and rinsed off the dust of the road.
This was so refreshing that slowly my anger was soothed. Then, when
I waded into the river up to my knees and the slow-flowing soft water
caressed my skin, I started to enjoy life again. Lost in this game, I
didn't notice that from the steps of the servants' house somebody
called me. On the way back to the barn an old woman waited on the
path and talked to me in broken German: 'She didn't sell you any
milk? The devil! I heard what she said to you, she is as bad as the
night. But do come to us. We have little, but always enough for somebody else to eat with us.'

So I was the guest of Ukrainian forced labourers. That evening I was
miserable to hear that for these victims of the Hitler regime nothing
had changed since the end of the horror. Day by day they did the same
hard labour, received the same poor food and hunger wages of the past
four years. I couldn't understand why they didn't rebel and make
demands. They were no longer in danger, as SS and 'Gestapo' power
had ended for good. They answered evasively and appeared depressed.
Only when the conversation turned to Soviet Russia and I told them
my story did they start to open up. Day and night they were afraid that
they would be forced to return to their homeland. 'Is it true that the
Western Allies collaborate with the Russian repatriation commissions?'
Would they be brought back by force to the Ukraine? They would prefer
to continue this dog's life here. Absolutely convinced of this, I started
to explain to them that the Western Allies in their area of occupation
would never permit kidnapping (for these repatriations were nothing
less). So I succeeded in calming down these despairing folk. At that
time I didn't foresee what, shortly afterwards, would overtake these
hunted people.

It was pitch dark and oppressively hot as one of them showed me,
with the help of a flashlight, the way to the barn. The big wooden gate
shut creakingly. For a while the hay rustled with my movements. Then
it became quiet. When my ear got used to the silence, I suddenly perceived
mysterious noises as I listened in the impenetrable darkness. From all
ends and corners I noticed rustling and low whistling. I tried to differentiate between rats, mice or bats, or did they give this strange concert
together? Let them . . . I felt comfortable in their company. How good
it was to be alone, all by myself, even in this dirty barn and no longer
with hundreds of women cooped up in one barracks. With the happy
feeling of being free I fell asleep . . . A roaring and rushing awoke me
from my beautiful dreams. A cloudburst was coming down and the rain

battered the big roof. I could think no more of falling asleep, for I was
tortured by an unbearable pain in my feet, as if all the bones had become
inflamed.

In the morning my ankles were swollen and walking was sheer torture;
much worse was cycling. In Celle they told me this was tendovaginitis,
which would heal only with total rest. Rest! No, that would have to come
later. First the end of the road must be reached. Impossible to interrupt
my journey when there were no more obstacles to overcome. I wrapped
a handkerchief tightly around each ankle and continued with crunching
tendons. It is a miracle what regained freedom makes the human being
capable of. One's strength is doubled and illness ignored. I rode slowly,
very slowly, in the direction of Hanover. The weather was murky and
added to my tiredness. Suddenly I was startled. From somewhere I heard
'Hello!' A woman in a ditch was waving. I got off the bike and she ran
towards me. Then I noticed that she wore the field-grey uniform of the
female SS guards.

Breathlessly she said, 'Can't you remember me? I am "Shenja"? That's
what the Polish women called me in Ravensbrück. Weren't you also once
in the Forest unit [*Waldkolonne*]? Aren't you called Grete?' She didn't
give me a chance to answer, pointed at her infected swollen face. 'Naturally,
I looked different then. But after such a long time in the Bunker I got
facial erysipelas and had to go to hospital in Schwerin.' Her voice trembled with suppressed tears.

'Yes, of course, now I remember! Didn't they then send you to the
Bunker because you had smuggled letters for Polish prisoners to their
relatives? And later on, didn't one prisoner from your unit flee? Wasn't
it like that?'

She nodded, in tears. 'Yes, exactly so. I sat in the Bunker until the
entire Ravensbrück camp was evacuated five weeks ago. Only then did
they let me out. What will become of me now? In Ulm, where I am at
home, they will immediately arrest me as a former concentration camp
guard.' She started to weep.

'But what are you thinking of? Why should they arrest you? Haven't
you helped so many prisoners and didn't you sit in prison month after
month because of your decency?' I tried to soothe her.

'Who would believe that?' she argued in a hopeless voice.

I sat next to 'Shenja' at the edge of the forest, wrote down the
addresses of former prisoners and advised her to write to them as soon
as the mails worked again. I also gave her my own address in Thierstein.
'But first of all, Shenja, you have to get different clothes. How can you
still run about in an SS uniform? You risk being beaten up or even
killed.'

'Maybe you're right, but I haven't thought of that at all because I didn't have a bad conscience. I didn't do anything bad to anybody.'

Gomorrha 1945

In Hanover I saw the first devastated large city. I pushed the bicycle over torn streets covered with pieces of broken glass. For kilometres on both sides there was nothing but the gaping holes of the ruins, remnants of factories with their bizarrely twisted iron frames. In this devastated city it was no longer spring. Even the sun shone yellow and evil, its brightness veiled by the dirty grey clouds of dust that the wind drove forward. Many people walked through the streets without houses and I asked myself, astonished, where they might all be living, where they came from and where they were going. Slowly I proceeded to the centre of the town and found there a welfare office for former 'KZ'-ers. The room was filled with the unrestrained crying of several gipsy women. They were searching for their husbands and sons. Words of consolation were no help: 'You surely will find them again . . .' Nobody believed it. There they stood, the freed, and had only one topic of conversation: 'Who were your comrades?' 'Did so-and-so survive?' 'When did they stop at your place to gas people?' 'Where you were, did they also shoot people in the end?' I listened to the conversation between two young men. The topic was women. 'For me the only possible one would be a former "KZ"-erin! Could you imagine marrying somebody else? What could we talk about? Only one who has gone through the same things could understand.'

As a person passing through I received money, coupons and a pack of cigarettes. In this devastated city, even for 'KZ'-ers there was no place to stay overnight. They recommended the bunker of the railway station for sleeping. I learnt that in Hanover there was an office of the International Red Cross and made my way there, full of hope now to be able at long last to write to my children in Palestine and let them know that I was still alive. In Mecklenburg I had made the first attempt to send a sign of life abroad. On the highway I talked to an American soldier who looked Jewish, described my situation to him and asked him to send a message to Jerusalem, as Germans could not use the mails. Almost a year later I was to learn that the soldier had carried out my request. It was different with my second attempt at the International Red Cross, where my request was rejected as presumptuous. KZ here, KZ there, a German had no right to use the services of this international aid organisation. 'If you have waited for so many years without sending your children a message, you can be patient somewhat longer,' were the parting words of the person behind the counter.

Later I stood in front of the remnants of the pompous central railway station of Hanover. The rain came pouring down. In the large forecourt, surrounded by fields of ruins and with asphalt scarred by the impact of fire-bombs, rose the lonely equestrian statue of King Ernst August as last witness of former splendour. The rainwater ran down in greenish rivulets over horse and rider, and only with an effort was one still able to decipher the writing at the bottom of the monument: 'To the father of the country from his grateful people.' I burst into tortured laughter. In those parts of the station – the waiting rooms, platforms and halls – whose roofs had resisted the bombs crowded a mass of refugees. Apathetic, grey, with wasted faces, they squatted anywhere or moved with slow mechanical steps as if dazed. Somewhere loud noises could be heard, mainly from young women showing off. I found it frightening to see how very chaotic times change the faces and the entire behaviour of women. The expressions and gestures of many seemed brutal and provocative, and not a few reminded me of the women prisoners in Siberia. Is it because of the ruthless struggle for existence, or do dictatorships create such types?

I was shocked to see the improvised vehicles of the refugees, on which they transported their belongings. Four small rollers with a board nailed on top and the vehicle was ready. Those who owned two bicycle wheels were in better shape. Of course, proper baby carriages were in great demand, not to mention an actual bike. But where should I put my most valuable possession, the bicycle, if I wanted to spend the night in the bunker? How could I prevent it from being stolen? I was astonished and moved when I noticed that in the chaos of the devastated station, into which it rained front and back, where no train departed or arrived, the office for the storage of hand luggage was still working as if nothing had happened. A decent railwayman picked his way back and forth among the puddles of rainwater and patiently filled in numbered tickets, cashing money and guarding the deposited treasures. Sacred German order! The bunker of the train station was overcrowded; without the KZ document of discharge I would have had no chance to get in. All the straw pallets were occupied, but I found a space nevertheless at one of the long wooden tables. On the plank beds lay women and children. Here, too, one slept on bunk beds. Indeed it is among the achievements of the Nazi regime, just like the one-storey barracks, Hitler's 'Barackstil' as we called it in the KZ. In the dim lighting of the bunker room I looked around the table company I had joined for one night. Most of them were soldiers, older ones. A few were already asleep, heads resting on arms. Others conducted a low, monotonous conversation. I listened as the man sitting opposite me informed his comrade that he was from Mannheim-Viernheim. Hearing the name of this town, I was reminded of the last despairing words of Grete Sonntag: 'Never again will I see my father and my mother . . .' I turned to the soldier. 'Do you by any chance know a family Faltersleben in Viernheim?' (Faltersleben was the maiden name of Grete Sonntag, and Änne was her real first name.) The soldier replied in a friendly way: 'I certainly do. We are near neighbours.' 'Then perhaps you also know how Mr and Mrs Faltersleben are? Are they in good health? Do you know?' There came the astonished reply: 'Now, listen, if you know these people, don't you also know that the old one has been dead for several years? Anyway, why are you interested in the family? Are you from Viernheim?' 'No, I'm not, but I was together with Änne and I wanted to beg that when you get home you will tell Mrs Faltersleben what happened to her daughter.' Suddenly no trace of friendliness remained in the face of the soldier. He looked reserved and suspicious, so that I stopped feeling like talking. Then he started again: 'Änne, I have known Änne well and I also know how she is. Where exactly do you claim to have seen the girl? She hasn't been in Germany for over ten years; don't tell me any fairy tales.' 'No, that's not what I'm doing. I saw her for the last time in Siberia.' Then I told him about our time together in the camp. His face turned more disconsolate by the minute. As I finished he bent over the table and said in a bitter tone, 'And that happened to a loyal Communist like Änne? That's impossible. Perhaps the Nazis didn't lie when they wrote about such things in the newspapers, for instance about the show trials? And all those years we had thought that – thank God – at least Änne was safe. She's made it, she can live in a Socialist country. And how often have I wished also to have had such luck . . .'

By six in the morning I was already on my bike, shivering, riding on the highway that leads to Hildesheim. I was interested to see, on the walls along the route, Nazi slogans from the last years of the war, painted in white or black. '"*Volk*" to the Guns!' was written in huge letters, or 'Better Dead than Slaves!' Everywhere, sometimes even still on the advertising pillars from which rags of paper hung, a black figure threatened; at first I thought it was an advertisement for a detective novel until the subtitle 'The enemy is listening' put me right.

The Last Lap

Not half an hour had passed since I had left the outskirts of Hanover when a long-dreaded disaster occured. I had a flat tire and owned neither glue nor rubber. Far and wide there were no houses. It was only after a while that buildings could be seen in the distance – a lonely farm. Perhaps I could get help there. An old man, the owner of the farm, met my plea for the repair of the damage with a categorical question: 'What can you pay for it?' I offered money, which he turned down as an imposition. Then I offered my pack of cigarettes, whereupon he agreed haughtily. The son carried out the repair, the old man took the cigarettes. But when he noticed that two cigarettes in the pack were missing, although I had spoken about a full pack, he started shouting, outraged and full of indignation, and declared that the agreement didn't hold any longer. He even ordered his son to undo what he had already finished. I started begging and the farmer made new demands. Eventually the old villain got out of me a fountain pen, Inka's goodbye present when I left Ravensbrück.

In Hanover I had learnt that a train ran between Hildesheim and Göttingen. As a former 'KZ'-ler I received a ticket, so I succeeded in arriving in Göttingen on the same day. Late in the evening I was in a strange town without any street lighting. It was completely dark; no light could be seen from the road, even from the blocks of flats. The window panes broken during the bombardments had been replaced by cardboard or plywood. I faced the problem of where to stay overnight. A passer-by advised me to enquire at the police station. I went in, full of inhibitions. Behind a barrier sat an older officer. I got my document of discharge out of the bag and put it in front of him. Due to the continuous unfolding and refolding, the piece of paper had been torn and separated into four pieces. The policeman took the pieces, read them carefully line for line and looked at me from behind his glasses. Wagging his head and in tones of genuine fatherly indignation he rebuked me: 'How could you treat a document so carelessly! Don't you know that this document is worth gold?'

Flabbergasted, I searched for an apologising explanation. Suddenly I felt ten years old and had been reprimanded by a teacher because of untidy exercise books. And without realising, I stood up straight in front of the policeman, pressing my arms to my side, just like in Ravensbrück. For minutes I forgot that I was a free person. The friendly policeman fetched a large pot of glue, carefully chose a piece of pliable white cardboard, cut it fussily and stuck on to it the so carelessly destroyed valuable document. Then he wished me good luck in freedom and ordered a younger colleague to put me up in his apartment for the night. After this experience the auxiliary police had lost its terror for me, and until my final return home they proved to be excellent accommodation agents.

In imprisonment one forgets what life in freedom is like really. There remains only a vague picture. My own picture of longing was a forest path overgrown by grass, shaded by the leaves of early summer, on which gold-green patches of sunlight lay. During my ride through the Thüringer Wald, this dream turned into reality. Through the lovely valley my road followed the curves of a mountain stream. It was June and the meadows were strewn with flowers. Their glowing green contrasted with the dark background of mountain slopes covered by pines and fir trees. At one point the little stream flowed in a large curve away from the road and I crossed the fragrant meadow to the bushes along its bank. The bushes formed niches where one could hide so as not to be seen from the road, and a flat rock formed an ideal bathing spot. Both banks were so densely overgrown by trees and bushes that the stream remained in deep shadow. Its rushing swallowed up all other noises. Over rounded rocks the water shot in little falls, creating currents and cascades, and dark whirlpools towards the bank. Carefully I let myself slide in, holding on with both hands to a rock, and let the stream pull away my body. In the cold water, the joy of my own body returned to me, that simple joy of life that I had long forgotten.

It was late afternoon when I pushed my bike slowly uphill. Once again the tyres worried me and I stopped to examine them. At this point a biker jumped off his machine next to me and enquired in a friendly way whether by any chance I had a flat tyre. We started talking and he told me that he was coming home from a successful foraging excursion that had yielded two bottles of home-distilled gin. One word followed another and then we sat laughing at the side of the road and tasted his laboriously acquired treasures. In front of us at a turn of the valley rose a shattered viaduct. My friendly host was a builder of bridges and, with much astonishment, I gathered from his increasingly excited stream of words that he was convinced great times were now beginning for him. In his imagination he saw all the destroyed bridges rising in their old splendour. He himself would rebuild many of them, and that would be the big chance of his life. At the side of the road in the evening sun he gushed on about scaffolding and filigree columns, and about planning and installing, and made fun of all those who lamented at the sight of so many destroyed bridges. It was not the future business that inspired him, however, but rather the prospect of a never-ending wealth of projects. When saying goodbye he recommended a watermill in the valley where he had friends who could give me a place for the night: an old house full of women and children, owners and refugees crowded into a narrow space. The miller's wife regarded the bustle like a hermit looking at the travelling company that by accident has been lost in his forest. She didn't let anybody disturb her quiet or destroy her optimism. 'Anything is

anyway only temporary. Soon we will again have normal times.' When
I was leaving she extended a cordial invitation to spend my vacation at
her place next year. 'Vacation' did she say? There would never again be
such a thing.

One clear summer's day surpassed another in beauty. I enjoyed riding
my bike slowly along the high road, admiring the sunny chessboard of
fields stretching to the chain of hills of the Frankenwald, visible pale blue
on the horizon. I caught myself thinking that this journey should never
end.

Near Saaldorf fate caught up with me in the shape of the destroyed
bridge. Someone showed me the way to the place where a ferry crossed.
I discovered it standing on a hill that reached down steeply to the river.
It was high time as the ferry was just approaching my bank. As so often
in those days of total disillusion, I was taken over by the feeling that
this ferry was my last chance to reach the other bank. A curving path,
as narrow as it was steep, led down to the landing place. I let the bike
rush and got around a few curves with great difficulty, then fell head
over heels with all my might. One leg was stuck in the bike, the crash
was so fierce that during the first minutes I didn't even feel any pain,
but stood up and limped to the ferry with the last of my strength. But
then it had happened: my leg refused to function. Friendly people brought
me to a Red Cross station of the American Army where a medic put on
a professional Unna's paste dressing and urged me to spend a few days
in bed because I, as he claimed, also had water on the leg in addition
to the dangerous injury. Although this was troubling, on the highway
one has no time to be ill, especially when the goal is so close at hand.
I had to reach Hirschberg that day, because then only two days would
separate me from my final destination Thierstein.

With many thanks for the assistance I limped away. What a blessing
a bike is. Even with a bad leg, one can get ahead. But the pain was darkening the world for me and only with great effort did I reach the small
town of Hirschberg towards evening. On the main street stood an auxiliary policeman. I hoped he would help me quickly to find quarters for
the night. I received neither a yes nor a no to my enquiry, but a somewhat excited question: 'Are you a Political?' And as I nodded he asked
hesitatingly, 'Perhaps even a Communist?' I winced and replied, 'I used
to be . . .' He didn't let me continue, grabbed my hand and on his face
appeared an expression of fanatical admiration and submissiveness.
'Comrade!' he implored, 'you have to come to my house. You have to
be our guest. You have suffered for us . . .' I felt sick. Compassion and
antipathy struggled within me, but compassion won and I agreed. What
torture it is to be admired as a martyr. The 'comrade's' neighbours

arrived, cake was being baked and genuine coffee appeared as if by a miracle. At last they told me in complete confidence what was filling their hearts. With glowing faces they told me about their preparations for the reception of the Red Army, because now there existed no more doubt that Thüringen would become Communist. They wanted to meet the Soviet comrades with banners and red flags.

On the next day I had to cross the Bavarian frontier, which was no easy undertaking. The Americans had put up roadblocks on all the transit roads, because they wanted to guard against a new stream of refugees coming from Thüringen, set in motion by the rumours about the advance of the Russians. The son of the Communist auxiliary policeman led me over secret paths into Bavarian territory up to the Autobahn. About this Nazi achievement I had until then known only from hearsay, and now it lay before me deserted, its bridges blown up and grass sprouting out of its broken concrete. Until now I had ridden many hundreds of kilometres on decayed roads, rutted paths and byways, up hill and down dale. After these the Autobahn appeared to me as a real miracle. It was as if one were gliding along and could easily conquer immeasurable distances.

I spent the last night in Gefrees, the first and only time on this journey in a hotel. But I couldn't fall asleep. So near my goal I was suddenly seized by fear. What would happen if my mother wasn't in Thierstein. I didn't even know if she was still alive. Maybe she was buried under the ruins of her house. That soldier in Fürstenberg had told me that Hans-von-Seeckt Street in Potsdam had been bombed to bits. Towards morning my fear rose to panic. In my imagination I saw the village of Thierstein also in ruins.

At the crack of dawn I left the hotel and started the journey, tired and bruised, full of bad premonitions.

Immediately after Gefrees I noticed a bent old man who, laboriously, was filling in with gravel the deep holes in the rutted highway. Hesitantly I approached him and asked, 'Do you perhaps know the village of Thierstein?' He looked up and wiped his teary eyes with the back of his hand, blinking and examining me, and said in Franconian dialect, 'That I do!' In a sinking voice I continued, 'Was Thierstein destroyed?' I stared at the mouth of the old man, who waited far too long with his answer. At long last I heard the voice as from afar: '*Ei ja*, that is burnt down.' The blood froze in my veins and my own voice gave out. I had to know more, but the man turned back to his gravel and left me standing. I moved the bike nearer to him and begged him: 'Please, tell me, did the entire village burn down? Also the house of Johannes Thüring?' But the old man apparently thought that he had talked enough about this topic and with a 'that I don't know!' he turned his back on me. I went a few more steps uphill, threw the bike into the ditch and let myself fall down, my face hidden in my hands. The sharpening of the scythes, this much-loved sound of early summer, could be heard across the meadows as if they were making fun of my pain. Now everything was finished. Why continue riding . . . ?

But then something occurred that may belong to the most peculiar psychic changes that happen during long imprisonment. The prisoner reacts to the blows of fortune in an abnormal way. That certainly is due to the fact that he has to suffer them in uninterrupted sequence. They hit him to the bone and for a short time inescapable despair tears him apart. But amazingly quickly he tends to recover. He has lost the capacity to remain for long in deep disappointment. His unconscious reaction causes him to push it aside as quickly as possible. And that was what happened to me now. A moment earlier I had lain on the ground at the end of my tether and had given up. A few minutes later I stood up and made an unbelievable decision: should Thierstein really be lying in ruins, should I not find any of my family there, I would go to Potsdam. I had to be certain about the fate of my mother.

When trying to stand up, my body would not obey me. With legs trembling and short of breath, I tried to ascend the steep road with the bike. I had to be sure. In a meadow they were mowing. I approached the farmers and received confirmation of the bad news. Yes, Thierstein really had burnt down. They all knew this. Some talked about the entire village, others only about half of it. An SS formation had fortified themselves in the village cemetery and had shot at the advancing Americans, who replied with artillery fire, and the village went up in flames.

With an aching heart I rode on. My strength waned the closer I came to the now feared goal. Needing drinking water near a farm, I almost didn't dare ask. Lost in painful thoughts, I reached a range of hills from where one had a view of the surrounding mountains and villages. At a distance of only a few kilometres I noticed above a dark forest of fir trees the high roof of the tower of the castle ruin of Thierstein. The village itself was hidden by trees. Twenty-five years ago I had seen it for the last time. Oddly enough, the view of the top of this tower awak-ened my hope and with new courage I reached the foot of the Thiersteiner mountain. In a field next to the road shone the white kerchief of a countrywoman. I leant the bike against a tree and slowly walked towards her. I felt as if I were now expecting my sentence: 'The house of Johannes Thüring is one of the few houses of the village that have not been destroyed. And there live your mother, your sister, your brother-in-law Dr Fleiss, and many children.' Tears streamed down my face, I sobbed and stammered incoherent words, so that the farmer's wife fell silent in shock as I flew to the bike dumbstruck. In a daze I managed the ascent to the mountain effortlessly, rushed through the village street with its empty gaping windows, the old village well in the market place and up to the house of my grandparents. In the yard stood my sister, who cried out when I fell into her arms. From above on the steep wooden stairs at the entry to the house my mother's voice, which had turned old, called over and over again, 'Has she really come? Has she really come . . . ?'

INDEX